Kierkegaard and Levinas

Indiana Series in the Philosophy of Religion
Merold Westphal, *editor*

EDITED BY
J. AARON SIMMONS
AND DAVID WOOD

Kierkegaard and Levinas

Ethics, Politics, and Religion

INDIANA UNIVERSITY PRESS
Bloomington and Indianapolis

This book is a publication of

Indiana University Press
601 North Morton Street
Bloomington, IN 47404-3797 USA

http://iupress.indiana.edu

Telephone orders 800-842-6796
Fax orders 812-855-7931
Orders by e-mail iuporder@indiana.edu

© 2008 by Indiana University Press
All rights reserved

No part of this book may be reproduced or utilized in any form or by any means, electronic or mechanical, including photocopying and recording, or by any information storage and retrieval system, without permission in writing from the publisher. The Association of American University Presses' Resolution on Permissions constitutes the only exception to this prohibition.

The paper used in this publication meets the minimum requirements of American National Standard for Information Sciences—Permanence of Paper for Printed Library Materials, ANSI Z39.48-1984.

Manufactured in the United States of America

Library of Congress Cataloging-in-Publication Data

Kierkegaard and Levinas : ethics, politics, and religion / edited by J. Aaron Simmons and David Wood.
    p. cm. — (Indiana series in the philosophy of religion)
    Includes bibliographical references and index.
    ISBN 978-0-253-35258-3 (cloth : alk. paper) — ISBN 978-0-253-22030-1 (pbk. : alk. paper) 1. Kierkegaard, Søren, 1813–1855. 2. Lévinas, Emmanuel. I. Simmons, J. Aaron, date II. Wood, David, date
    B4377.K5527 2008
    194—dc22

                                                                              2008021268

1 2 3 4 5 13 12 11 10 09 08

To a continued conversation between neighbors

Contents

Acknowledgments

We would like to thank Merold Westphal (series editor) and Dee Mortensen (senior sponsoring editor) for their continuous support of this volume. The index was prepared by Alison Sven.

The essays by Merold Westphal and Martin Matuštík have appeared previously in journals. We thank the editors of those journals for allowing us to reprint those essays here.

- Merold Westphal, "The Many Faces of Levinas as a Reader of Kierkegaard," *Revista Portuguesa de Filosofia* (2008).
- Martin Matuštík, "'More Than All the Others': Meditation on Responsibility," *Critical Horizons: A Journal of Philosophy and Social Theory* 8, no. 1 (August 2007): 47–60.

Abbreviations

Kierkegaard

(CA) *The Concept of Anxiety: A Simple Psychologically Orienting Deliberation on the Dogmatic Issue of Hereditary Sin.* Ed. and trans. Reidar Thomte and Albert B. Anderson. Princeton: Princeton University Press, 1980.

(CD) *Christian Discourses and the Crisis;* and *A Crisis in the Life of an Actress.* Ed. and trans. Howard V. Hong and Edna H. Hong. Princeton: Princeton University Press, 1997.

(CI) *The Concept of Irony with Continual Reference to Socrates.* Ed. and trans. Howard V. Hong and Edna H. Hong. Princeton: Princeton University Press, 1989.

(CUP) *Concluding Unscientific Postscript to Philosophical Fragments.* Vol. 1, *Text.* Ed. and trans. Howard V. Hong and Edna H. Hong. Princeton: Princeton University Press, 1992.

(E/O I&II) *Either/Or.* Vols. *I and II.* Ed. and trans. Howard V. Hong and Edna H. Hong. Princeton: Princeton University Press, 1987.

(EUD) *Eighteen Upbuilding Discourses.* Ed. and trans. Howard V. Hong and Edna H. Hong. Princeton: Princeton University Press, 1990.

(FSE) *For Self-Examination,* in *For Self-Examination / Judge for Yourself!* Ed. and trans. Howard V. Hong and Edna H. Hong. Princeton: Princeton University Press, 1990.

(FT) *Fear and Trembling;* and *Repetition.* Ed. and trans. Howard V. Hong and Edna H. Hong. Princeton: Princeton University Press, 1983.

(JC) *Johannes Climacus,* in *Philosophical Fragments / Johannes Climacus.* Ed. and trans. Howard V. Hong and Edna H. Hong. Princeton: Princeton University Press, 1985.

(JFY) *Judge for Yourself!* in *For Self-Examination / Judge for Yourself!* Ed. and trans. Howard V. Hong and Edna H. Hong. Princeton: Princeton University Press, 1990.

(JP) *Søren Kierkegaard's Journals and Papers.* Ed. and trans. Howard V. Hong and Edna H. Hong. Princeton: Princeton University Press, 1967–1978. Citations by volume and entry number.

(PC) *Practice in Christianity.* Ed. and trans. Howard V. Hong and Edna H. Hong. Princeton: Princeton University Press, 1991.

(PF) *Philosophical Fragments* in *Philosophical Fragments / Johannes Climacus.* Ed. and trans. Howard V. Hong and Edna H. Hong. Princeton: Princeton University Press, 1985.

(SLW)   *Stages on Life's Way.* Ed. and trans. Howard V. Hong and Edna H. Hong. Princeton: Princeton University Press, 1988.

(SUD)   *The Sickness unto Death: A Christian Psychological Exposition for Upbuilding and Awakening.* Ed. and trans. Howard V. Hong and Edna H. Hong. Princeton: Princeton University Press, 1980.

(TA)   *Two Ages.* Ed. and trans. Howard V. Hong and Edna H. Hong. Princeton: Princeton University Press, 1978.

(TDIO)   *Three Discourses on Imagined Occasions.* Ed. and trans. Howard V. Hong and Edna H. Hong. Princeton: Princeton University Press, 1993.

(UDVS)   *Upbuilding Discourses in Various Spirits.* Ed. and trans. Howard V. Hong and Edna H. Hong. Princeton: Princeton University Press, 1993.

(WA)   *Without Authority.* Ed. and trans. Howard V. Hong and Edna H. Hong. Princeton: Princeton University Press, 1997.

(WOL)   *Works of Love.* Ed. and trans. Howard V. Hong and Edna H. Hong. Princeton: Princeton University Press, 1995.

Levinas

(AT)   *Alterity and Transcendence.* New York: Columbia University Press, 1999.

(BPW)   *Basic Philosophical Writings.* Ed. Adriaan T. Peperzak, Simon Critchley, and Robert Bernasconi. Bloomington: Indiana University Press, 1995.

(BTV)   *Beyond the Verse: Talmudic Readings and Lectures.* Trans. Gary D. Mole. Bloomington: Indiana University Press, 1994.

(CPP)   *Collected Philosophical Papers.* Trans. Alphonso Lingis. Pittsburgh: Duquesne University Press, 1987.

(DF)   *Difficult Freedom: Essays on Judaism.* Trans. Seán Hand. Baltimore: Johns Hopkins University Press, 1990.

(DEH)   *Discovering Existence with Husserl.* Trans. Richard A. Cohen and Michael B. Smith. Evanston, Ill.: Northwestern University Press, 1998.

(DEHH)   *En découvrant l'existence avec Husserl et Heidegger.* Paris: Librairie Philosophique J. Vrin, 1949.

(EI)   *Ethics and Infinity: Conversations with Philippe Nemo.* Trans. Richard A. Cohen. Pittsburgh: Duquesne University Press, 1985.

(EE)   *Existence and Existents.* Trans. Alphonso Lingis. Pittsburgh: Duquesne University Press, 2001.

(EN)   *Entre Nous: Thinking of the Other.* Trans. Michael B. Smith and Barbara Harshav. New York: Columbia University Press, 1998.

(GDT)   *God, Death, and Time.* Trans. Bettina Bergo. Stanford: Stanford University Press, 2000.

(HO)   *Humanism of the Other.* Trans. Nidra Poller. Urbana: University
            of Illinois Press, 2003.
(LR)   *The Levinas Reader.* Ed. Sean Hand. Oxford: Blackwell, 1997.
(GWCM)   *Of God Who Comes to Mind.* Trans. Bettina Bergo. Stanford:
            Stanford University Press, 1998.
(OE)   *On Escape.* Trans. Bettina Bergo. Stanford : Stanford University
            Press, 2003.
(OTB)   *Otherwise Than Being, Or Beyond Essence.* Trans. Alphonso Lin-
            gis. Pittsburgh: Duquesne University Press, 1997.
(OS)   *Outside the Subject.* Trans. Michael B. Smith. Stanford: Stanford
            University Press, 1993.
(PN)   *Proper Names.* Trans. Michael B. Smith. Stanford: Stanford Uni-
            versity Press, 1996.
(RTB)   *Is It Righteous to Be? Interviews with Emmanuel Levinas.* Ed. Jill
            Robbins. Stanford: Stanford Univeristy Press, 2001.
(TIHP)   *The Theory of Intuition in Husserl's Phenomenology.* Trans.
            André Orianne. Evanston, Ill.: Northwestern University Press,
            1995.
(TO)   *Time and the Other.* Trans. Richard A. Cohen. Pittsburgh:
            Duquesne University Press, 1987.
(TI)   *Totality and Infinity: An Essay on Exteriority.* Trans. Alphonso
            Lingis. Pittsburgh: Duquesne University Press, 1969.
(UH)   *Unforeseen History.* Trans. Nidra Poller. Urbana: University of Il-
            linois Press, 2004.
(US)   "Useless Suffering." In *The Provocation of Levinas: Rethink-
            ing the Other.* Ed. Robert Bernasconi and David Wood. London:
            Routledge, 1988, 156–67.

Kierkegaard and Levinas

Introduction: Good Fences May Not Make Good Neighbors After All

J. Aaron Simmons and David Wood

At first glance, Levinas and Kierkegaard make an odd couple. The historical distance between the two spans the gap between the modern and postmodern worlds. One lived through the horrors of technology's abuses, while the other sat precariously at the edge of technology's promise. One was a somewhat orthodox Jew who claimed that his philosophical and religious authorships should not be confused and even assigned them to separate publishers. The other was a radically unorthodox Christian who would simultaneously publish "aesthetic" works under pseudonyms and "edifying discourses" under his own name.[1] Later he would claim that his entire authorship had been devoted to the question of how to become a Christian. The thought of one is defined by a critique of ontology and resistance to the idea of the subject; the thought of the other is a complex account of how "subjectivity is truth." For one, ethics is first philosophy and priority is given to the other person. For the other, ethics is at times "suspended" in the name of the religious, and priority is given to God. More personally, one was married with children and was involved in the public life of his city, culture, and religion, while the other spent most of his life recovering from a broken engagement and, despite attempts at public involvement, was considered something of a recluse and a social oddity.

Attempting to cover over these differences in the hope of eliminating the dissonance that emerges when Levinas and Kierkegaard are considered together would be to miss the value that lies in the uniqueness of each thinker. However, assuming an irresolvable discord is to be deaf to the moments of harmony that do ring forth, even if they are never sustained for long.[2] The trajectory of their thinking clearly overlaps at various points.

Religious Concern: While they represent different religious traditions, they each exemplify a sustained engagement with Tertullian's famous question: "What has Athens to do with Jerusalem?" Although on the surface they offer decidedly different readings of such scriptural events as the Akedah and emphasize different aspects of the love command, they are both examples of how such material can, and perhaps should, sustain philosophical discussion rather than be relegated to theology. The question of disciplinary adequacy runs throughout the works of both men and serves to contest the ease with which we embrace them as philosophers. What we mean by "philosophy" is precisely at stake in their thought. Despite the discrepancies between the way in which they view the relationship between their religious and philosophical writings, that they both have such dualities in their corpus illuminates more of a commonality than a divergence.

Style, Writing, and Pedagogy: The writing of both thinkers displays an experimental component. They both stress the multifaceted and dynamic structures of language and allow their texts to perform their arguments as well as straightforwardly present them. When Levinas distinguishes between the vocative (accusative) and the constative (nominative) elements in language, he does so with an eye toward human relationships and not simply with a concern for the philosophy of language. Similarly, when Kierkegaard addresses his edifying discourses to "that single individual" *(hiin Enkelte),* he does so to illustrate the way in which a reader is not simply a given, but rather a singular accomplishment. While Levinas claims that we must torture language in the attempt to "say" *(dit)* the "saying" *(dire),* Kierkegaard also focuses on the limits of language by emphasizing the role of dialogical performativity and differentiating between "direct" and "indirect" communication. The performative aspect of their works illustrates the way in which they both took seriously the pedagogical responsibility that comes with philosophizing. For each of them, writing was a way of opening the reader to his or her own possibilities and hence serves as an *occasion* for truth, rather than a mere *offering* of the truth as finished.[3] As Kierkegaard's Johannes Climacus says, drawing on Lessing, if God offered the truth in one hand and in the other offered perpetual striving toward the truth, he would choose the continuing path instead of instantly arriving at the destination. Kierkegaard and Levinas jointly offer such paths while forcing the reader to recognize that the destination, if achievable at all, is only attainable after a lifetime of struggle and work. Hence, reading Levinas and Kierkegaard calls us to action and engagement, rather than detached speculation, which far too often can serve as an excuse for quietism.

Contestation of Western Ontology: Levinas and Kierkegaard share a suspicion of the Western ontological tradition. It is not entirely wrong to say that what Levinas found so problematic in Heidegger echoes what Kierkegaard found so problematic in Hegel.[4] Interestingly, their critiques of each respective philosophical forerunner are made in the name of ethics. For Kierkegaard, Hegel's totalizing system was unable to account for the singularity of the individual. For Levinas, the all-encompassing way in which Heidegger understood the ontological difference never allowed for the possibility of alterity. Even though Levinas claimed that Kierkegaard asserted the singularity of the I while he, Levinas, asserted the singularity of the Other, they sing with one voice when it comes to resistance to totality, thematization, and systematicity. Thus, they *jointly* contest the absorption of the Other into the Same.

Ethico-Political Critique: Stemming from their resistance to systematicity,

Levinas and Kierkegaard also form something of a united front against the idea of established institutions that are fixed and finished. The discussions of temporality that pervade their work illustrate the dynamism with which they view truth and justice. Levinas's idea of the *lapse* is structurally similar to Kierkegaard's conception of repetition, each expressing the ineliminable task of hermeneutics in the political realm. Although the particular objects of their critical focus were different—Levinas targeted political institutions generally, while for Kierkegaard it was the established church—their respective critiques rest on the fact that no historical manifestation can ever be adequate to the call of responsibility. The duty to the other person, although demanding existential action here and now, is never reducible to my specific actions, nor could my actions ever fulfill the requirement. Infinite responsibility demands unending practice and an open-ended relationship with the future. Similarly, in Kierkegaard's case, the singular relationship with God can never be encapsulated in a particular socio-historical community, even though participation in such a community is the only way in which such a relationship can be lived. There is always an uneasy gap between obligation and its implementation.

Truth and Justification: Levinas is not persuaded by Kierkegaard's insistence on subjectivity as truth, but he does note the importance of Kierkegaard's move away from truth as "triumphant" and toward truth as "persecuted." Mirroring the resistance to "the establishment," and perhaps implicit in it, the new conception of truth that Levinas and Kierkegaard share is one that runs counter to the history of rationality that characterizes philosophy from Parmenides to Hegel. Truth is no longer linked to certainty, but instead to risk; no longer to arrogance and power, but instead to humility and invitation. This leads both Levinas and Kierkegaard to rethink the role of justification. Justification is no longer an assured possession enabling one to act without doubt or anxiety. Rather, justification becomes an unfulfilled desire that continually motivates self-scrutiny. If there is no innocent "place in the sun" on which to stand, the announcement "here I am" becomes one of risking oneself by standing at all. Appropriation is always an ordeal, as Abraham's reception of God's command demonstrates, and action is always undertaken *with fear and trembling.*

Biographical Convergences: Although one should be wary of allowing a philosopher's biography to over-influence a reading of the philosopher's work, in the case of Levinas and Kierkegaard there are several points worth considering. In the first place, they were both raised in religious homes and communities. This religious heritage not only provided their thinking with something of an archive from which both constantly drew, but it also shaped the impact that specific events would have on their mature thought. For Levinas, coming to grips with a God who, as Elie Wiesel says, remained silent during the Shoah would deeply mark the way in which he would incorporate God into his own thought. Understanding God as "Transcendent to the point of absence" was perhaps not merely a result of a philosophical commitment. For Kierkegaard, the "great earthquake" of his father's confession of sin against God affects his own thinking for years. Perhaps the God of *Works of Love* should be understood, at least in part, as a response to the terrifying God of his youth. In the second place, both were in a sense strangers in their own land. Levinas was a Lithuanian Jew in post-Christian France. Kierkegaard, although economically and socially one of Denmark's elite, became ostracized in both the press and the community to which he belonged. The fact that, for each, philosophy was devoted to all who are marginalized and occluded by a totalizing speculative philosophy cannot be detached from the personal struggle for identity that each confronted.

Even if we grant all of the above points of contact and harmonic convergences between the thought of Levinas and Kierkegaard, what are we to make of the decisive split between ethics and religion (or the other person and God) that divides them? Doesn't a chasm open here that consigns all of the above to triviality? Again, attempting to cover over the important differences between the two thinkers would be a mistake; neither ethics for Levinas nor religion for Kierkegaard are commonplace understandings. Ethics, for Levinas, cannot be equated to either of the classical ways of understanding it: What is the good life? (Socrates), What ought I do? (Kant). Instead, both of these questions are within the domain that Levinas terms "the political." Similarly, for Kierkegaard, religion is not simply a familial heritage (as was the case in much of nineteenth-century Denmark) or an expression of submission to a particular historical creed. Moreover, faith is not to be understood as simply a weak form of knowledge that must be believed in because it cannot be proven. Kierkegaard understood religion to be an "absolute relation to the Absolute" and faith to be a complete risk of one's subjectivity in the face of the "power that constitutes it." The point is this: Levinas and Kierkegaard may disagree on the priority we should give to ethics or religion, but how they understand these options radically re-invigorates the discussion of priority itself. Perhaps what Levinas means by "ethics" and Kierkegaard means by "religion" are not so far apart after all? Perhaps they are, but in such a way as to resist an easy identification between Levinasian ethics (and the question of how to act) and Kierkegaardian religion (and the question of what to believe). In either case, an engagement between the two thinkers is crucial for taking steps toward thinking ethics in the wake of the Holocaust and religion after the "death of God."

Levinas and Kierkegaard are thus key interlocutors for coming to grips with the "post" in postmodernity.[5] By bringing them into dialogue with one another we hope to performatively animate what it means to be children of a mixed parentage with a family tree that has both Greek and Hebrew limbs. As Derrida writes, quoting James Joyce, "Jewgreek is greekjew. Extremes meet."[6]

At stake in both the dissonance and resonance between Levinas and Kierkegaard are most of the pressing issues of contemporary society and contemporary philosophy. In a world where globalization simultaneously announces the expansion of human rights and the evaporation of the particularity of individuals and cultures, the question of singularity continues to press and the Levinasian and Kierkegaardian insights continue to resound. In a time when navigating the troubled waters of religious pluralism and religious exclusivity often means addressing concerns of alienation and militaristic hostility, the ethics of Levinas and the religion of Kierkegaard are instructive examples of how to speak truth to power by linking up justice with hospitality. Living in a world where race, gender, ethnicity, sexuality, and even species continue to set challenges to social harmony and sustainable political life, the fundamentally relational conception of ontology that we find in both Levinas and Kierkegaard speaks profoundly. Further, questions of how to think and speak after foundational metaphysics has been contested continue to demand our attention. Levinas and Kierkegaard remind us that taking for granted the move beyond metaphysics can be just as dangerous as not seeing the need to make such a move in the first place. They call us to a constant project of envisaging and re-envisaging how to think about justification without the arrogance of classical foundationalism, about normativity while being suspicious of universality and objective claims to legitimacy, and about communication while recognizing the social embeddedness of all language. Although pervasive in its application, deconstruction has yet to be adequately applied to epistemology; Levinas and Kierkegaard offer profound resources for doing just this.

By bringing these two "neighbors" into conversation, the goal is much more than one of historical interest and philosophical novelty. It is an attempt to re-invigorate the contemporary philosophical dialogue by inviting us, as Wittgenstein once said, "back to the rough ground." The rough ground on which Levinas and Kierkegaard both stand is the space in which ethics may be thought without guarantees, faith may be appropriated without rigid apologetics, truth may be embraced without certainty, justice may be championed along with humility, and objectivity reconceived in the light of subjectivity. With these goals in mind, the thinkers contributing to this volume represent a rich and diverse range of backgrounds, specializations, and philosophical styles. The distinctive achievement of this volume is in the opportunity it provides for Levinas scholars to engage Kierkegaard, and Kierkegaard scholars to engage Levinas, even as Levinasians and Kierkegaardians engage each other. The conversation between neighbors should, then, be a dialogue on two levels: between Levinas and Kierkegaard, and between those who bring them together in the contemporary debate.

Before concluding, a few words about the contemporary literature on Levinas and Kierkegaard are in order. Over the past decade, awareness of the importance of reading Levinas and Kierkegaard together has grown rapidly. The philosopher who has had the most impact in this area is Merold Westphal, who has dedicated several essays to the engagement between Levinas and Kierkegaard in addition to writing extensively on each individually.[7] In 2001 Jamie Ferreira published a commentary on Kierkegaard's *Works of Love* in which she argues that "Kierkegaard's commitments to notions of commanded love, duty, and infinite debt to the other bring his ethic into productive conversation with those in our day who, like Levinas, argue for the precedence of ethics over ontology."[8] Patrick Sheil's *Kierkegaard and Levinas: The Subjunctive Mood* and Westphal's *Levinas and Kierkegaard in Dialogue* will be two of the first book-length projects considering Kierkegaard and Levinas together.[9] Other than these few examples, engagements between Kierkegaard and Levinas have either been scattered throughout books devoted to other topics[10] or confined to journal articles.[11] Up to this point there has not been an edited volume entirely devoted to developing a conversation between them.[12] This collection remedies this lack by bringing together the leading scholars from the disciplines of philosophy and religion.

Giving the lie to the old adage that "good fences make good neighbors," this book demonstrates that only when such fences are torn down can conversation flourish. We take this collection to be a step toward such philosophical and political promise in that it establishes a dialogue across generations, academic disciplines, religious traditions, and philosophical perspectives. Importantly, however, this collection will only succeed if it also invites the reader to enter the conversation. In the end, "that single individual" to whom Kierkegaard wrote might be commensurable to the "neighbor" whom Levinas addresses.

The volume proceeds as follows. Part 1, *Levinas on Kierkegaard,* contains essays by Merold Westphal and J. Aaron Simmons.

The problematic reading of Kierkegaard that one finds in the Levinasian corpus is notorious. However, it has not received the careful attention it deserves. In "The Many Faces of Levinas as a Reader of Kierkegaard," Merold Westphal remedies this situation. Westphal argues that Levinas's reading of Kierkegaard is not as straightforwardly bad as it might, at first, seem. Indeed, Levinas's reading is multifaceted and, hence, as Westphal suggests, presents a multi-*faced* Levinas. Of course, this might be what one would expect from the philosopher who claims that the origin of signification is the face of the Other. Detailing this multiplicity, Westphal has occasion to give a careful consideration to the way in which Levinas and Kierkegaard are both deeply at odds with each other and yet continue to deeply resound at crucial junctures. The first face that Levinas presents, Westphal argues, is the one that exposes Levinas's lack of care with Kierkegaardian texts and, indeed, demonstrates his poor exegetical ability. According to Westphal, Levinas acts as if he never read *Works of Love* and does not seem to give any sensitivity to the way in which the "ethical" in Kierkegaard is a complex notion that requires careful attention to the play of pseudonyms within the authorship as a whole. Nonetheless, with the second face, we begin to see a Levinas who is crucially aware of the deep divergences of their respective philosophical positions. In particular, Levinas does not miss the reversal of priority that Kierkegaard gives to the relation between oneself, God, and the Other. In addition to these two Levinases, Westphal contends, there emerges a third that is appreciative of Kierkegaard even though substantive differences between their thought continue to abound. Levinas applauds Kierkegaard's privileging of interiority and also the critique of Idealism that it announces. The fourth face is the Levinas who is critical of the Kierkegaardian project because of its egoism and its violence. Westphal is quick to note that these are charges that a Kierkegaardian ought not too quickly dismiss. He spends the rest of the chapter attempting to provide at least the beginnings of a Kierkegaardian reply. Regarding the charge of egoism, Westphal looks to both *Works of Love* and also the discourse entitled "The Expectancy of an Eternal Salvation" as resources for recognizing Kierkegaard's commitment to the neighbor as integral to the life of faith. Regarding the charge of violence, Westphal demonstrates that the equivocation that Levinas displays in his understanding of Kierkegaardian notions of "ethics" actually prohibits Levinas from seeing the profound commonalities that underlie his and Kierkegaard's resistance to ethics understood as *Sittlichkeit*. Moreover, the disagreement between the way in which God is understood by the two thinkers yields a situation in which Levinas might see violence and a Kierkegaardian might see a limitation, and indeed arrogance, regarding how God talk is allowed in philosophical discourse. In conclusion, Westphal recognizes that although neither thinker gives us a clear politics, both serve to open spaces in which the future of politics might be understood as where justice and love are considered together.

Drawing on Westphal's chapter, in "Existential Appropriations: The Influence of Jean Wahl on Levinas's Reading of Kierkegaard," J. Aaron Simmons attempts to provide something of a back story for why Levinas reads Kierkegaard as he does. Simmons does this by turning to the French existentialist appropriation of Kierkegaard found in the works of Levinas's close friend and philosophical interlocutor, Jean Wahl. In order to set the stage for considering the influence of Wahl, Simmons begins by claiming that Levinas is best understood as an ambivalent reader of Kierkegaard. Due to his tendency to be highly selective in what he appropriates from other philosophers, Levinas both praises and criticizes Kierkegaard's philosophy without really giving it the rigorous hearing it requires. Illuminating this ambivalence, Simmons considers each of the interpretive strains that characterize Levinas's reading of Kierkegaard. First, Levinas claims that Kierkegaard opens a "new modality of the true." Levinas's point here is that Kierkegaard rightly resists the totalizing tendencies of Hegel and thereby also refuses to pay homage to systematicity. Emphasizing the singular, Kierkegaard's philosophy is not about "truth triumphant," Levinas insists, but about "truth persecuted." Simmons gives particular consideration to Levinas's reading of the Kierkegaardian notions of subjectivity as a "tensing on oneself" *(tension sur soi)*, and of God as both radically transcendent and yet presented as a humble servant. Second, Levinas also insists that it is not only problematic but actually violent for Kierkegaard to surpass ethics in favor of religion. In response to each interpretive strain, Simmons offers a reading of Kierkegaard to demonstrate that, although we should not understate the distance between the two thinkers regarding the priority given to the relationship with God in Kierkegaard and the relationship with the other person in Levinas, there is ample evidence in Kierkegaard's authorship to support the claim that he is much closer to Levinas's position than Levinas is willing to admit. For example, regarding the first interpretation, the idea of subjectivity as a "tensing on oneself" is shown to be precisely what Kierkegaard, following Luther, would have understood as the definition of sin and not of proper selfhood. Similarly, regarding the second interpretation, Simmons notes the similarity between Levinasian ethics and Kierkegaardian religion. Having outlined Levinas's reading of Kierkegaard, Simmons then moves on to consider what he takes to be the primary source of Levinas's ambivalence: the work of Jean Wahl. Simmons articulates three main aspects of Wahl's understanding of Kierkegaard that he takes to be relevant to Levinas's own: (1) the solitary individual alone before God, (2) the notion of overcoming the ethical, and (3) the turn to religion as a result of the consciousness of sin. In all of these aspects, Simmons demonstrates the way in which Wahl's existentialist commitments color his reading of Kierkegaard. Ultimately, even if Wahl's reading of Kierkegaard is not wrong, it is misleading and serves to produce a picture of Kierkegaard that, without supplemental considerations, Levinas would be right to criticize. Simmons concludes by claiming that although Levinas's interpretation of Kierkegaard is problematic, Levinasian criticisms are important calls to philosophical rigor and ethico-political attention by those who call themselves *Kierkegaardian*.

Part 2, *On Love and Transcendence,* comprises chapters by John Llewelyn, M. Jamie Ferreira, and Jeffrey Dudiak.

The main concern of John Llewelyn's "Who or What or Whot?" is the status that is given to the priority of God and/or the Other as it relates to the question of (obligation to) love our neighbor. Llewelyn begins by demonstrating the way in which Levinas and Kierkegaard seem to be quite disparate thinkers when it comes to the issue of inwardness and singular subjectivity. However, he quickly notes that, in other ways, they are not as far apart as it might initially seem. Both view the Other as the one that I am commanded to love and view God as the one who commands love of the neighbor. And yet for Levinas, it is also the neighbor who commands me to love my neighbor. For Llewelyn, this slight difference will make quite a difference. Arguing against getting lost in a competition between the ethical and the religious, Llewelyn focuses on the way that the ethico-religious functions in the thought of both philosophers. The key distinction is not that one eliminates ethics in favor of the religious while the other does the opposite, but that they have two different notions of subjectivity occurring in the reference to the religious: for Kierkegaard it is "I" and for Levinas it is "me." This creates a difference in what Llewelyn terms the "order of priority" between God and the Other. After detailing the main points within both Kierkegaard's and Levinas's understandings of God and/or the word "God," Llewelyn concludes by suggesting that both Kierkegaard and Levinas fail adequately to leave open the space for loving all our neighbors. They both continue to conceive the question of obligation (of the ethico-religious) as concerning the alterity of a "who": "Who is my neighbor?" However, Llewelyn contends that we would be better served to follow Derrida, who recognizes that our hospitality (the command to love the neighbor) extends to those who do not signify as personal whos. Instead, we should bring the personal who and the impersonal what together into "the archic yet anarchic pronoun 'Whot.'"

Expanding on the engagements between Levinas and Kierkegaard that were touched on in *Love's Grateful Striving*—a book-length commentary on Kierkegaard's *Works of Love*—in "Kierkegaard and Levinas on Four Elements of the Biblical Love Commandment" M. Jamie Ferreira offers a detailed point-for-point consideration of the ways in which the two thinkers understand and appropriate the four aspects of the love commandment. While Kierkegaard affirms all four components—the commandment/to love/the neighbor/as yourself—Ferreira notes that Levinas is hesitant about three of them. Focusing on the first three aspects of the commandment in tandem, Ferreira demonstrates that although both Kierkegaard and Levinas are in agreement regarding the unconditionality of the command, they seem to be at odds regarding the support given to the notions of *love* and *neighbor*. Whereas Kierkegaard understands the neighbor to be every person and is guided by the requirements of equality and kinship, Levinas worries about the way in which the term "neighbor" has become commonplace and thus has lost its weight. Preferring the term "other" *(l'autrui)*, Levinas suggests that we should not allow this relationship to become anything less than the relationship of absolute difference that it is. Similarly, Kierkegaard's comfort with the term "love" *(Kjerlighed)*, which he understands as a type of caring that mirrors God's care for us, is contrasted with Levinas's opposition to the term "love" in favor of the notion of responsibility. Despite these seeming disagreements, Ferreira claims that Levinasian ethics should be understood as "a commitment to the commandment of neighbor love." Before moving on to address the fourth aspect of the commandment, the "as yourself," Ferreira offers an extremely helpful analysis of how the accounts of each thinker can be used to supplement and even complement the account of the other. First, Levinas enriches Kierkegaard by stressing the neediness of the neighbor and the responsibility that love demands. At the same time, Kierkegaard enriches Levinas by emphasizing the love that should always guide our responsibility and by mitigating the possible claim that an infinite ethics is an unlivable ethics by introducing the distinctions between fulfillable tasks and completeable tasks and also between the idea of helping everyone and the idea of not excluding anyone. With respect to the final aspect of the commandment, Ferreira demonstrates that the difference between the two thinkers can be read as one more of emphasis than content. In order to demonstrate this claim, and also consider those areas where real substantive disagreement might be genuinely occurring, Ferreira turns her attention to the notions of responsibility and autonomy, the infinity of the demand, self-esteem and self-love, reciprocity, equality, justice, and self-sacrifice. In conclusion, Ferreira suggests that deeper than the superficial dissonance between the two thinkers there might lie an essential resonance between them.

Jeffrey Dudiak's chapter, "The Greatest Commandment? Religion and/or Ethics in Kierkegaard and Levinas," takes as its starting point the remarkable fact that Kierkegaard and Levinas are both thinkers who resist totality and yet diverge sharply on how this totality is best resisted. The two are at odds, Dudiak notes, on the priority that should be given to God and the Other. However, both agree that it is the relationship of responsibility that defines selfhood and provides the task of ethical existence. Inspired by Merold Westphal's claim that "what we say about God should have a direct bearing on our own self-transformation," Dudiak argues for what he terms a "parallelism," where the love of God and the love of the neighbor are simply "two ways of expressing" the same thing. Dudiak argues that although Westphal clearly decides in favor of Kierkegaard over Levinas, there is a need for a Levinasian reading in reply. Dudiak offers a quick synopsis of Westphal's argument, which centers on the articulation of three types of transcendence: cosmological, epistemological, and religious-ethical. He then turns his attention to Levinas's reading of Kierkegaard in order to provide the context in which to consider the way in which a Levinasian might reply to Westphal's Kierkegaardianism. The key aspect of Dudiak's account is that, for Levinas, Kierkegaard's requirement of God as the mediator between human beings, as well as the condition for love, simply returns the human other to the level of likeness to oneself. As such, Kierkegaard problematically suspends universality and is never able to return to it, whereas Levinas both suspends the universal in the name of the singular other *and* supports universality in the requirement of law. After offering a careful reading of the opening prayer of *Works of Love*, Dudiak moves on to his central claim: contra Westphal's contention, Levinas does not offer us an atheism, but instead an a/theism that allows for God to be thought otherwise than according to the old criteria of epistemological and cosmological transcendence. Hence, God, for Levinas, does not simply "exceed" my expectations and thereby remain transcendent, but actually "precedes" all experience through invocation.

Part 3, *Time, Alterity, and Eschatology,* contains chapters by David Kangas and Martin Kavka, Michael Weston, and John J. Davenport.

In "Hearing, Patiently: Time and Salvation in Kierkegaard and Levinas," David Kangas and Martin Kavka engage in a conversation that simultaneously performs the conversation between Levinas and Kierkegaard that this volume facilitates while also challenging the ease with which such a conversation could occur. Focusing on the reflections on patience offered in Kierkegaard's *Upbuilding Discourses* and the complex relationship between waiting, hearing, and embodiment that extends throughout Levinas's authorship, Kangas and Kavka explore the stakes of hearing a God not contaminated by being *within* history. While Kangas stresses a resonance between Levinas and Kierkegaard related to their notions of awaiting time itself (i.e., the temporal possibility of revelation), he nonetheless also admits crucial differences when it comes to the difference between the Jewish and Christian content of such revelation. In reply, Kavka brings together Levinas's "Reflections on the Philosophy of Hitlerism" and early writings such as *On Escape* and *Existence and Existents* in order to demonstrate how salvation takes a communal form in Levinas in a way that one struggles to find in Kierkegaard. The chapter concludes by revisiting the very question of what constitutes the neighborliness of Levinas and Kierkegaard—the very performance of conversation, a conversation that both constitutes and challenges, emerges as both an inaugural event and a critique of how the current debates have gotten started.

In "Kierkegaard, Levinas, and 'Absolute Alterity,'" Michael Weston argues that for both Kierkegaard and Levinas the I is identified as in need of salvation. That is, the I can only become a self due to the intervention of an "absolute other." Whereas the I in Levinas is saved from meaninglessness because of the traumatic encounter with the Other, the I in Kierkegaard is redeemed from the futility of an attachment to the temporal by an act of divine grace (the relationship to God). Despite the seeming congruence of the two thinkers' conceptions of selfhood as produced by the relation to alterity, Weston argues that both philosophers run into substantive obstacles. Levinas provides the seeds of his own turmoil in his explication of the *il y a*. Weston proposes that the *il y a* yields all of the necessary elements for the salvific relationship for which Levinas claims that we require the Other. As such, Levinas's phenomenological argument for the relation to the Other is, at least, superfluous and perhaps even fails to obtain sufficient warrant in the first place. In contrast, Weston claims that, according to Kierkegaard, one must appeal to grace in order to obtain the requisite salvation. However, recognizing that a philosophical argument could not adequately support such an appeal, Kierkegaard provocatively puts forth an alternative conception of selfhood. This alternative conception is one that Weston argues has been convincingly articulated by Blanchot and Derrida and which ought to be understood along the lines of the Levinasian *il y a*. For both Kierkegaard and Levinas, then, the relation to either the Other and/or to God is unnecessary given the reality of the relation to the *il y a*.

In "What Kierkegaardian Faith Adds to Alterity Ethics: How Levinas and Derrida Miss the Eschatological Dimension," John J. Davenport does three main things. First, he gives a very helpful rubric for understanding various interpretations of *Fear and Trembling* that all focus in one way or another on the "higher-ethics" being proposed in the text. Second, Davenport argues that *Fear and Trembling* cannot be read correctly without taking into consideration the "eschatological core of . . . religiousness in Kierkegaard's sense." Finally, Davenport levels a substantial critique on Levinas's and, even more directly, on Derrida's readings of Kierkegaard in particular and their understandings of ethics in general. Davenport locates three trajectories of higher-ethics readings of *Fear and Trembling*: (1) the strong divine command interpretation, (2) the agapic command ethics interpretation, (3) aretaic love ethics interpretations. Davenport focuses primarily on a particular strain of interpretations that depend on both the agapic command interpretation and also one particular aretaic love interpretation, "alterity ethics." As examples of thinkers who advocate this sort of reading, Davenport turns to Levinas and Derrida. Before offering his critique of the Levinasian-Derridean version of alterity ethics, however, Davenport sets the stage by articulating the components of the eschatological dimension that he finds in Kierkegaardian faith. Davenport stresses Abraham's confidence that he will get Isaac back. Although such a belief is literally "absurd" given that it flies in the face of the impending reality of Isaac's death, Davenport claims that this simply opens the space for better understanding Kierkegaard's devotion to the idea that the moral law can only be fulfilled with the aid of grace, as practiced in light of the eschatological horizon of God's promises. The problem with both Levinas's and Derrida's readings of Kierke-gaard is that they eliminate this eschatological dimension in favor of a singular relation to the other person that no longer requires any real relation to God. Hence, both eliminate "the distinctive element in Kierkegaardian faith." More problematically, however, by ignoring the eschatological element, they also fail to appreciate the real insight of the agapic ethical ideal itself. The rest of the chapter is devoted to demonstrating the failings of Derridean ethics in light of this eschatological appreciation.

Part 4, *Ethico-Political Possibilities,* features chapters by Edith Wyschogrod, Zeynep Direk, Stephen Minister, and Martin Beck Matuštík.

Edith Wyschogrod brings Levinas and Kierkegaard together around the idea of upbuilding in "The Challenge of Justice: The Ethics of 'Upbuilding.' " Inter-secting such themes as subjectivity, singularity, God, and legality, Wyschogrod begins by offering an interpretation of upbuilding and the role it plays in Kierkegaard's authorship. Stressing the way in which upbuilding both lifts up to the heights and roots down to the depths, Wyschogrod sets the stage for con-sidering the way in which self hood is for both Kierkegaard and also especially for Levinas a position of powerlessness and dispossession while also being a po-sition from which we are able to move toward the other in love. Hence the single individual is not formed in triumph, but in persecution. As Wyschogrod aptly notes, for Kierkegaard the road that is upbuilding is not one that is hard, but hardship is precisely the road that upbuilds. This quality of hardship is one that Wyschogrod finds to be resonant with Levinas's notion of being for-the-Other. The self does not primarily fear for itself, but fears for the Other. Rather than producing quietistic resignation that stifles, this fear serves to motivate and propel to action. Having worked through Kierkegaardian and Levinasian sub-jectivity, Wyschogrod then turns her attention to the question of justice and le-gality. In the same way that upbuilding challenges any easy subjective grasp, but instead challenges the very stability of the self, the call to justice demands law but also contests its adequacy. Looking to a particular understanding of the re-lationship between Halakhah and Aggadah, Wyschogrod argues that, for Levi-nas, the law must constantly expose its limitations and in so doing open the space in which its original ethical intent continues to signify. In conclusion, Wyschogrod returns to the idea of upbuilding as it relates to the life lived in service to the Other—striving for justice. Here, she brings Levinas and Kierke-gaard together (and yet exposes important divergences between their thought) by considering the way in which both thinkers desire an end for the hardship of ethical life, but both recognize the way in which an achievement of the desire actually eliminates the upbuilding character of life itself. Hence, for Kierke-gaard, the task is to actually find out what God wants of me—what it is that I am to do. For Levinas, the task is to try to live up to God's command to "re-spond to the cry of the Other."

In "Levinas and Kierkegaard: Ethics and Politics," Zeynep Direk provides a substantive treatment of the way Kierkegaard and Levinas are both "thinkers of the political." Direk begins with a thorough account of the complexity of

Levinas's engagement with and reading of Kierkegaard. Beginning with Derrida's claim in "Violence and Metaphysics" that, contra Levinas's reading of Kierkegaard, "the philosopher Kierkegaard does not *only* plead for Søren Kierkegaard," Direk suggests that in order to understand the Levinasian rationale for thinking that does offer such a self-interested plea we must go back to his critique of Idealism. Direk gives significant weight to the role Franz Rosenzweig played in shaping Levinas's understanding of Kierkegaard in relation to Hegel. Although not recognized as such by Levinas himself, Direk argues that Kierkegaard is "present as an interlocutor at every crucial step that Levinas takes in [*Totality and Infinity*]." After demonstrating the complex relationship between these two thinkers, Direk turns to consider the specifically political aspect of their respective philosophies. Focusing on the role of history, hereditary sin, and relation of self-knowledge and the absolute relation to the Absolute, articulated in such works as *The Concept of Anxiety* and *Fear and Trembling*, along with a consideration of the relationship between singularity and universality in *Totality and Infinity* and the critique of freedom offered in "Reflections on the Philosophy of Hitlerism," Direk proposes that both Kierkegaard and Levinas stand together in resisting the "politics of identity" as reducible to a problematic, even violent totalization. The crucial distinction between the two, according to Direk, is that Kierkegaard allows for a relation with God beyond ethics, which, for Levinas, is simply "demonic" in that it precludes openness to other human beings. Although Direk notes that for both thinkers the question of religion is always already political, Direk concludes the essay by highlighting Levinas's challenge to the way in which Kierkegaardian religion did not adequately understand responsibility and hence is not able to serve as a complete account of the relation between subjectivity, ethics, and politics.

Stephen Minister's "Works of Justice, Works of Love: Kierkegaard, Levinas, and an Ethics Beyond Difference" articulates the way in which Levinas and Kierkegaard each go beyond the superficial stereotypes and quick interpretations that they too often have received. Minister contests the charge of rampant, asocial individualism in Kierkegaard and political vacuity in Levinas, suggesting that both thinkers provide a way forward for questions of ethical and political life. Minister stresses that for both Levinas and Kierkegaard, the goal of philosophy is to indicate the task that confronts each person in her or his ethico-religious subjectivity. Neither thinker stops at "difference and singularity" but goes on to "articulate possibilities for meaningful action and commitment." The chapter is divided into two main sections—one dealing with the way Levinas understands justice to operate in the world of lived existence, and one that takes up Kierkegaard's ethical account in *Works of Love*. Minister's consideration of Levinas focuses on three main thematics: (1) the way in which the face and the "third party" both function to provide something of a Levinasian theory of human nature, (2) a close reading of how the command "thou shalt not kill" serves as the primary example of how ethical responsibility requires specific interpretation and application in particular situations, and (3) the importance of critique for both Levinas and Derrida in opening the space for a better tomorrow. Drawing on the work of Merold Westphal, Jamie Ferreira, and Nel Noddings, among others, Minister locates three ways in which Kierkegaard also builds on his notion of subjectivity to recommend our specific responsibilities to others: (1) responsiveness to the other's material needs, (2) encouragement of proper self-love, and (3) support of the other's love of her own neighbors. In this chapter the rubber hits the road, as it were, regarding the political consequences of Levinasian and Kierkegaardian philosophy. Unwilling to allow their "exaggerated reputations" to hold sway, Minister combines careful textual analysis with rigorously provocative suggestions for a life to be lived on the basis of their work.

In the final chapter of this volume, " 'More Than All the Others': Meditation on Responsibility," Martin Beck Matuštík provides a sustained reflection on the concrete stakes of responsibility as understood in three ways: Jan Patočka's "finite responsibility," Derrida's Kierkegaardian "emphasis on the infinite dimension of responsibility," and further "ethico-existential variations on in/finite responsibility," drawing on Levinas, Dostoyevsky, and Kierkegaard. Responding to Havel's claim that responsibility must translate into action, Matuštík considers the above conceptions of responsibility in relation to the political specifics of Charta 77—a manifesto for human rights in Czechoslovakia that was issued by Havel, Patočka, and Hájek. Matuštík argues that by considering the way in which Dostoyevsky, Derrida, and Patočka stand as critical resources for bridging Kierkegaard and Levinas, we can see that both Kierkegaard and Levinas support the Havelian conception that responsibility is to be understood not as an abstraction, but as a personal response of one's own subjectivity. Matuštík begins with a testimony of sorts, and in this way situates the chapter itself as something of an ethical response in its own right. After introducing the issues and central questions of ethical responsibility and political action, he moves on to consider Patočka's notion of finite responsibility. For Patočka, Matuštík claims, authentic subjectivity occurs when there is a movement beyond the orgiastic demonic and a call to a sustained contestation of absolute stability of meaning. As Matuštík writes, "Patočka views human history as nothing else but the trembling of any given, thus finite certainty of meaning." Thus there is an intersection in Patočka between subjectivity and political orders in that both are constituted in the act of being responsible for their own histories—histories that are ever made and remade in this act itself. Having articulated the basics of Patočka's position, Matuštík moves on to consider the way in which Derrida reads this position as being "an existential, flat-footed Christian notion of responsibility." Stressing the aporetic dimension of all responsibility and all relations to others, Derrida allows for a radicalization of the "sober responsibility" described by Patočka. Matuštík suggests, however, that although Derrida is helpful for keeping the stakes of personal and political relations in clear view, and even though Derrrida takes himself to be safeguarding the valuable insights of Patočka, his account goes too far and actually forces responsibility into undecidability rather than making the undecidable constantly bear on the necessity of concrete decision and political action. Matuštík wonders whether Derrida does not make the world just a bit heavier than we can bear. As a corrective of this Derridean "ir/responsible undecidability," Matuštík turns to the Kierkegaardian-Levinasian-Dostoyevskyan responsibility that he finds to underlie the spirit of Charta 77. For Kierkegaard, Levinas, and Dostoyevsky, as well as for Patočka and Havel, what we find is the necessity of an "existentially lived responsibility" that can never become derailed by an "abstract conceptual aporia," but instead constantly calls the self to specific finite acts. Importantly, however, Matuštík is quick to indicate that these acts are not themselves products of divine guarantees and foundational justifications. Instead, they are expressions of the fear and trembling that Kierkegaard and Levinas repeatedly describe. In conclusion, Matuštík turns his attention to the religious implications of this conception of responsibility—which he understands to be always already "ethico-religious." When considered in the light of the "useless suffering" experienced at Auschwitz, Matuštík contends that the Christian God must be understood according to a "low Christology." The uselessness of this suffering can never be justified according to a theodicy. Instead, what becomes apparent is that "the Christian God . . . revealed in low Christology" and "the Jewish God . . . encountered only indirectly in the love of one's neighbor" are one and the same God. Kierkegaard and Levinas should not be read as at odds either ethically or religiously. In the end, both view God as found in the relation to others—a relation that always demands our diligent attention and considered action. Kierkegaardian Christianity and Levinasian Judaism are both expressions of how the call of the widow, the orphan, the stranger, and the political dissident demand a taking up of one's history (whether nationally or individually) by acting in the present in order to respond to this history and open a new future in which useless suffering is lessened. It is in this way, Matuštík argues, that I continue to be more responsible than all the others. The "someone" who "must begin," as Havel writes, is me.

Notes

1. The terms "orthodox" and "unorthodox" are intentionally ambiguous. Surely Kierkegaard's "attack on Christendom" was in the name of trying to restore something like orthodoxy to what he considered to be rampant indifference. However, if orthodoxy is understood etymologically as having to do with common opinion, Kierkegaard was certainly unorthodox.

2. Of course it should be noted that when read in the light of Rosenzweig it might be the perpetual dissonance that makes for such an enlivening conversation of alterities. For him, a happy harmony between Levinas and Kierkegaard is the very temptation to be avoided.

3. To borrow from Heidegger, we might say that they both "leap ahead" *(vorauspringen)* of their reader rather than "leaping in" *(einspringen)* for them (see §26 of *Being and Time*).

4. Importantly, it could be claimed that, for Levinas, the critique of Heidegger is more aptly a critique of Hegel.

5. For a consideration of how Kierkegaard relates to both aspects of the term "post-

modernity," see Martin J. Matuštík and Merold Westphal, eds., *Kierkegaard in Post/ Modernity* (Bloomington: Indiana University Press, 1995).

6. Jacques Derrida, "Violence and Metaphysics," in *Writing and Difference*, trans. Alan Bass (Chicago: University of Chicago Press, 1978), 153.

7. See especially Westphal, *Levinas and Kierkegaard in Dialogue* (Bloomington: Indiana University Press, 2008); Westphal, "Levinas, Kierkegaard, and the Theological Task," *Modern Theology* 8, no. 3 (July, 1992): 241–61; Westphal, "Transparent Shadow: Kierkegaard and Levinas in Dialogue," in *Kierkegaard in Post/Modernity*, ed. Martin J. Matuštík and Merold Westphal (Bloomington: Indiana University Press, 1995), 265–81; Westphal, "Levinas' Teleological Suspension of the Religious," in *Ethics as First Philosophy: The Significance of Levinas for Philosophy, Literature, and Religion*, ed. Adriaan T. Peperzak (New York: Routledge, 1995), 151–60; Westphal, "Commanded Love and Divine Transcendence in Kierkegaard and Levinas," in *The Face of the Other and the Trace of God*, ed. Jeffrey Bloechl (New York: Fordham University Press, 2000), 200–33; Westphal, "Divine Excess: The God Who Comes After," in *The Religious*, ed. John D. Caputo (London: Blackwell, 2002), 258–76.

8. M. Jamie Ferreira, *Love's Grateful Striving: A Commentary on Kierkegaard's "Works of Love"* (Oxford: Oxford University Press, 2001), 12.

9. Patrick Sheil, *Kierkegaard and Levinas: The Subjunctive Mood* (Ashgate, 2008); Merold Westphal, *Levinas and Kierkegaard in Dialogue* (Bloomington: Indiana University Press, 2008).

10. See Jill Robbins, *Altered Reading: Levinas and Literature* (Chicago: University of Chicago Press, 1999), especially chap. 6; Hent de Vries, *Religion and Violence: Philosophical Perspectives from Kant to Derrida* (Baltimore, Md.: Johns Hopkins University Press, 2002), esp. chap. 2; Michael Weston, *Kierkegaard and Modern Continental Philosophy: An Introduction* (London: Routledge, 1994), esp. chap. 7; Mark Dooley, *The Politics of Exodus: Kierkegaard's Ethics of Responsibility* (New York: Fordham University Press, 2001), esp. 206ff.; John D. Caputo, *Against Ethics: Contributions to a Poetics of Obligation with Constant Reference to Deconstruction* (Bloomington: Indiana University Press, 1993); and Claudia Welz, "Reasons for Having No Reason to Defend God: Kant, Kierkegaard, Levinas, and Their Alternatives to Theodicy," in *Wrestling with God and with Evil: Philosophical Reflections*, ed. Hendrik M. Vroom (New York: Rodopi, 2007), 167–86.

11. See J. Aaron Simmons, "Politics as an Ethico-Religious Task: Kierkegaard and Levinas on Religion in the Public Square," *Soundings* 89, no. 1–2 (Spring-Summer 2006): 1001–1018; Brian Treanor, "God and the Other Person: Levinas's Appropriation of Kierkegaard's Encounter with Otherness," *Proceedings of the American Catholic Philosophical Association: Person, Soul, and Immortality* 75 (2001): 313–24; Mark Dooley, "The Politics of Exodus: Derrida, Kierkegaard, and Levinas on 'Hospitality,'" in *International Kierkegaard Commentary: "Works of Love,"* ed. Robert L. Perkins (Macon, Ga.: Mercer University Press, 1999), 167–92; Peter Kemp, "Another Language for the Other: From Kierkegaard to Levinas," *Philosophy and Social Criticism* 23, no. 6 (1997): 5–28; Gitte W. Butin, "Encounter with the Other: A Matter of Im/Mediacy," *Kergma und Dogma,* 45 (October-December 1999), 307–16; Brian T. Prosser, "Conscientious Subjectivity in Kierkegaard and Levinas," *Continental Philosophy Review* 35 (2002): 397–422; Stephen M. Minister, "Is There a Teleological Suspension of the Philosophical? Kierkegaard, Levinas, and the End of Philosophy," *Philosophy Today* 47, no. 2 (Summer 2003): 115–25; Christopher Arroyo, "Unselfish Salvation: Levinas, Kierkegaard, and the Place of Self-Fulfillment in Ethics," *Faith and Philosophy* 22, no. 2 (April 2005): 160–72; Gary

Foster, "The Representative Other: Confronting Otherness in Kierkegaard, Levinas, and Ricoeur," *Philosophical Writings* 25 (Spring 2004): 19–29; Jacques Colette, "Levinas et Kierkegaard: Emphase et paradoxe," *Revue Philosophique de Louvain* 100, no. 1–2 (February-May 2002): 4–31; Jeffrey Stolle, "Levinas and the Akedah: An Alternative to Kierkegaard," *Philosophy Today* 45, no. 2 (Summer 2001): 132–43; Andrea Hurst, "Kierkegaard, Levinas, and the Question of Escaping Metaphysics," *South African Journal of Philosophy* 19, no. 3 (2000): 169–87.

12. This is strange indeed, considering the fact that collections have been published treating Kierkegaard and MacIntyre, Kierkegaard and deconstruction, Levinas and Lacan, Levinas and Buber, and Levinas and the eighteenth century. Bringing Levinas and Kierkegaard together is more about picking up the scattered threads and weaving them into a piece of art than of starting a new quilt from scratch. See John J. Davenport and Anthony Rudd, eds., *Kierkegaard After MacIntyre: Essays on Freedom, Narrative, and Virtue* (Chicago: Open Court, 2001); Elsebet Jegstrup, ed., *The New Kierkegaard* (Bloomington: Indiana University Press, 2004); Jonathan Rée and Jane Chamberlain, eds., *Kierkegaard: A Critical Reader* (Oxford: Blackwell, 1998); Sarah Harasym, *Levinas and Lacan: The Missed Encounter* (Albany: State University of New York Press, 1998); Peter Atterton, Matthew Calarco, and Maurice Friedman, eds., *Levinas and Buber: Dialogue and Difference* (Pittsburgh, Pa.: Duquesne University Press, 2004); Melvyn New, Robert Bernasconi, and Richard A. Cohen, *In Proximity: Emmanuel Levinas and the Eighteenth Century* (Lubbock, Tex.: Texas Tech University Press, 2001).

Part One.   *Levinas on Kierkegaard*

1   The Many Faces of Levinas as a Reader of Kierkegaard

Merold Westphal

Face 1

Levinas is not always a good reader of Kierkegaard. For example, he credits Kierkegaard with bringing to European philosophy "the possibility of attaining truth through the ever-recurrent inner rending of doubt" (PN, 77). In light of the polemic against modern philosophy's preoccupation with doubt by Kierkegaard and his pseudonyms, one is left flabbergasted.[1] Again, Levinas tells us that "in protesting against the absorption of subjectivity by Hegel's universality, [Kierkegaard] bequeathed to the history of philosophy an exhibitionistic, immodest subjectivity" (PN, 76). In the light of the emphasis by Johannes de Silentio and Johannes Climacus on the secret hiddenness of faith, one is once again reduced to bewilderment. Or again, Levinas distinguishes his critique of the state (and by implication the whole social order that Hegel calls ethical life or *Sittlichkeit* and Kierkegaard's pseudonyms call the ethical stage or existence sphere) from Kierkegaard's because his is not to be based on "all the worries that an individual may have in a State. That would be to return to the egoism against which Reason is right" (TH, 23). Are we to believe that the polemic against the ultimacy of the state in *Fear and Trembling* is based on Abraham's egoistic desire not to be hemmed in by society's oppressive rules?

Perhaps Levinas' most sustained misreading of Kierkegaard concerns the meaning of the ethical. Sometimes he is clear that by the ethical stage which is to be teleologically suspended in faith, Kierkegaard (whom he doesn't distinguish from his pseudonyms) does not mean pure practical reason in either its Platonic sense as the recollection of eternal truth or the Kantian sense of the self-legislation of universal norms, as timeless and as socially unsituated as Plato's forms; he rather means the laws and customs of one's people, what Hegel calls *Sittlichkeit*. Thus he describes the ethical stage as one "at which the inner life is translated in terms of legal order, carried out in society, in loyalty to institutions and principles and in communication with mankind" (PN, 67). But he wonders whether "the true ethical stage is correctly described by Kierkegaard as generality and equivalence of the inner and the outer" (PN, 69; cf. 76). The faith in which *Sittlichkeit* is teleologically suspended "does not open man to other men but to God, in solitude," and for this reason "carries within it an irresponsibility, a ferment of disintegration" (PN, 70). The transition from the ethical to the religious "begins the disdain for the ethical basis of being, the somehow secondary nature of all ethical phenomena that, through Nietzsche, has led us to the amoralism of the most recent philosophers" (PN, 72). Yes, friends, Kierkegaard is to blame for Nietzsche and his followers!

Of course, Levinas shares Kierkegaard's critique of the ultimacy of the laws and customs of one's people, which he calls war, politics, history, and reason (TI, 21–22) and is just as eager to see it teleologically suspended in something higher. But for him this higher is the individual's responsibility for the human Other, which he calls *diacony* (PN, 73–74). In a glorious non sequitur, Levinas concludes that since Kierkegaard wants to transcend the ethical stage (which the two agree as identifying as *Sittlichkeit*), he "seems not to have experienced" the uniquely individual responsibility for the Other which exceeds what my society asks of me. In other words, Kierkegaard has no other notion of the ethical than the Hegelian ethics portrayed in *Either/Or II* and suspended in *Fear and Trembling*.

Levinas writes as if he had never even heard of *Works of Love*, much less read it.[2] But he does seem aware of the Climacus writings, to which he makes apparent reference. If he had read *Postscript* more carefully, he would have found in the midst of a crucial text about the religious stage a different notion of the ethical. There the theory of the three stages becomes at once twofold (objectivity and subjectivity) and fourfold (aesthetic and speculative objectivity over against ethical and religious subjectivity). Here the ethical is not left behind by the religious but stands in closest relation to it. The critique of the system, especially in its world-historical dimensions, is designed to keep open the space of the ethical (CUP, 133–59). This is not Levinas' ethics of diacony, and Climacus will speak here of "my ethical relationship with God," rather than with my neighbor (CUP, 140, 157). But it is an ethics of uniquely individual, unconditional responsibility beyond the laws and customs of my people, and it is precisely in terms of this responsibility to God that my responsibility to love my neighbor opens up in *Works of Love*. There are at least three senses of the ethical in the corpus, not just one, as Levinas supposes.

Face 2

I suspect that if Levinas applied for admission to one of our graduate programs and submitted as a writing sample an essay including these readings of Kierkegaard, we would dismiss him out of hand, shaking our heads and asking, Who taught this kid to read, anyway? So, when Levinas writes, "It is not I who resist the system, as Kierkegaard thought; it is the other" (TI, 40; cf. PN, 73), we are suspicious. Is this another sloppy reading? The only mere I in Kierkegaard's corpus is the aesthetic self; the ethical self is mediated by the social system,[3] and the religious self is never alone but always alone—before God *(coram deo)*. Outside the aesthetic the self in Kierkegaard's corpus is always essentially relational. Does Levinas think it is the aesthete whom Kierkegaard sends out as his David against the twin Goliaths of speculation and Christendom? Is he unaware that it is God as *Ens Alterissimum* who disturbs the system and that the Knight of Faith is the locus of this disruption solely by being obedient to the divine command?

In a word, or rather two, no and no. Levinas knows that it is not a matter of aesthetic subjectivity. "Kierkegaard could not resort to the particularity of feeling and enjoyment, as opposed to the generosity of the concept. The state he called esthetic, and which is that of sensible dispersion, leads to the impasse of despair in which subjectivity loses itself" (PN, 67). Moreover, he is fully aware that Kierkegaardian subjectivity is religious and that Kierkegaard and his pseudonyms insist on the priority of the God relation.

There is in fact a double sense in which the God relation comes first for Kierkegaard. On the literary front, he spends a lot of time describing it from a variety of angles before he gets to the ethics of neighbor love in *Works of Love,* and he complains bitterly that readers expect him to say everything at once.

> Despite everything people ought to have learned about my maieutic carefulness, by proceeding slowly and continually letting it seem as if I knew nothing more, not the next thing—now on the occasion of *[Upbuilding Discourses in Various Spirits]* they will probably bawl out that I do not know what comes next, that I know nothing of sociality. The fools! Yet on the other hand I owe it to myself to confess before God that in a certain sense there is some truth in it, only not as people understand it—namely, that continually when I have first presented one aspect clearly and sharply, then the other affirms itself even more strongly.
>
> Now I have the theme of the next book. It will be called:
> Works of Love (JP, V 5972)[4]

As a Christian writer deeply immersed in Scripture, Kierkegaard knows that the first table of the Ten Commandments (Ex. 20: 1–17) and the first commandment in Jesus' summary of the law (Mark 12:28–34) concern our relation to God, while the second table and the second commandment in Jesus' summary concern our relation to our neighbors. So he proceeds methodically from what is first to what is second. He is a foundationalist, not in the epistemic sense of building the edifice of knowledge on a *fundamentum inconcussum* of absolute certainty, but in the biblical sense of knowing the difference between building on theocentric rock and building on anthropocentric sand (Matt. 7:24–27).

When he finally turns to "sociality" and the ethics of commanded neighbor love, we discover a second way in which the God relation comes first. God is both the commander and the enabler of neighbor love and, as such, is always the middle term between myself and my neighbor (WOL, 57–58, 67, 77, 107, 119, 121, 142). Thus the command of neighbor love is grounded in the notion of equal kinship of all "to God in Christ. For Christianity teaches me that both I and my neighbor are equally created by God and equally redeemed by Christ" (WOL, 69). I cannot properly perceive either myself or my neighbor without first seeing us in this double relation to God.[5] By reversing this order and insisting that I relate first to my neighbor, Levinas accurately identifies the most fundamental divergence between himself and Kierkegaard. Now it is the human Other who is the middle term between me and God.

> I do not want to define anything through God because it is the human that I know. It is God that I can define through human relations and not the inverse. The notion of God—God knows, I'm not opposed to it! But when I have something to say about God, it is always beginning from human relations . . . I do not start from the existence of a very great and all-powerful being. Everything I wish to say comes from this situation of responsibility . . . And anything that I could go on to say about God . . . starts from this experience, and not the inverse. The abstract idea of God is an idea that cannot clarify a human situation. It is the inverse that is true . . . ultimately my point of departure is absolutely nontheological. I insist upon this. It is not theology that I am doing, but philosophy.[6]

Perhaps the reason Levinas does not begin with God is that he is an atheist. If we fill in an ellipsis in the passage just cited, we read, "Everything I wish to say comes from this situation of responsibility which is *religious insofar as the I cannot elude it. If you like, it is like a Jonah who cannot escape.*"[7] If "religion" is simply the name for the fact that responsibility is inescapable, then not only do we not start from God as "a very great and all-powerful" Creator, who may also be a righteous Lawgiver and a merciful, all-loving Redeemer, but we will not end with such a God either. For if we did, "religion" would surely signify our relation to that God.[8]

Face 3

Be that as it may, we now have two Levinases, one who reads Kierkegaard rather badly and one who understands him well enough to see precisely where they most basically differ. Out of this second Levinas there emerges a third, one who appreciates Kierkegaard despite their differences. To give just one example, but a deep and persuasive one, he welcomes Kierkegaard's defense of subjectivity and interiority, not only against the naturalisms that would reduce it to "objective Being" but especially against the idealism that would let the subject "be absorbed by the Being that this subject uncovered," an absorption based on the assumption that "Being was the correlate of thought" (PN, 66). Hegelian idealism posits "truth that triumphs—that is, that leads to discourse . . . But to discern in that discourse—in that *possibility of speaking* . . . a distant *impossibility* of discourse . . . to sense . . . the end of philosophy, ending in a political totalitarianism in which human beings are no longer the source of their language, but reflections of the impersonal logos, or roles played by figures: all this constitutes the value of the Kierkegaardian notion of existence and its deeply Protestant protest against systems" (PN, 68).[9] As leery as he is of the teleological suspension of the ethical, he finds an important truth in Abraham's silence in Problema 3 of *Fear and Trembling*. By contrast with the self of the philosophers,[10] the self of Abraham is the kind that knows itself to be bound by an unconditional and ineluctable obligation.

Face 4

It may be, however, that the most interesting Levinas, as a reader of Kierkegaard, is the one who, as a kind of prosecutor, levels two accusations that are too serious to be ignored or lightly dismissed, even if they turn out on analysis to rest on misreading. The grand jury, we might say, has decided that the matter should come to trial. Whether we are offended at the critique of human aspirations to autonomy, both as intellect and as will, to be found in the Kierkegaardian corpus (and perhaps doubly offended that Climacus and Anti-Climacus should name this offense as such) or, by contrast and with Levinas appreciate its unmasking of the arrogance that masquerades as Enlightenment or as Reason (read Modernity, if you like), we are likely to be surprised by a central theme of Levinas' counter-critique: the charge that Kierkegaardian subjectivity is a form of egoism. We are unprepared for Levinas' description of Kierkegaardian subjectivity "as a tensing on oneself" or as "existence tensed over itself" (PN, 67; cf. 72) and puzzled that he describes this tension as "the anxiety of A for A . . . of the Same in its care for the Same" (PN 68) and as "a kind of torment over oneself" (PN, 76). Not that the Kierkegaardian self is relaxed and at ease or that there is any shortage of anxiety and torment—but "over itself"?

Levinas responds to our puzzlement. He wants to defend a self "without its resistance to system [whether speculative or social] manifesting itself as the egoist cry of the subjectivity, still concerned for happiness or salvation, as in Kierkegaard" (TI, 305). The self tensed on or over itself is the Christian self defined by its "thirst for salvation" which "consumes itself with desires" that the world cannot satisfy (PN, 67). We hear here an echo of Augustine's "you made us for yourself and our hearts are restless until they rest in you."[11] When Levinas speaks of the pagan sources of this experience, it becomes clear that he is speaking of happiness and salvation on the far side of death, the eternal happiness with which Johannes Climacus is concerned.[12] Echoing, perhaps, Climacus' claim that it is sin that makes God "absolutely different" from the human self (PF, 44–47), he portrays the Kierkegaardian subject as "begging for forgiveness and salvation" (PN, 70).[13] This egotism, he insists, is not an "ugly vice" but simply Spinoza's *conatus essendi* at work, or the *Jemeinigkeit* of Heidegger's *Dasein*, whose being is always at issue for it (PN, 70–71).

In response to Spinoza's *conatus* and Heidegger's *Jemeinigkeit*, Levinas regularly plays Climacus: these systems have no ethics. So this is a devastating comparison. How can Kierkegaard reply? He might begin by quoting C. S. Lewis, substituting ethics where Lewis speaks of politics. "We are very shy nowadays of even mentioning heaven. We are afraid of the jeer about 'pie in the sky,' and of being told that we are trying to 'escape' from the duty of making a happy world here and now into dreams of a happy world elsewhere. But either there is 'pie in the sky' or there is not. If there is not, then Christianity is false, for this doctrine is woven into its whole fabric. If there is, then this truth, like any other, must be faced, whether it is useful at political meetings or no."[14] Since it is a major task, if not *the* major task of Kierkegaard's authorship as a whole to distinguish Christianity both from the speculative system called Hegel and the social system called Christendom in order to clarify what is involved in becoming a Christian, Kierkegaard might simply tell us that since the idea of eternal happiness is woven into the very fabric of Christianity, he can neither ignore nor abandon it. Because God is demanding love, faith is simultaneously obedience to God's commands and trust in God's promises.

Sound as this response may be, it can be taken as an acknowledgment: "Guilty as charged. In its promise of eternal happiness, Christianity addresses itself to the egoism of those who see death as the ultimate threat to their *conatus* or their *Jemeinigkeit*." Levinas might well add, "Just as we have learned not to trust those for whom honesty is only the best policy, so we should be leery of those for whom faith is the best policy, a life insurance policy for eternity."

If, however, we allow Lewis a few more sentences, we get the elements of a further response: "Again, we are afraid that heaven is a bribe, and that if we make it our goal we shall no longer be disinterested. It is not so. Heaven offers nothing that a mercenary soul can desire. It is safe to tell the pure in heart that they shall see God, for only the pure in heart want to. There are rewards that do not sully motives." This is an echo of Augustine's *Dilige, et quod vis fac*—Love and do what you please.[15] For Kierkegaard and Augustine, the inescapable responsibility of the Christian is expressed in Jesus' twofold summary of the law: we are to love God with our whole heart, and we are to love our neighbor as ourselves. Since both Augustine and Kierkegaard hear this "as yourself" as signifying the inseparability of proper self-love from proper neighbor love,[16] the task, and surely it is the task of a lifetime, is triple: to learn to love God aright, to learn to love myself aright, and to learn to love my neighbor aright. Just to the degree that the self has become this threefold love, it can safely be told to do as it pleases. For it has become a radically decentered self; it is no longer a selfish self and its inclinations are no longer in conflict with its duties. So far from its desire for salvation being the egoism of a naturalistic *conatus essendi* or an existential/ontological *Jemeinigkeit*, it is rather the desire to make permanent and perfect the welcoming of the Other, both divine and human, into a self which recognizes that both are already an essential part of its own identity.[17]

Like Kant and those puritans whose God spends eternity worrying lest someone somewhere should be happy, Levinas is allergic to eudaemonism of any sort.[18] By failing to notice that the interests of the self are not necessarily interests for the self[19] and that the one who finds satisfaction in being fair and happiness in being generous is not an egoist, Levinas gives to his own ethics a grimness it does not need.[20]

A complete Kierkegaardian answer to Levinas' charge, however, cannot rest with the general claim, however sound, that eudaemonism is not inherently egoistic. For a theological eudaemonism could be ethically irresponsible when it comes to human interrelations. Thus, for example, the recurring question whether various forms of mysticism are morally bankrupt. The full answer will have to make fully explicit what was presupposed in the preceding discussion, namely, that the God to whom the Kierkegaardian self turns for salvation is the very God who commands us to love our neighbor unconditionally. This is not to say that those who call themselves Christians might not think that salvation is a ticket both to eternal happiness and to a moral holiday here and now. Especially in a Lutheran context, there can be the temptation to interpret justification by faith so as to make works of love unnecessary. But Kierkegaard vigorously repudiates this reading of Luther, most overtly in *For Self Examination* and *Judge for Yourself*, but most extensively in *Works of Love*. Authentic faith will have to be "faith working through love" (Gal. 5:6).

For the present, with reference to the latter work, only three observations. (1) Kierkegaard writes of the essays that make up this book, "They are *Christian deliberations,* therefore not about *love* but about *works of love*" (WOL, 3). (2) He does not attribute to his readers that perfection of love that would warrant the permission "do as you please." So in the first series he presents a deontological ethic of neighbor love that emphasizes its commanded character and its challenge to every improper self-love. The responsible self is under unconditional obligation to and for the neighbor. (3) In emphasizing the priority of the God relation, he does not disguise its privacy, what Climacus calls its hidden inwardness. So he writes, "Shut your door and pray to God—because God is surely the highest." But he does not leave it at that. Instead he continues, "when you open the door that you shut in order to pray to God and go out the very first person you meet is the neighbor, whom you *shall* love" (WOL, 51). God and the soul, it would seem, have a good deal of business to conduct in private, and doubtless some of this involves the confession and forgiveness of sins and the promise of eternal life. But as I open the door to go back into the world, the last thing God does is to remind me that the very first person I meet is my neighbor, whom I *shall* love.

If we pay sufficient attention to the corpus as a whole, we will not arrive at *Works of Love* entirely unprepared. Kierkegaard introduced Johannes Climacus and his question about the relation of eternal happiness and historical knowledge on June 13, 1844. Just five days earlier, on June 8, he published three upbuilding discourses, including one entitled "The Expectancy of An Eternal Salvation." It is a meditation on a "pie in the sky" text, 2 Corinthians 4:17–18:

Our hardship, which is brief and light, procures for us an eternal weight of glory beyond all measure.
Because we do not esteem the things that are seen but the things that are unseen, for the things that are seen are temporal, but the things that are unseen are eternal.[21]

Kierkegaard knows how the "pie in the sky" objection runs. If you talk to people about eternal life they become so heavenly minded they are no earthly good. So he wants to discuss "what consequences the expectancy of an eternal salvation has for this earthly, troubled life" (EUD, 254). If this expectancy does not work in two places at once, namely in heaven and on earth, "then it is fraudulent, the craftiness of a sick soul that wants to sneak out of life, and is not the authentic presence of a healthy soul in the temporal; then it is not the expectancy of the eternal but a superstitious belief in the future" (EUD, 259). So he specifies two ways in which this expectancy should work on earth.

First, "the expectancy of an eternal salvation will help a person to understand himself in temporality" (EUD, 259). It does so by bringing "comfort beyond measure" in the midst of life's troubles. It is "a refuge in distress, a fortress that life cannot take by storm" and the believing soul "returns from this conception strengthened" (EUD, 263). Kierkegaard does not specify what Paul's troubles are, but they are familiar enough. Later in the same epistle Paul gives a frightening list of beatings, imprisonments, stoning, and, perhaps most serious of all, anxiety for the churches he has founded (2 Cor. 11:23–29). These are not the ordinary vicissitudes of life. They are all work related, the hazards of apostolic ministry. Paul didn't choose this line of work for the perks or the good working conditions. It was a matter of obedience to a call from God and of love for those to whom he preached the gospel. So if in the face of great sufferings he does not lose heart (2 Cor. 4:1,16) but is strengthened, he is strengthened for a ministry of obedience to an unconditional obligation before God and of love for those who are strangers to him (and often a royal pain once he gets to know them—the Corinthians, for example).

Second, "the expectancy of an eternal salvation will reconcile everyone with his neighbor, with his friend, and with his enemy in an understanding of the essential" (EUD, 265). The essential, of course, is eternal life, but it is not a zero-sum game. It is a good which "in being possessed does not shut out anyone else." So whoever is "properly concerned" about heavenly happiness "will not want to shut anyone out" (EUD, 266). There follows a polemic against those who are eager to shut out all who do not meet the conditions of entry as defined by themselves. They understand that the expectancy of eternal salvation should work both in heaven and on earth, but they take this to mean that they are to play God (or at least St. Peter) both then in heaven and now on earth. When they pray, "Your will be done on earth as it is in heaven" (Matt. 6:10), they reserve to themselves the right to define this will for God.

This second principle of reconciliation and non-exclusion is far from being a full-fledged ethic of neighbor love. But by seeing the hope of eternal happiness as essentially *including* an attitude of reconciliation with both neighbor and enemy and *precluding* any desire to exclude them from the highest good, it tells us, Kierkegaard included, that the authorship is essentially incomplete as long as it focuses only on the individual's relation to God, whether that be deontologically in terms of obligation and obedience or teleologically in terms of hope for heavenly happiness. We will be on the lookout for *Works of Love*.

There is another sense in which at least the beginning of a response to Levinas' concern does not have to wait until we get to *Works of Love*. Levinas asks whether "a part of that authenticity Kierkegaard has made appealing to us does not consist in the forgetting and sublimating of that same tension on oneself that still defines Kierkegaardian subjectivity; and *whether a renunciation of self should not accompany that desire for salvation* so underrated by systematic philosophy" (PN, 71, emphasis added). A careful reader of the corpus would notice a double renunciation corresponding to the double command to love God and neighbor. There is the radical renunciation of all selfish self-love required by the neighbor love commandment as developed in *Works of Love*. But already in the earlier presentations of the religious stage, which involves the individual's loving obedience to God, a multiple and dramatic renunciation of self accompanies the desire for salvation. We can put the question this way: what sort of self-renunciation and transformation is required if the expectancy of eternal life is not to be "a superstitious belief in the future" either as "the craftiness of a sick soul that wants to sneak out of life" or the will to power of those who wish to preside over both earth and heaven (EUD, 259)? Kierkegaard's answer will be his version of "It is safe to tell the pure in heart that they shall see God, for only the pure in heart want to."

It would be an anachronism to attribute to Abraham a hope for eternal happiness in either the Platonic sense of the soul's immortality or the Jewish/Christian sense of the resurrection of the body. Still, we can assume that he hopes for the fulfillment of God's covenant promises to and through his descendants.[22] But his faith is not just the belief that God will be good to him. It involves, as Silentio tells the story, a multiple renunciation. He must leave behind his homeland to become "an alien in the promised land," and in the process leave behind his "worldly understanding" relative to which his emigration was entirely "unreasonable" (FT, 17).[23] He had to be, like the Knight of Infinite Resignation, willing to give up without resentment that which was dearest to him. But more than that, he had to be willing not just to *give up* his beloved son but to *do him in*, and, unlike the tragic hero, to be willing to do so without the comfort of the universal, the shared understanding that the family must sacrifice for the good of the larger community. And just because the social universal is the ground of the rational universal, the form of life which gives rise to the public language game, he is unable to explain and justify his willingness to Sarah, or Isaac, or Eliezer, but must remain silent. As the Knight of Faith, Abraham does not appear as an egoism tensed on itself, but as a deeply decentered self. Long before Nietzsche (not to mention Kierkegaard) shattered the Cartesian cogito,[24] Abraham's cogito is shattered by the demands of the living God, along with the *conatus* of which it is the expression.

The epistemic resignation signified in *Fear and Trembling* in terms of such notions as absurdity, paradox, madness, unreasonableness, and silence is more fully thematized in *Philosophical Fragments*. There faith is explicitly linked to the hope of eternal happiness, but also to revelation as distinct from recollection, which means that the self not only does not have the truth but does not have the capacity to recognize it even if face-to-face with it. So far from being the autonomous, self-sufficient, and, if you like, masculine self implicit in the notion of recollection and developed in the rationalisms, empiricisms, and pragmatisms of modernity, the believing soul is entirely dependent on God to give both the truth and the capacity to recognize it as such. Since the (re) production of this capacity is an act on a par with creation, Climacus calls it a miracle. And, as if to add insult to injury, he insists that I am in this predicament through my own fault, that I am in the untruth by virtue of sin, and that repentance and rebirth are an integral part of that miracle by which the truth can be recognized as such by faith. No wonder Climacus presents offense rather than doubt as the alternative to faith. As if he had been reading Levinas, he sees to it that the hope of salvation is accompanied by a renunciation of self-sufficiency, both epistemic and moral. The self needs both forgiveness and a teaching that goes beyond the maieutic.

Climacus continues to thematize eternal happiness in *Postscript*. There the three moments of existential pathos that make up Religiousness A involve a radical renunciation of the selfish self. This is perhaps most clearly seen in the analysis of suffering as perpetual dying to immediacy, but it is also present in the surrounding moments, resignation and guilt. And the point of the long analysis of these three moments is not just to show that Socrates can be religious without the help of Christianity, but more importantly, that Christianity cannot be religious without Socrates. To put it less paradoxically, Religiousness A is the context, the *how*, without which the specifically Christian *what* concerning the absolute paradox of the God-man, is not even religious, but a mixture of aesthetic and speculative elements posing as religion. Levinas may not be much interested in this renunciation because it has nothing immediately to do with the ethical relation to the widow, orphan, and stranger, in short, the neighbor. But shouldn't he at least acknowledge that a very significant renunciation of self does accompany the desire for salvation precisely in that pseudonym most focused on eternal happiness.

The second renunciation, the one involved in commanded neighbor love, is most fully expressed in the sustained assault on selfish self-love in *Works of Love*. But, as already noted, Levinas seems wholly ignorant of this text. Like too many others, he stops reading with the first authorship, assuming that Kierkegaard has said all he needs or wants to say by the time he finishes *Postscript*. It's a bit like complaining that Kant is unaware of moral responsibility because one finds no ethics in the First Critique. By neglecting the second authorship, and especially those writings that deal with Religiousness C, as I call those works in which Christ becomes not only the paradox to be believed but also the prototype to be imitated,[25] he overlooks the place where he and Kierkegaard are in deepest agreement, in spite of their difference over the priority of the God relation, and offers a seriously flawed critique of Kierkegaardian subjectivity as an egoism tensed on or over itself.

If I do not treat this reading of Kierkegaard *simply* as a misreading, it is for three reasons. First, it reminds us of a basic hermeneutical principle, the importance of reading the whole of Kierkegaard's authorship if we are properly to understand any of its parts. Particular texts have regularly been read in the light of their biographical, social, and cultural context, but too frequently they have not been read in the context of the authorship as a whole. It's a bit too neat, but heuristically we can say that the so-called first and second authorships correspond to the first and second commandments of Jesus' summary of the law and that only together do they give us an account of what used to be called "the whole duty of man" (Eccl. 12:13, KJV).

Second, as we discover how this reading is a misreading, we discover the deep, if formal agreement between Kierkegaard and Levinas. The responsible self, in each case, is tense, not relaxed and at ease in Zion (see Amos 6:1–7); and in both cases this tension derives not from a natural, self-centered *conatus essendi* but from a desire directed precisely toward that Other who radically relativizes that *conatus,* denying autonomy both to its cogito and to its will to power. They disagree most obviously on who this Other, in the first instance, is. But just because of the deep agreement that underlies this by no means shallow disagreement, it becomes possible to read them not just against each other but with each other, asking how the tension between them can be a creative one and not just a train wreck. We can ask what dangers each might avoid by learning from the other.

Third, and as an example of the second point, Levinas' concern that hope of eternal happiness may lead me to neglect the widow, the orphan, and the stranger points to a very real danger in the Kierkegaardian position, one not entirely absent from Christian history. It can be illustrated by the national energy policy recently announced by the George W. Bush administration. Hoping to hit a home run with the voters, President Bush made sure to touch all the bases. He talked about (1) increased exploration for oil and gas, (2) increased use of nuclear energy, (3) expedited authorization process for new power plants, (4) conservation, (5) research and development for alternative, renewable sources of energy, and (6) environmental protection. The plan was met with widespread suspicion (or in some quarters, perhaps, confident hope) that he was serious about only the first three and was merely paying lip service to the last three. The proof of the pudding, it was said, would be in actions taken. What gets funded and at what levels? What legislation is proposed and opposed? What regulatory decisions are made? Whose side in legal disputes does the Justice Department take?

The text is as pure as the driven snow, and in response to the skeptics, the administration pointed to its provisions addressing their concerns. But the text is one thing, its implementation another. I am reminded of the Soviet official I once heard defend the human rights record of the Soviet Union on the grounds that its constitution guaranteed human rights. I have tried to show that the Kierkegaardian corpus is as pure as the driven snow, that it clearly affirms the Johannine principle that we cannot pretend to love God, whom we have not seen, if we do not love our brothers and sisters whom we have seen (1 John 4:20–21). Levinas' prophetic skepticism may be unfair to the text, but it is the ever-needed reminder that pure texts are not the same as pure hearts nor profession the same as practice. Those who emphasize the priority of the God relation and the derivative character of the neighbor relation always need to do more than affirm the inseparability of the first and the second commandment.

They need to be especially vigilant against the temptation to allow "second" to come out as "secondary," to slide, at least in practice, into less important or peripheral or even optional.

Alongside the complaint that Kierkegaardian subjectivity, precisely in its religiousness, is a form of egoism, is a second complaint too serious to be quickly dismissed, namely, that precisely in its religiousness it is also a form of violence. In expressing his appreciation of the way in which this subjectivity resists both political and speculative totalitarianism, Levinas wonders whether it "does not lead us to other forms of violence" (PN, 68–69). Part of what he has in mind is a "verbal violence" in which, like Nietzsche, Kierkegaard "philosophizes with a hammer" (PN 76). The philosopher who resists the tyranny of totality with the trauma of transcendence in the manner that Levinas does is not in a very good position to complain about the "tone" (PN, 72) of his predecessors' writing. It's a case of the pot calling the kettle black.[26] Still, we cannot dismiss this charge on that ground, for it is not primarily a question of rhetoric. Ironically, it is the religious as such that links Kierkegaard to Nietzsche, as we hear in a passage partially cited above.

> It is not just a question of literary form. Violence emerges in Kierkegaard at the precise moment when, moving beyond the esthetic stage, existence can no longer limit itself to what it takes to be an ethical stage and enters the religious one, the domain of belief. This latter is no longer justified in the outer world. Even within, it is at once communication and solitude, and hence violence and passion. Thus begins the disdain for the ethical basis of being, the somehow secondary nature of all ethical phenomena that, through Nietzsche, has led us to the amoralism of the most recent philosophers. (PN, 72)[27]

There is a serious equivocation here. The ethical stage *(Sittlichkeit)* is not identical with the "ethical basis of being" for Kierkegaard any more than politics is identical with the ethical relation for Levinas. We encounter it again in the following passage, in which the first appearance of ethical order signifies *Sittlichkeit,* while the second signifies the ethical relation. "Kierkegaard has a predilection for the biblical story of the sacrificing of Isaac. Thus, he describes the encounter with God as a subjectivity rising to the religious level: God above the ethical order! His interpretation of the story can doubtless be given a different orientation. Perhaps Abraham's ear for hearing the voice that brought him back to the ethical order was the highest moment in this drama" (PN, 74; cf. 77). But let us not simply dismiss his anxiety simply on the grounds of this carelessness. What bothers Levinas about *Fear and Trembling* is the fear that there the religious does preempt not just "the ethical state" but "the ethical basis of being" itself. Levinas here seems to side with those biblical scholars who have sometimes suggested that the point of the story is to reinforce Israel's repudiation of child sacrifice as practiced by Canaanite cults.[28] This would bring the story of the Akedah (binding of Isaac) into line with the sixteen other passages in the Hebrew Bible where such practices are condemned.[29]

Attractive as such a solution may seem, it simply brushes aside two awkward features of the story common both to the biblical version and to Silentio's. First, although it becomes clear that God never intends for Abraham actually to sacrifice Isaac, God does command him to do so. Second, Abraham demonstrates his willingness to obey this command, not in words but in three days' worth of deeds (Gen. 22:4).[30] While Abraham is stopped from killing Isaac, he is not rebuked; and it is this Abraham that is the hero of faith in Genesis, in subsequent biblical texts[31] and, most importantly in the present context, in *Fear and Trembling*. Silentio does not find Abraham's greatness in his hearing and obeying the voice of God when it was easy, when he was told to save Isaac, but in his hearing and obeying the voice of God when it was terrifyingly difficult. Far from seeking to minimize the *horror religiosus* (FT, 61) of the situation, Silentio insists on it with a rhetoric that makes Levinas uneasy and tells us, "I have seen the terrifying face to face" (FT, 33). Eventually he relates the Abraham story to Luke 14:26, in which Jesus says, "If any one comes to me and does not hate his own father and mother and wife and children and brothers and sisters, yes, and even his own life, he cannot be my disciple." Silentio adds, "This is a hard saying. Who can listen to it?" (FT, 72).

In the text it is clear that the ethic which is to be teleologically suspended in faith is the Hegelian *Sittlichkeit*, the laws and customs of one's people. Against Hegel and a complacent Christendom that finds in him an ideological spokesman, Silentio insists that the will of God is not necessarily identical with the laws and customs of any people but is, for faith, a higher norm which relativizes the latter whenever there is a conflict between what "we" think is right and what God says is right. As we have seen, Levinas (1) sometimes recognizes that this is the target of the text (which he attributes to Kierkegaard) and (2) shares Kierkegaard's desire to deprive every *Sittlichkeit* of its claims to absolute authority. So what's his beef? If we distinguish the ethical^S (= *Sittlichkeit*) from the ethical^L (= the ethical relation as Levinas understands it), as Levinas is not careful to do, the complaint would read like this: although only intending to relativize the former, by allowing a religious legitimation of Abraham's intent to kill Isaac, converting it from murder to sacrifice, Kierkegaard has expressed his disdain for the latter, thereby helping to give us Nietzsche and post-Nietzschean amoralism both political and philosophical. By teleologically suspending the ethical^S in the religious instead of in the ethical^L, Kierkegaard opens the door to a violence that cannot be accepted.

Here once again Levinas identifies with pinpoint accuracy the deepest disagreement between himself and Kierkegaard. This is another dimension of the debate over the priority of the God relation. According to the theistic view that governs *Fear and Trembling*, whatever God commands is right. This article of faith is independent of the debate over divine command theory.[32] Whether it is God's command that makes whatever is commanded right, as a nominalist/voluntarist tradition would insist, or, on the other hand, God commands it on the basis of seeing it to be in conformity with the divine essence, as a realist/intellectualist tradition would insist, both sides agree that God cannot command anything that is wrong. So if God commands Abraham to sacrifice Isaac, Abraham is right to obey, just as he is right to obey when God tells him to stay the knife. As Augustine puts it, "But when you suddenly command us to do something strange and unforeseen, even if you had previously forbidden it, none can doubt that the command must be obeyed, even though, for the time being, you may conceal the reason for it and it may conflict with the established rule of custom in some forms of society; for no society is right and good unless it obeys you. But happy are they who know that the commandment was yours."[33] Silentio makes Abraham happy in this sense. Without telling us how it happened, he stipulates that Abraham "knew it was God the Almighty who was testing [prøvede] him . . . but he knew also that no sacrifice is too severe when God demands it—and he drew the knife" (FT, 22). For Augustine, Silentio, and Kierkegaard, we do not ultimately know what is right until we know what God has commanded.

Levinas is worried, as we all should be, about claims to religious sanction for violence. The holy wars of yesterday and today are frightful indeed. So over against theism's moral empiricism, he places a moral a priorism. His critique of Kierkegaard's violence comes in the form of the priority of ethics to theology. We can know ahead of time that God could not possibly command some things, in this case the killing of Isaac.[34]

One objection to this move would go like this. Levinas has not given us an ethics. He tells us that the face of the Other speaks (TI, 66) and that it says "you shall not commit murder" (TI, 199, 216, 262, 303). But to know precisely what this excludes one would have to discover what justice requires by figuring into one's calculations, not just the legitimate demand of the Other but also the legitimate claims of the Third (and Fourth, etc.). Since Levinas has not done this, nor claimed to have done so, his objection has the force of "I (or We) don't approve of this." While that is not morally irrelevant, the point to notice is that his disapproval derives no support from his powerful account of the structure of moral transcendence. Moreover, if he were to preclude the possibility that in Abraham's case God might be the Third, whose requirements trump those of both Abraham and his community, that would make it clear that the atheism of which he sometimes speaks is not penultimate but ultimate and that so far from ethics being first philosophy for him, it depends on a prior ontology, one that excludes from being the kind of God Abraham, Silentio, and Kierkegaard presuppose.[35]

Another way to put this objection would be to notice the ontotheological character of Levinas' response. At the heart of Heidegger's critique of the ontotheological constitution of metaphysics (by which he means not the ethical relation Levinas calls metaphysics but the theoretical posture Levinas calls ontology) is the question, "How does the deity enter into philosophy?" For metaphysics or ontotheology, "the deity can come into philosophy only insofar as philosophy, of its own accord and by its own nature, requires and determines that and how the deity enters into it."[36] Levinas would seem to belong to this tradition. God can be taken up into his discourse only within the limits of an understanding of the ethical that is established without reference to God but which dictates the terms of God's involvement. As with Kant, God can be introduced after the fact to offer moral support to the philosopher's morality, but only on condition that God's voice is silenced during the establishment of that morality.[37]

Ironically, there is something quintessentially modern about this strategy for keeping religion from legitimizing violence. At the metaphysical (Levinas' ontological) level, we find it in Lessing, not only in *Nathan der Weise* but also in *On the Proof of the Spirit and of Power*,[38] a text of no small importance to the writings of Johannes Climacus. In the latter text Lessing argues against the possibility that Jesus is God incarnate on the grounds that his idea of God precludes a priori the possibility of any historical revelation to that effect. At the ethical level, as already noted, Kant makes Jesus into the highest instantiation of a moral ideal established within the limits of reason alone, which, in this case, means without reference to God. In both cases the desire was to create a purely rational and thus universal religion by eliminating those elements of positivity that made such historical religions as Judaism, Christianity, and Islam, or within Christianity, Catholicism and Protestantism, essentially different from each other, and, as such, the potential basis (all too frequently actualized) for religiously warranted violence. There is an element of déjà vu in Levinas' revival of this strategy.[39]

In itself, of course, this irony is not an objection. The objection would be that there is a certain arrogance in the notion that philosophy, whether in the form of ontotheologically constituted metaphysics or in the form of ethics, can dictate the terms on which God can be allowed into human culture. Is this not an act of (attempted) violence against God, *lèse majesté* against the only Ultimate Majesty? That would be the Kierkegaardian charge to which Levinas (or his enthusiasts) would need to reply if his critique is to have the force he wishes. He might reply that human majesty is the Ultimate Majesty, but then his God talk would lose much of its intended force and he would be exposed as a crypto-Feuerbachian. Or he might explain the relation of his God to moral right and wrong in some other way. Is God an independent variable on the moral scene or just a name for the depth dimension of the human self by virtue of which it has moral authority? Obviously Levinas is not in a position to provide the needed clarification, but Levinasians need to fish or cut bait on this issue.

There is another irony here. Later, in *Otherwise Than Being*, Levinas gives the basis for a very Kierkegaardian response to his objection. There he presents the trauma of transcendence in terms of the same's obsession with and being taken hostage by the other, whose claims radically put the same in question. But he insists that this is without slavery or alienation (OTB, 11, 105, 112, 114, 118, 138). The alterity in question demands "a sacrifice without reserve ... the sacrifice of a hostage designated who has not chosen himself to be hostage, but possibly elected by the Good ... But being Good it redeems the violence of its alterity" (OTB, 15).[40] Levinas can object to Silentio's Abraham only to the degree that he is sure Abraham's God is not the Good. This is a fundamental point of divergence between Levinas and Kierkegaard, and it is at least as much ontological as it is ethical.[41]

The point of this argument is not to let Kierkegaard and Kierkegaardians off the hook. I have suggested above that Levinas and Kierkegaard need each other as prophetic voices to alert each other to the dangers inherent in their own prophetic philosophies. Levinas' complaint about violence poses a challenge to which Kierkegaard (or his enthusiasts) need to say more than they have. Of course the point of *Fear and Trembling* is not that we become Knights of Faith by killing our children, or by trying to until God stops us. But if we read *The Book on Adler* as a commentary on *Fear and Trembling,* it represents the clear acknowledgment that Kierkegaardian faith can offer no a priori guarantees that divine revelation will restrict itself to human expectations or to our deepest sense of what makes sense.[42] In Kierkegaardian perspective, that is just a way of saying that there really is a God? How, then, is the faith that lives before the God of Abraham to be kept from being the launching pad and legitimizer of holy war and the cultural imperialism that is its sidekick?

I believe Kierkegaard has resources for replying to this challenge. Doubtless they will involve the notion that the Good and the True are something to die for rather than to kill for. But developing these resources will have to be a task for the future. For the present, I conclude with an observation and a challenge. Both Levinas and Kierkegaard offer powerful critiques of the politics of their day (and ours). With prophetic boldness they shake the foundations rather furiously. But neither gives us a politics. In a certain sense I suppose it's just as well, for had they done so the result would be of limited usefulness to us both because their situations were quite different from ours and because, partly for that reason, they probably have political biases from which we would prefer to be free. Another reason why it's just as well should be fairly obvious. This lacuna in their writings gives to those of us who find our own thought challenged and nurtured by theirs both the opportunity and perhaps the responsibility to develop what we might call a Levinasian politics of justice and a Kierkegaardian politics of love. Nor should we take the contrast between justice and love too seriously. For Levinas increasingly speaks the language of love alongside the language of justice,[43] and Kierkegaard makes it clear that love is the debt we owe to the neighbor.

Notes

This chapter first appeared in *Revista Portuguesa de Filosofia* (2008). It is reprinted here by permission.

1. See the satires of JC and FT, 5–7; also PC, 81 n. 18, where Anti-Climacus complains that in modern philosophy "the practice has been to use the category 'doubt' where the discussion should be about 'offense.' The relation of personality to Christianity is not

to doubt or to believe, but to be offended or to believe . . . Instead of deterring and calling people to order by speaking of being despairing and being offended, [modern philosophy] has waved to them and invited them to become conceited by doubting and having doubted." In the light of what is to follow, it is worth noting that three times in this passage this defect is identified as "ethical" and not merely as "religious." Clearly this is not The Ethical that is teleologically suspended in FT.

2. Jamie Ferreira writes that "Levinas's concentration on the account of the ethical found in Kierkegaard's pseudonymous writings (*Fear and Trembling* and *Either/Or*) obscures the commonality between them on the character of the ethical relation to the other, which appears as soon as we turn to *Works of Love.*" *Love's Grateful Striving: A Commentary on Kierkegaard's* Works of Love (New York: Oxford University Press, 2001). Perhaps she is too kind. It is not a matter of concentration, as if there were an unbalanced emphasis, so much as oblivion—total blackout. But I agree with her that the result is most unfortunate.

3. This is the I that is We and the We that is I in terms of which Hegel defines Spirit. See *Hegel's Phenomenology of Spirit,* trans. A. V. Miller (Oxford: Clarendon, 1977), 110–11.

4. Among the texts included in the volume to which Kierkegaard here refers is one entitled "An Occasional Discourse," better known as "Purity of Heart Is to Will One Thing," which continues the analysis of the religion of hidden inwardness (though not by name) developed in *Postscript.*

5. I have developed the theme of God as the middle term between me and myself in "Transcendence, Heteronomy, and the Birth of the Responsible Self," in *Levinas and Kierkegaard in Dialogue* (Bloomington: Indiana University Press, 2008), chap. 6.

6. "Transcendence and Height" in BPW, 29–30. Is it not a strange notion of philosophy that rules out by definition, that is, a priori, the possibility that the God relation is integral to my self-relation and neighbor relation and that neither of the latter two can be properly understood apart from the former? Kierkegaard would agree that the idea of God as a very powerful being is abstract and not much help in clarifying the human situation. While he always presupposes God as creator, his point of departure is not power but demanding love.

7. "Transcendence and Height," in BPW, 29, emphasis added.

8. Perhaps Derrida is more candid. He also thinks that responsibility is inescapable, but he acknowledges that he "quite rightly passes for an atheist." *Circumfession* in *Jacques Derrida,* trans. Geoffrey Bennington (Chicago: Chicago University Press, 1993), 155.

9. For other expressions of appreciation, see TH, 15; "Enigma and Phenomenon" in BPW, 71, 76; and PN, 78.

10. Kant being an important exception.

11. *Confessions,* I, 1.

12. Is Levinas unaware that the hope of bodily resurrection, which is the Christian form of hope for eternal happiness, had its origin in pre-Christian Judaism, not in Platonic and pre-Platonic doctrines of the soul's immortality?

13. Anti-Climacus puts it a bit differently. Echoing the Pauline imperative, "be reconciled to God" (2 Cor. 5:20), he writes that Christianity not only "by means of the Atonement wants to eliminate sin as completely as if it were drowned in the sea" but also commands, "Thou shalt believe in the forgiveness of sins" (SUD, 100, 115).

14. *The Problem of Pain* (New York: Macmillan, 1962), 144–45.

15. *Tractatus in epistolam Joannis ad Parthos,* 7, 4, 8.

16. For Augustine, see *De Trinitate*, VIII, 4, 9 and XIV, 4, 18. For Kierkegaard, see WOL, 18, 22–24, 107.

17. I have discussed this internal relation of the self to its Others, both for Levinas and Kierkegaard, in "Transcendence, Heteronomy, and the Birth of the Responsible Self."

18. Climacus, who is not so allergic, nevertheless recognizes and rejects the eudaemonism that is merely sensualism (CUP, 403 n.). For a nicely nuanced analysis of Kierkegaard's relation to the eudaemonism of the Aristotelian tradition, see John Davenport, "Towards an Existential Virtue Ethics: Kierkegaard and MacIntyre," in *Kierkegaard After MacIntyre: Essays on Freedom, Narrative, and Virtue*, ed. John J. Davenport and Anthony Rudd (Chicago: Open Court, 2001).

19. Rawls makes this distinction somewhere in *A Theory of Justice*.

20. Part of the difference here may be simply that Levinas does not believe in any afterlife. It sounds that way when he writes, "But death is powerless, for life receives meaning from an infinite responsibility, a fundamental *diacony* that constitutes the subjectivity of the subject—without that responsibility, completely tendered toward the Other, leaving any leisure for a return to self" (PN, 74). Levinas' responsibility in the face of death is importantly different from Heidegger's resoluteness in the face of death; but neither involves the hope of eternal life. The fact that Levinas can only conceive of a return to self as "leisure" perhaps explains why there is no "as yourself" in his version of "you shall love your neighbor." See EN, where he does use the language of neighbor love.

21. I cite the text as it appears in the Hongs' translation at EUD, 261 and 266.

22. As spelled out in Genesis 12, 15, and 17.

23. We might call Silentio's exegesis Alexandrian in that he gives an allegorical meaning to Abraham's emigration, namely the leaving behind of his worldly understanding. But it is equally Antiochene in that the literal or historical meaning, the departure from his homeland, is not only of intrinsic importance but also integrally involved in substance and not only as sign with the allegorical meaning. See Sandra M. Schneiders, "Scripture and Spirituality," in *Christian Spirituality: Origins to the Twelfth Century*, ed. Bernard McGinn, John Meyendorff, and Jean Leclerc (New York: Crossroad, 1988).

24. See Paul Ricoeur, *Oneself as Another*, trans. Kathleen Blamey (Chicago: University of Chicago Press, 1992), 11–16.

25. Especially WOL, PC, FSE, and JFY. For the introduction of the concept of Religiousness C, see "Kierkegaard's Teleological Suspension of Religiousness B," in *Foundations of Kierkegaard's Vision of Community*, ed. George Connell and C. Stephen Evans (Atlantic Highlands, N.J.: Humanities, 1991).

26. In fairness to Levinas it should be noted that these comments, from 1963 and 1966, precede his most violent rhetoric, which belongs to *Otherwise Than Being* (1974) and essays associated with it. The first version of "Substitution," which became chapter 4 of *Otherwise Than Being* appeared in 1968. From at least that point on violent rhetoric is a Levinasian trademark.

27. Cf. PN, 76: "That harshness of Kierkegaard emerges at the exact moment when he 'transcends ethics.'"

28. See, for example, John Bright, *A History of Israel* (Philadelphia: Westminster, 1959), 92. For the rejection of this reading, see Gerhard von Rad, *Genesis*, rev. ed. (Philadelphia: Westminster, 1973), 238–29; and Walter Brueggemann, *Genesis* (Atlanta: John Knox, 1982), 185–86.

29. Louis Jacobs cites these passages in "The Problem of the *Akedah* in Jewish

Thought," in *Kierkegaard's "Fear and Trembling": Critical Appraisals,* ed. Robert L. Perkins (University: University of Alabama Press, 1981), 1. This essay gives a nice overview of the rich variety of interpretations of Genesis 22 in the Jewish tradition.

30. Silentio makes it four days. See FT, 10, 12. In American law, such actions would be sufficient to convict Abraham of conspiracy (if it were possible, legally speaking, to conspire with God), even if the act itself did not occur.

31. Romans 4; Galatians 3; and Hebrews 11.

32. For an overview with a helpful bibliography, see Janine Marie Idziak, "Divine Command Ethics," in *A Companion to Philosophy of Religion,* ed. Philip L. Quinn and Charles Taliaferro (Cambridge, Mass.: Blackwell, 1997). So far as I can see, *Works of Love* is neutral on this question, as is Phil Quinn's "The Divine Command Ethics in Kierkegaard's *Works of Love,*" in *Faith, Freedom, and Rationality: Philosophy of Religion Today,* ed. Jeff Jordan and Daniel Howard-Snyder (Lanham, Md.: Rowman & Littlefield, 1996). Both focus on the commanded character of love in the Christian tradition, but without making the command into that which makes love right. The question of the *Euthyprho,* so far as I can see, is left unanswered. Since Quinn defends divine command theory elsewhere, his title can be a bit misleading.

33. *Confessions,* III, 9 (Pine-Coffin translation).

34. The theist also knows a priori that God cannot command evil, but until she knows what God commands does not know whether the killing of Isaac is good or evil. Thus for Silentio, it will be sacrifice if God commands it and murder otherwise.

35. For Levinas' claims to the contrary, see, in addition to TI, "Is Ontology Fundamental?" in BPW; "Ethics as First Philosophy," in LR.

36. *Identity and Difference,* trans. Joan Stambaugh (New York: Harper & Row, 1969), 55–56. For my account of Heidegger's critique, see the title essay of *Overcoming Onto-Theology: Toward a Postmodern Christian Faith* (New York: Fordham University Press, 2001).

37. This is similar to what Habermas means by the linguistification of the sacred. The discourse in which moral norms are established is one from which God is excluded. See *The Theory of Communicative Action,* vol. 2, *Lifeworld and System: A Critique of Functionalist Reason,* trans. Thomas Mc Carthy (Boston: Beacon, 1987), 46–108. But unlike Kant and Levinas, Habermas does not try to introduce God into moral discourse for motivational effect after all the normative work has been done.

38. To be found in *Lessing's Theological Writings,* trans. Henry Chadwick (Stanford, Calif.: Stanford University Press, 1957).

39. The same can be said about Derrida's attempt to revive the Kantian project. See "Faith and Knowledge: The Two Sources of 'Religion' at the Limits of Reason Alone," in *Religion,* ed. Jacques Derrida and Gianni Vattimo (Stanford: Stanford University Press, 1998); and Derrida, *Specters of Marx: The State of the Debt, the Work of Mourning, and the New International,* trans. Peggy Kamuf (New York: Routledge, 1994).

40. Cf. OTB, 43, where Levinas speaks of "a disinterestedness imposed with a good violence," and OTB, 123, "In this trauma the Good reabsorbs, or redeems, the violence of non-freedom."

41. For Levinas "ethics is not at all a layer that covers over ontology, but rather that which is in some fashion more ontological than ontology" (GWCM, 89–90). One might put this by saying that it is only as a radical ethical claim on me that the human Other *is.* But whether there *is* a non-human other to whom I am absolutely obligated and whose goodness redeems the violence of a command like the one given to Abraham—that question is not the Levinasian ethical as "more ontological than ontology" but rather a

more traditional ontological question, though fact and value are as inseparable here as for an ethics that is "more ontological than ontology."

42. Need one mention the paradox motif that runs through the corpus?

43. Especially in EN.

2 Existential Appropriations: The Influence of Jean Wahl on Levinas's Reading of Kierkegaard

J. Aaron Simmons

Levinas as an Ambivalent Reader of Kierkegaard

Whereas Martin Heidegger is at his best when he is reading other philosophers, Emmanuel Levinas is not. Despite his early success at interpreting Husserl for a French audience,[1] with his own philosophical maturity came a waning of such deep readings in favor of using other thinkers as foils or as problematically superficial points of support for his own original thinking.[2] Borrowing Heidegger's useful distinction between *going counter to a thinker* and *going to a thinker's encounter*,[3] often Levinas just goes and gets what he needs from a text whether this be positive, as in the case of his reading of Rosenzweig, or negative, as in the case of Hegel or Heidegger. If only it were this easy.

When it comes to Levinas as a reader of Kierkegaard, as Merold Westphal points out in chapter 1 of this volume, we cannot just conclude that Levinas is a "bad" reader, even if there are moments when this seems to be the best possible characterization.[4] Offering the examples of Levinas's claim that Kierkegaard is preoccupied with doubt, Levinas's notion of "immodesty," the bizarre thought that Kierkegaard's Abraham is motivated by an egoistic revolt against the state, and ultimately the misconception of Kierkegaard's frozen "ethical stage" that appears throughout Levinas's comments, Westphal admits that he

> suspect[s] that if Levinas applied for admission to one of our graduate programs and submitted as a writing sample an essay including these readings of Kierkegaard, we would dismiss him out of hand, shaking our heads and asking, Who taught this kid to read, anyway?[5]

However, at the very moments when he appears to be at his most superficial, Levinas often makes a deeply significant point about a thinker that illuminates a strikingly "good" reading.[6] Consider that while Levinas tends to equate Hegel and Heidegger, he does so by obviously over-simplifying their thought *and yet* he simultaneously displays a deep appreciation of the trajectories in their thinking that invite such a reductive equation. Given this dynamism, even if it is often problematic, we might conclude that when Levinas gets a thinker *wrong,* he frequently does so in the *right* way. Bad readings may still produce profitable results. However, what a sustained consideration of Levinas's own thinking demonstrates is that we can never be satisfied with this instrumental relation to others. The ends never *justify* the means, but there may be times in which inadvertently certain means that would not otherwise be commended produce good outcomes.

For these reasons, we should not conclude that Levinas is just a bad reader of philosophy in general, and Kierkegaard in particular, but instead merely that he is an *ambivalent,* or a *highly selective,* one. For example, Levinas often finds something helpful in a text or thinker and either pulls it out of context and stretches its meaning for his own purposes (e.g., the repeated use of the line from Dostoevsky),[7] or occasionally even straw-mans an idea or a thinker in order to facilitate his own philosophical point (as, I believe, is often the case with his reading of Kierkegaard).

There is perhaps no thinker for whom Levinas's ambivalence is more pronounced than Kierkegaard. For Levinas, Kierkegaard is both the best example of a kindred spirit in the project of resisting totality and systematic philosophy, and the worst example of someone who relegates ethics to a secondary role. Both of these interpretations are understandable. Regarding the critique of totality, Kierkegaard and Levinas stand in something of a transitive relationship. Kierkegaard's entire philosophy can be read as a contestation of Hegel's systematic elimination of singularity. Drawing on the above example, we can see how this relationship mirrors Levinas's own relationship to Heidegger. Given that it is hard to differentiate between Hegel and Heidegger in Levinas's thought, we should expect to see resonances between Kierkegaard and Levinas inasmuch as they both resist the philosophical movement toward any overarching unified synthesis.

To push this point one step further, Levinas claims that one of the greatest influences on his own thinking is Franz Rosenzweig. Indeed, he notes that Rosenzweig's *Star of Redemption (Stern der Erlösung)*[8] is "a work too often present in *[Totality and Infinity]* to be cited" (TI, 28). Levinas reads Rosenzweig's philosophy, which is essentially "a discussion of Hegel," as being "a radical critique of totality" (EI, 75–76).[9] Since Levinas claims that a critique of Hegel is the starting point of his own thought, it would only be surprising if there *were not* a significant overlap between his and Kierkegaard's thought. Mark Taylor also notes this resonance between Kierkegaard and Levinas when he observes that "in criticizing Hegel's notion of the subject, Levinas implicitly aligns himself with Kierkegaard's critique of Hegelian philosophy."[10]

However, just as Kierkegaard's critique of totality suggests a connection with Levinas, his conception of religion provides a stumbling block for Levinas's wholehearted embrace of him. Due to Kierkegaard's theory of the progression of "stages along life's way," which clearly seems to posit the religious as higher than the ethical, it is not difficult to see why Levinas seeks to contest this aspect of Kierkegaard's philosophy. Although there is ample evidence in Kierkegaard's authorship to support Levinas's frustration, to say that Kierkegaard only has one static conception of ethics that is decidedly trumped by religion is perhaps the most problematic point in the Levinasian interpretation. Thus, building on Merold Westphal's work tracing the relation between Kierkegaard and Levinas, I will further develop Levinas's reading of Kierkegaard and point out both the aspects of it that are right on target (i.e., the idea of the singularity of subjectivity and the priority of God to the Other), and then briefly indicate where his reading does not just miss the bull's-eye, but fails to hit the target altogether (i.e., the static and solitary conception of ethics and the violence of a self-absorbed subjectivity).

Before proceeding, it is important to note a particular obstacle in attempting to give a thorough account and evaluation of Levinas's reading of Kierkegaard, namely, Levinas just does not write much about Kierkegaard. The most sustained reflection he provides is in his collection of short essays about various philosophical and literary thinkers, *Proper Names*.[11] In it we find a revised version of the comments that he made at the 1964 UNESCO Kierkegaard Vivant conference,[12] along with the reprint of a 1963 essay that was originally published in German.[13] Levinas offers two main interpretative lines for reading Kierkegaard. Being characteristically ambivalent, the first champions Kierkegaard's conception of a "new modality of truth," while contesting his conception of an "immodest subjectivity." The second is a biting critique that Levinas finds flowing out of the ontology that is coordinate with Kierkegaardian subjectivity, namely, surpassing the ethical is fundamentally violent to other people. I will consider each in turn and then offer a few suggestions as to where Levinas's interpretation finds its philosophical roots—the work of Jean Wahl.

Interpretation 1: A New Modality of the True

Levinas opens his 1965 essay "Enigma and Phenomena" with a characterization of Western ontology:

> As a speech directed upon the present, philosophy is an understanding of being, or an ontology, or a phenomenology. In the order of its speech it encompasses and situates even what seemed first to contain this speech or overflow it, but which, when present, that is, discovered, fits into this logos, is ordered in it, even making what is discernible of the past or of the future in the present enter into it. Being and speech have the same time, are contemporary. To utter a speech that would not be anchored in the present would be to go beyond reason. Beyond what is discernible in the present only meaningless speech would hold forth.[14]

According to Levinas's description, ontology brings being *(ontos)* and speech *(logos)* into identity. This identity has important consequences for Western philosophy. As the "love of wisdom," philosophy is essentially a search for truth. To be a philosopher is, on this account, to be the person who adheres to Socrates' instruction to "follow [the] beloved wherever it may lead" (*tōi erōmenōi akolouthein hopē an ekeinos hupagē*).[15] The path to truth is thus a path on which we can be led by the "evidence" of logic and argument. According to this evidence, Levinas asks the pressing question, "Does not the primacy of ontology among the branches of knowledge rest on a most obvious evidence?"[16] The "evidence" to which Levinas refers can be put simply as the idea that when we inquire into the truth, we inquire into the way things *are*. When coupled with Parmenides' claim that to know the truth is to know that that which is, is, and that which is not, is not, we can easily see the logic of Levinas's conclusion regarding the identity between being and speech. Only that which *is* can properly be an object of knowledge, and only that which can be known can be spoken about. Moreover, that which is must have its being in the present, for to deny this is to deny the law of non-contradiction. The connection between being, speech, and the present, is, then, the primary triad of Western philosophy. It forms what Derrida calls its "logocentric" character.

Accordingly, truth is recognized by the Greeks, as well as all those who continue to follow in their footsteps, as "divine." As Aristotle notes in the *Metaphysics*, "The most divine knowledge is also most worthy of honor."[17] The highest truth is the truth pertaining to the knowledge which "would be the only kind or the most appropriate kind for God to have."[18] Truth is thereby *triumphant* since it is identified with the very being of God. The philosopher who knows the truth thus "occup[ies] the divine perspective on the world, or at least peek[s] over God's shoulder."[19] Philosophy is essentially privileged due to its objectivity. This historical trajectory finds its culmination in the idealism of Hegel. Arriving at "the absolute truth and all truth," philosophy finally reaches absolute unity in "the Idea that thinks itself."[20] Truth finally triumphs as "Absolute Knowledge" when *Geist* comes to self-consciousness of itself:

> The *goal*, Absolute Knowing, or Spirit that knows itself as Spirit, has for its path the recollection of the Spirits as they are in themselves and as they accomplish the organization of their realm. Their preservation, regarded from the side of their free existence appearing in the form of contingency, is History; but regarded from the side of their (philosophically) comprehended organization, it is the Science of Knowing in the sphere of appearance: the two together, comprehended History, form alike the inwardizing and the Calvary of absolute Spirit, the actuality, truth, and certainty of his throne, without which he would be lifeless and alone.[21]

Levinas summarizes the Hegelian position as the "absorption" of the "human subject" by Being. Triumphant truth means the triumph of Reason to which "the subject . . . [has handed] over its last secrets" (PN, 66). Against the backdrop of this triumphant truth, privileged perspective, and absolute openness, Levinas locates the philosophical importance of Kierkegaard.

The Secret Anxiety of Kierkegaardian Subjectivity

According to Levinas, European thought owes "the strong notion of existence" to Kierkegaard (PN, 66). Rather than be persuaded by the totalizing movements of idealist metaphysics, Kierkegaard attempted to maintain absolute secrecy. What could contest the all-consuming eye of metaphysical objectivity? What could withstand the never-ending probes of philosophical inquiry? What could dethrone triumphant truth? For Kierkegaard it is the radical interiority of human subjectivity. The interiority of the self is a land into which the conquering force can gain no access. The classical triad of Being, speech, and presence, that defined the absolute status of truth, is exhausted in the domain of exteriority. "Exteriority cannot match human interiority," Levinas surmises from Kierkegaard. "The subject has a secret," he continues, "for ever inexpressible, which determines his or her very subjectivity" (PN, 67). Levinas is quick to point out that this secret is not simply a secret that has yet to be told. It is instead a secret that "remains of itself inexpressible" (PN, 67).

Subjectivity is not simply locked until the right key is found to open it; it is locked by a clasp for which there is no key. Levinas will contend that this inexpressible secret of Kierkegaardian subjectivity is "identifiable especially with the burn of sin" (PN, 67). The reference to Christian theology is not a slip of the pen. Levinas's equation between the radical interiority of subjectivity and the burn of sin is due to his conviction that Kierkegaard's philosophy goes beyond "philosophical notion[s]" themselves by "return[ing] to the Christian experience" (PN, 67). The experience that Levinas terms "Christian" is the biblical notion of a "thorn in the side" (PN, 67),[22] which continues to call the self to itself. Subjectivity is defined by a fundamental anxiety for itself and its condition in existence, namely, its sinfulness. Kierkegaardian subjectivity is, according to Levinas, best understood as a "*tensing on oneself*" *(tension sur soi)* (PN, 67, italics in the original).[23]

If there was any doubt as to the philosophical ghosts that Levinas wished to conjure with this definition of subjectivity, it is quickly removed when Levinas proceeds to link the Kierkegaardian self that is turned in on itself with Spinoza's essential notion of self-perseverance from the *Ethics* and Heidegger's definition of *Dasein* as a being for whom its own Being is an issue that first appears in *Being and Time*.[24] Levinas's pairing of Kierkegaardian subjectivity with Spinoza's *conatus essendi* and the *Jemeinigkeit* of *Dasein* is certainly not a laudatory pronouncement. Both of the latter represent "the ugly vice" of egoistic ontology (PN, 70). It is as if Levinas is saying that the Kierkegaardian subject is fundamentally defined as being "for itself" *(für sich, pour soi)* and is never able to make the transition to being "for-the-other" *(pour l'autre)*.

Although there is much in Kierkegaard to invite a reading similar to that offered by Levinas above, the charge of egoistic subjectivity is hard to swallow when we consider the whole of Kierkegaard's authorship. Surely Levinas is right regarding the conception of subjectivity as an essential secret, and we can follow him without much hesitation on the idea of interiority's being non-subsumable into speculative totality. But even a cursory glance at *Fear and Trembling*, the only Kierkegaardian text Levinas seemingly has read, should indicate the lengths to which Kierkegaard's Johannes de Silentio will go to expose the dis-possession of Abraham's own subjectivity. Abraham's concern is constantly with God *and* Isaac, never just with himself. Were it true that Abraham was simply "tensed on himself," then why would God's command be an ordeal

(Prøvelse) for him? How could he be tried *(forsøges)* and tempted *(fristede)* if his concern were only for his own care (Heidegger) or perseverance (Spinoza)? The drama of the struggle is only possible because he is *not* egoistic.[25]

Moreover, it is difficult to see how Kierkegaard's own Lutheranism would allow him to conceive of subjectivity as a self-turned-in-on-itself.[26] For Luther, this is the very definition of sin.[27] To move out of one's sin and toward the redemptive grace of God is to move beyond this self-concern in the name of giving oneself over to God. If Levinas had overlooked the importance of the religious stage in Kierkegaard's articulation of the progression of subjectivity, then we might at least forgive him on this point due to sheer ignorance. However, as we will see momentarily, it is precisely the move beyond the ethical and into the religious that raises Levinas's most critical ire. Given Kierkegaard's explicit Lutheranism, the proper view of subjectivity (as religious) is always *kenotic*. An essential kerygma of Christianity is *kenosis*.[28] "Outside the aesthetic," Westphal rightly protests against Levinas's supposition, "the self in Kierkegaard's corpus is always essentially relational."[29]

Interestingly, Levinas seems to recognize the relational character of Kierkegaardian subjectivity when he asks whether "the exaltation of pure faith . . . is not itself the ultimate consequence of that still natural tension of being on itself that I have alluded to . . . as egotism" (PN, 70). With this passage Levinas shows his hand. Despite all indications to the contrary, Levinas is not really arguing that the Kierkegaardian self is isolated unto itself, but instead he is arguing against the way Kierkegaard conceives of relationality. The real problem is not that the self is self-absorbed, for Levinas's own statements recognize that there is always a tête-à-tête engagement even for the most solitary of Kierkegaardian subjects. Rather, what Levinas most stringently resists is the Other with whom the self is engaged—God, as opposed to the other person.

Kierkegaard's God and the Importance of Persecuted Truth

In "The Transparent Shadow: Kierkegaard and Levinas in Dialogue," Westphal notes that "for Levinas, recognizing the infinity of the neighbor is an essential prior condition to recognizing the infinity of God, while for Kierkegaard it seems to be the other way around."[30] This reversal of priority is, Westphal says elsewhere, "the most fundamental divergence between [Levinas] and Kierkegaard."[31] On this point, Levinas astutely recognizes how his thought is differentiated from Kierkegaard's. Moreover, he offers a very good understanding of the impact that Kierkegaard's God has on Kierkegaard's notion of truth. If the Western ontological tradition is characterized by the triumph of truth, Kierkegaard's philosophy affirms a truth that is "persecuted."[32] The highest example of this can be found in Kierkegaard's appropriation of the Christian incarnation. God comes to earth not as a king but as a servant. God does not enter human history riding a flaming chariot with purple robes of majesty trailing behind, but is instead greeted by shepherds and cattle in a manger.

Levinas uses Kierkegaard's God as an illuminative example of what he calls an "enigma": "What is essential here is the way a meaning that is beyond meaning is inserted in the meaning that remains in an order, the way it advances while retreating. . . . In an enigma the exorbitant meaning is already effaced in its apparition."[33] The Kierkegaardian God, Levinas writes,

> is revealed only to be persecuted and unrecognized, reveals himself only in the measure that he is hunted—such that subjectivity, despairing in the solitude in which this absolute humility leaves it, becomes the very locus of truth. The Kierkegaardian God is not simply the bearer of certain attributes of humility; he is a way of truth which this time is not determined by a phenomenon, by the present and contemporaneousness, and is not measured by certainty.[34]

Notice how Levinas opposes Kierkegaard's conception to everything that characterized the classical notion of truth (power, communicability, certainty, and presence). The persecuted God of "Enigma and Phenomena" is the enigma that expresses the persecuted truth of *Proper Names*.

Levinas claims that the idea of persecuted truth is a direct result of Kierkegaard's radical notion of belief. Traditionally, belief is simply understood as a weak version of knowledge. It is what we almost know or know to a certain degree, but not what we actually and properly know. We believe in what we do not have enough evidence to call knowledge. Kierkegaard challenges this idea from the start. As long as knowledge is given priority in this way, logocentrism remains intact. Levinas nicely articulates this by saying that "belief is not, [for Kierkegaard], an imperfect knowledge of a truth that would be perfect and triumphant in itself. In his view, belief is not a small truth, a truth without certainty, a degradation of knowledge" (PN, 77). Instead, Kierkegaard refuses to set belief in opposition with knowledge, for this would just be an opposition between certainty and uncertainty. The actual opposition, Levinas insists, is "between truth triumphant and truth persecuted." This alteration opens what Levinas will call a "new modality of the true" (PN, 78; CPP, 66). Kierkegaard's "completely new" idea can be simply expressed as the inherent link between transcendence and humility.

Persecuted truth is an idea that Levinas can wholeheartedly support. Unfortunately, right at the moment when it seems that he is beginning to see the connection between his and Kierkegaard's thought, he turns on his heels and goes in the opposite direction. As noted earlier, the main split between Levinas and Kierkegaard is regarding their different loci of relational priority. Although Levinas will champion the new modality of truth opened by Kierkegaard, and celebrate his resistance to Hegelian totalization, Levinas ultimately returns to the charge of egoistic subjectivity when he considers the priority that Kierkegaard gives to the religious sphere. Having just claimed that it is due to Kierkegaard's radicalized notion of belief that persecuted truth begins to appear, Levinas makes a startling suggestion: "Violence emerges in Kierkegaard at the precise moment when, moving beyond the esthetic stage, existence can no longer limit itself to what it takes to be an ethical stage and enters the religious one, the domain of belief" (PN, 72). It is as if Levinas completely reversed the phrase from Hölderlin:

> But where the danger threatens
> That which saves from it also grows.[35]

Right where the saving idea of persecuted truth emerges there hides the dangerous, perhaps even "violent" notion of a "suspension of the ethical."

Interpretation 2: The Problem of Surpassing Ethics

There is hardly a more antithetical idea to Levinas's philosophy than the proposition that ethics could or should be suspended. Yet this is exactly what it appears that Kierkegaard requires in the highest stage of human existence—religious subjectivity. Receiving its most sustained treatment in *Fear and Trembling*, Johannes de Silentio argues that only by virtue of such a "teleological suspension" could Abraham be viewed as anything other than a murderer. "By his act," Silentio writes, Abraham "transgressed the ethical altogether and had a higher τέλος outside it, in relation to which he suspended it" (FT, 59). The higher telos to which Silentio refers is Abraham's "absolute duty" to God.[36] An absolute duty is only possible through an absolute relation; for only then would the duty be immediate. Mediation is the greatest threat for Abraham. If his relation to God is mediated by something (or someone) else, then he is lost. This is the paradox of Abraham's existence. As a particular existing individual, he stands higher than the universal itself. Silentio expresses this situation thus:

> During the time before the result, either Abraham was a murderer every minute or we stand before a paradox that is higher than all mediations. The story of Abraham contains, then, a teleological suspension of the ethical. As the single individual he became higher than the universal. This is the paradox, which cannot be mediated (FT, 66).

To be without mediation is also to be without public expression. Mediation is the condition of possibility for communicability. For this reason, Silentio constantly claims that he cannot understand Abraham, and that Abraham's situation is a secret even to Abraham himself. Devoting the entire third Problema to the question of communication, Silentio asks whether Abraham was justified in remaining silent. If Silentio answers this question in the affirmative, he simply repeats the difficulty he seeks to address. Justification is itself a public enterprise. I justify myself *to another*. To be justified unto oneself is similar to having a radically private language: it is a conceptual impossibility that runs aground in lived experience.[37] In Abraham's case, Silentio has already claimed that if there is such public expression then Abraham is condemned as nothing but a murderer. However, on the other hand, it would be wrong to conclude that Abraham is simply unjustified. To be unjustified is to fail to be justified and as such it is a negative expression for the same thing. Both justification and its failure operate according to the same universal logic—a logic that is public, communicable, and necessary. Hence Silentio's answer to the question of justification is more than a simple neither/nor; it is a contestation of the universal, of the general, of the public *as* the highest criterion.

"Now we are face to face with the paradox," Silentio announces. "Either the single individual as the single individual," he continues, "can stand in an absolute relation to the absolute, and consequently the ethical is not the highest, or Abraham is lost: he is neither a tragic hero nor an esthetic hero" (FT, 113). Abraham's silence is neither aesthetic—which would be demanded in order to save another rather than sacrifice another—nor is it ethical—which would be demanded only as a "human prescience" that would expect the same from each and every other person in the same situation (FT, 112). Both of these silences are contingent: the person remaining silent *chooses* to do so. The silent aesthete could always cease to be aesthetic by speaking; the silent ethicist could always be unethical by proffering forth. Abraham is different. "Abraham remains silent—but he *cannot* speak," Silentio insists. His silence is rightfully unjustified according to the standards of ethical behavior, but his silence does not answer to this standard. His silence is not simply required of him; it defines him. "And," Silentio concludes, "even if he understood all the languages of the world, even if those he loved also understood them, he still could not speak—he speaks in a divine language, he speaks in tongues" (FT, 114).[38]

What can we glean from this? It would appear that Abraham is unavailable for public criticism, beyond the scope of justification, defined by a paradoxical relation that is incommunicable and absolutely resistant to any attempt at understanding. What all of this amounts to, for both Silentio *and also for Levinas,* is that Abraham is situated *beyond* ethics. Allow me to quote a rather lengthy passage from the opening of Problema 1 in which Silentio defines "ethics."

> The ethical as such is the universal, and as the universal it applies to everyone, which from another angle means that it applies at all times. It rests immanent in itself, has nothing outside itself that is its τέλος but is itself the τέλος for everything outside itself, and when the ethical has absorbed this into itself, it goes not further. The single individual, sensately and psychically qualified in immediacy, is the individual who has this τέλος in the universal, and it is his ethical task continually to express himself in this, to annul his singularity in order to become the universal. . . . If this is the highest that can be said of man and his existence, then the ethical is of the same nature as a person's eternal salvation, which is his τέλος forevermore and at all times, since it would be a contradiction for this to be capable of being surrendered (i.e., teleologically suspended), because as soon as this is suspended it is relinquished, whereas that which is suspended is not relinquished but is preserved in the higher, which is its τέλος (FT, 54).

This definition of the ethical hearkens back to Hegel's definition of "ethical life" in *The Philosophy of Right:*

> The integration of these two relative totalities [i.e., the good and conscience] into an absolute identity has already been implicitly achieved in that this very subjec-

tivity of pure self-certainty, aware in its vacuity of its gradual evaporation, is identical with the abstract universality of the good. The identity of the good with the subjective will, an identity which therefore is concrete and the truth of them both, is Ethical Life.[39]

Levinas is cognizant of the Hegelian conception of ethics that is being deployed here by Silentio and can be found throughout part 2 of *Either/Or*.[40] Levinas's description of Kierkegaard's ethical stage is best understood as what Hegel terms *Sittlichkeit*. It is a stage "at which the inner life is translated in terms of legal order, carried out in society, in loyalty to institutions and principles and in communication with mankind" (PN, 67).[41] Levinas focuses on the key aspects of what he takes to be Kierkegaard's notion of religious subjectivity as distinct from ethical subjectivity: the inability of translation into public understanding (speaking in tongues), the individual being higher than the general (paradox), absolute duty to God rather than human laws and institutions.

Yet Levinas is just as resistant to *Sittlichkeit* as is Kierkegaard.[42] His entire philosophy is devoted to rejecting ethics as nothing but a social morality that eliminates all singularity in the absorptive movement of totalization. Levinas is adamant that ethics is a "consciousness of a responsibility toward others" that "far from losing you in generality singularizes you, poses you as a unique individual, as I" (PN, 76). However, rather than seeing resonances between his own radicalized view of ethics and Kierkegaard's radical notion of religion, Levinas absolutely resists any such connection and instead claims that "Kierkegaard seems not to have experienced [the singularizing potential of infinite ethical responsibility], since he wants to transcend the ethical stage" (PN, 77). For someone whose thought is committed to ethics as "first philosophy," Levinas is unable to accept anything that looks like a movement beyond or past ethics. This is an unfortunate result and it ultimately leads to some of the worst moments in Levinas's reading of Kierkegaard.

Depending on the misguided idea that Kierkegaardian subjectivity is defined by a "tensing on oneself," Levinas proceeds to suggest that the religious stage is "at once communication and solitude, and hence violence and passion" (PN, 72). Referencing the inability of the religious self to justify itself "in the outer world," Levinas moves quickly from secrecy to violence. This slippery slope culminates in the shocking claim that Kierkegaard's philosophy "begins the disdain for the ethical basis of being, the somehow secondary nature of all ethical phenomena that, through Nietzsche, has led us to the amoralism of the most recent philosophers" (PN, 72). Levinas repeats this sentiment in his comments at the Kierkegaard Vivant conference: "It is Kierkegaard's violence that shocks me. The manner of the strong and the violent, who fear neither scandal nor destruction, has become, since Kierkegaard and before Nietzsche, a manner of philosophy" (PN, 76). Utterly flabbergasted, Westphal responds to this charge by saying, "Yes, friends, Kierkegaard is to blame for Nietzsche and his followers."[43]

Acting as if he had never even heard of *Works of Love*, Levinas dismisses

Kierkegaard as fundamentally violent. This is a difficult charge to accord with Levinas's own admitted respect for Kierkegaard's attempt to defend the individual from the onslaught of the Hegelian system. In a strange reversal of direction, or what Westphal calls a "glorious non sequitur,"[44] Levinas contends that in the attempt to help the individual escape the Hegelian "slaughter-bench"[45] of history, Kierkegaard actually ties the knots holding her down even tighter. Concretely, we can best see this aspect of Levinas's critique in his re-reading of the Akedah.

Recounting Kierkegaard's text as a "descrip[tion of] the encounter with God as a subjectivity rising to the religious level," Levinas throws his hands up at the suggestion of a "God above the ethical order" (PN, 74; cf. 77). The "highest moment" of the dramatic encounter is not, for Levinas, the raising of the knife, as Silentio suggests, but instead is when Abraham is able to "hea[r] the voice that brought him back to the ethical order" (PN, 74; cf. 77). If we see that Abraham's ability to hear this voice is actually the point of the text, then we can see the elevation of infinite responsibility for the other who lies on the altar as the true expression of subjectivity. On this account, Abraham is not to be praised for going beyond the ethical, but to be praised for having the "sufficient distance" from his blind obedience to the command to kill his son that was required for him to stay his hand (PN, 77).[46] For Levinas, this interpretation is more consistent with the rest of the biblical narrative, especially Abraham's dialogue with God on behalf of the just who might be present in the damned cities of Sodom and Gomorrah (PN, 74; cf. 77).

Oddly, twice Levinas claims that Kierkegaard never references this other passage and hangs quite a bit of his critique on this fact. However, Silentio does mention Abraham's pleading for the righteous in Sodom and Gomorrah and he does so in a very Levinasian vein (one that continues to contest Levinas's understanding of Kierkegaardian subjectivity): "But Abraham had faith. He did not pray for himself, trying to influence the Lord; it was only when righteous punishment fell upon Sodom and Gomorrah that Abraham came forward with his prayers" (FT, 21). Surely this passage should have the double effect of illuminating Levinas's superficial reading of *Fear and Trembling,* and also give us pause in being too quick to conclude that Kierkegaard is guilty of overlooking the essential responsibility to the other person that Levinas terms "diacony."

A Source of Levinas's Ambivalence[47]

Having articulated the ambivalent way in which Levinas reads Kierkegaard, I will now consider what I find to be the most influential source for his reading: Jean Wahl's existentialist appropriation of Kierkegaard.[48] The influence of Jean Wahl on Levinas is hard to overstate. Wahl was one of the first French Kierkegaard scholars and his expansive *Études Kierkegaardiennes* (*Kierkegaardian Studies*) first appeared in 1938.[49] Not only did Levinas dedicate *Totality and Infinity* to Wahl, he also speaks of him, along with Dr. Nerson and M. Shoshani, as "one of my privileged interlocutors."[50] Additionally, in the "disparate inventory" that Levinas calls his "biography," he refers to "the intellectual, and anti-intellectualist, refinement of Jean Wahl and his generous friendship, regained after a long captivity in Germany," and also to the "regular conferences since 1947 at the Collège Philosophique which Wahl founded and inspired" (DF, 291).

Levinas's relationship with Wahl was one of genuine friendship as well as intellectual respect. In the Talmudic essay, "Being a Westerner," Levinas says that Wahl is "a man curious to examine every new idea while stubbornly defending every valuable idea" (DF, 47). Moreover, in the essay devoted to Wahl in *Proper Names,* Levinas goes as far as saying that Wahl "has read all the books and everything valid (and sometimes even invalid) that has been said in philosophy" (PN, 111). Levinas's personal respect and intellectual admiration of Wahl come together in the memorial essay entitled "Jean Wahl: Neither Having nor Being," which is contained in *Outside the Subject.* Therein, Levinas speaks about Wahl's presence, person, poetry, philosophy, and his influence both inside and outside the walls of the academy. In all cases, according to Levinas, Wahl contested the detached speculations of abstract philosophical thought so characteristic of Western philosophy. For Levinas, Wahl was a thinker of the concrete, the immediate, the lived, and the felt, whose thought was "already an anticipation of Husserl's phenomenology!" (OS, 70). "In many cases," Levinas notes, "Jean Wahl may be defined as the child's question within the Trojan walls of thought" (OS, 71).

Jean Wahl and the Existentialist Appropriation of Kierkegaard

In her 1999 book, *Altered Readings,* Jill Robbins suggests that "Jean Wahl's role in French philosophical life, and in Levinas's philosophical life in particular, should be acknowledged."[51] Mark Taylor makes a similar comment in *Altarity* when he argues that Levinas drew much of his thinking from his friend and Kierkegaard scholar, Jean Wahl. "It is clear," Taylor writes, "that Levinas has learned and borrowed much from his long-time friend."[52] Robbins mounts a convincing case regarding the main aspects of Wahl's thought that reappear in Levinas. She claims that there the main point of contact between Wahl and Levinas is regarding the idea of transcendence as dualistic.

> First, Wahl's description of transcendence, as a relation that absolves itself from the relation . . . is brought to bear on *Totality and Infinity*'s account of transcendence, and Wahl's particular term, transascendance, is explicitly evoked there. . . . Second, for Wahl, the individual is transcended not just by the 'up-above' *[en haut],* and 'beyond' *[au delà]* of *transascendance* but also by the 'down below' *[en bas],* which is expressed by Wahl's corresponding term *transdescendance.*[53]

Thus, for Wahl, transcendence is always a *transcendence-with-direction.*[54] To transcend is to move beyond, but moving beyond can be both toward the higher and the lower. Transcendence names a confrontation with otherness on both sides of the ontological spectrum. Transcendence is thus possible for the being who can both go above and go below its own being rather than simply being a property of divinity (whether conceived as the *summum bonum* or the *ens perfectissimum*). Wahl's notion of *transascendance* and *transdescendance* can be found throughout Levinas's authorship as it relates to the characterization of the Other and the response of the self. Transcendence is dynamic for Jean Wahl, and in the hands of Levinas this dynamism becomes the very life of the ethical encounter.

Consider the following passage from *Totality and Infinity:* "The nakedness of the face is destituteness. To recognize the Other is to recognize a hunger. To recognize the Other is to give. But it is to give to the master, to the lord, to him whom one approaches as 'You' [*Vous*] in a dimension of height" (TI, 75). Here we find Levinas's typical characterization of the face as both the *most destitute* and simultaneously the *most high*. The Other is transcendent in two directions: by being the widow, the orphan, and the stranger that I nonchalantly pass on the street, and also by being the very infinitude of the infinite. The master who commands is also the servant who bows low. The dynamism of the Other is repeated in the response of the self. Levinas repeatedly reminds us that the face cannot appear as such. It should not be confused with the eyes, brow, chin, or nape of the neck—its *transascendance* is precisely located in the inability of the subject to locate the face in representation. However, Levinas also claims that the face confronts me in the eyes of every other person. My obligation to the face of the Other is not an obligation to an abstraction, but to the concrete needs of the person who faces me. The face's *transdescendance* is found in its concrete embodiment in this or that needy person. The ambiguity of the face owes its very orientation and articulation to Jean Wahl.

In addition to Robbins and Taylor, Hent de Vries also comments on the distinct traces of Wahl on Levinas's reading of Kierkegaard.[55] In *Religion and Violence,* de Vries provides an extended consideration of Levinas's reading of Kierkegaard as it centers on the drama of Genesis 22. Although de Vries draws heavily on Wahl's reading of the tension between the divine and the demonic due to their both being "above the general," he does not give any sustained indication as to how, and the ways in which Wahl's interpretation of Kierkegaard is central for Levinas's own. Similarly, Taylor notes Wahl's influence only in a footnote. Although Robbins does offer the helpful account of the Wahlian legacy in Levinas's understanding of transcendence, she does not give any extended consideration of Wahl's appropriation of Kierkegaard. What is lacking in the literature is an account of aspects in Jean Wahl that serve to explain Levinas's ambivalent relationship with Kierkegaard. While deeply indebted to the bread crumb traces left in these other texts, in what follows I will attempt to sketch the main lines of Wahl's interpretation of Kierkegaard that centrally figure into Levinas's reading.

The three main aspects of Jean Wahl's appropriation of Kierkegaard that, I believe, are explanatory for Levinas's reading are (1) the solitary individual alone before God, (2) the notion of overcoming the ethical, and (3) the turn to religion as a result of the consciousness of sin. In all three of these aspects, the overriding influence on Wahl's own understanding is his affiliation with French existentialism. The first might be reconceived as a focus on isolation and *Angst*, the second as singular responsibility (what Sartre calls "anguish"),[56] and the third as an attempt to overcome anxiety through passion. Hence we should realize from the outset that Wahl's reading of Kierkegaard is essentially existentialist. The main tendencies that he locates in Kierkegaard are the very same that he goes to great lengths to highlight in the thought of his contemporaries (e.g., Jaspers, Marcel, Sartre, Heidegger). As he writes in *Philosophies of Existence*, "the philosophy of existence springs from the essentially religious meditations of Kierkegaard."[57]

The Solitary Individual Alone Before God

It is not hard to arrive at the conclusion that solitude is central to Kierkegaard's philosophy. By most accounts, *Fear and Trembling* is a lengthy consideration of Abraham's secrecy and his inability to communicate with the rest of the world. Going as far as having Johannes Climacus claim that "subjectivity is truth," Kierkegaard displays more than just a superficial devotion to the solitary individual who must appropriate truth for herself rather than participate in the social appropriation of objectivity. Additionally, given that Kierkegaard repeatedly dedicates his work to "that single individual" *(hiin Enkelte)*,[58] it is easy to see that Kierkegaard is deeply committed to the radically individual, the singularity of the individual, the singularity that stands in opposition to the totality of systematicity. His entire critique of Hegel centers on Hegel's apparent conclusion that there was no singularity that could not be incorporated into the totality of *Geist*. For Kierkegaard, what gets lost in Hegel's system is precisely "me" as unique, as myself and no other, as essentially alone in myself rather than ultimately being caught up in the dialectical logic of the *Aufhebung*. Given this pervasive consideration of the solitary individual who stands in singular resistance to the system, it is understandable that Wahl would read Kierkegaard as resistant to the idea of social integration and communitarian concerns.

"In the province of existence, Kierkegaard believes, the individual can only hear his own voice"; Wahl writes, "he cannot, properly speaking, join the society of other men; he must take his secret to the grave."[59] The individual is a secret unto himself. The reason for this is, according to Wahl, located in Kierkegaard's conception of subjectivity as a fundamental concern about oneself. "To understand truth, according to Kierkegaard, is to appropriate it for oneself, to produce it, and at the same time to be infinitely interested in it. Kierkegaard's thought," Wahl continues, "is dominated by the idea of an infinite concern about oneself" *(Ce qui domine Kierkegaard, c'est l'idée d'un souci infini de soi)*.[60] He echoes this conception of Kierkegaardian subjectivity in *A Short History of Existentialism* where he claims that "the existent individual, as Kierkegaard defines him, is first of all he who is in an infinite relationship with himself and has an infinite interest in himself and his destiny."[61]

These passages convey both an important insight into Wahl's existentialist understanding of Kierkegaard's notion of subjectivity and also into Levinas's frustration with it. First, defining subjectivity as an "infinite concern for oneself" is resonant both with Heidegger's early notion of *Dasein* as a being who questions its own being and with his idea of authenticity (and Sartre's latter appropriation of it) being wrapped up in taking up oneself as a kind of self-project. If the self is ontologically defined by self-concern, then this leads to a type of existential *anxiety* that is as unavoidable as it is inescapable. This connection between the idea of concern and anxiety, which are not so closely aligned in English, become more apparent in the French. The term *souci* can mean both a *concern for* something, and an *anxiety about* something—in the sense of being worried about it.

The ethical and political implications of this idea are immediately apparent. If the self is defined by its concern for itself, and this concern is read as worrying about (being anxious about) oneself, then the life of the individual is not primarily a matter of living with others, but of coming to grips with one's own existence. Authenticity becomes an ethically problematic conception rather than a mere value-neutral claim regarding self-actualization. For Levinas, self-worry ultimately amounts to other exclusion. To be absorbed by oneself is to fail to be absorbed by the Other. The struggle for authenticity is tantamount to ignoring the neediness of other people. On this reading, Kierkegaard's subjectivity is simply one more case of ontology's marginalization of ethics in the name of self-promotion. The language of "infinite concern about oneself" is also reflected in Levinas's own characterization of Kierkegaard. As we saw above, Levinas understands Kierkegaardian subjectivity to be essentially immodest and ultimately should be read as a "tensing on oneself" *(tension sur soi)* (PN, 67). This tensing is Levinas's attempt to convey what Wahl indicates here as an "infinite concern" *(un souci infini)*.[62] Both are expressions for a subjectivity that is turned inward. This interiority is precisely the space of ethical exclusion that Levinas contests from the outset. That there was ever such a withdrawn subjectivity is the myth that *Otherwise Than Being* sets out to dispel.

The apparent source for Wahl's reading of Kierkegaard on this point is the notion of truth as subjectivity that is most clearly articulated in the *Postscript*. There Climacus defines truth as "*An objective uncertainty, held fast through appropriation with the most passionate inwardness*" (CUP, 203, italics in original). Moreover, Climacus claims that "the difficulty of existence is the existing person's interest, and the existing person is infinitely interested in existing" (CUP, 302). Given these two passages, we might simply conclude that Wahl's reading is uncontroversial. However, although Wahl does make proper reference to Kierkegaardian texts, his focus on the solitude of the individual becomes problematic due to the sheer lack of consideration of, to borrow from Connell and Evans, "the foundations of Kierkegaard's vision of community."[63] If Levinas is guilty of not having read enough Kierkegaard, Wahl is guilty of not being able to differentiate between the pseudonyms and adequately account for the variant, and even contradictory, positions reflected by the various personages to whom Kierkegaard gives shape.[64]

If Wahl's reading of Kierkegaardian subjectivity is illuminated by the places where he finds it to closely resemble the thought of Heidegger, even more is illuminated by considering the places where Wahl finds Kierkegaard and Heidegger to diverge. He outlines the distinctions as follows:

> We can see that the philosophy of Heidegger contains a certain number of heterogeneous elements. The notion of the experience of anguish, and marked Kierkegaardian influences, lead to a definition of human existence as anxious, bent over itself *[courbée sur elle-même]*, making plans. On the other hand, the Heideggerian individual is in-the-world, an idea which is foreign to Kierkegaard and may have come in part from Husserl.[65]

What emerges in this passage, and is then further developed in *Philosophies of Existence,* is the idea that Kierkegaard lacked several key aspects that are subsequently found in the thought of Heidegger and likewise Jaspers—intersubjective engagement with other people and with history.[66] Wahl suggests that what Jaspers and Heidegger add to Kierkegaard is the idea of relationships with other people. Both of the latter thinkers argue that the individual is only possible within a history shared with others. There is no individual "alone before God" without being an individual in a historical tradition *(Geschichtlichkeit).* If the self is not to be understood as a Kantian transcendental unity of apperception or the Fichtean "absolute ego," which Climacus will call the fictitious "I-I," then the self must be understood as embedded in society and history—both of which are intrinsically public. Moreover, Jaspers makes the idea of communication central to his thought, which allows him to open space for a direct encounter with the other person. Similarly, Heidegger says that *Dasein* is always already *Miteinandersein.* Alternatively, according to Wahl, Kierkegaard only permits this encounter to be "indirect" and mediated through the relation with God.

Given Levinas's almost wholehearted rejection of Heideggerian ontology, which he finds totalitarian (in both the philosophical and political senses) due to its focus on the power of *Dasein*—the power to become authentic, to stand in the clearing of being, to move from the "first" to the "other" beginning, and so on—it is easy to see why he would reject Kierkegaard if he understood him to be doing the same thing. For Levinas, the Heideggerian vocabulary is one that constantly asserts ideas such as representing, grasping, comprehending, using, and projecting—all of which prefer the self to the Other. Wahl's presentation of Kierkegaard is one that finds Heidegger to be much less individualistic, much more engaged with other people, much more dis-possessed of selfhood, than Kierkegaard. Wahl goes as far as claiming that "the philosophy of Heidegger is an expansion, and in a certain sense, a negation of Kierkegaardian individualism."[67] It is understandable, then, that influenced by such a reading, Levinas finds Kierkegaard to be a thinker who is congenial to the project of affirming the Other rather than the Same (Kierkegaard qua critic of Hegel), and yet opposed to the ethical preference of the other person rather than the self (Kierkegaard qua radical "existentialist" individualist).

Having seen how Levinas would be troubled by Kierkegaard's inability to recognize the immediacy of the encounter with the Other as exposed in the alternative reading of Genesis 22 Levinas offers, we can also see how Wahl's articulation of Kierkegaard's notion of the God relation would yield a Levinasian rejection of such an idea. Although I will consider the idea of a "teleological suspension of the ethical" by the religious as well as the notion of sin as the motivation for faith below, it will suffice for our purposes here to simply see how it is that, according to Wahl, the relationship to God is really a matter of a proper relationship with oneself. For Levinas, God appears[68] in the ethical encounter. For Wahl's Kierkegaard, the Other only appears as a secondary consideration in the religious encounter. The God relation is primarily the condition of subjective anxiety and the promise for triumph over it. By relating to God, the way out of one's isolation is made manifest. However, according to Wahl, this does not yield a community: "Never are we as alone as in our confrontation with God."[69] The individual enters a "private relation with God" *(un rapport privé avec Dieu)*.[70] It is for this reason that Wahl describes the religious stage as the "domain of great solitude" *(le domaine de la grande solitude)*.[71] For Levinas, the idea of being *alone* with God misunderstands God *and* the other person.

Overcoming the Ethical

For Wahl, neighbor love comes only after existential subjectivity has become religious subjectivity. Only subsequent to one's proper relation with God is there a possibility for proper relation with other people. As Wahl writes:

> In the domain of subjectivity there is something else besides the individual in the first person singular. Great as his solitude may be, Kierkegaard carries on a sort of passionate dialogue: there is a second person, the person he addresses, and over and above the first and second persons there is God, conceived not as a he, but in such a way as to render possible, by invocation and prayer, the relationship between the first person and the second. *For Kierkegaard all true love is grounded in the love of God.*[72]

For Levinas, any interruption of the relation with the Other, even if this interruption is said to be the word of God, is essentially violent; Levinas's second interpretation of Kierkegaard is entirely devoted to this point. There is violence when there is conditionality and mediation introduced into the relation with the neighbor. This violence is due to the fact that for Levinas it is impossible to transcend the ethical except through self-delusion.

As I suggested above, Levinas is unable, or perhaps just unwilling, to see the resonances between his notion of "ethics" and Kierkegaard's notion of "religion." Let me suggest that one of the main reasons for this is the way in which Wahl presents Kierkegaard's "teleological suspension." Consider the following passage:

> To choose the ethical is to become a part of the community, find a vocation, marry, perform some function in life. But on the other hand, Kierkegaard believes that there is something higher than all this, higher than the ethical; this belief finds its practical expression in the breaking of his engagement, its philosophical expression in *Fear and*

Trembling. For there is what Kierkegaard calls a 'suspension of the ethical', a suspension prompted by the fact that I hear the voice of God, and *God can absolve us even from our moral obligations.*[73]

Levinas might have been more disposed to allow for a connection with Kierkegaard's notion of the religious if it had not been for the way in which he seems to follow Wahl's conception of the religious as an "absolution" of moral obligation. The entire philosophy of Levinas might adequately be summarized as the refusal of any possibility of eliminating obligation. Responsibility for the other person is definitive of existence rather than a mere addition to it. Hence, to absolve oneself of moral obligation is to cease being a self at all. Similarly, the idea that God's voice is the highest that can be heard is identical to the claim that the human voice is not the highest. Wahl indicates that in the relation with God, there is no human company nor can the human voice even be heard. Gone is the Levinasian idea of original "sociality," and in its place we have "me in my intimate individuality and God in his supreme authority" *(C'est moi dans mon individualité intime, c'est Dieu dans son autorité suprême).*[74] If hearing God means turning a deaf ear to one's neighbor, then Levinas is quick to say that he will have none of it.[75]

If Wahl's emphasis on existentialist individualism is due largely to his failure to differentiate between the pseudonyms, his rather static presentation of the ethical is due in part to his lack of differentiation between various conceptions of the ethical in Kierkegaard's authorship.[76] These two problematic tendencies are not unrelated. The various conceptions of ethics that appear throughout Kierkegaard's thought are specifically presented pseudonymously. The static conception of the ethical as nothing but a Hegelian understanding of *Sittlichkeit* also anticipates Wahl's static understanding of the religious as an overcoming of it through the consciousness of sin.[77]

The Turn to Religion as a Result of the Consciousness of Sin

Merold Westphal suggests that by reading Levinas's essays "Philosophy and the Idea of Infinity" and "Phenomenon and Enigma" together we might say that "Levinas has a philosophy of sin without salvation."[78] What Westphal points to in this passage is the way in which Levinas "has abstracted not just from the specifically Christian 'salvation drama' of Kierkegaard, but from any drama which gives to God a decisive agency in human affairs and envisages a fundamental alteration of experience as we now endure it."[79] The result, Westphal contends, is that Levinas "seems to share with Hegel and with the secular postmodernists the conviction that 'it doesn't get any better than this.'"[80] Although I do want to tentatively contest the way in which this conclusion seems to indicate that Levinas falls solidly in line with a type of Panglossian resignation that would yield extremely problematic political results (if not downright political complacency),[81] where Westphal hits the nail on the head is on the issue of Levinas's resistance to the idea of salvation. Divine salvation for Levinas is simply another way to fail to live under the weight of the command from/to the Other. Salvation, I would argue, is for Levinas simply too closely aligned with the idea of a "good conscience," which is, to his mind, the first step toward ethical indifference and political complacency.[82]

Earlier, I demonstrated how Levinas's critique of Kierkegaard amounts to the charge of fundamental violence. Although initially a fairly superficial response to Kierkegaard's idea of "teleologically suspending the ethical," Levinas's charge is exacerbated due to the way in which he seems to attribute to Kierkegaard, and the majority of Western Christianity for that matter, a view of religion as a reprieve. On Levinas's reading, religion in Kierkegaard is a way of avoiding the infinity of the ethical demand. There are two reasons for this, both of which, I believe, can be traced to Wahl's comments on Kierkegaard's notion of the God relationship.

First, if the idea that religion is a singular relationship to God is not carefully couched in a complex understanding of God's relationship to each and every other person, it can give the impression that it is also a relation from which the other person is excluded (Isaac in Abraham's encounter with God). Second, if the move to religion is a response to the consciousness of sin—a consciousness that is just as present in Levinas as it is in Kierkegaard—then it can be read as a mere strategy of quietist impotence. On this view, the move to religion would be understood as the realization that since I cannot do anything on my own to overcome my sinfulness, I must fall into the arms of God and trust in divine forgiveness. The problem with this way of understanding it, as Levinas rightly demonstrates, is that if the relation to God is conceived as simply being a way to save oneself, salvation is inherently egoist. We might cast this in a more Levinasian perspective if we said, Only the Other's needs matter; even if it means my own destitution. Ultimately, I think that both of these readings of Kierkegaard's conception of the God relation are misguided. The solitude of one's exposure before God is what singularizes me *as solely responsible* and as such the neighbor is best understood as a gift from God. Likewise, the idea of religion as a response to the consciousness of sin does not mean that we leave behind a guilty conscience, but it might allow us to slightly adjust the often devastating hyperbole of Levinasian responsibility.

Both of the above components can be clearly located in Jean Wahl. As already noted, for Wahl, the Kierkegaardian God relationship is best understood as a relation to oneself. Even the anxiety of the individual, a radically interior concern, is due to the reflexive relation with God. "The existent individual," Wahl notes, will be "essentially anxious, and infinitely interested in respect to his existence because an eternity of pains or an eternity of joys depend upon his relation with God."[83] Here we see the characteristic conception of "tensing on oneself" coupled with religious expectation. Notice, however, that it is an expectation for oneself. Again, it is not that Wahl is clearly saying what Kierkegaard does not, it is just that his rather monolithic presentation skews Kierkegaard into a very static existentialist philosopher who retreated to religion due to an inability to adequately deal with the struggles of existence. Regarding the issue of religion as an escape from sin, Wahl comments,

> Kierkegaard is the man who, through the act of sinning, sees himself standing before God. To be conscious of sin . . . is to see oneself standing before God, and for Kierkegaard, as for Luther before him, the idea of "standing before God" is one of the fundamental categories.[84]

Wahl not only finds religion to be a conceptual escape for the Kierkegaardian subject, but also he claims that it is a personal escape for Kierkegaard himself. "In Kierkegaard's case," he writes, "there is failure in his very life, and it is to overcome this failure that he resorts to God, turns to transcendence."[85] Whether Wahl is referring to the "great earthquake" Kierkegaard experienced in relation to his father or to the broken engagement with Regine Olsen, the specifics are not important. What is crucial, however, is that Wahl has no trouble interpreting Kierkegaardian texts in the light of Kierkegaard's biography. Surely there is something to be gained by taking into account the various personal details that may have had an effect on Kierkegaard's thinking, but to claim, as Wahl does in his introduction to a French translation of *Fear and Trembling* (*Crainte et tremblement*), that the two main questions of *Fear and Trembling* (what is the relation between the individual and the real and between the individual and time?) are really Kierkegaard's attempt to question whether or not he can marry his fiancée, is just going too far.[86]

All of the above points regarding Wahl's reading of Kierkegaard are summarized in a passage at the end of *Kierkegaardian Studies* where Wahl gives the "Kierkegaardian definition of existence." To exist is "to choose; to be passionate; to become; to be isolated and to be subjective; to be infinitely concerned about oneself *[souci infini de soi]*; to know sin; and to be before God."[87] When confronted with such a definition, it becomes easy to see how Levinas could be ambivalent about Kierkegaard. Nowhere in this summary is there mention of the way in which being subjective is isolated only in the uniqueness of one's encounter with God, an encounter that ruptures the possibility of standing alone in the world. Absent is a consideration of being with others (e.g., *Works of Love*) that always accompanies being before God (e.g., *Fear and Trembling, Sickness unto Death*). There is no mention of the levels of the ethical that appear across the pseudonyms (e.g., *Either/Or, Practice in Christianity, Judge for Yourself!*). Moreover, Wahl does not consider the possibility that the necessities of choice, passion, and becoming are all components of how one takes up one's subjectivity as not being simply an infinite concern about oneself, but rather a self-emptying move toward other people because of God's self-emptying move toward "me" (the kerygma of *kenosis*). Because of this, Wahl's Kierkegaard is ultimately static in his existentialism and fundamentalist in his Christianity, neither of which is an accurate description of the dynamism and relationality that pervade Kierkegaard's authorship.

Despite the need for a more careful consideration of the Kierkegaardian position, we must not overlook the way in which Levinas's critiques are genuine worries for all those who would champion subjectivity over alterity and quickly advocate the move to religion (although Kierkegaard does neither). Although I have attempted to explain why Levinas would misunderstand Kierkegaard in this way (given Wahl's conception), these misunderstandings keep open the wounds that we must not be too quick to bandage.

Notes

1. See Levinas, TIHP, DEHH; for some later collected papers on Husserl, see DEH.

2. It could be argued that Levinas is in breach of his own standards of ethical interaction. Expecting that all previous thinkers should have been concerned with what concerns him is to preclude his being open to the orbit of their thinking. If the long and short of Levinas's thought is an infinite responsibility to the other, he would seemingly feel a greater weight to read others responsibly. Alternatively, however, such commentators as Jacques Derrida and Jill Robbins suggest that the only way to read someone is to misread her or him. See Derrida, "At This Very Moment in This Work Here I Am," in *Re-Reading Levinas,* ed. Robert Bernasconi and Simon Critchley (Bloomington: Indiana University Press, 1991), 11–48; and Robbins, *Altered Reading: Levinas and Literature* (Chicago: University of Chicago Press, 1999). Although I am persuaded by the contention that there cannot be one true reading of a particular figure to the exclusion of all other interpretations, nonetheless, we should not forget that there are better and worse misreadings.

3. Martin Heidegger, *What Is Called Thinking?* trans. Fred Wieck and J. Glenn Gray (New York: Harper, 1968), 77. The actual phrases are "go to their encounter" *(entgegen gehen)* and "go counter to them" *(dagegen angehen).* David Wood, "Glimpses of Being in Dasein's Development: Reading and Writing after Heidegger," is a very good consideration of Heidegger precisely on this point in *Time After Time* (Bloomington: Indiana University Press, 2007), 102–16.

4. Merold Westphal, "The Many Faces of Levinas as a Reader of Kierkegaard," included as chapter 1 of the present volume.

5. Ibid., 22.

6. See Heidegger's discussion of what counts as thought-provoking in "What Calls for Thinking," in *Basic Writings,* rev. and exp., ed. David Farrell Krell (San Francisco: HarperSanFrancisco, 1993), 369–91.

7. Levinas's phrasing of this quote varies in his authorship: "Each of us is guilty before everyone for everyone, and I more than the others" (OTB, 146); "Every one of us is guilty before all, for everyone and everything, and I more than others" (BPW, 102).

8. Franz Rosenzweig, *The Star of Redemption,* trans. Barbara E. Galli (Madison: University of Wisconsin Press, 2005).

9. Levinas echoes this claim in *Totality and Infinity:* "We were impressed by the opposition to the idea of totality in Franz Rosenzweig's *Stern der Erlösung*" (28); and also in "Franz Rosenzweig: A Modern Jewish Thinker": "Rosenzweig's thought presents itself as a revolt against Hegel" (OS, 53).

10. Mark C. Taylor, *Altarity* (Chicago: University of Chicago Press, 1987), 204.

11. The original was published as *Noms propres* (Editions Fata Morgana, 1975). There are scattered references to Kierkegaard throughout Levinas's authorship. Most of these are merely instances of name-dropping and display the same sort of straw-manning that

I mentioned above. However, in addition to *Proper Names,* there are three other places where Levinas will at least give, if not a thorough consideration, a slightly more extended one than usual. These essays are: "Enigma and Phenomena" in CPP, "Franz Rosenzweig: A Modern Jewish Thinker" in OS, and a letter that Levinas submitted to the *Bulletin de la Société française de Philosophie* in 1937 that has been translated and reprinted in UH.

12. The proceedings of this conference were published by Gallimard in 1966 under the title *Kierkegaard vivant,* and they contain an address by René Maheu followed by essays by Jean-Paul Sartre, Jean Beaufret, Gabriel Marcel, Lucien Goldmann, Martin Heidegger, Enzo Paci, Karl Jaspers, Jean Wahl, Jeanne Hersch, and Niels Thulstrup. Additionally, the text records two roundtable discussions that contain the interventions by Levinas.

13. Originally in *Schweizer Monatshefte* 43 (1963).

14. Levinas, "Enigma and Phenomena," in CPP, 61.

15. Plato, *Euthyphro,* in *Complete Works,* ed. John M. Cooper (Indianapolis: Hackett, 1997), 14c–d.

16. Levinas, "Is Ontology Fundamental?" in BPW, 2.

17. Aristotle, *Metaphysics,* trans. Richard Hope (Ann Arbor: University of Michigan Press, 1952), 983a5.

18. Ibid., 983a10.

19. Merold Westphal, *Overcoming Onto-Theology: Toward a Postmodern Christian Faith* (New York: Fordham University Press, 2001), 6.

20. G. W. F. Hegel, *The Encyclopaedia Logic,* trans. T. F. Geraets, W. A. Suchting, and H. S. Harris (Indianapolis: Hackett, 1991), §236.

21. G. W. F. Hegel, *Phenomenology of Spirit,* trans. A. V. Miller (Oxford: Oxford University Press, 1977), §808.

22. See Numbers 33:55; Joshua 23:13; Judges 2:3; 2 Corinthians 12:7.

23. I grant that this is a rather strange phrase in both English and French. Although I am staying consistent with Michael Smith's translation, it could also be understood as a "pressing on oneself." Either way, for Levinas, the crucial aspect is that the self constantly recurs to itself rather than going toward the Other.

24. Benedict Spinoza, *Ethics,* trans. W. H. White and rev. A. H. Stirling (Hertfordshire, U.K.: Wordsworth Classics, 2001), pt. 3, proposition 6: "Each thing, in so far as it is in itself, endeavours to persevere in its being." Martin Heidegger, *Being and Time,* trans. Joan Stambaugh (Albany: State University of New York Press, 1996): "*[Da-sein]* is ontically distinguished by the fact that in its being this being is concerned *about* its very being" (10).

25. For an extended consideration of this point, see J. Aaron Simmons, "What About Isaac? Rereading *Fear and Trembling* and Rethinking Kierkegaardian Ethics," *Journal of Religious Ethics* 35, no. 2 (Spring 2007): 319–45.

26. On this point, I am following Jamie Ferreira's instruction that "we should assume Kierkegaard is in theological agreement with Luther except for those places where he specifically notes otherwise." *Love's Grateful Striving: A Commentary on Kierkegaard's "Works of Love"* (Oxford: Oxford University Press, 2001), 19; cf. 23.

27. See Bernhard Lohse, *Martin Luther's Theology: Its Historical and Systematic Development,* trans. and ed. Roy A. Harrisville (Minneapolis: Fortress, 1999), esp. pt. 3, "Sin."

28. *Kenosis* is the theological idea that God empties Godself in the personhood of Christ. See Philippians 2:7–8. For an example of how Christianity can be reconciled with postmodernism through the idea of a kenotic God, see J. Aaron Simmons, "Is Con-

tinental Philosophy Just Catholicism for Atheists? On the Political Relevance of *Kenosis*," *Philosophy in the Contemporary World* 15, no. 1 (Spring 2008). See also Gianni Vattimo, *Vattimo's Belief,* trans. Luca D'Isanto and David Webb (Stanford, Calif.: Stanford University Press, 1999); Vattimo, *After Christianity,* trans. Luca D'Isanto (New York: Columbia University Press, 2002); Vattimo and Richard Rorty, *The Future of Religion,* ed. Santiago Zabala (New York: Columbia University Press, 2005).

29. Westphal, "Many Faces of Levinas," 22–23.

30. Merold Westphal, "The Transparent Shadow: Kierkegaard and Levinas in Dialogue," in *Kierkegaard in Post/Modernity,* ed. Martin J. Matuštík and Merold Westphal (Bloomington: Indiana University Press, 1995), 273. This claim is a constant refrain in Westphal's work: "For Levinas . . . infinity is human, while for Kierkegaard it is divine" ("Levinas's Teleological Suspension of the Religious," in *Ethics as First Philosophy: The Significance of Emmanuel Levinas for Philosophy, Literature, and Religion,* ed. Adriaan T. Peperzak [New York: Routledge, 1995], 151–60, 159). We may wonder, however, whether Westphal's description is appropriate to Levinas's thought. For Levinas, it is crucial that God can never be "recognized" as such. And yet, especially in his later work, Levinas does talk about the shadow of God's passing, which may be read as the way in which we recognize God without ever claiming that our comprehension is adequate to God's non-presence. Moreover, although there is some ambiguity throughout Levinas's authorship, whether we can even differentiate between the "infinity of the neighbor" and the "infinity of God" is an open question.

31. Westphal, "Many Faces of Levinas," 24.

32. When considering the cash value, as it were, of this term, we should remember that for Kierkegaard, the truth of Christ could never be separated from Christ's material and historical existence. Hence "persecuted truth" is always already wrapped up in the destitution of the personhood of Christ rather than merely being a claim about the structural impossibility of achieving systematic and "triumphant" truth.

33. Levinas, "Enigma and Phenomena," in CPP, 66.

34. Ibid., 66–67.

35. Friedrich Hölderlin, "Patmos," in *Selected Poems and Fragments,* trans. Michael Hamburger, ed. Jeremy Adler (London: Penguin, 1998), 231. Heidegger quotes this passage in "The Question Concerning Technology," in *The Question Concerning Technology and Other Essays,* trans. William Lovitt (New York: Harper & Row, 1977), 28.

36. See Problema 2 in FT.

37. Diane Perpich makes a similar point regarding justification and Levinas in *The Ethics of Emmanuel Levinas* (Stanford, Calif.: Stanford University Press, 2008).

38. The connection between Silentio's reference to "speaking in tongues" in this passage and Levinas's repeated use of the idea of prophecy is a connection that has yet to be pursued. Consider 1 Corinthians 14:1–6, where prophecy is contrasted with tongues in that the former speaks to other people while the latter speaks to God: "He that speaketh in an *unknown* tongue edifieth himself; but he that prophesieth edifieth the church" (KJV). Before deciding in Levinas's favor over and against Kierkegaard, due to the public quality of prophecy and the private nature of tongues, it is important to remember that, under his own name, Kierkegaard wrote numerous *edifying* discourses. This should give us pause in equating Kierkegaard's position with that of Silentio. The relation between public edification and private expression might be more dynamic that Levinas would otherwise suggest—or a quick reading of Kierkegaard's *Fear and Trembling* will allow.

39. G. W. F. Hegel, *The Philosophy of Right,* trans. T. M. Knox (Oxford: Oxford University Press, 1962), §141. See also part 3 of this text, "The Ethical Life."

40. Consider Judge Wilhelm's argument that the individuality which characterized the aesthetic stage be overcome by entering into ethical institutions, particularly marriage.

41. Compare this to Hegel's description in paragraph 144 of *The Philosophy of Right*: "The objective ethical order, which comes on the scene in place of good in the abstract, is substance made concrete by subjectivity as infinite form. Hence it posits within itself distinctions whose specific character is thereby determined by the concept, and which endow the ethical order with a stable content independently necessary and subsistent in exaltation above subjective opinion and caprice. These distinctions are absolutely valid laws and institutions."

42. For a sustained argument regarding why it is *Sittlichkeit* that Kierkegaard primarily sets out to challenge, see J. Aaron Simmons, "What About Isaac? Rereading *Fear and Trembling* and Rethinking Kierkegaardian Ethics."

43. Westphal, "Many Faces of Levinas," 22.

44. Ibid.

45. G. W. F. Hegel, *Introduction to "The Philosophy of History,"* trans. Leo Rauch (Indianapolis: Hackett, 1988), 24.

46. See Genesis 18:16–33.

47. Surprisingly little research has been done tracing the French reception of Kierkegaard. Notable exceptions include Jacques Message, "Remarques sur la reception de *Begrebet Angst* en France," *Kierkegaard Studies* (2001): 323–29; Denis de Rougemont, "Kierkegaard en France," *Nouvelle Revue Francaise* 46 (June 1936): 971–76. De Rougemont does an excellent job of arguing that, due to the order in which Kierkegaard's works were translated into French, three problematic views of his thought arose. He was seen as being (1) immoral, (2) nihilistic, and (3) anti-Christian. He goes on to say that the importance of Kierkegaard's religious writings was overlooked to the detriment of French interpretation. Moreover, if one does account for the religious elements of Kierkegaard's later work, it is clear, de Rougemont contends, that "Subjectivity is not subjectivism" (974, my translation). It is not the vague, uncontrollable sentiment so characteristic of romanticism and anarchy (974). With his assessment I am in complete agreement. As demonstrated below, Jean Wahl's understanding of Kierkegaard (and thereby Levinas's own) tends to track toward the very problematic accusations that de Rougemont highlights (with the possible exception of anti-Christianity).

48. Although it is beyond the scope of the present chapter, I would also suggest that the other main source of Levinas's reading of Kierkegaard is Franz Rosenzweig's engagement with Kierkegaard in *The Star of Redemption,* trans. Barbara E. Galli (Madison: University of Wisconsin Press, 2005), 13–14, 25.

49. Jean Wahl, *Études Kierkegaardiennes,* 2nd ed. (Paris: Librairie Philosophique, 1949). All subsequent references are to *Kierkegaardian Studies,* and all translations are my own.

50. Levinas, "Reality Has Weight," in RTB, 160.

51. Robbins, *Altered Reading,* 101.

52. Taylor, *Altarity,* 185.

53. Robbins, *Altered Reading,* 102–103.

54. See Jean Wahl, *L'expérience métaphysique* (Paris: Flammarion, 1965); Wahl, *La pensée de l'existence* (Paris: Flammarion, 1951); Wahl, *Existence humaine et transcendance* (Neuchâtel: Éditions de la Baconnière, 1944).

55. Hent de Vries, *Religion and Violence: Philosophical Perspectives from Kant to Der-*

rida (Baltimore, Md.: Johns Hopkins University Press, 2002), especially chap. 2: "Violence and Testimony: Kierkegaardian Meditations."

56. See Jean-Paul Sartre, *Existentialism and Human Emotions* (New York: Philosophical Library, 1985), 18–20.

57. Jean Wahl, *Philosophies of Existence: An Introduction to the Basic Thought of Kierkegaard, Heidegger, Jaspers, Marcel, Sartre,* trans. F. M. Lory (London: Routledge & Kegan Paul, 1969).

58. This phrase is used throughout Kierkegaard's authorship (see the indexes for EUD, PC, FSEJF, FT, CA, CUP, WOL, CD, UPVS, TDIO, WA).

59. Wahl, *Philosophies of Existence,* 76.

60. Ibid., 83.

61. Jean Wahl, *A Short History of Existentialism,* trans. Forrest Williams and Stanley Maron (New York: Philosophical Library, 1949), 4.

62. In his introduction to *Crainte et tremblement* (Paris: Aubier, 1984), vi, Wahl actually refers to the "individual's extreme tension" (*la tension extrême de l'individu*). All translations from this text are my own.

63. George B. Connell and C. Stephen Evans, eds., *Foundations of Kierkegaard's Vision of Community: Religion, Ethics, and Politics in Kierkegaard* (Atlantic Highlands, N.J.: Humanities, 1992). Although this text was published over a decade ago, it continues to be one of the most important collections of essays devoted to what is often overlooked in Kierkegaard's thought—his commitment to political critique, social organization, and communal life.

64. A footnote in his introduction to *Crainte et tremblement* indicates that he is aware of this. He acknowledges that several commentators have claimed that the notion of ethics in *Fear and Trembling* is more a product of Johannes de Silentio than Kierkegaard (iv–v n. 1). However, the sheer fact that Wahl notes this rather than incorporating it into his own exposition supports my supposition as to his occlusion of the distinct variance between pseudonyms.

65. Wahl, *Short History of Existentialism,* 24.

66. Wahl, *Philosophies of Existence,* 21–23. Consider Wahl's claim: "To the Kierkegaardian position, which *shuts the individual up,* as it were, within his subjectivity and his subjective relationship with God, Jaspers and Heidegger bring the idea of what they call *Geschichtlichkeit*—the individual's deep historicity" (ibid., 51, my emphasis).

67. Wahl, *Short History of Existentialism,* 20.

68. "Appears" is not exactly the right term, but it must suffice here, with reservations.

69. Wahl, *Philosophies of Existence,* 76.

70. Wahl, introduction to *Crainte et tremblement,* v, xi.

71. Ibid., v.

72. Wahl, *Philosophies of Existence,* 77, my emphasis.

73. Ibid., 57–58, my emphasis.

74. Wahl, introduction to *Crainte et tremblement,* vi.

75. Ibid., v. The actual passage is: "*on n'y pénètre pas 'de compagnie'; on n'y entend pas de voix humaine.*"

76. In his introduction to *Crainte et tremblement,* Wahl indicates that he is aware of the fact that a suspension of the ethical in the name of the religious is not an elimination of it, but instead a re-instantiation of it. He recognizes that entering the religious sphere both suspends the ethical and at the same time, affirms it in a new way (xx). However,

this passage only suggests that Wahl understands the Hegelian notion of the *Aufhebung* that is being deployed in *Fear and Trembling*. The ethical is understood in the same way but appropriated on the hither side of the God relation rather than being an obstacle to it. Elsewhere Wahl comes closer to recognizing the dynamism of Kierkegaardian ethics when he admits that "we have perhaps not given enough attention to the importance [Kierkegaard] accords to love" (*Philosophies of Existence,* 79). Unfortunately, Wahl leaves this at a mere recognition of a failure rather than actually attempting to fill in the gap that he has otherwise left open. Similarly, although Wahl devotes an entire chapter of *Kierkegaardian Studies* to "The Christian Life and Its Categories," he leaves the idea of Christian ethics as differentiated from the Hegelian social morality of *Fear and Trembling* underdeveloped.

77. His description of the ethical in Kierkegaard anticipates Levinas's own understanding of it as nothing but *Sittlichkeit*. He describes it as "the state of the citizen and the married man" (*Kierkegaardian Studies,* 72).

78. Westphal, "Transparent Shadow," 278.

79. Ibid., 277.

80. Ibid.

81. Diane Perpich and I have argued elsewhere that this complacency is precisely what Levinas sets out to overcome. See J. Aaron Simmons and Diane Perpich, "Making Tomorrow Better Than Today: Rorty's Dismissal of Levinasian Ethics," *Symposium* 9, no. 2 (Fall 2005): 241–66. For considerations of the practical political results of Levinasian philosophy, see Stephen Minister, "Works of Justice, Works of Love: Kierkegaard, Levinas, and an Ethics Beyond Difference"; and Zeynep Direk, "Levinas and Kierkegaard: Ethics and Politics," which are both included in the present volume.

82. In this chapter I am unable to give this difficult issue the attention it requires. Recognizing that it is an argument that needs further clarification, I would suggest that without some conception of salvation (or perhaps more properly, without a notion of grace) Levinas's philosophy is unable to give an adequate account of the way in which the Good is lived in the relation to the other person. For now, though, I want to use this brief excerpt from Westphal's argument to illuminate Levinas's suspicion of the religious if it is construed as anything like an escape. For rich considerations of the way grace, salvation, and eschatology function in Kierkegaard and Levinas, I encourage the reader to see John Davenport, "What Kierkegaardian Faith Adds to Alterity Ethics: How Levinas and Derrida Miss the Eschatological Dimension"; and David Kangas and Martin Kavka, "Hearing, Patiently: Time and Salvation in Kierkegaard and Levinas," in this volume.

83. Wahl, *Short History of Existentialism,* 6.

84. Wahl, *Philosophies of Existence,* 19.

85. Ibid., 73.

86. Wahl, introduction to *Crainte et tremblement,* i.

87. Wahl, *Kierkegaardian Studies,* 361.

Part Two.

*On Love and
Transcendence*

3   Who or What or Whot?

John Llewelyn

I

When Kierkegaard stated, "The metaphysical, the ontological, is *[er]*, but it does not exist *[er ikke til]*," he drew the line that separates him from Hegel and both of them from Levinas (SLW, 476). His Danish does this distinctly. On the one hand, the preposition *til*, "to," indicates a relation between subjectivity and otherness that, Kierkegaard maintains, cannot be subsumed within the sphere of being or essence. On the other hand, while agreeing with Kierkegaard's denial, Levinas argues against Kierkegaard (and Heidegger) that the ec-static, ex-sistent to-ness and toward-ness of the relation indicated by Kierkegaard's preposition presupposes an inward-ness without which there can be no relations. This in-wardness is not the inwardness of subjectivity as Kierkegaard describes it. It stems not from the singular individual's decision and free will, but from finding itself subjected to and responding to another's command. Before investigating this difference more closely, let us review briefly the Hegelian conception they agree in rejecting.

Hegel teaches that the other is the negative of the same, "the necessary other," as Kierkegaard calls it. In *The Concept of Anxiety* Kierkegaard applies to Hegel a criticism he has heard made of Schelling. Having affirmed that the negative is the evil, it is a short step to a position in which transitions in logic are declared illogical because they are evil and transitions are declared unethical in ethics because the evil is the negative. "In logic they are too much and in ethics too little . . . If ethics has no other transcendence, it is essentially logic. If logic is to have as much transcendence as common propriety requires of ethics, it is no longer logic" (CA, 13). It is to this panontologism that Levinas too is objecting when he writes that "the fundamental fact of the ontological scission into same and other is a non-allergic relation of the same with the other" (TI, 305/282).[1] To say that this "relation is non-allergic is to say that it is not a relation in which there is a conflict between forces. Hence the quotation marks when he writes that "the 'resistance' of the other does not do violence to me, does not act negatively; it has a positive structure: ethical" (TI, 197/171). The other resists me in being undesirable, because he or she is my accuser. This resistance is also a resistance to system "without its resistance to system manifesting itself as the egoist cry of the subjectivity, still concerned for happiness or salvation, as in Kierkegaard" (TI, 305/282).

II

For both Kierkegaard and Levinas the other is the one I am commanded to love. For both Kierkegaard and Levinas the other is my neighbor. According to both Kierkegaard and Levinas I am commanded to love my neighbor by God. According at least to Levinas I am commanded to love my neighbor also by my neighbor. Furthermore, God commands me to love my neighbor as I love myself. "You shall love your neighbor as yourself" (Lev. 19:18, Matt. 22:39). You *shall* love your neighbor. I *do* love myself. According to Kierkegaard self-love is part of all preferential love, whether the latter be friendship or erotic love. These are forms of temporal love. They fall short of commanded love as the temporal falls short of the eternal. But if they fall short through being forms of self-love, how can I be commanded to love my neighbor as myself? Only if self-love can be unselfish.

"The concept 'neighbor,'" Kierkegaard writes, "is actually the redoubling of your own self; the 'neighbor' is what philosophers call 'the other,' that by which the selfishness in self-love is to be tested" (WOL, 21). The friend or the beloved are nearest to me by preference. Their being near to me is exclusive of others. My love ceases to be exclusive only when the other is as near to me as I am near to myself. As such the other is my neighbor. The selfishness and Narcissism of preferential love is superseded by a love of oneself as neighbor to a neighbor. The former love differs from the latter in that while in the former love I make demands on the beloved, in the latter love demands are made on me. The latter love is a test of the former in that the beloved as neighbor makes demands on me *as myself* a neighbor, as one who loves the other *as myself*. There therefore appears to be no difference between the beloved as neighbor making demands on me as neighbor and my making them on myself as neighbor. This would follow from Kierkegaard's subsumption of these demands under the commandment "You shall love your neighbor as yourself."

Levinas observes that in Buber's and Rosenzweig's translation of the Hebrew version of this commandment its last word, *kamocha,* "as yourself," is separated from the beginning of the verse, yielding "Love your neighbor; this work is (as) yourself" (GWCM, 91/144).[2] The work will be the work of love, but *my* love, not, as in Kierkegaard's interpretation, the love of God or the love that God is. Kierkegaard writes, "In erotic love and friendship, preferential love is the middle term; in love for the neighbor, God is the middle term" (WOL, 58). That is to say, the other is your neighbor on the ground of equality before God (WOL, 60). With this we seem to reach what for Levinas would be a stumbling block, a double difficulty, partly a difficulty relating to the difference between Kierkegaard's Christian construal of God, partly a difficulty relating to God independently of that construal.

Kierkegaard's concept of God is a stumbling block for Levinas on account of what Kierkegaard calls the absurdity of the absolute paradox that God became man. In Kierkegaard's concept of God the way to Christ is the way to God and the way to God is the way to Christ. The way to Christianity is guarded by the incarnation. And the incarnation is an offensive absurdity. Its offensiveness is essential to Christianity. It is not, however, because the incarnation offends Levinas's Judaism that he cannot as a philosopher follow Kierkegaard. It is because no positive religion, including Judaism, can be the key to an understanding of ethicality. "The Other is not the incarnation of God, but precisely by his face, in which he is disincarnate, is the manifestation of the height in which God is revealed" (TI, 79/51). The key to the understanding of ethicality is the "Western," Greek idea of the Good beyond being. "If it has played no role in the Western philosophy issued from Aristotle, the Platonic idea of the Good ensures it the dignity of a philosophical thought—and it therefore cannot be traced back to any oriental wisdom" (TI, 218/194). If the offense that Kierkegaard holds to be essential to Christianity were not the incarnation but the crucifixion, there might be a chance of building a bridge from him to Levinas by going back from the crucifixion to what Christian theologians call its prefiguration in the story of Abraham and Isaac told in the Hebrew Bible. This chance is weakened by the fact that Christ was crucified but Isaac was not killed. The chance is still further weakened by the fact that in his reading of Kierkegaard's account of the story of Abraham and Isaac, Levinas says that primacy should have been given to the restitution of the purely ethical relationship after the angel of the Lord cried, "Lay not thine hand upon the lad." That is to say, independent of the difficulty raised for Levinas as a Jew by Kierkegaard's Christian conception of God, is the difficulty for Levinas that Kierkegaard not only ends with a positive religion but *begins* there too, with God, rather than with an ethics of the other human being.

III

This statement of how Kierkegaard and Levinas differ from each other in one respect raises the question whether, notwithstanding the latter's emphasis on the importance of the return to ethicality in the story of the events on Moriah, he himself retains a place for a religiousness that he does not oppose to ethicality. At the very least he would want to retain for ethicality the sense of binding that the second syllable of the word "religion" is commonly taken to signify, whether or not this signification is supported by etymology. The opposition between the ethical and the religious is starker in those places in Kierkegaard's writings, for instance, the *Concluding Unscientific Postscript,* where so many of the references to the ethical are references to general objective ethics as conceived by the Hegelians. He is there writing about ethics particularly as *Sittlichkeit,* custom, practice, morals as mores. Levinas maintains that the generality and historicality of ethics or morals thus understood is conditioned or quasi-conditioned by what he calls the ethical. For Kierkegaard it is animated by the religiousness in which the finite collides not only dialectically but also paradoxically with the absolute otherness of the transcendent infinite. He calls this Religiousness B. Levinas would call it Christianity. But it would not be making too crude an assessment of the difference at this point between the two thinkers if we said that both aim to find room for what, using a locution Kierkegaard employs, we could describe as the ethico-religious.

For both Kierkegaard and Levinas the second word of this hyphenated expression evokes the individual in his or her first person singularity. But while for Kierkegaard in this context this first person singularity is that of the I, for Levinas it is that of the me. For Levinas the first person singularity is that of the I when I am the one that seeks to enjoy myself; it is the first person singularity of the self of the world of happiness in time as distinguished by Kierkegaard from eternity. One of Levinas's criticisms of Kierkegaard is that the projective character he attributes to the enjoyment of worldly life carries over into what in Kierkegaard corresponds to what St. Paul describes as the new life or at least into what Kierkegaard describes as the serious matter of choosing not between good and evil, but between choosing between good and evil and not so choosing: between decisiveness and indifference. Choosing or deciding is an act of free will, and an act of will relates to what will or will not be. Such an act, Levinas maintains, depends on a passivity which, if it has any intentionality at all, has an intentionality that is reversed, whether intentionality be understood as an intending to do something or in the broader phenomenological sense in which all so-called mental acts or states of consciousness are intentional in that they are directed at an objective or accusative. The primary accusative, Levinas holds, is the first person singular in the accusative case: me, the one whose very selfhood is due to its being singled out, elected, by the other one who accuses me of not fulfilling my duty. My selfhood is not a matter of consciousness. If it is not misleading to speak in the Levinasian context of selfhood being constituted—for in this context constitution is also deconstitution of consciousness—the constitution of my selfhood is due to duty or, to use the term that Levinas prefers, to responsibility, meaning by this the absolute responsibility without which no specific relative duties are ethical.

Kierkegaard defines this responsibility or answerability *(Ansvar)* in terms of God and his laws. The religiousness and the responsibility that goes with it is the religiousness of a religion, albeit that this responsibility is spelled out in terms of responsibilities to my neighbor, the other human being. The responsible love that helps my neighbor is the love that helps my neighbor to love God. Similarly for my neighbor's love of me. Not least when my neighbor is my wife. "This the world can never get into its head, that God not only . . . becomes the third party in every relationship of love but really becomes the sole object of love, so that it is not the husband who is the wife's beloved, but it is God, and it is the wife who is helped by the husband to love God, and conversely, and so on" (WOL, 120–21). The world can never get into its head that for the truly loving husband and wife God is between them when they are in bed. They make up a threesome. But the third, God, is love. And the third is first where the love between husband and wife is love of the other as neighbor. This is what distinguishes the Knight of Resignation from the Knight of Faith in the "Preliminary Expectoration" in *Fear and Trembling*. The Knight of Resignation, unlike the Knight of Faith, thinks erroneously that he can give up the girl and without giving up himself hope to graduate to faith (FT, 44–45).

"Ultimately, love for God is the decisive factor; from this originates (*stammer*) love for the neighbor," Kierkegaard writes (WOL, 57). As though with this sentence in mind Levinas writes about the word "God": "What matters here is that it is from the relation with the other, in the depth of Dialogue, that this inordinate word has significance for thought, not vice-versa."[3] This difference in order of priority stands even when allowance is made for two facets of Kierkegaard's exposition that may seem to be passed over in Levinas's explicit and implicit criticism.

First, does not the place Kierkegaard leaves for grace mean that a moment of reversal must be admitted by what was called earlier the projective structure of Kierkegaard's interpretation of first personal subjectivity? Does this not to some extent forestall Levinas's critique by admitting a so to speak "in-static" interference into the centrifugal ec-staticness that he finds in Kierkegaard's account of the self, as he finds it and finds it objectionable in Heidegger's analysis of *Dasein?* However, grace does not meet the requirement of perspicuity that Levinas believes ethicality imposes, and without which there would be no safeguard against fanaticism.

> When I maintain an ethical relation I refuse to recognize the role I would play in a drama of which I would not be the author or whose outcome another would know before me; I refuse to figure in a drama of salvation or of damnation that would be played in spite of me and would make play of me. (TI, 79/52)

Here Levinas is manifesting the distrust in which Kierkegaard and Kant hold the insobriety of enthusiasm and *Schwärmerei*. Grace would belong to the realm of "mysterious designs." Therefore it could not belong to the realm of the ethical or indeed of the ethico-religious.

Levinas's analysis of Kierkegaard's notion of the first person singular as ecstatic or projective may appear to need qualifying also in order to do justice to Kierkegaard's exclamation: "*You* shall, *you* shall love the neighbor. O my listener, it is not *you* to whom *I* am speaking; it is *I* to whom eternity says: *You* shall" (WOL, 90). In so far as the pattern here is that of being addressed it resembles that of the *you* addressing the *me* as described by Levinas. But what Kierkegaard here calls eternity is not what he refers to earlier in *Works of Love* as "the *first you*" (WOL, 57), meaning the neighbor as neighbor in contrast to the *alter ego* of erotic love or friendship who, despite his or her otherness, is still the self-loving I. By eternity here is meant God. Now late in *Totality and Infinity* Levinas writes about eternity as follows:

> The dream of a happy eternity, which subsists in man along with his happiness, is not a simple aberration. Truth requires both an infinite time and a time it will be able to seal, a completed time. The completion of time is not death, but messianic time, when the perpetual is converted into the eternal. Messianic triumph is the pure triumph; it is secured against the revenge of evil whose return the infinite time does not prohibit.

Is this eternity a new structure of time, or an extreme vigilance of the messianic consciousness? The problem exceeds the bounds of this book. (TI, 284–85/261)

Although it is a special problem concerning eternity that Levinas declares out of bounds in his book concerning the ethical, and although the ethical itself breaks the bounds of being and knowledge, no problem or mystery concerning eternity can belong to the ethical Exteriority which the subtitle of *Totality and Infinity* announces is the topic of that book. The eternity of what Kierkegaard calls inwardness is beyond the bounds of that book for the same reason.

Nevertheless, Levinas grants, "The movement that leads to the other human being leads to God."[4] The ethico-religious leads to religion. And provided the priority of the movement that leads to the human is preserved the religion to which it leads is the superior form of religion. "Everything that cannot be reduced to an interhuman relation represents not the superior form but the primitive form of religion" (TI, 79/52). The word "reduced" reproduced here from the published translation should be interpreted, with its Latin original in mind, as "led back." The French text has *se ramener,* which itself leads back to the "leads" *(mène)* of the sentence cited at the beginning of this paragraph. God and be-godded religion cannot be reduced to the ethicality of interhuman relations in the sense that there is no more to religion than these relations. It cannot be in terms of such be-godded religion that the religiousness of the ethico-religious in Levinas is to be understood. To understand Levinas in this way would be to reduce his notion of the ethico-religious to Kierkegaard's in the sense that it would be to say at least that the other as God is the way to the other as human being. When the risk is taken of transferring Kierkegaard's expression "ethico-religious" to the Levinasian context, the second component must be given a sense that is not defined only through the idea of God. It includes the sense Levinas gives to "metaphysics" when he writes, "In metaphysics a being is in a relation with what it cannot absorb, with what it cannot, in the etymological sense of the term, comprehend" (TI, 80/52). Metaphysics is *meta-phusis,* beyond being.

The ethico-religious is the ethico-metaphysical and vice versa for Levinas: "For the relation between [the] being here below (*l'être ici-bas*) and [the] transcendent being (*l'être transcendant*) that results in no community of concept or totality—a relation without relation—we reserve the term religion" (TI, 80/52). That is to say, (the) transcendent being is beyond being, and because (the) transcendent being is related, albeit unrelationally, to (the) being here below, the latter too is beyond being. But the beyond of being is the Good, not God. More precisely, for Levinas the beyond of being is God only if God is the Good. Kierkegaard too sometimes refers to the Good and to God as though they were interchangeable, but only where the Good is defined in terms of God. Thus at the beginning of the third chapter of *Purity of Heart,* after citing the epistle to James 4:8 ("Draw nigh to God, and he will draw nigh to you"), he adds this explanation: "For only the pure in heart can see God, and therefore draw nigh to Him; and only by God's drawing nigh to them can they maintain this purity.

And he who in truth wills only one thing can will only the Good."[5] The Platonic Good is Levinas's guide to the ethical, and, as has been seen, the ethical is an exteriority where all is aboveboard. It is the realm of frankness and sincerity. What Levinas refers to as "the final secret of being" (TI, 80/52) is that there is no secret in the realm of the ethical. This realm is ethico-religious as against the realm of the political, because the latter is the field in which the struggle for equality and reciprocal recognition takes place (TI, 35/64). Politics aims at a happy totality. That totality is made possible and impossible or unpossible—otherwise possible—by the infinity of Desire which interrupts it. It is for the latter that Levinas reserves the word "religion," meaning by this "the surplus possible in a society of equals, that of glorious humility, responsibility, and sacrifice, which are the condition for equality itself." "Religion . . . is the ultimate structure" or, "if one may so put it, de-structure." This de-structure is testified to by texts from Holy Scripture, for example by Micah 1:3–4: "For behold, the Lord cometh forth out of his place, and will come down, and tread upon the high places of the earth. And the mountains shall be molten under him, and the valleys shall be cleft, as wax before the fire, and as the waters that are poured down a steep place." But the power of such texts to stand witness to the ultimacy of religion as de-structure or dis-structure or cata-strophic structure does not depend upon their Scriptural authority.[6] In that regard it is, to borrow a phrase and a title from Kierkegaard, without authority.

Even in studies devoted to the exegesis of Torah, Talmud, and other texts of the Jewish religious tradition, it must be possible to express what is testified by them in Greek, meaning by that discourse of philosophy transmitted from Athens, not least in what Levinas hears in Plato's doctrine of the Good beyond being. This beyond is the beyond of the title of those readings and discourses Levinas collects under the title *L'au-delà du verset*.[7] His title is not *Au-delà du verset, Beyond the verse*. It is *The Beyond of the Verse*. The beyond is *in* the verses of Scripture. In their words is their transcendence. But the transcendence of the word is the deed. It is, to borrow again the words of another of Kierkegaard's titles, works of love. And the love is love of the other in both senses of that genitive, and of the other in two senses too: the other human being, *Autrui* or *l'autre*, and the Other, *l'Autre*, meaning God.

IV

A warning was given above against inferring that Levinas would have the other take over the work of the Other as just distinguished. Although because of his confessional commitment to Christianity Kierkegaard is unable to allow this, it cannot be only because of Levinas's confessional commitment to Judaism that he is unable to dispense with the word "God." There are philosophical reasons why he cannot do this, Greek reasons, and not ones derived simply from the fact that the Greeks needed the word. Levinas says that the word "God" is extraordinary. But without it we should be unable to understand ordinary words. Or, rather, we should be unable to understand that all ordinary words are extraordinary, not only those that carry their extraordinariness on the face, but words in daily use like "good-bye" and "adieu." The transcendence of words is their being for the other, *pour l'autre*. What is added, we may ask, if, having said, "For the other human being" we go on to say, as Levinas does, "And thereby unto God," *Pour l'autre homme et par là à-Dieu?*[8] What is the force of this "thereby"? Does it link the for-the-other to the unto-God chronologically or ontologically? This is a question that is raised in Descartes's Third Meditation, so frequently referred to by Levinas, where the answer seems to be that the idea of the existence of the self that is conscious of itself, the *pour-soi*, is prior in the temporal order of discovery to the idea of the existing God, while God is prior to the self ontologically. But what Levinas's "thereby" signifies is neither in the *ordo cognoscendi* nor in the *ordo essendi*. It signifies in the space of *dés-inter-essement* in the etymological sense of this word. On page 9 of the 1982 edition of *L'au-delà du verset* where this is said there are two typographical curiosities that may not be unintended misprints.[9] Instead of *dés-* the published text has *dès-*, which usually means "from" in a temporal sense. But a misprint so apt that one hopes it is intended is *éthymologique* [*sic*]. For it is ethics or the ethical, *l'éthique*, that disorders both the order of being and the order of knowing, the ethical not as exclusive of the religious, but as leading us and Descartes both to the idea of God and to the God that comes to the idea, *Dieu qui vient à l'idée*. The God that comes to the idea cannot be comprehended in any idea or finite mind, as Descartes confirms when he breaks off ratiocination and instead offers a prayer in praise of God's majesty. Levinas would say that prayer, *oraison*, is a reason, *raison*, that is prior to rationalist ratiocination.

The rationalist Descartes is of course interested in establishing the existence of God. Kierkegaard treats the establishing of God's existence almost as an irrelevance. He is content to say that he knows God exists because his father told him so.[10] This question of how we know God exists is deliberately set aside by Levinas. He states at the beginning of the foreword to *De Dieu qui vient à l'idée* that this book makes no pretense to deal with the question of the existence or non-existence of God, or indeed with the question whether it makes sense to talk of deciding one way or the other. His approach is phenomenological, and phenomenology suspends questions of existence. Levinas's non-dogmatic quasi-theological phenomenology has in common with the rationality of Descartes's theological ontology that it seeks "a reasonable way to speak of God."[11] It does this by binding back speaking about God into one human being's speaking to another. It shows that the abstractness of the Other as God is given meaning through being placed within the context of concrete relations with the human other.[12]

One illustration of this passage from the abstract to the concrete is a passage to a dimension of otherness that has not yet been mentioned. At the end of the essay entitled "Meaning and Sense" a reference is made to Exodus 33, God's words to Moses: "And it shall come to pass, while my glory passeth by, that I will put thee in a cleft of the rock, and will cover thee with my hand while I pass by: And I will take away mine hand, and thou shalt see my back parts; but my face shall not be seen." Levinas's gloss on God's not showing his face is that God shows himself only by his trace, where a trace is to be understood in terms of God's having passed and—in contrast with what is representable by an image or sign—of his never having been present and never being capable of becoming present to view, not even to the mind as an objective. Viewing and visibility are out of the question precisely because the "thereby" (*par là*) cited above does not usher in a being or the being of a being. It marks that the meaning of the word "God" is our addressing ourselves to the other human being. Address is not a relation to an object or objective. It is being face-to-face. This is not strictly a relation, but the precondition of relationality.[13] Levinas then gives an ethical exegesis of the words cited above from Exodus: "To go toward Him is not to follow this trace, which is not a sign; it is to go towards the Others (*les Autres*)."[14] But there has already taken place in Levinas's text, if not quite a reversal of this humanizing move, a reaching back to what makes the move possible, to a kind of compromise (which is also a com-promise), a common origin of alterity which he calls illeity. The third-personality (*il*, "he") of this neo-logism is apt because it is in the trace of illeity that we go towards the plural Others.

It would be more accurate to say that illeity is not a neologism, but a neographism. For it alludes to a Scripture beyond the biblical Scripture that Levinas takes as his clue. Parallel to the philosophical and ethical issue at stake here is the doctrine invoked by Levinas that the Torah stands as a safeguard against a too familiar proximity to God.[15] Tangential to this doctrine is the Kabbalistic doctrine that God is the Torah.[16] He reminds us too of the place in the *Phaedrus* (275) where we read that—like God in Exodus 33—the author of a piece of writing or of a drawing is typically unavailable and unanswerable to the reader or viewer. And it is in this Platonic dialogue that we find the theory of knowledge as recollection illustrated by the analogy of truths written on the wax of the mind. Kierkegaard too harks back to this theory in order, like Levinas, to substitute an ethical transcendentalism for the epistemological immanentism of Plato's theory of *anamnesis*. In Kierkegaard's case, this transcendentalist alternative is what he calls repetition *(Gjentagelse)*. Repetition does not retrieve something remembered. It is directed not simply toward a temporal future and past. It is directed to eternity. And it is teleological, as confirmed by the thought in *Fear and Trembling* of a teleological suspension of the ethical. Although illeity is not recollected, neither is it teleological. Yet the absolute past of its immemoriality is matched by an absolute futurity. So if illeity is an origin, as Levinas says it is, while denying it any cosmogonic or cosmological status, it could be regarded as the common origin of doctrines found in the Hebrew and Greek traditions. This brings us to a critical question. Would the absolute otherness of this common origin offer a way of getting behind and subverting the Other called God?

Pertinent to this question are the following rhetorical questions from *Purity of Heart:* "For, after all, what is eternity's accounting other than that the voice of conscience is for ever installed with its eternal right to be the exclusive voice? What is it other than that throughout eternity an infinite stillness reigns wherein the conscience may talk with the individual about what he has done of Good or evil."[17] There is mention of conscience and of good and of evil here, but there is no mention here of God. So is Kierkegaard contemplating the possibility of an ethics of eternity that is ethico-religious but neither an ethics of generality in the style of Hegel nor an ethics of religion? No. For, in the paragraph preceding the one in which he may seem to be leaving an opening for this possibility he has written: "In eternity . . . each one shall render account to God as an individual." And here the name of God is being used essentially, not borrowed as a manner of speaking as it seems to be when Levinas employs the expression "judgment of God" for the judgment that calls me to a justice more exacting than that of the universal judgments of history (TI, 246–47/224–25). As in the sentences cited from Kierkegaard, the Hegelians are again being targeted. But Levinas would acknowledge Nietzsche as well as Kierkegaard to be a marksman alongside himself, except that the eternity of Nietzsche's eternal return of the same is neither the eternity that gets mentioned in the sentences just cited from Kierkegaard nor the eternity that gets mentioned toward the end of *Totality and Infinity* only in order that its author may tell us that it raises a problem that exceeds the frame *(cadre)* of this book. Has not the book been treating throughout problems that exceed any frame? This is a question that exceeds the frame of this essay. I therefore pass, as that book does, to some conclusions, or, as Kierkegaard might say, to a concluding unscientific postscript, pausing only to observe in passing that a postscript is something that exceeds a frame, and that this can be said of the entirety of Kierkegaard's *Concluding Unscientific Postscript* as confidently as it can be said of his collection of nothing but prefaces entitled *Prefaces*.

V

If with Kierkegaard we give priority, ethico-religiously speaking, to the Other as the God of Christianity over the other as the other human being, are we not in direct conflict both with secular ethics and with any religion which, like Levinas's, does not give a central place to the Incarnation? The conflict will not flare up into warfare if the Christian, the Jew, and the Muslim not only tolerate one another but listen to one another. Levinas purports to keep his Jewish faith separate from his thinking of ethicality. This thinking helps us to understand how not only tolerance but active listening to and welcoming the other as stranger can happen. It opens a way, as Christianity also does, to loving the enemy, but it does so without requiring that that love be offered only on condition that the Christian or Jewish or Islamic doctrine be accepted as fundamental in ethico-religious intersubjectivity and sociality. To accept a doctrine as fundamental is to accept it not merely as a doctrine or theoretical tenet, but in one's actions and, Kierkegaard would say, as an "existence communication."

Kierkegaard keeps his Christian faith separate from his thinking of unregenerate Hegelian ethicality, but that faith is the heart of his thinking of ethicality as given back dialectically in the absurd paradoxicality of Religiousness

B, in which eternal happiness is at one and the same time, or, rather, at the intersection of time and eternity, worldly suffering. In Religiousness A happiness is the telos one hopes to achieve via suffering. It takes this end to be achievable through things of this world, the world understood as a totality to which these things belong together with the individual. It is a religiousness of immanence, and its pathos is aesthetic. Hence it is available to the pagan. None of this means that Religiousness A does not share with Religiousness B a consciousness of culpability. Without that there would be little plausibility in the proposal I hereby make that Kierkegaard's Religiousness A be taken together with Levinas's description of the ethico-religious as pointers toward a Derridian notion of religiousness that is more comprehensive than those proposed by Kierkegaard and Levinas yet is no less demanding on the singular individual than are their teachings regarding the ethico-religious. It is this demandingness that distinguishes the proposed revision both from paganism as conceived by Levinas when he distinguishes the sacred (*le sacré*) from the holy (*le saint*), and from paganism as conceived by Kierkegaard when he dismisses paganism: "The highest well-being of a happy immediacy, which jubilates joy over God and all existence, is very endearing but not upbuilding and essentially not any relationship with God" (CUP, 560 n.). It is not essentially a relationship with God according to Kierkegaard because in place of existentiality it puts "all existence," that which is comprehended. The paradox and the absurd "are employed aesthetically with regard to the marvelous among many other things, the marvelous that certainly is marvelous but that nevertheless can be comprehended" (CUP, 558–59).

Derrida demonstrates that the greater comprehensiveness of a religiousness beyond religiousness as portrayed by either Kierkegaard or Levinas does not mean that it is a religiousness in which everything can be comprehended. He keeps open the path to a greater comprehensiveness by observing that the question "Who is my other?" begs a question. He asks us to ask instead "Who or what is my other?" To put this in Levinas's terms, he questions the opposition between the sacred and the holy. Levinas's word *saint* translates the Hebrew *kadosh*, meaning separated. But the Hebrew word can also mean sacred. Derrida invites us to follow this hint of the Hebrew when he expands the scope of what Levinas first calls reversed or inverted intentionality but comes to think of rather as an interruption of intentionality and its noetic-noematic structure. Intentionality implies consciousness and, on Levinas's interpretation of it, consciousness implies a synthetic unity of apperception over against an objective accusative. In responsibility this objective accusative of what is said or what appears (*apparaît*) becomes the subject's appearing (*comparaît*) as though in a court of law, except that I am found culpable not on account of anything I have done or left undone, not because of a contravention of a law, but simply through my excluding the singular other from my singular place in the sun. Derrida reopens the question whether this excluded other is divine, human, animal, vegetable or mineral, whether we must extend what he calls paradoxically democracy to come "to the whole world of singularities, to the whole world of humans assumed to be like me, my compeers . . . even further, to all nonhuman living beings, or again, even beyond that, to all the nonliving, to their memory, spectral or otherwise, to their to-come."[18]

My other, according to Levinas, is someone, a he or a she, who can speak. Derrida invites us to consider whether no less other than the other who can speak is the other who cannot speak, the it on behalf of which it is therefore my responsibility to speak, however unimaginably other the other may be. So unconditional is the welcome this ultimate other invites me to make that its alterity cannot be marked by the paleonym or pronym "God" or by the neographism "illeity" unless these markers are undecided as between who and what. Following the suggestion made by the relative pronoun in "Our Father *which* art in Heaven . . ." in the King James version of Luke 11:2, this undecidedness could be marked by the neographism "whot."

In the phenomenological description of the experience that manifests the speculative system that Hegel constructs occur moments when alterity is the alterity of a who, for example, the alterity of my master. But as the dialectic of "the necessary other" who negates and elevates me progresses, the personal Who becomes an impersonal What, for example the alterity of the impersonal and universal "absolute master" called death. Kierkegaard and Levinas seek to save the Who in its singularity. So too does Derrida. But he seeks to save also the What. Not principally the What of essence nor the Hegelian What that is singular through being an ultimately single and all-comprehensive It, but a What that respects the plurality of unique Its. This fails to be marked by Levinasian illeity, of which the third-personality is indeed that of the third person, whether another human being or God. To do justice to the singularity both of human and all non-human others, a justice that is done by neither Levinas nor Kierkegaard, Derrida is in effect inviting us to give asylum in our thinking of what he calls the New International democracy to come to a barbarism, neither Greek nor Hebrew nor Arabic nor yet English, neither simply spoken nor simply written, at the heart of the chiasmus of logos as saying and of logos as said, the archic yet anarchic pronoun "Whot."

Notes

1. The second page number refers to the French original, *Totalité et infini: Essai sur l'extériorité* (The Hague: Nijhoff, 1980).

2. The second number refers to the French original, *De Dieu qui vient à l'idée* (Paris: Vrin, 1982).

3. Levinas, "Dialogue," in GWCM, 151; "Le dialogue," in *De Dieu qui vient à l'idée*, 230.

4. Levinas, "Dialogue," in GWCM, 148; "Le dialogue," in *De Dieu qui vient à l'idée*, 227.

5. Søren Kierkegaard, *Purity of Heart Is to Will One Thing: Spiritual Preparation for the Office of Confession*, trans. Douglas Steere (London: Collins, 1966), 47; see also p. 161.

6. Levinas, "God and Philosophy," in GWCM, 199 n. 15; "Dieu et la philosophie," in *De Dieu qui vient à l'idée*, 110 n. 9.

7. BTV, French original: *L'au-delà du verset: lectures et discours talmudiques* (Paris: Minuit, 1982).

8. Levinas, GWCM, xv, *De Dieu qui vient à l'idée*, 13.

9. Levinas, BTV, xii, *L'au-delà du verset*, 9.

10. JP, IX A 118.

11. Levinas, BTV, xiv, *L'au-delà du verset*, 11.

12. Levinas, GWCM, xiv, *De Dieu qui vient à l'idée*, 11.

13. GWCM, 150–51/230.

14. Emmanuel Levinas, *Humanism of the Other*, trans. Nidra Poller (Urbana: University of Illinois Press, 2006), 44; *Humanisme de l'autre homme* (Montpellier: Fata Morgana, 1972), 63.

15. Emmanuel Levinas, "Loving the Torah More Than God," in DF, 144; "Aimer la Thora plus que Dieu," in *Difficile liberté: essais sur le judaïsme* (Paris: Albin Michel, 1976), 192.

16. Zohar, II, 60a.

17. Kierkegaard, *Purity of Heart*, 163.

18. Jacques Derrida, *Rogues: Two Essays on Reason*, trans. Pascale-Anne Brault and Michael Naas (Stanford: Stanford University Press, 2005), 53; *Voyous: Deux essais sur la raison* (Paris: Galilée, 2003), 81.

4 Kierkegaard and Levinas on Four Elements of the Biblical Love Commandment

M. Jamie Ferreira

Important initiatives have already been made in bringing Kierkegaard and Levinas together for comparison, especially in the work of Merold Westphal and Michael Weston.[1] In my commentary on Kierkegaard's *Works of Love*—his lengthy examination of the biblical commandment of neighbor-love—I brought in briefly aspects of Levinas's ethics in order to illuminate Kierkegaard's commitment to the notion of an infinite debt to the neighbor and his rejection of certain notions of reciprocity.[2] The present volume, dedicated entirely to a comparison (and contrast) between Levinas and Kierkegaard, provides an opportunity for me to develop and extend the ways in which I think their ethics illuminate each other—in particular, by focusing more closely on four aspects of their response to the classical Judeo-Christian formulation of the love commandment. Both Jewish and Christian Scriptures propose a commandment in which we are to love our neighbor as ourselves: "You shall love your neighbor as yourself. I am the Lord" (Lev. 19:18); "You shall love your neighbor as yourself" (Matt. 22:39; Mark 12:31; Gal. 5:14). Although both Levinas and Kierkegaard agree that it is a commandment, something required rather than superogatory, they are intriguingly different in their responses to other elements of the formulation. Kierkegaard's response to the classical formulation of (1) the *commandment* (2) to *love* (3) the *neighbor* (4) *as yourself* is to affirm unambiguously all four elements, whereas Levinas expresses some ambivalence and/or reservation about three of those elements. These contrasting responses provide a fruitful opportunity to reconsider what is at stake for each of them and whether they differ substantively or merely terminologically, and in what follows I want to develop and solidify my comparison between Levinas and Kierkegaard on all four elements of the neighbor-love commandment, namely, command, love, neighbor, and as yourself.

Agape as Commanded Responsibility to/for the Neighbor

Kierkegaard

Kierkegaard's *Works of Love,* consisting of fifteen deliberations written in 1847 on the biblical commandment of neighbor-love, offers a detailed examination of both the character of the commandment as such and the ways in which it can be expressed or violated.[3] The second deliberation, a tripartite in-depth formal (almost legalistic) study (IIA, B, C) of the commandment "You shall love the neighbor" focusing on the terms "shall," "neighbor," and "you," explores the absolute obligatoriness and scope of the commandment. Kierkegaard unpacks the "shall" of the commandment in terms of its unconditional bindingness: the love it commands "does not stand or fall with the contingency of its object" (WOL, 39). Moreover, the command is unconditionally inclusive, both with respect to the object of the command (the "neighbor" as every single human being) and the subject of the command (the agent as every single human being).

The "neighbor" is understood as every person, "the whole human race, all people, even the enemy, and [we are] not to make exceptions, neither of preference nor of aversion" (WOL, 19). The inclusiveness of the object of love is a function of two commitments held by Kierkegaard: equality and kinship. First, the neighbor is an affirmation of absolute human equality: "He is your neighbor on the basis of equality with you before God, but unconditionally every person has this equality and has it unconditionally" (WOL, 60). Second, the neighbor is an affirmation of "the kinship of all human beings" (WOL, 69). In other words, the inclusiveness of the category of neighbor is intended to guarantee that no one can ever say of someone that he or she is excluded from the realm of their responsibility—there are no legitimate exceptions. The commandment to love everyone is not seen as the impossible task of caring for everyone, but the possible task of not excluding anyone (the next one, the nearest one) who presents himself or herself to me in need. Kierkegaard also takes pains to insist that the equality of every human being does not obscure his or her concrete distinctiveness—the response that is commanded depends on the particular concrete situation of the needy person (as exemplified in the story of the Good Samaritan).[4]

Conceptually distinguishing "preferential" and "nonpreferential" love in Deliberation IIB, Kierkegaard makes clear that love as a preferential feeling cannot be commanded; what is capable of being commanded—in contrast to erotic love *(Elskov)* and friendship *(Venskab)*—is a kind of caring *(Kjerlighed)*. Although the bindingness of the obligation is absolute, the caring can take different forms, depending on the needs of the person, and the forms can do justice to special relations.[5] Interestingly, *Kjerlighed* is the same Danish word used by Kierkegaard to describe God's love. Kierkegaard insists that this caring for others is expressed in "sheer action," in concrete action—it has fruits even though it cannot be judged by the success of its outward accomplishments.[6] For all these reasons it seems clear that commanded love, for Kierkegaard, is an active caring (as opposed to feeling or affection) for others to which we are unconditionally obligated. Moreover, the neighbor is, Kierkegaard says, "what thinkers call 'the other' " (WOL, 21), and construing neighbor-love as distinct from preferential love is Kierkegaard's way of safeguarding the genuine alterity of the other, so that the other is not "the other I" but rather "the first you" (WOL, 57).

Kierkegaard and Levinas on Elements of the Love Commandment 83

Kierkegaard also considers the command in terms of a never-ending debt that cannot be repaid. We have, he says, a "duty to remain in love's debt to one another" (WOL, 175). Our responsibility to others is seen as an infinite debt: "love is most correctly described as an infinite debt"; "the one who loves by giving, infinitely, runs into infinite debt" (WOL, 176, 177). Moreover, Kierkegaard judges that the task proposed by the commandment is able to be achieved, despite its being infinite, so the question is in what way we can meaningfully claim that an infinite task can be fulfilled. For Kierkegaard, despite his Lutheran appreciation of sin, the commandment can be fulfilled; "eternity," he says, "calmly assumes that every person can do it and therefore asks only if he did it" (WOL, 79). Obviously he is assuming that it is done, and only done, with God's grace; one example he likes to use to indicate both that we can love and why we can love is from his journals: "It is like a child giving his parents a present, purchased, however, with what the child has received from his parents" (JP, 2:1121, 10). Christ is "the prototype oriented to the universally human, of which everyone is capable" (JP, 2:1939, 372), so fulfillment of the Christian requirement means "imitation" of Christ's love, "of which everyone is capable" because of grace. The infinity of our obligation is, he insists, an extreme but accurate expression for the rigor of duty, but it is "not a fanatical expression" (WOL, 187); despite its "immeasurability" he affirms that "in everything done for you by the one who loves, in the least little triviality as well as in the greatest sacrifice, there is always love along with it" (WOL, 181). Thus the infinity of the debt does not mean that the commandment can never be fulfilled in the sense that we can never truly love an other person or perform a genuine work of love. Rather than denoting the impossibility of a genuine act of love, the infinity of the commandment means that the task can never be completed—Kierkegaard insists that we can never say "now I have paid my debt," or even made an "installment payment" on it (WOL, 178). He explains that the refusal to see our obligation to others as an infinite debt amounts to enthroning economic notions of "bookkeeping" and "calculation" (WOL, 178) and "comparison" (WOL, 182–85). Thus Kierkegaard employs, though implicitly, the distinction between a work that achieves a certain quality and a work that is completed, which we can call the distinction between a fulfillable task and a completeable task.[7]

Levinas

Like Kierkegaard's, Levinas's understanding of our obligation to the needy other emphasizes its unconditionality: "the *I* before the Other is infinitely responsible."[8] It is an "unlimited deficit," a "debt" that cannot be a matter of "book-keeping."[9] But it may appear inappropriate to evaluate Levinas's response to the commandment of neighbor-love since he has expressed some ambivalence about both the terms "love" and "neighbor." We need to reconsider this to determine if the difference is substantive or not.[10] First, Levinas expressed reservations about the term "love." He learned early on, he says, to "distrust the compromised word 'love,'" choosing instead to speak of "the responsibility for the Other, being-for-the-other" (EI, 52). Repeatedly he distances himself from the term "love" which he considers "worn-out and debased," preferring instead "the harsh name for what we call love of one's neighbor," namely, "responsibility for my neighbor."[11] But even in the same essay (indeed on the same page) where Levinas expresses his preference for the idiom of "responsibility" for the neighbor, rather than the idiom of love, he continues to speak of "love of one's neighbor," which he defines as "love without Eros, charity, love in which the ethical aspect dominates the passionate aspect, love without concupiscence."[12]

Levinas's reservations about the word "love" for the neighbor are perhaps due to the fact that it can too easily fail to portray what is at stake—it can fail to announce strongly enough that "I am *ordered* toward the face of the other," who "*commands*" me (OTB, 11, emphasis mine); my response is his "*right*" (BPW, 167, emphasis mine).[13] Still, as we saw above, despite his preference for the harsh view of love as responsibility for the other, Levinas does return time and again[14] to the language of love as long as it is acknowledged that "there is something severe in this love; this love is commanded."[15] In fact, in his later work, Levinas goes so far as to say, "That which I call responsibility is a love, because love is the only attitude where there is encounter with the unique." He writes in particularly striking terms that the "idea of the face is the idea of gratuitous love" and suggests that faith is "believing that love without reward is valuable," that "commanding love signifies recognizing the value of love in itself," and that "God is a commandment to love . . . the one who says that one must love the other."[16]

Levinas also occasionally expressed hesitation about whether the term "neighbor" is the best one to use. Sometimes this is because it seems to obscure or obliterate the fact of difference,[17] and sometimes because it may have lost its legitimate shock value and become taken for granted.[18] Despite this, he nevertheless persisted in using it from his earliest to his latest writings: "It is as a neighbor that a human being is accessible—as a face"; "in this call to responsibility of the ego by the face which summons it, which demands it and claims it, the other *(autrui)* is the neighbor."[19] Levinas equates the two categories: "the neighbor, the responsibility to the other."[20] The term "proximity of the neighbor" means for him "the responsibility of the ego for an other, the impossibility of letting the other alone faced with the mystery of death."[21] Given that rationale (mortality), no one is excluded from the category of "neighbor."

In sum, Levinas has what he calls "a grave view of *Agape* in terms of responsibility for the other,"[22] and he details how "the Other becomes my neighbor precisely through the way the face summons me, calls for me, begs for me, and in so doing recalls my responsibility, and calls me into question."[23] Thus, despite his specific reservations, it is obviously appropriate to construe his ethic as a commitment to the commandment of neighbor-love.

Complementarity of Their Accounts

Thus far, we can say that Levinas's account complements Kierkegaard's in two main ways. First, it makes clear that in one sense our neighbor, any neighbor, is always in need, in the sense of always vulnerable to death. This might be seen as itself a weakness in Levinas's account, namely, that since he does not provide adequate criteria for distinguishing between the generic threat of mortality and other instances of suffering, his view may entail an implausible leveling or raising of all indiscriminately. Second, and more importantly, when we see how rich the notion of responsibility is for Levinas, it is easier to understand Kierkegaard's account of the commandment. Kierkegaard is speaking of a love which can be commanded—and he is well aware that preference or inclination cannot be commanded. Still, it might be difficult for us to imagine "love" without preference, whereas the idea of responsibility for the other does not initially raise as many questions as "love" does about the relevance of preference. Obligation and responsibility go together more easily in our minds than obligation and love. If we see the heart of the obligation for Kierkegaard as one of responsibility for the other (rather than inclination or affection), it does not seem so difficult to understand why no one can be excluded (i.e., why preference cannot be a criterion for our responsibility) and it does not seem so difficult to understand why both the wife and the friend are at the same time the neighbor.[24]

On the other hand, the emphasis on love in Kierkegaard's account can complement Levinas's account. There is some value in not simply limiting the language of relation to the language of responsibility. After all, responsibility can be fulfilled grudgingly, hatefully. Perhaps this sad truth accounts for the extremely negative reaction readers often have to Levinas's notion of the self as a "persecuted hostage" in responsibility.[25] This phrase seems to describe a very unloving situation, putting us at odds with the neighbor—a relation which we would normally condemn. But Levinas makes it clear that "the Other is not a being we encounter that menaces us or wants to lay hold of us" (TO, 87). In fact, Levinas's notion of hostage has ties with the notion of host[26] and reminds us not only of the early descriptions he used of the self as open in "hospitality" to the other in *Totality and Infinity,* but also of the way he later ties hospitality to the extreme sacrifice of "giving to the other the bread from one's mouth"[27] and designates his own ethics as "the ethics of the welcome."[28] The terms "hospitality" and "welcome" remind us of the graciousness with which responsibility should be fulfilled. Levinas explicitly ties responsibility and gracious gift together when he recognizes that the responsibility of which he speaks "is not a cold juridical requirement." Rather, "it is all the gravity of the love of one's fellowman—of love without concupiscence" and it is accomplished "through all the modalities of *giving.*"[29]

Moreover, Kierkegaard, as we saw above, employs two distinctions that can mitigate the criticism that an ethic of infinite demand is too extreme, that it is unlivable ethic. First, Kierkegaard's employment of a distinction between a fulfillable task and a completeable task can illuminate Levinas's assumptions about the infinite demand. Like Kierkegaard, Levinas insists that we can never say the task is completed: "One is never quits with regard to the other." Explaining the "infinity in the ethical exigency," he insists that "at no time can one say: I have done all my duty" (EI, 105). The task is not completeable. But Levinas also allows that we can do what is commanded in the sense that we can respond to the other appropriately. Acknowledging that "the great objection" to his thought is the question, "Where did you ever see the ethical relation practiced?" he replies as follows: "its being utopian does not prevent it from investing our everyday actions of generosity or goodwill toward the other: even the smallest and most commonplace gestures, such as saying 'after you' as we sit at the dinner table or walk through a door, bear witness to the ethical."[30] He elaborates: "I remember meeting once with a group of Latin American students, well versed in the terminology of Marxist liberation and terribly concerned by the suffering and unhappiness of their people in Argentina. They asked me rather impatiently if I had ever actually witnessed the utopian rapport with the other that my ethical philosophy speaks of. I replied, 'Yes, indeed—here in this room.'"[31] Levinas's appreciation that even in simple gestures we can express genuine "pity, compassion, [and] pardon" (OTB, 117) accounts for his willingness to say that "I am he who finds the resources to respond to the call," the call of the "the poor for whom I can do all and to whom I owe all" (EI, 89). All in all, for Levinas the responsibility he describes has a paradoxical "extraordinary everydayness" (OTB, 141).

On both accounts, even though the task is never finished, it is fulfillable. We can express genuine love or compassion at a given time, whether it is helping the wounded person we find on the sidewalk, opening the door lovingly for another, or forgiving someone without humiliating him or her.

Second, Kierkegaard's implicit distinction between helping everyone and not excluding anyone can also be used to illuminate Levinas's assumptions about the unconditional scope of the command. The commandment cannot oblige us to help everyone everywhere, since that is an impossible task—we cannot affect everyone, we cannot be everywhere, and for each one we help there is another we cannot help at the same time or with the same resources. The unconditional scope of the command, in both ethics, is best understood as precluding the legitimacy of ever saying to anyone who presents him- or herself in need to me that I have no obligation in that situation.

For the moment it is enough to note that, although there may be important differences between their accounts, Levinas and Kierkegaard both appreciate that the two accents—love and responsibility—need to be part of a full account of relation to the neighbor. Levinas's preference for the language of "responsibility for the other" clarifies Kierkegaard's understanding of "*commanded* love," and Kierkegaard's preference for the language of love keeps in focus the graciousness of giving in "commanded *love*." Moreover, the infinity of the task expressed by the commandment can for both thinkers be understood in ways that make it ethically demanding without being impossible. Having underlined the commitments they share, I turn now to an element of the formulation of the love commandment that seems to place them in opposition.

Kierkegaard's Commitment to the "As Yourself"

Kierkegaard is not afraid in *Works of Love* to unambiguously affirm that what he calls the love commandment's "little phrase, *as yourself*" (WOL, 17) is as important to his account as the three other elements. He spends seven pages examining this little phrase, and his discussion reveals that the "as yourself" serves five main purposes—it is meant (1) to "open the lock of self-love," (2) to teach a person "proper self-love," (3) to be a standard for our love of others so that it is not less than love for ourselves, (4) to be a standard for our love for others so that it is not more than love for ourselves, and (5) to remind us that we have been loved by God.

He boldly announces the first message of the "as yourself": "if one is to love the neighbor *as oneself*, then the commandment, as with a pick, wrenches open the lock of self-love and wrests it away from a person" (WOL, 17). He soon makes it clear, however, that wrenching open and wresting away the lock of self-love means opening up a restricted self-love, not eliminating self-love. He does this by his affirmation of "proper self-love" (WOL, 18).

Kierkegaard has no hesitation in affirming the possibility of what he calls "proper self-love." In fact, he deduces it from the commandment to love the neighbor as yourself. Luther claimed that the commandment's "as yourself" shows man "the sinful love with which he does in fact love himself, as if to say: 'You are completely curved in upon yourself . . . a condition from which you will not be delivered unless you altogether cease loving yourself, and forgetting yourself, love your neighbor."[32] Kierkegaard, however, reminds us in no uncertain terms that "if the commandment is properly understood it also says the opposite: *You shall love yourself in the right way.* Therefore, if anyone is unwilling to learn from Christianity to love himself in the right way, he cannot love the neighbor either" (WOL, 22).

Although Kierkegaard is exceedingly sensitive to the dangers of perversions of self-love (which he terms "selfish self-love," WOL, 151), he assumes that without "proper self-love" one cannot properly love anyone else. The point of the commandment of neighbor-love *(Kjerlighed),* he notes, is to "guide" (WOL, 67) the love *(Kjerlighed)* which is placed in us by God, so that we do not exclude anyone from it.[33] He is commending opening the "lock," which is done by rendering love *inclusive* rather than exclusive and competitive. In other words, there is an exercise of self-love which is to be opened up, yet there is clearly a right way to love oneself.

The second message Kierkegaard finds in the "as yourself" is a heightening of the message of "proper self-love," namely, the reminder that sometimes people do not sufficiently love themselves. He writes that just as often as he feels the need to pull in the reins on one person's selfish self-love, he feels the need to open another person to proper self-love: "Whoever has any knowledge of people will certainly admit that just as he has often wished to be able to move them to relinquish self-love, he has also had to wish that it were possible to teach them to love themselves" (WOL, 23). He bemoans the unnecessary tragedy of a person who "does not know how to love himself rightly," and concludes: "When someone self-tormentingly thinks to do God a service by torturing himself, what is his sin except not willing to love himself in the right way? And if, alas, a person presumptuously lays violent hands upon himself, is not his sin precisely this, that he does not rightly love himself in the sense in which a person *ought* to love himself?" Christianity reminds a person to "love his neighbor as himself, that is, as he ought to love himself," because "selfishly not willing to love oneself in the right way" is just as bad as "selfishly loving oneself" (WOL, 23).

But more is at stake in the commandment's qualification, "as yourself," than legitimating proper self-love; the "as yourself" requires in addition that we use love of self as an index or standard for our love for another. That is, to one who asks, "How shall I love my neighbor?" the commandment "will invariably go on repeating the brief phrase 'as yourself'" (WOL, 20). Kierkegaard here follows Luther, who instructs in the "Lectures on Galatians" (1535): "if you want to know how the neighbor is to be loved and want to have an outstanding pattern of this, consider carefully how you love yourself."[34] What does this pattern involve? Luther's answer is that it requires positive readings of the seven commandments relating to our treatment of others. It requires that we support, help, increase, protect, and preserve, in addition to abstaining from harm, and we are "commanded to further" the welfare of the other because this is what we would wish for ourselves.[35] Luther's "short conclusion" to the Ten Commandments contains a simple model of how the "as yourself" functions: "Everybody seeks love and friendship, gratitude and assistance, truth and loyalty, from his neighbor. And all these are what the Ten Commandments require of us."[36]

Similarly, many of the later deliberations in *Works of Love* explicitly assume a certain model of our love of self. For example, Kierkegaard works with the assumption that we want to be treated with respect, want not to be treated condescendingly, and that we forgive ourselves our false starts and weaknesses. All of these provide a pattern or model, so that we are never at a loss as to "how" to love the neighbor. In this way the third message of the "as yourself" is to keep us from loving the other *less* than we should.

But the "as yourself" as standard also has an obverse side. The fourth message is to keep us from loving the other *more* than we should. Kierkegaard actually anticipates the possible objection that loving the neighbor "as oneself" is not as "high" as loving the neighbor *more than oneself* (WOL, 18). His explanation of why the "highest" is loving another "as yourself" is revealed in the examples that he uses. To love another more than yourself means that one fulfills the other's desire even though one thinks it is harmful to the other: "If you can perceive what is best for him better than he can you will not be excused because the harmful thing was his own desire" (WOL, 20).[37] Moreover, if one refuses to give up the beloved "if the beloved required it," that is, if it was for the beloved's good—one is not loving the beloved as one ought to love oneself (WOL, 21).

Works of Love, in sum, clearly distinguishes between a "selfish self-love" (WOL, 151) that is at odds with the good of the other and a "proper self-love" (WOL, 18) that both encompasses the good of the other and is the measure of the good of the other. But for Kierkegaard there is yet another dimension to the phrase "as yourself." The fifth message of the "as yourself" is a reminder that, as Kierkegaard notes repeatedly in Works of Love, we have been loved by God; "as yourself" translates into "as you yourself have been loved" by God. It is, in other words, a reminder of God's enabling gift of love—that I can love because I am loved.

Levinas's Reservation About the "As Yourself"

Let's turn now to Levinas's response to the "as yourself," which is the locus of what is perhaps the biggest difference in their responses to the classical formulation of the love commandment.[38] Much of what Levinas says might be taken to imply that he could not allow an "as yourself" to be a part of the love commandment. His claims that the persecuted self "empties itself" of itself, "divests itself," and is "hostage" (OTB, 111–28) support his conclusion that "in ethics, the other's right to exist has primacy over my own."[39] The "subordination" and "dissymmetry" (or "asymmetry") to which he refers is extreme: "My duty to respond to the other suspends my natural right to self-survival" and "If there was only the other facing me, I would say to the very end: I owe him everything."[40] Moreover, Levinas did at least once explicitly consider the "as yourself" and appeared to think that the idea of loving your neighbor "as yourself" implied that "one loves oneself most." This is revealed in the course of an interview in which he was asked the following question: "Cannot moral experience be translated as an experience of the other as identical to oneself? . . . [that] corresponds to the imperative . . . 'Love your neighbor as yourself'?"[41] His response is intriguing; he was, he says, "perplexed" by the biblical text (and implies that the translators should have been more perplexed) and asks "What does the 'as yourself' signify?" He imagines Buber and Rosenzweig saying to each other "does not 'as yourself' mean that one loves oneself most?" and sees their rejection of that implication as the reason for their alternative translation, "Love your neighbor; he is like you." Levinas, however, isn't satisfied with that and proposes yet another alternative translation. Given his hermeneutical principle that it is only when the "entirety of the Bible becomes the context of the verse that the verse resounds with all its meaning," he concludes that the Bible as a whole "always" posits the "priority of the other in relation to me." His alternative translation, therefore, emphasizing the "priority of the other" goes as follows: "Love your neighbor; this work is like yourself; love your neighbor; he is yourself; it is this love of the neighbor which is yourself." It is unclear why Levinas should assume that "as yourself" would imply that one loves oneself more than the other ("loves oneself most"), but as long as he does it is understandable why he would reject it. However, it is possible to reject that particular reading of the "as yourself" without rejecting the "as yourself" altogether. The question remains whether there is a way in which the "asymmetry" of the ethical relation and the priority of the other can be appropriately maintained without jettisoning all facets of an "as yourself," and whether Levinas avails himself of it.

The "as yourself" implies a kind of equality, and presumably Levinas wants to downplay any kind of equality that seems to put limits on one's responsibility for the other; equality seems at odds both with any notion of the priority of the other and the subordination of the self. Moreover, he may feel the need to reject emphasis on the "as yourself" because when the phrase reminds us of the other's equal status, it also serves to remind us at the same time of the other's equal status *as commanded.* The equality implied by the "as yourself" tends to allow us to put the spotlight on the other's responsibility—she too is commanded to love her neighbor—and it thus allows us to begin to compare and calculate obligations. It promotes the kind of bookkeeping arrangement that Levinas criticizes. Thus resistance to the "as yourself" serves two different functions: first, to deflect attention from the self (as when Levinas retorts that the other's obligation to me is "his affair," not mine [EI, 98]); second, to focus attention on the self by forestalling the escapist tendencies we have to shift attention to the other's obligation. All of the above might account for Levinas's unwillingness to explicitly appeal to or affirm the "as yourself."[42]

An Assessment

Both Kierkegaard and Levinas affirmed an infinite obligation to the neighbor and both feared the dangers of a "bookkeeping" mentality in ethics, of calculation and comparison, yet Kierkegaard explicitly highlighted and appealed to the "as yourself" of the love commandment, and Levinas explicitly expressed perplexity and reservation about it. Is the difference merely terminological or is it substantive? Did Levinas reject the "as yourself" or did he merely refuse to emphasize it? Is there a difference in the practical response required of us on each account?

Let's reconsider the most obvious prima facie difference between what Levinas and Kierkegaard say. Levinas says, You should love the neighbor more than yourself. Kierkegaard says, You should love the neighbor as yourself. Given Kierkegaard's commitment to equality, his formulation seems to imply that you should *not* love your neighbor more than yourself. And, as we saw earlier, he does explicitly say this. This seems a substantive and straightforward disagreement with Levinas. However, we could as well phrase the implication of Kierkegaard's commitment to equality as follows: When you love the neighbor as yourself, the principle of equality implies that *you must not love yourself more than your neighbor.* Levinas would of course agree. Phrased this way it seems like a substantive agreement between them—neither wants you to love yourself more than your neighbor.

There is, however, clearly a difference of emphasis, of accent, and one explanation of that could be the different dangers sensed by each thinker, and the different audience each is confronting. Perhaps after the Shoah (and Freud) it is callous or dangerous to remind people to love themselves. Or perhaps we could say that Levinas did not necessarily think it was illegitimate to love our self, but rather that the audience to whom he saw himself speaking did not seem to him to need a reminder about love of self. Perhaps a Jewish sense of worth and self-esteem are so natural that Levinas assumes them, does not need to argue for them, whereas Lutheran (or Pietistic) Christianity's message of abjectness and depravity impels Kierkegaard's sad recognition of the need for a corrective message. In order to decide if the difference is substantive, one must ask whether Levinas would explicitly reject any of Kierkegaard's commitments and his rationale for the "as yourself." Does Levinas deny the equality of all human beings to which Kierkegaard is committed? Does he deny that there is a legitimate kind of self-love, a legitimate self-esteem?

Importantly, Levinas's emphasis on asymmetry was intended to clarify the ethical relation between us, rather than to engage an ontological agenda by denying any sort of ontological equality. Levinas is perfectly willing at times to admit that the other, the neighbor, is an equal. Early on he concedes that "the poor one, the stranger, presents himself as an equal," even though she "approaches me from a dimension of height . . . equality is founded" (TI, 213, 214). In his later work, he affirms the legitimacy of the way in which "I am approached as an other by the others, that is, 'for myself.'" "'Thanks to God,' I am another for the others" (OTB, 158). This acknowledgment is repeatedly echoed in his insistence on equity and justice and "equality between those that cannot be compared."[43] There is a kind of equality implied in Levinas's legitimation of justice that precludes any simplistic contrast with Kierkegaard on equality. In effect, there does not seem to be a substantive difference in this regard. For Kierkegaard the legitimacy of self-love and the "as yourself" is in part a matter of consistency. If we cannot exclude anyone, we cannot arbitrarily exclude ourselves; similarly, if one has reverence for God's creation or God's gifts, one must have reverence for one's self as well. Whether or not Levinas would agree, one could say that his acknowledgment of equality and justice is a de facto acceptance of at least one significant aspect of the rationale for an "as yourself."

Another rationale for the "as yourself" to which we can assume Kierkegaard was committed is the argument that it is part of our duty to others to maintain our self, in order to be able to support those in need. In his "Treatise on Good Works" (1520), Luther explicitly argues that it is a duty to care for oneself since to fail to take care of oneself is to become a murderer of oneself: anyone whose immoderate sacrifice is ruining his strength "will be regarded as a man who takes no care of himself, and, as far as he is able, he has become his own murderer."[44] This latter rationale is one that is easily available to Levinas on his own terms. His commitments to the "ethics of the welcome" and his understanding of hospitality (of "hands which give"[45]) can be said to support a functional equivalent of the "as yourself."

Could Levinas accept Kierkegaard's view that we are not commanded to love the other more than ourself? It is certainly possible that if Levinas accepted Kierkegaard's description of the adoration and idolatry that loving the neighbor more than oneself amounts to, he would find himself on Kierkegaard's side of the question, If "to speak of loving another person more than oneself . . . would mean, despite one's insight that this would be harmful to him, doing it *in obedience* because he demanded it, or *in adoration* because he desired it" (WOL, 20), there is reason to think that Levinas too would reject that reading of love. Levinas translates the duty "not to kill" more generally as the duty not to do harm to another: "you shall not jeopardize the life of the other."[46] So he would presumably agree that unconditional love for others does not mean fulfilling all their desires, even those harmful to themselves. Nor does such love, he insists, constitute a recommendation of suicide (EI, 121).

Do we then have only a difference of emphasis, in which each could accept what the other says, though he did not explicitly say it (given his audience and purpose)? Are we left only with the following conclusion: if we believe that "he that is not against us is with us" (Luke 9:50), we can accentuate their commonality; if we prefer to think that "he that is not with me is against me" (Luke 11:23), we can accentuate their divergence. Does a reconsideration of the "as yourself" provide any evidence of a genuinely substantive disagreement between them?

One possible substantive difference might have to do with the connection Kierkegaard makes between the "as yourself" and God. It might seem as if the question of God is the obvious place for a contrast between Kierkegaard and Levinas, insofar as the one is Christian and the other Jewish. Beyond that, of course, there is the issue of whether Levinas's deontologized "trace of God" differs from the God to whom Kierkegaard prays in *Works of Love*. Finally, there is the question whether they differ on the immediate versus mediated role of God; I have addressed this question elsewhere,[47] suggesting that there is more commonality than is usually thought. Still, it does seem that Kierkegaard's understanding of the "as yourself" can reveal a potential dissimilarity. As I noted earlier, "as yourself" reminds us that the Author of our being, the one who commands us, is also the source of love in us. Kierkegaard takes seriously the richness of the commandment's formulation as revealed in a New Testament variation: "A new commandment I give you, that you love one another: that as I have loved you, you also love one another" (John 13:34). The result is that he appreciates two variants of the commandment's "as yourself": (1) as (you ought to love) yourself and (2) as (you) yourself (have been loved). Not only does the love commandment provide the yardstick and sample of love of the neighbor (not less or more than proper self love), the second variant reminds us that God has loved us first, that God is the origin and source of the love in us which God commands us not to limit preferentially. I can only love because I am loved: I cannot love of my own resources, on my own initiative, so to speak. But by the same token, I can love because I am loved: my creation is a kind of gifting of love. The "as yourself" reminds me both of my createdness and of the gift of love to me, and so takes me out of myself, exteriorizes and desubjectifies my response to the other. Levinas, by contrast, effectively equates an acknowledgment that "God loves me" with a selfish concern with "my salvation."[48]

In sum, the fifth message of the "as yourself," according to Kierkegaard, is the reminder of God's enabling gift of love, and this paradoxically reminds me about myself precisely in order to take my attention away from myself by encouraging me in my striving to love the other. When the commandment is construed without the encouragement provided by the reminder that we are loved and so are able to love, it could suggest that the individual is left to his own resources. Deliberately downplaying the "as yourself" is Levinas's way of trying to turn us away from ourselves toward the other, but his refusal to explicitly affirm love of self may reveal a theological difference between him and Kierkegaard with respect to creation and autonomy. Ironically, the effort to focus only on the self's responsibility can, despite its good intentions, return the spotlight to the self. On the one hand, Levinas's emphasis on the initiative of the other is a response precisely to an overemphasis in the culture on human autonomy and independence, yet his ethic promotes a kind of autonomy (I alone am responsible [EI, 100–101]). That is, the effort to prevent our obsession with assessing the other's obligation carries with it the threat of taking our attention away from the other altogether, by enshrining another kind of self-centeredness in making the self supreme in its agency of loving. Levinas's understandable fear of reminding us of the first dimension of "as yourself" (we are both equal, and equally commanded) because it is open to the danger of calculation and comparison and limits on our responsibility, carries in its train a failure to remind us of the second dimension (we are both loved equally and infinitely)—a failure to remind us of our ability through God's gracious gift of love to fulfill the command and our dependence on God's gift.

In this respect, then, it could be argued that consideration of the "as yourself" reveals one possible locus of substantive disagreement between Kierkegaard and Levinas—a substantive difference of opinion insofar as radical responsibility entails radical autonomy. Levinas's emphasis on how only I can answer the neighbor's needs may signal a theological divergence on the meaning of hope and humility. On the other hand, it might be that this is the only consistent position once a substantive theo-ontology is rejected.

Another point of comparison: it could also be argued that Kierkegaard's appreciation of the second variant—love others as God has loved you—provides an account of why the demand is an infinite one that differs from Levinas's. However egoistic we are, we might not in fact construe self-love as infinite or want to be loved by others infinitely, so loving others as we love ourselves or loving others as we want to be loved by them do not necessarily imply an infinite task. That is, it is not immediately obvious why we finite beings could ever have an infinite responsibility to other finite beings. Kierkegaard's appeal to the second variant provides a straightforward answer to why the task is an infinite one. In the case of Levinas, there is a little more ambiguity (or richness?). Although it could be argued, as I have done elsewhere, that Levinas also relies on the notion of God (the "trace of God") to account for the "infinity" of the demand generated by a finite being,[49] such a "trace" may well have different theological implications for notions of ability and autonomy.

A final point of comparison is relevant to the discussion of reciprocity. In both thinkers, the position on reciprocity is somewhat nuanced. Although known for rejecting the reciprocity he saw in Buber's account and insisting on asymmetry, Levinas at times affirms a "reciprocal relationship" in which "I am another for the others" (OTB, 158). Kierkegaard also rejects reciprocity, but what he is referring to is what he calls "repayment-love." Nevertheless, he does appeal to a notion of "like for like."[50] In fact, both Levinas and Kierkegaard appeal repeatedly to the biblical notion that one gains one's life by losing it.[51] However, there may be a substantive difference between Levinas and Kierkegaard related to this concerning the notion of the response of the other to our gift. Levinas's notion of a gift "without return" includes an extreme position on the nullifying effects of the gratitude of the receiver; he suggests that even the return of gratitude would seem to invalidate the genuineness of my giving to the other. Although Kierkegaard sometimes sounds like he holds this as well, his position is more flexible, allowing a return to be appreciated and even enjoyed, so long as it is not made a condition of the giving.[52]

In conclusion, it seems clear that an appreciation of the ethics of both Levinas and Kierkegaard depends on an appreciation of their understandings of the infinity of the demand, of self-esteem or self-love, of reciprocity and mutuality, and of equality, justice, and self-sacrifice. In this chapter I have suggested that analysis of the biblical formulation of the love commandment common to them both is a fruitful *entrée* into all of these questions, and that such analysis suggests that comparison and contrast between them be made only with caution. If we wanted to, we could easily formulate the ethics of Kierkegaard and Levinas in a way that gave the appearance of a radical substantive opposition between them. We could say, for example, that Kierkegaard's ethic of love included the affirmation of the "as yourself" and of equality, as well as the element of a "like for like," while Levinas's ethic of responsibility saw the "as yourself" with suspicion, and affirmed a radical dissymmetry in the ethical relation, explicitly rejecting the notion of reciprocity. In light of the above, however, it should be clearer just in what way both superficial descriptions would be true, but nevertheless mightily misleading.

Notes

1. Merold Westphal, *Levinas and Kierkegaard in Dialogue* (Bloomington: Indiana University Press, 2008); Westphal, "Commanded Love and Transcendence in Levinas and Kierkegaard," in *The Face of the Other and the Trace of God: Essays on the Philosophy of Emmanuel Levinas,* ed. Jeff Bloechl (New York: Fordham University Press,

2000); Westphal, "Levinas, Kierkegaard, and the Theological Task." *Modern Theology* 8 (July 1992): 241–61; Westphal, "The Transparent Shadow: Kierkegaard and Levinas in Dialogue," In *Kierkegaard in Post/Modernity,* ed. Martin Matuštík and Merold Westphal, 265–82 (Bloomington: Indiana University Press, 1995); Michael Weston, *Kierkegaard and Modern Continental Philosophy* (London: Routledge, 1994). Calvin Schrag suggests the fruitfulness of cross-reading Levinas and Kierkegaard with respect to matters of transcendence and unconditional love; *The Self After Postmodernity* (New Haven: Yale University Press, 1994), 146.

2. *Love's Grateful Striving: A Commentary on Kierkegaard's* Works of Love (Oxford: Oxford University Press, 2001), 48–50; 124–26; 134. The bulk of the commentary is an explication and defense of the plausibility of Kierkegaard's ethic.

3. The deliberations in *Works of Love* form two series, henceforth designated as 1:X or 2:X.

4. The emphasis on distinctiveness is found in *Works of Love*, I–IV, II–IV; Good Samaritan (p. 22).

5. For more on this, see M. Jamie Ferreira, *Love's Grateful Striving*, esp. chap. 6, sec. 3.

6. In *Works of Love* the emphasis on concrete action is found in 1:IIIA (98–100); the distinction between fruits and outward achievements over which we have no control is begun in 1:I and extended in 2:VII.

7. I have elsewhere defended such a distinction in terms of Kant's distinction between a "'supreme" good and a "perfect" good within the category of highest good. See Ferreira, *Love's Grateful Striving*, 125.

8. Levinas, "Existence and Ethics," in PN, 74. References to specific Levinasian essays from collected volumes will be cited in notes and references given to the name of the particular essays themselves.

9. These categories are found repeatedly in Levinas's thought, but in particular, see "God and Philosophy," in BPW, 144–45; and OTB, 124–25.

10. I draw here on M. Jamie Ferreira, "'Total Altruism' in Levinas's 'Ethics of the Welcome,'" *Journal of Religious Ethics* 29, no. 3 (Fall 2001): 446–47.

11. "Philosophy, Justice, and Love," in EN, 103.

12. "Philosophy, Justice, and Love," in EN, 103. See also "Peace and Proximity," in BPW, 167.

13. "Peace and Proximity," BPW, p. 167 (emphasis mine).

14. "Peace and Proximity," BPW, 169; "God and Philosophy," BPW, 140.

15. "Philosophy, Justice, and Love," EN, 108.

16. "The Paradox of Morality: An Interview with Emmanuel Levinas," in *The Provocation of Levinas*, ed. Robert Bernasconi and David Wood, 168–80 (London: Routledge, 1988), 174, 176–77.

17. See "Transcendence and Height," BPW, 27.

18. "Perhaps because of current moral maxims in which the word *neighbor* occurs, we have ceased to be surprised by all that is involved in proximity and approach" (OTB, 5).

19. "Is Ontology Fundamental?" BPW, 8; "Peace and Proximity," BPW, 167. Levinas equates "face" with the "forsakenness" of the other ("God and Philosophy," BPW, 141).

20. "God and Philosophy," BPW, 142.

21. "Peace and Proximity," BPW, 167.

22. "Philosophy, Justice, and Love," EN, 113.

23. "Ethics as First Philosophy," in LR, 83.

24. "In erotic love and friendship, preserve love for the neighbor," WOL, 62; "Your wife must first and foremost be to you the neighbor," WOL, 141.

25. The neighbor is "the persecuted one for whom I am responsible to the point of being a hostage for him" (OTB, 59), yet "this responsibility against my will . . . is the very fact of finding oneself while losing oneself" (OTB, p. 11). This positive notion of hostage is apparent in the claim that "it is through the condition of being hostage that there can be in the world pity, compassion, pardon, and proximity" (OTB, p. 117).

26. For more on this dual notion of hospitality, see M. Jamie Ferreira, " 'Total Altruism' in Levinas's 'Ethics of the Welcome,' " 454–55. Also, Levinas says that "in my essays, the dis-quieting of the Same by the Other is the Desire that shall be a searching, a questioning, an awaiting: patience and length of time, and the very mode of surplus, of superabundance" ("Questions and Answers," in GWCM, 81; for more on the relation between the surplus of desire and persecution, see M. Jamie Ferreira, " 'The Misfortune of the Happy': Levinas and the Dimensions of Desire," *Journal of Religious Ethics* 34, no. 3 (September 2006).

27. "Hospitality, the one-for-the-other in the ego, delivers it more passively than any passivity from links in a causal chain. Being torn from oneself for another in giving to the other the bread from one's mouth is being able to give up one's soul for another" (OTB, 79). This refers back to his earlier comment: "To give, to be-for-another, despite oneself, but in interrupting the for-oneself, is to take the bread out of one's own mouth, to nourish the hunger of another with one's own fasting" (OTB, 56).

28. "Dialogue: Self-Consciousness and the Proximity of the Neighbor," in GWCM, 151.

29. "The Philosophical Determination of the Idea of Culture," in EN, 186.

30. "Dialogue with Emmanuel Levinas," in *Face to Face with Levinas,* ed. Richard A. Cohen (Albany: SUNY Press, 1986), 32. Levinas repeatedly makes this particular kind of reference to "commonplace gestures." See also EI, 89; and OTB, 117.

31. "Dialogue with Emmanuel Levinas," 33.

32. "Lectures on Romans" (1515–16), in *Luther's Works* (St. Louis, Mo.: Concordia, 1972), 25: 513.

33. He writes, "Eternity's *shall* binds and guides this great need so that it shall not go astray" (WL, 67). Note that his main contrast is between preferential love *(forkjerlighed,* covering both erotic love and friendship) and non-preferential love *(kjerlighed).*

34. "Lectures on Galatians" (1535), in *Luther's Works,* ed. Jaroslav Pelikan (St. Louis, Mo.: Concordia, 1964), 27:57.

35. "A Short Exposition of the Decalogue," and "A Short Exposition of the Decalogue, Apostle's Creed, and Lord's Prayer," in *Reformation Writings of Martin Luther,* trans. Bertram Lee Woolf (New York: Philosophical Library, 1953) 1:71–99, 74.

36. Ibid., 1:75.

37. One must always, of course, strive against the danger of a patronizing arrogance in this regard.

38. Here I draw on M. Jamie Ferreira, " 'Total Altruism' in Levinas's 'Ethics of the Welcome,' " 447–48.

39. "Dialogue with Emmanuel Levinas," 24.

40. "Dialogue with Emmanuel Levinas," 24; "Questions and Answers," in GWCM, 83.

41. "Questions and Answers," in GWCM, 90.

42. Levinas's reluctance to affirm the "as yourself" is not required by the original Hebrew formulation, which can support the reminder that we are both commanded to love and both created by or in love, and thus enabled to love. I explain this in "Total Altruism," 450.

43. "Questions and Answers," in GWCM, 82.

44. "The Treatise on Good Works" (1520), in *Luther's Works; The Christian in Society, I,* ed. James Atkinson (Philadelphia: Fortress, 1966), 44:15–114, 108.

45. "God and Philosophy," in BPW, 144.

46. "Dialogue with Emmanuel Levinas," 24.

47. "Levinas and Kierkegaard on Triadic Relations with God," in *Gazing through a Prism Darkly: Reflections on Merold Westphal's Hermeneutical Epistemology* (forthcoming).

48. "The Paradox of Morality," 177.

49. "Levinas and Kierkegaard on Triadic Relations with God."

50. Kierkegaard, WOL, 181, 376, 380–86; for more on this, see Ferreira, *Love's Grateful Striving.*

51. Levinas, "Dialogue with Emmanuel Levinas," 27; also, "this responsibility against my will . . . is the very fact of finding oneself while losing oneself" (OTB, 11). Kierkegaard, WOL, 268, 362.

52. For more on this, see Ferreira, *Love's Grateful Striving,* 163–64.

5 The Greatest Commandment? Religion and/or Ethics in Kierkegaard and Levinas

Jeffrey Dudiak

> Then one of them, which was a lawyer, asked him a question, tempting him, and saying, Master, which is the great commandment in the law? Jesus said unto him, Thou shalt love the Lord thy God with all thy heart, and with all thy soul, and with all thy mind. This is the first and great commandment. And the second is like unto it, Thou shalt love thy neighbor as thyself. On these two commandments hang all the law and the prophets.
>
> —Matthew 22:35–40 (KJV)

Love God and Love Your Neighbor: What Is the Problem?

Rare indeed is a contemporary Continental philosopher of religion who does not have both Søren Kierkegaard and Emmanuel Levinas, however he or she might weight a preference for one over the other, as significant points of reference. I am far from the first to have learned much from both. The critique—shared but unique—that each makes of totality thinking, of "philosophy as comprehension" (and so of "philosophy"), in the name of the other/Other, the totally other, who resists, breaks through, and breaks up comprehension and the whole to which thought tends and aspires, and to whom we are called to answer as singular selves, locates these two thinkers in a shared ethico-religious space in which the self-same is radically decentered by an overwhelming invasion of transcendence that remains recalcitrant to any attempt to reassume or domesticate it, beyond any attempt to bring it within the control, bounds, or predictability of a system.

And yet, despite these evident parallels, these neighbors, for all of their proximity, are far from speaking in a unified voice but are divided by diverse religious sensibilities, or highly diverse sensibilities toward the religious, perhaps irrevocably so. Or so it seems. Indeed, it could be argued that what is most dear to each is—precisely as *most* dear—highly problematic to the other, to the point of creating a perhaps irreparable rift—at least theoretically speaking—between them. For those of us who love them both, perhaps a lingering reflection on the space of this difference can teach, inspire, and provoke us further still.[1]

The point of ostensive contention here is a crucial one, one of transcendence and love, or one of the relative priority of one of these with respect to the other, or the relationship between faith and ethics, between my relationship with the transcendent God and my love of, or responsibility for, my fellow humans. Put succinctly, Kierkegaard is of the opinion that ethics, or at least ethics of the highest kind as love of neighbor, is only possible if it follows from, or has as its condition of possibility, our *prior* love of God; Levinas is of the view that an insistence upon a *prior* responsibility to God precisely blocks the unlimited responsibility for the neighbor which he refers to as ethics. For Kierkegaard, the God relationship is to be prior to and is to govern my relationship to my neighbor, whereas for Levinas it is my ethical relationship to the other that sets the table for anything I might make of my relationship to God.[2]

These characterizations represent much broader and well-entrenched viewpoints (at least on the surface and in the popular mind, even a well-educated popular mind) and reflect a difference that makes a difference—one with bite, with implications for how we are to live both with God and neighbor in our world. We are all too familiar these days with the specter of the "holy warrior" (of whatever religious persuasion) and with the reaction against it, a specter that divides our race between those who so identify the good with God that anything that God requires is justified,[3] and those who fear that the preceding model is the very recipe for violence and who therefore want either to reject God (and with God at least *this* alibi for violence) or, insofar as they are theists, not identify the good with God, but "God" (or at least what will be permitted to pass under that name) with the good. At the extremes we find a fundamentalism in which the good is dissolved in God and, at the other end, either a thoroughgoing laicism or a theological liberalism in which God is dissolved in the good. But even as these positions soften toward a more moderate middle—in which God only demands what we by nature know to be good, for example—it is difficult to see how one could avoid, at least in religious practice, making some kind of call, one way or the other, with respect to this ("theological")[4] version of the Euthyphro problem. Either God voluntaristically defines the good along with all else, and for the good we take our lead from God, blindly trusting that when God demands even what appears to be evil it is in fact the good by the very fact of its being demanded by God, or else there is something higher than God from which we take our lead regarding even God, and God is not "God" (at least the one conceived by orthodox theology) after all.[5]

Of course, this is not what we want, at least those of us who cannot (for whatever reasons) give up on God and yet want to be able to give an (ethical) account of ourselves to those who do not share our faith. This is not what we want, those of us who envision the love of God and the love of neighbor as complements, as each an augmentation of the other in a mad (non)economy of love in which love for one does not come at the expense of but breeds the love of the other—like the eros of the couple that engenders the child: from love more love, more to be loved and to be loving in its turn.[6] My articulation of this, out of my Christian heritage and commitment, is to attempt to hear in Jesus' version of the greatest commandment a case of parallelism, in which the love of God and love of neighbor are two ways of expressing the same, in which as identical, neither can be the means to or the result of the other. And yet, if to love God and to love neighbor are equivalents, does it follow that the neighbor is God? If so, have we again collapsed God (faith) into the good (ethics)? Still, if we insist on a separate act of "loving God," can we really, given God's renowned jealousy, avoid turning the love of neighbor into a secondary matter, a result? Levinas has certainly been accused of the former, and Kierkegaard boldly claims the latter as an antidote to that.

Transcendence and Self-Transcendence: A Rubric

As a way of approaching these issues, I borrow, as a heuristic rubric for the discussion to follow, a provocative thesis from Merold Westphal, the principal thesis of his book *Transcendence and Self-Transcendence*: "What we say about God should have a direct bearing on our own self-transformation. Descriptions of divine being and prescriptions for human becoming are flip sides of the same coin. Within this paradigm, I propose to explore the transcendence of God in strict correlation with human self-transcendence."[7] This rubric is helpful in that it puts forth a thesis *à propos* the "relation to God—relation to neighbor" relation, and does so in a way that favors Kierkegaard and is critical of Levinas, important here to provide a Kierkegaardian voice critical of Levinas to counter-weigh (1) Levinas's own critical comments on Kierkegaard (which Kierkegaard was himself unable to provide by dint of his untimely death over a century too soon) and (2) my own prejudices for Levinas over against Kierkegaard in this encounter.[8] I will therefore provide here a brief summary of Westphal's text, to which I will later have recourse.

The text opens with an illuminating analysis of ontotheology in which Westphal argues that Heidegger's charge of ontotheology, contrary to popular employments of the term maligning anything "theological," does not apply to theism per se, does not simply correlate with any ontology that includes God as (a) Being, but only to a theism for which God functions as a term by means of which reality is comprehended and therefore dominated by the human agents availing themselves of such a God, or a theism that is false to itself in making human being the center rather than God, who here is reduced to humanity's tool.[9]

Westphal then moves on to describe three kinds of transcendence, each in turn a building on and a developing of its predecessor: cosmological transcendence, epistemological transcendence, and religious-ethical transcendence. Cosmological transcendence holds that God exists beyond the world (although is also involved in it), or, that while the being of the world depends for its existence on God, God does not depend for his existence on the being of the world. In this section, Westphal attempts to illustrate (rather than demonstrate,

it seems to me)[10] his thesis negatively by providing a reading of two thinkers, Spinoza and Hegel, who deny a transcendent God and correlatively (caus-
ally?) deny self-transcendence, deny a self whose center is outside of itself, and
one that would permit an ethics of the other, or a love of the other that is not
grounded in self love.

The next kind of transcendence, epistemological transcendence, in addition
to affirming the cosmological transcendence of God, and as a hedge against
the temptations of ontotheology, affirms in addition the resistance of God to
human knowledge. God cannot be brought under the auspices of human comprehension and control, and we humans remain oriented to a God who is always beyond our reach. Here Westphal shows how the teachings of Pseudo-
Dionysus, Aquinas, and Karl Barth on the epistemological transcendence of
God correlates in these thinkers with a movement toward a self-decentering,
self-transcending ethics.

Ethical self-transcendence reaches its fullest expression when Westphal articulates religious-ethical transcendence—the third and highest level of transcendence—as the act, the practice over against the theory, of self-transcending,
as the site at which the self is called on to respond to—even to make itself in response to—an inbreaking of transcendence that radically moves it off its own
center and orients it toward the other/Other, making the self what it is in this
very movement. It is here, at the apogee of the study, that Levinas and Kierkegaard are put forth as representatives, respectively, of ethical and religious (or,
collectively, ethical-religious) transcendence, and where the crucial differences
between them—despite their similarities—come to the fore. For while Westphal
clearly has a deep appreciation for Levinas (and includes him as one of the two
figures in this culminating section of his study), in the end he wonders whether
Levinas really has a place in this study on transcendence and self-transcendence,
as Westphal suspects that "Levinas may well be an atheist" (i.e., someone who
denies cosmological transcendence). The "hero" of the study is Kierkegaard,
whose affirmation of the transcendence of God—not only in theory but in active faith[11]—is the very foundation of his ethics, of his self-transcendence or
decentering with respect to the neighbor, or love.

Westphal's work deserves further attention in its own right[12] (and will surface again both tacitly and explicitly in what follows), but I wish to employ it
here mainly as a launching pad into a discussion of some of the issues around
transcendence and love that surface in a Kierkegaard-Levinas encounter. For
while Kierkegaard would, it seems, strongly endorse Westphal's thesis, Levinas
would deny it (at least in its stronger, causal form, I will argue)—which is why,
of course, Kierkegaard stands as the dénouement of Westphal's study, while
Levinas is, in the end, abandoned by it. Indeed, more than merely denying it,
Levinas claims that Transcendence as employed by Kierkegaard not only does
not lead to ethical self-transcendence (to the ethical de-centering of the self
over against the human other), but is precisely an impediment to it. As Levinas
might put it, What one does *not* say about God (or at least does not say in the

first instance, prior to the encounter with the human other) is in direct correlation with self-transcendence. How so?

Transcendence and Love: An Impediment?

Levinas's direct comments on Kierkegaard, occupying only a few pages,[13] are at once appreciative and critical. On the plus side, Levinas credits Kierkegaard with two genuine, philosophical innovations: (1) the strong notion of a separated subject and (2) the articulation of a new view of the truth as a persecuted truth (as opposed to triumphant truth). Against the dominant, Hegelian thought of his day (and perhaps thereby against the predominant tendency of the philosophical tradition as a whole), in which the subject was absorbed in the universality of the System, the product and in the service of an impersonal logos, Kierkegaard, according to Levinas, rehabilitated with incomparable force the unicity and singularity of the subject. The subject "has a secret," an inexpressible interiority recalcitrant to an all-consuming exteriority, which Kierkegaard, on Levinas's view, identifies with the burning of sin which no rational or universal discourse is able to recover or extinguish. Kierkegaard's subject is an "existence tensed over itself, open to the outside in an attitude of impatience and of waiting—an impatience that the outer world (of people and things), wrapped in a relaxed, impassive thought, cannot satisfy. And beyond that thirst for salvation, there is an older tension of the human soul (perhaps for this reason 'naturally' Christian) that consumes itself with desires."[14] This tension on itself, this anxiety, is the very subject, the egoism, me.

But if the notion of a separated subject protects interiority against absorption in exteriority, Kierkegaard's second innovation, the idea of a persecuted truth, protects the transcendent from being absorbed by the immanent. On Levinas's reading, Kierkegaard's persecuted truth is not built on the desire to overcome doubt, that drive which animates triumphant truth, but takes in "the ever recurring inner rending of doubt" as a constitutive element, as "part of the evidence itself."[15] The faith/belief *(la croyance)* that corresponds to this persecuted truth is thus not a lesser form of knowledge, one to be surpassed, for example, in absolute knowledge. Faith/belief does not take the part of the uncertain over against the certainty of knowledge; it introduces an alternative form of truth, namely, a truth that does not deliver itself as phenomena: "Here with Kierkegaard something is manifested, yet one may wonder whether there was any manifestation. . . . Truth is played out on a double register: at the same time something essential has been said, and, if you like, nothing has been said."[16] This persecuted truth, operating as it does under a "permanent rending," "allows us, perhaps, to put an end to the game of disclosure, in which immanence always wins out over transcendence; for once being has been disclosed, even partially, even in Mystery, it becomes immanent."[17] A separated subject in relation to a non-assumable exteriority: no reader of Levinas can fail to recognize the resonance with his own thinking that Levinas finds in Kierkegaard, and the reason for his appreciation of it. And yet there is also that in Kierkegaard which troubles Levinas.

Levinas's criticism of Kierkegaard comes down to his being shocked by the violence he finds in the latter, reflected, he thinks, in the immodesty of the Kierkegaardian subject (presumably because this subject need not answer for itself to the other, as we shall see), and in the Kierkegaardian style that has infected post-Kierkegaardian philosophy, even that of Kierkegaard's detractors.[18] "The manner of the strong and the violent, who fear neither scandal nor destruction, has become, since Kierkegaard and before Nietzsche, a manner of philosophy. One philosophises with a hammer."[19] And so, while Levinas applauds Kierkegaard's opposition to the violence of totality, he hears and fears in Kierkegaard the introduction of "another violence." And this other violence that Levinas finds in Kierkegaard, takes hold, Levinas posits (and this is especially significant for what is at stake in this essay), "at the precise moment where he [Kierkegaard] 'bypasses the ethical'"[20] for the religious stage. What Levinas certainly has in mind here (one can scarcely imagine otherwise) is the famous "teleological suspension of the ethical" that faith demands, as outlined in *Fear and Trembling*. Indeed, here the hero of faith, Abraham, harkens to the voice of God alone, turning a deaf ear (as torturous as it is for him to harden himself to do so) to the human other and others—in this case his own familial flesh. In this move into the religious stage that describes the movement of faith, which is clearly the highest and greatest, the ethical—the stage of the universalities of reason and of communal obligations—is "bracketed" in favor of something higher: the absolute command of God, the absolute relation (the relation that is "absolved" of every other concern) with the Absolute. So when God commands that Isaac be put to the knife by Abraham's own hand, faith obeys. Abraham in faith, as the hero of faith, is willing to sacrifice, must sacrifice, along with Isaac, ethics. It is not that the ethical here is negated exactly, since from the perspective of ethics Abraham's intended act is still murder (and all of his fatherly obligations remain in place), but it is suspended, "put out of play" by a higher calling that, from the point of view the religious, at least, transforms the act of murder into an act of sacrifice. Here, then, what Levinas might be taken as criticizing in Kierkegaard is the reversal of Dostoyevsky's often quoted dictum: "If God is dead, then all is permitted," now rendered as, "If God (as the Absolute into which I enter into an absolute relation in faith) is *alive*, then all (which God commands, however irrational, however unethical) is permitted, nay, required." So, if God commands you, then head for the hill (Moriah). But if God commands someone else, then head for the hills (and with any luck, not Moriah).

There is a strong sense in which Levinas *is*, and perhaps justifiably, concerned here with the break with reason and with the communal bonds that faith represents over against the universality of ethics, a faith that in the face of ethics cannot but appear as purely individual, arbitrary, even *self*ish (and Kierkegaard has Johannes de Silentio illustrate that from the outside the Knight of Faith is indistinguishable from a tax collector). The Knight of Faith, having suspended the general (the presupposition of language and shared communication), *cannot* explain himself, and thus need not (to the point where the very attempt to do so is a temptation). The section of *Fear and Trembling* whose title is the query: "Is there a teleological suspension of the ethical?" is followed by another: "Is there an absolute duty to God?," and yet another: "Was it ethically defensible for Abraham to conceal his undertaking from Sarah, from Eleazar, and from Isaac?" The nay to the latter follows from the yea to the former two. It was ethically indefensible because cut off from ethics, "the universal as such." Ethically indefensible but religiously necessary. Any accountability to the human other is rendered, in the turn away from the universality of terms that would permit it, precisely impossible. For Levinas, on the contrary, the moment of "apology," answering not only for but to the other, giving an account of myself, is constitutive of ethics. Ethics has, for Levinas, as an essential moment, an explaining of myself to the other who lies outside of myself, and a seeking for his "investiture" (TI, 84–90), and this requires recourse to the reasons that will function within a universal/communal context.[21]

But Levinas is neither advocating for a mere return to the ethical of which Kierkegaard's religion is the suspension, nor arguing that any movement beyond the universal is either illusory or evil (i.e., bad violence). Levinas is not going Hegelian. On the contrary, Levinas is at least as fearful of the violence of the universal (his word for this is "totality") as is Kierkegaard. Indeed, in advocating for ethics against the (at least perceived) violence of the religious, Levinas proposes a shift in the definition of ethics. For, "it is not at all certain that ethics is where he [Kierkegaard] sees it."[22] Ethics is, in its deepest moment, for Levinas (as is well-known), not at all a matter of universal imperatives (rational or communal), but my obligation to respond to the face/call of the other in his/her vulnerability that precisely interrupts any recourse I might have to a general system that would allow me to determine, in advance, what I owe and do not owe to the neighbor. To the other's need I am obligated to respond, without excuse or deflection: *hineni, me voici,* "here I am," the same response Abraham makes to the call of God in Genesis 22:1 and 22:11 (and, significantly, also to Isaac at 22:7), as Levinas is well aware. And for Levinas, this "ethics as consciousness of a responsibility toward others . . . far from losing you in generality, singularizes you, poses you as a unique individual, as I."[23] And elsewhere: "To be myself means, then, to be unable to escape responsibility."[24] Levinas is arguing that the encounter with the human other performs as well as that with the divine Other (as in Kierkegaard) the breakup of the totality,[25] but without the violence of isolating the self from the neighbor in a personal (i.e., purely individual) relationship with God.

But if "ethics is not," for Levinas, "where he [Kierkegaard] sees it," a case could be made that for Kierkegaard "ethics [in its most profound sense] is not where he [Kierkegaard himself] sees it [at first]" either, or at least not where he in the guise of Johannes de Silentio[26] leaves it in *Fear and Trembling.* For Kierkegaard, there is ethics, and then there is ethics.[27] Taking up Kierkegaard's cause here against Levinas's charge that Kierkegaard "exceeds" or "oversteps" [dépasse] ethics for faith, Westphal imagines Kierkegaard's response as being: "Wait 'til I'm finished," meaning that while it may well be the case that *Fear and Trembling* is devoid of an ethics, that does not mean that there is not an ethics to be had, and *Fear and Trembling* was neither the only nor the last book that Kierkegaard would write. Westphal further complains that Levinas "writes as if he had never heard of this book [*Works of Love*],"[28] Kierkegaard's passionate and compelling ethical tome, suggesting, of course, that *Works of Love* supplies (at least in part, and perhaps preeminently among the works that make a contribution to this) the ethics that Levinas believes to be missing. It is true that Levinas does write as if he had never heard of *Works of Love*, and perhaps he had not (I cannot say one way or the other). The question is whether that makes any difference to his point. On the one hand, it would certainly seem to, since faced with the text of *Works of Love* it would be absurd in the extreme to claim that Kierkegaard has no ethics, to accuse him of leaving ethics behind for religion (or at least teleologically suspending it in a way that did not allow it to return to the center stage of his concerns), to claim that neighbor love for him is not of the highest importance (or of the second highest importance if we keep *Fear and Trembling* in mind). Indeed, neighbor love is—and this is a point as central to *Works of Love* as any—an absolute command!

Still, it is important to remember that this Kierkegaardian ethics is no mere return to the ethical order of reasoned and reasonable universal obligation that would take hold once again after the abatement of the terrible call of God to faith by which it had been suspended. Kierkegaard's ethics is not a return to the ethical order *on this side of faith*, but emerges out of faith *on the other side*, as it were, as that which does not precede but is the result of loving God. The move from faith to ethics is not a stepping back down into the ethical (as universal), but a horizontal movement—the extension/continuation of the God-relation (the love of God) into an ethical relation (the love of neighbor). For the *Works of Love* are not a universal ethics but a specifically and self-consciously Christian ethics. An ethics of self-sacrificial love makes no more sense from the perspective of rational universality than do any of the commands of God addressed to the Knight of Faith, and this because this ethics is not the ethics teleologically suspended in faith, but an ethics that *follows* from the God-relation that is the *result* of faith and its obedience. And how could it be otherwise, for we have learned from Kierkegaard, across the teachings of Climacus in *Philosophical Fragments*, that the self cannot but remain ensnared in the self-focus of sin—except by the giving of the condition for faith, along with faith itself, by God. Without the giving of the condition for love along with love, the self could be no more decentered toward the other than toward God. The God-relation precedes, as the very condition of possibility for, ethics. *Works of Love* is neither the rational derivation of a universal ethics (*Moralität*) nor a communally grounded ethics[29] (*Sittlichkeit*), but an ethics of love, in which my obligation is not to a rule valid for all, but God's command to *me* to love my neighbor to the point of self-sacrifice, with or without my neighbor's reciprocation—an ethics of agape. Despite Levinas's allergy to the term "love" (especially in the earlier works), one cannot but notice a certain confluence between the descriptions of the works of love for the neighbor and Levinas's stress on my responsibility—before myself—to the neighbor. Whatever specific similarities and dissimilarities a careful study might turn up—and the respective contexts out of which the works of these authors emerged are both near (both are biblical) and far (Jewish over against Christian)—it seems to me, at least, that their respective notions of ethics as an anarchic self-giving to the neighbor are at least in the same neighborhood.

But the *source* of these ethics are all important, both to Kierkegaard and to Levinas. The *source* of the ethics/works of love is, as Kierkegaard stresses time and again, the love of God; my love of the neighbor is the command of God, is my obedience to God.[30] My first love/obligation is for/to God, and my love/obligation of/to the neighbor is a side effect of that, a love of others commanded by the Other, who is to be the first "object" of my love, and a necessary condition of my love of neighbor. In the words of *Works of Love:* "Ultimately, love for God is the decisive factor; from this originates love for the neighbor ... the Christian love commandment commands loving God above all else, and then loving the neighbor" (WOL, 140).[31]

It is this necessary interjection (this mediation—ironic given Kierkegaard's consistent mockery of mediation)[32] of "God" between me and my neighbor—which, for Kierkegaard, is the very condition of possibility for an ethics, a Christian ethics of agape, to which Levinas objects, that he fears, in which he sees an impediment to ethics (as infinite responsibility to the other), and the threat of "another violence," however edifying these reflections[33] on my responsibilities to the neighbor offered in *Works of Love.* But how so, given that in Kierkegaard's ethics I am decentered toward the other, turned toward the other in the service of love, as I am, *mutatis mutandis,* decentered by, and called to responsibility for, the other in Levinas?

One of Levinas's prevailing concerns is that the other be respected as "other," that is, allowed to speak for himself *(kath'auto)* and not reduced to "the same," that is, to another version of myself, able to be treated as another me, or as I myself would like to be treated, wherein I would "love my neighbor as myself."[34] To treat the other as the same, to reduce the other to another (like) myself, is the very violence that ethics overcomes. My suspicion is that Levinas's concerns regarding Kierkegaard, and the violence he finds in him, stem not so much from a perceived lack of ethics in Kierkegaard but from an ethics that, precisely by insisting on God as its fulcrum, in effect reduces the other to the same.

One gets the feeling in reading Kierkegaard (or should I speak here only for myself?) that while God is Totally Other, the neighbor is presumed to be mostly like me. We human beings are all pretty much the same, all pretty much in the same position, over against the Mystery of the utterly transcendent God. Entranced by the blazing glory of the heavens, we human beings stand together, shoulder to shoulder (and not face-to-face), on the earth. Indeed, how could God as Totally Other, as the object of my faith/belief, not overwhelm and negate any other other, not reduce to all but zero the *relative otherness* (and for Levinas there can be no such thing in ethics, and so this is an ethical if not strictly logical oxymoron) of any other in comparison to the infinite otherness of God, and, correlatively, reduce to all but zero the weight of demand placed on me by a neighbor next to the infinite command of the Infinite? And is this not exactly what happens in Kierkegaard/Silentio's reading of the Abraham and Isaac story? Here any ethical call that might issue from the human other is suspended by the demands of faith, by this teleology that trumps any and everything else. Do we not here feel the very stiffening of resolve and the onset of the pious myopia that are the germ of religious violence? For God may well turn me toward the other in love (as in the *Works of Love,* and thank God) . . . but he may also call me to Moriah, and the paradoxical love/hate transacted there (as in *Fear and Trembling,* and thank God here too, I guess). For when it is God who is the Other *par excellence,* and the human other is only a little bit other (*par impossible* for Levinas), when ethics finds its bearings in a theonomy, rather than in the face, that is perhaps the risk we run.

But if, in relation to the absolute otherness of God, in relation to the Absolute, the human other appears as largely the same, that I need to ethically relate to the human other by means of God produces (or so I am positing Levinas's concerns might lead us to believe) a correlative reduction of this human other to the same. Recall how Levinas sums up the main trajectory of the philosophical tradition (and it would require a blithe spirit indeed to think that the theological tradition deviated much from it): "Western philosophy has most often been an ontology: a reduction of the other to the same by the interposition of a middle and neutral term that ensures the comprehension of being" (TI, 43). And on the previous page we find: "This mode of depriving the known being of its alterity can be accomplished only if it is aimed at through a third term, a neutral term, which itself is not a being; in it the shock of the encounter of the same with the other is deadened" (TI, 42). He then goes on to list "a concept thought," "sensation," and "Being" as candidates that have, in the tradition at different times, played the role of this third term. Now, Levinas is speaking here of cognition, not ethics (or of a cognition that dominates ethics), but my suspicion is that Levinas would see Kierkegaard's "God" or "Christian ethics/works of love" as plausible candidates to play the role of this "neutral third term" within the ethical sphere. The power of the third term is that it purports to govern both terms (me and the other) as independent of either (and so neutrally), but in such a way that my access to it (which I discover across its governance of me, and so which "I find in myself" (TI, 44)) gives me a certain comprehension of (both understanding of and power over) the other, and this *prior* to my actual encounter with him/her. Here the other is "given" to me prior to being "given" to me. And is this not the role that God, and the ethics that come at the command of God, play *à propos* the human other in Kierkegaard? Is not God a neutral third (governing me and the other), who is found "in myself" (across my personal relationship with him), and whose commands for works of love delineate in advance (prior to the actual encounter with the other) what my responsibility to the other is, namely, love?[35] Here the other demands of me only that which, even prior to his arrival, I already find in myself (i.e., in my own relationship with God, which is closed to the other). And does this not precisely deaden the shock of the actual encounter with the other insofar as I am not here obligated by the other to respond to the other, but obligated to God for the other (or by God to the other), already equipped with my obligations before the encounter? And is this not precisely the reduction of the other to the same as Levinas envisions it? Here, paradoxically, it is not the lack of an ethics that is an impediment to "ethics," but precisely the presence of an ethics (i.e., a set of commands [or even a single one] that prescribes *in advance* what one's obligations to the other will be, meaning that the encounter with the other will in fact always be an encounter with a same).

And this is why it is important to understand that for Levinas too, as for Kierkegaard, there is ethics, and then there is ethics, and to try and sort out the relations between a number of things all here moving about under the same name. For if Kierkegaard distinguishes Christian ethics from universal ethics, Levinas too distinguishes his ethics of absolute responsibility for the other from universal ethics, or what he also refers to as justice. In each case, there is an ethics that transcends ethics as a rationally derived, communally shared set of moral prescriptions. But unlike for Kierkegaard, where Christian ethics (whose condition is the love of God) is contrasted with the rules for humans generally (universal ethics) as the higher to the lower, for Levinas ethics as my singular responsibility for the other is contrasted with universal ethics as the condition to the conditioned. That is, for Levinas, "ethics" proper is not a positive command at all, but something more like a susceptibility to being commanded. And that is why, however much Levinas's ethics of responsibility might appear to parallel (or at least resonate with) Kierkegaard's ethics of agape in terms of "content" (the non-reciprocal service of the neighbor, etc.), the nearer "parallel" remains that between Levinas's ethics and Kierkegaard's religion[36] as each an openness to the other/Other. Kierkegaard's Christian ethics is already a beginning filling out of the commands for which openness to the Other is the preparation; Levinas's ethics is that openness itself. And this has deep implications for the relationship that "ethics" (Christian ethics, or the ethics of responsibility to the neighbor) in each case has to ethics as universal obligation. For Kierkegaard Christian ethics, following from the God-relation, cannot be for everyone, but are commanded of the faithful in a manner that remains transcendent (like the faith it follows) above any universalizable ethics (even if all those failing to follow them are at fault). But for Levinas, (the) ethics (of responsibility) are the calling of all qua human (even if they fall first and hardest upon "me"),[37] and rather than being elevated above universal ethics as a higher order of orders, is rather that which both undergirds and undermines universal ethics itself—for my responsibility to the neighbor is simultaneous with my responsibility to my neighbors, and thus the "measures" of justice take hold (the reason for reason), and thus the need to (continually re)constitute a "universal" ethics in community with all others.[38] This move back to the universal appears no where in Kierkegaard. Unlike in Kierkegaard, where religion suspends universal ethics, and universal ethics are "replaced" by Christian ethics for those who love God, in Levinas ethics as responsibility both suspends (calls into question in response to the face as singular) and supports (calls for the constitution of justice as a response to the others) universal ethics, as law. And this is why Levinas chides Kierkegaard's "suspension" of the ethical order despite the fact that Levinas's "ethics" are not there either, and why he reads the Abraham drama of Genesis 22 against Kierkegaard, not as God's call to transcend the ethical order but as God's call to return to it:

> In his [Kierkegaard's] evocation of Abraham, he describes the encounter with God at the point where subjectivity rises to the level of the religious, that is to say, above ethics. But one could think the opposite: Abraham's attentiveness to the voice that led him back to the ethical order, in forbidding him to perform a human sacrifice, is the highest point in the drama. That he obeyed the first voice is astonishing: that he had sufficient distance with respect to that obedience to hear the second voice—that is the essential.[39]

Does Ethics Harbor Transcendence After All?

> How could love be rightly discussed if You were forgotten, O God of Love, source of all love in heaven and on earth, You who spared nothing but gave all in love, You who are love, so that one who loves is what he is only by being in You! How could love properly be discussed if You were forgotten, You who made manifest what love is, You, our Saviour and Redeemer, who gave Yourself to save all! How could love be rightly discussed if You were forgotten, O Spirit of Love, You who take nothing for Your own but remind us of that sacrifice of love, remind the believer to love as he is loved, and his neighbor as himself! (WOL, 20)[40]

Kierkegaard insists that the love of God is a prerequisite for a love ethic, that if God is left out of the picture, there is in fact no love at all (even if there is an illusion of love).

> *Worldly wisdom thinks that love is a relationship between man and man. Christianity teaches that love is a relationship between: man—God—man, that is, that God is the middle term.* However beautiful the love relationship has been between two or more people, however complete all their enjoyment and all their bliss in mutual devotion and affection have been for them, even if all men have praised this relationship—if God and the relationship to God have been left out, then, Christianly understood, this has not been love but a mutual and enchanting illusion of love. *For to love God is to love oneself in truth; to help another human being to love God is to love another man; to be helped by another human being to love God is to be loved.* (WOL, 112–13)

One might then expect Kierkegaard to say that Levinas's rejection of God as the necessary "middle term" for ethics—on which Kierkegaard insists[41]—would have to translate into the conclusion that Levinas does not, and in principle could not, despite any illusions, have ethics, or at least not an ethics of agape, although what Kierkegaard would in fact say in this situation can only be a matter of educated speculation. In lieu of Kierkegaard's own contributions to a direct discussion with Levinas, I am—as I have already indicated—grateful for the contributions of Merold Westphal, who (while still generous to Levinas) clearly takes Kierkegaard's side in this encounter, and to whose work I have recourse here as an aid and spur to my discussions. For it seems to me that Kierkegaard would indeed affirm, with Westphal (which is not surprising given that Westphal's reading of Kierkegaard would have contributed to its formation in the first place), the central thesis of Westphal's *Transcendence and Self-Transcendence* introduced earlier: "What we say about God has a direct bearing upon our ethical self-transcendence." For if "what we say about God" can be taken as basically equivalent to "not forgetting the God of love," and "our ethical self-transcendence" can be taken as basically equivalent to "rightly discussing love" (which presumably has something to do with actual loving), then Kierkegaard's opening prayer to *Works of Love* as quoted (in part) above can be taken as another way of saying what Westphal is saying in *Transcendence and Self-Transcendence* (and indeed, the latter is perhaps naught but a more propositional paraphrase of the former).[42]

Let us look, then, at how Westphal approaches Levinas in light of this implication. For after acknowledging that Levinas provides a "splendid heuristic" for what will follow as the culmination of the study (Kierkegaard as the paradigm of the work's central thesis), Westphal worries that "Levinas is not a leading candidate for consideration in an essay about the transcendence of *God*,"[43] one whose thesis posits a correlation between the transcendence of God and self-transcendence, in that for Levinas "God does not appear as an independent agent . . . [and so] is of no direct help in our inquiry into the nature of divine transcendence."[44] He elaborates:

> The transcendence with which Levinas concerns himself is that of the human other *(Autrui),* the widow, the orphan, and the stranger, the neighbor whose face I see and not God whose face I do not. There is plenty of God talk in Levinas's writings, but apart from its secondary role, it may well be that he is an atheist. He regularly transfers such terms as absolute, infinite, revelation, height, and glory from their usual theological home to serve as descriptions of the human other, and it is far from clear that he affirms a personal God, who, distinct from the world and its human inhabitants, is a creator, lawgiver, and redeemer. It often sounds as if 'God' is a name for the depth dimension in my neighbor which puts me in question with a summons to justice and even, in later writings, love.[45]

And then with the question, "But what if the other were God?"[46] Westphal closes his chapter on Levinas and moves on to his analysis of Kierkegaard, for to "try to think God as the voice that addresses us from on high" is, Westphal maintains, "exactly what we find in Kierkegaard."[47]

On the one hand, Levinas does little to contest, and a lot to confirm, these Kierkegaardian fears about forgetting God, speaking in *Totality and Infinity* about the "separated subject" necessary to ethics as naturally "atheist" (TI, 58),[48] denying in *Otherwise Than Being and Beyond Essence* that God is an "alleged interlocutor" (OTB, 158), and strongly suggesting the priority of ethics to the God-relation in the very title of one of his Talmudic readings, "Loving the

Torah More Than God" (in DF). Westphal's characterization of Levinas in the preceding does indeed ring true, both in letter and in tone. And yet—curious thing!—if the God-relation is the necessary condition for an ethics that would decenter me toward the other, if the love of God is required for the love of neighbor, and Levinas lacks the former, he should not have the latter either. If it is ridiculous to argue that Kierkegaard does not have an ethics, it would be at least as ridiculous to argue that Levinas does not have ethics, and one that is not precisely the decentering of the self toward the other. Levinas's thought is not just a "splendid heuristic," but probably the single most passionate philosophy of irremissible responsibility for the other in the Occidental tradition. So, either the thesis that the God-relation is the very condition of possibility for an other-oriented ethics, an ethics of agape, is wrong, or else Levinas does, in his ethics, despite appearances perhaps, rely on the God-relation after all. While a case could, and perhaps even should, be made for the first possibility, this is not what we find in Levinas. I propose that what we do find, despite Levinas's protestations against Kierkegaard, is something rather closer to what Kierkegaard is saying about the necessary relationship between God and ethics than it first appears—provided that we come to "think" God not as at the other end from us of an "intentional" relationship (as we find in Kierkegaard), be that an "inverse intentionality,"[49] but as prior to *any* intentionality.

For indeed, if the Kierkegaardian/Westphalian thesis is correct and there is a positive relationship (causal—a necessary condition!—in Kierkegaard, sometimes causal and sometimes more of a correlation in Westphal) between the transcendence of God and the decentering of the self toward the neighbor, then should not the decentering of the self in Levinas lead us to suspect, not the lack of a transcendent God but a correlatively transcendent God? As is well known, the self in Levinas is described in terms (often criticized) denoting a hyperbolic self-transcendence, an openness to the other called by Levinas a "passivity more passive than all passivity," referred to as "fission," to the point of being "hostage" to the other. If the passivity of the self in Christianity is described as being a slave to Christ (Paul's *doulos christou*), Levinas's self is even more slave in being assigned (by God, I am arguing) to be hostage to every human other, unable even to gather itself in its identity as servant of an identifiable and unified other from which its assignation to others flows. Levinas's "me" (*moi*, in the accusative!) is sold into slavery to each and every other by a God who can only be traced across a transaction completed before its birth and against which it has no appeal. Here the self does not lose itself to find itself in the face of God; it loses itself to find itself always again at a loss. If self-transcendence is found in hyperbolic form, should this not, on the argument that ties ethical self-transcendence to our relation with God, correlate with a relationship to a hyperbolically transcendent God?

This is indeed, I suggest, what we find in Levinas. God, in Levinas, is the name for that which binds me irremissibly to the other human being, or is this binding itself, in a binding that is one of the core meanings of religion. "God" is, moreover, *required* here—for without God turning me toward the other, the "good violence" (OTB, 43) of the other's interruption of my egoism would simply be "violence," to be avoided and not, as Levinas describes it, "desired."[50] But, as that which turns me toward the other, God withdraws from my focus and turns my focus to the ones, my neighbors, to whom I am assigned. "The Infinite is not in front of its witness, but as it were outside, or on the 'other side' of presence, already past, out of reach, a thought behind thoughts which is too lofty to push itself up front" (OTB, 149). Here God transcends, and hyperbolically so, the situation in which God is at work. Indeed, in Levinas one does not speak of (or to) God directly, as if God were, in Levinas's phrase, "an alleged interlocutor," but only indirectly. It is not here that God does not speak, and not that God does not speak to me personally, but does so always across my obligations to the others to whom God binds me, such that it is only across this having been bound that God, as Levinas says, "comes to the idea."[51] On this view, the theological language in Levinas is not ornamental, but an acknowledgment of God as an appropriate theological designation for the "ethical fact" of my being bound irremissibly to my neighbor in responsibility, even if the word "God" itself is late on the scene, even if, as Levinas says, "the word God is still absent from the phrase in which God is for the first time involved in words" (OTB, 149),[52] and even if God only becomes an object of thought "after the fact."[53]

Such a schema differs radically from that of "the-ism" (and a reader sensitized by Levinas cannot but suspect in every "ism" a totalizing gesture), which I am defining here as any thinking, or living, that has God as its thematic focus (Kierkegaard's "not forgetting," Westphal's "what we say about God") in relation to which everything else (e.g., our relations to human others) takes on the meaning—derivative and thus secondary—that it does, and as "thematic" rests on, in the broadest sense of the term of a *logos* about the *theos*, "theo-logy." For Levinas, I am suggesting, does not offer us an atheism in theological language, but an a/theism that respects the transcendence of God—and the correlative decentering of the self—so thoroughly that theists, like Kierkegaard and Westphal, whose entire way of thinking requires an existing God to anchor all of its other terms (including and especially that of the thinker him- or herself), cannot but suspect in it an atheism. For the God who addresses me indirectly is not necessarily no God, but (as per Westphal's own trajectory) perhaps an even more transcendent God than that of theism, more Wholly Other than the God who can be relied on to center the picture, more "God" than the God who is, more "the divine God," to borrow Heidegger's phrase, or, in Levinas's own phrase, "a God not contaminated by Being" (OTB, xliii) than the God of theism.

By why do theists not recognize this God, one that the logic of correlation between a God-relation and ethics (given Levinas's ethics of responsibility) should suggest? It is, I propose, because in theism, which rests on the presupposition of a cosmologically transcendent God (to return to Westphal's rubric), the indicative (the being of God) is prioritized over the imperative (the call of God), and that Levinas reverses this priority. Let us remind ourselves of the opening and governing gesture of Westphal's text, of the claim that "what we say about God [what Westphal refers to as the indicative] should have a direct bearing on our own self-transformation [what Westphal refers to as the imperative]," which I am taking as a restatement of Kierkegaard's claim that not forgetting God is a precondition for love of neighbor, even if Kierkegaard speaks of loving God here rather than speaking of God (even while he has a lot to say about God). Here the "strict correlation" between (divine) transcendence and (human) self-transcendence, between the indicative and the imperative, is given a "causal" force: the indicative has a "direct bearing" on the imperative. For theism (as I am defining it here), it is God as transcendent (to which we respond in faith), as Wholly Other, that is the precipitating cause of self-transcendence (ethics), and Westphal offers us here, as the organizing principle of his book, three models of transcendence and their implications for the possibility of self-transcendence, not a phenomenology of self-transcendence, and its implications for our ideas about divine transcendence. Levinas is closer to the latter, I would argue, offering us a quasi-phenomenology of the otherwise-than-being across which God comes to the idea. Which comes first, the indicative or the imperative? Theism gives a certain priority to the indicative. Levinas gives us an imperative that does not presuppose any indicative.

Clearly this precedence of the imperative over the indicative—where, as Levinas puts it variously, "ethics is first philosophy," "ethics precedes ontology," and "truth presupposes justice"—has profound consequences for the meaning of both cosmological and epistemological transcendence, for here every claim that we make about God, including any claim we make about the being (or non-being) of God (as of anything else), answers to, has as the test of its truthfulness, my ethical relationship with the neighbor. Remember that for Levinas (as already mentioned) the ethical relation is neither *beyond* the limits of knowledge (although from the perspective of knowledge it is that too) nor beyond—in the sense of higher than—being, but *foundational* for knowledge, as for everything that *is*. For instance, "the given," the object of ontological and epistemological focus, is, for Levinas, tied to "giving," to the offering of what is mine to the other creating a common object, creating, in fact, any object and objectivity at all. So for Levinas, unlike for theism, our idea of Transcendence does not affect our capacities for self-transcendence, our self-transcending affects (I would say even *effects*) our ideas of Transcendence.

Since for "theism" (I am speaking here more to Westphal's schema than of Kierkegaard per se, although I am arguing that Kierkegaard does not differ on these points substantially) a cosmologically transcendent God is foundational to epistemological transcendence, which is in turn foundational for ethical/religious transcendence, on this way of thinking one cannot quite get one's head around Levinas's precedence, giving it full rein. Westphal states the obvious: if there is a call, there must *be* a caller, there must *be* something, in the case of theism someone, who calls, and if we are going to make any sense of this situation, we need to be able to say something, however humbly and inadequately, about this caller (and there appears to me little doubt that in Kierkegaard it is the *revealed* God of Christianity who is this caller). Granted, for both

Westphal and Kierkegaard, the personalness of the call should, and does, transform what we should say, and Westphal informs us that, having passed through ethical/religious transcendence, we realize that "while recognizing that they point to an important truth," the impersonal metaphysical categories for God must "point beyond themselves to personal ('moral') categories *that are more nearly adequate to their intended referent.*"[54] So "King" and "Father" are more nearly adequate than "Prime Mover" when we are speaking of God, for example. But adequacy to its object (even if that object turns out to be a subject), the adequacy of our representations of the object to the object, still governs this epistemology, even if (as in Kierkegaard) this "knowledge" remains at the level of faith/belief, even if the "persecuted truth" produced requires subjective commitment as integral to the process. It is true that for theism ethical/religious transcendence (that calls us to action and not only knowledge) transforms, even radically, the *content* of our knowledge of God, but does not fundamentally change the model that conceives of God as a *noema* of our "intentions" (be they "knowledge" or "belief"); faith/belief still *aims at* an "object" (it is faith/belief *in God*).

It is as a challenge to this model, a challenge to the "obvious" claim that behind the call there must be a caller, that I read what might be called Levinas's epistemological transcendence, wherein ethics precedes, and does not simply supplement, cosmological transcendence. If Levinas can be said to retain the idea of adequation for knowledge, the ultimate test of a truth claim's adequacy is not its correspondence to an object, but whether or not it is an ethically adequate offering in the face of the need of the other, in the face of the face, and this goes also for theistic/theological truth claims. But theology, God talk, presents us with an additional challenge on Levinas's scheme, because God (the God who is already at work before the word God is pronounced, and God becomes an object of belief) is not an object, a thing, a Being about which one could make truth claims, not even the Highest Being of theism. Neither, of course, is the human other in Levinas. It is in the face of, or face-to-face with, the human other that objects are constituted, and knowledge about them becomes possible; we never properly have knowledge of the human other qua ethical subject. And God for Levinas, we recall, at least on my reading, is the name for that which binds me to the other. Perhaps we could say here that ethical responsibility for the other is the condition of possibility for my/our knowledge of objects, for the very constitution of objects, and God is the condition of possibility for my ethical responsibility. If the human other already transcends knowledge in being foundational for it, then so much more does God, who is yet another step removed—*behind*—the relationship of knowledge conceived of as adequation, or any intentional act that would be the co-ordination—given or achieved—of an aim and an aimed at. Epistemological transcendence, in the sense of God's transcending of our epistemological categories, is not for Levinas, as it is for theism, the "too far, too much" of a real but inadequate knowledge of God, but a recognition that God, as the condition of possibility for the condition of possibility for knowledge, as prior to knowledge, is not the sort of thing—not a thing at all—that is subject to being known, but functions in an entirely different, and non-comparable, modality. God on Levinas's scheme is Wholly Other not in "permanently *exceeding*" and surprising my expectations,[55] yet still being subject to my experience, but Wholly Other in *preceding*, in evoking or invoking, my experience itself (not as a puppet master manipulating the scene—for Levinas there is no "world behind the world"—but as the spirit that animates the scene itself.

For Levinas, God has always already withdrawn behind my having been assigned to the other. This does not remove God's mystery, for what could be more mysterious than a God who is not an object for knowledge (or one who is not an object of knowledge until very late in the game, and then only across a certain "betrayal," OTB, 151), nor does it remove revelation, even if it is not God here who is revealed. This does not mean, either, that we cannot "know" God, but we must carefully distinguish (Westphal too refers to these terms) between believing-in/knowing-about (an epistemological concern) and biblical knowing (a spiritual, intimate familiarity), as a participation in the life of God, in the Life that is God (as Michel Henry might put it).[56] And this does not mean that we need not worry about being faithful to God, but we must carefully distinguish between belief-about (an epistemological concern) and faith as faithfulness, wherein we understand that we are most faithful to God not by focusing on God, but by setting our focus on that to which God turns us.

The Love of God

My guess, in conclusion, is that we misconstrue the argument as one between Kierkegaard and the priority of the love of God on the one side, and Levinas's rejecting God to emphasize responsibility to the neighbor on the other. For Levinas affirms, with theism, I am claiming, the necessity of God for ethics, but this God is not the God of theism (perhaps "is not" *tout court*), not the "object" of faith/belief, and not the necessary "middle term" in human relationships. Levinas's argument is not with God, but with the God of theism, the God of whom we can and must think and/or speak before we can ethically encounter the human other, the God who becomes my first obligation rather than the God who obligates me, first and foremost, to the other. Indeed, Levinas's argument with Kierkegaard may be first of all an argument with a schema in which God is thought in such a way that God could be in potential competition with the neighbor for my attentions in the first place. Indeed, as removed from my intentional focus, as that which—prior to any intentional act, and always behind my back—rather turns my focus to the other, Levinas removes God from being a competitor for my focus, my devotion, my love. Here, then, is a response to the problem of the "greatest commandment" being segmented into two commandments whose both/and tempts us toward, ultimately and in practice, an either/or, or a one before the other. For perhaps to love the other in God's love does not require being in love with God, with the concomitant risk of the latter relationship's dangerous clandestinity. But this Levinasian "solution," or this "solution" inspired by Levinas, comes at a price: we are no longer able to be blindly responsible *to* the God of our theism but must be responsible (to our fellows) *for* the God of our theism—and *that* requires fear and trembling of the highest order.

Notes

1. As Kierkegaard and Levinas are both thinkers of "difference," perhaps the difference between them should not ultimately trouble us. Perhaps each "needs" the difference that, with respect to his own thought, the "other" represents. I am, despite the investigations that follow, open to taking their differences *à propos* each other as finally productive.

2. This is a live issue for me in my own religious life. I was raised an evangelical Quaker (generally more theologically conservative and biblically oriented), but for the past twenty years have worshiped with non-programmed Friends (generally more theologically liberal, and more peace and justice oriented). I am equally comfortable in either community and have a concern to work toward reconciliation, both in myself and in the larger Quaker community, between these two emphases, which represent an issue that goes well beyond my own faith tradition.

3. This makes for some strange political bedfellows, a complicity without cooperation between, for example, the Taliban and certain American fundamentalists, who share more with each other than what divides them, even if on their own view the thing that divides them is the only important thing.

4. Of course the Euthyphro problem is already "theological" in Plato's version, but takes on a different aspect in monotheism, when Plato's theology becomes Judeo-Christian theology.

5. Accepting the latter as a good thing rather than as something over which we despair and probing its implications seems to me to be *a part* of what Caputo is up to in *The Weakness of God,* although the text has layers that go beyond just that. John D. Caputo, *The Weakness of God: A Theology of the Event* (Bloomington: Indiana University Press, 2006).

6. Compare the sections entitled "Phenomenology of Eros," "Fecundity," and "The Subjectivity in Eros" in TI, 256–73.

7. Merold Westphal, *Transcendence and Self-Transcendence: On God and the Soul* (Bloomington: Indiana University Press, 2004), 2. Although I will focus on only this work here, it contains a small part of what Westphal has to say about the Kierkegaard-Levinas relationship. Michael R. Paradiso-Michau has compiled a list of thirteen articles or books, already published or forthcoming, in which Westphal has dealt with this relationship, beginning in 1992.

8. This prejudice is best stated up front and is evident in my article: Jeffrey Dudiak, "Religion with an Impure Heart? Kierkegaard and Levinas on God and Other Others," in *The Hermeneutics of Charity: Interpretation, Selfhood, and Postmodern Faith,* ed. J. K. A. Smith and H. Venema (Grand Rapids, Mich.: Brazos, 2004), 185–96.

9. This analysis is not, moreover, irrelevant to what Westphal will say about the relationship between Kierkegaard and Levinas, as it will function as one of his main apologies for Kierkegaard over against the concerns of Levinas—an attempt to defend an ontologically conceived God against the charge of ontotheology, or over against Levinas in particular, to defend a cosmologically transcendent God (who exists) against the charge

of a "God contaminated by Being," against the charge that a conception of a cosmologically transcendent God is necessarily totalizing.

10. Even if it is the case (and I am not doubting this here) that a number of thinkers (in this case two) who deny (the) transcendence (of God) also deny ethical self-transcendence, this does not demonstrate a *necessary* link between the two denials, and especially not a causal one. This would not even be demonstrated should *every* thinker who denies the transcendence of God also deny ethical self-transcendence, unless the mechanism of the connection were revealed.

11. Or at least his theory of active faith, so the matter remains unstraightforward, retaining the ambiguities and aporias that accompany any philosophy critical of philosophy.

12. I tried to provide some of that in an unpublished paper presented at the Institute for Christian Studies on March 16, 2005, entitled, "Transcending God with Levinas: Reading Westphal's *Transcendence and Self-Transcendence* Back-words," an invited paper to a conference on "Intelligibility of the Transcendent: Thinking with Levinas about God, Philosophy, and Education." Some of the structural problems with the current essay stem from the fact that it is an attempt to rewrite this earlier essay that examined Westphal's readings of Levinas in light of Kierkegaard as an essay examining the Kierkegaard-Levinas relationship more directly, rather than starting from scratch.

13. Emmanuel Levinas, *Noms propre* (Fata Morgana, 1976). "Existence et éthique," 77–87; "A propos de 'Kierkegaard vivant,'" 88–92. Emmanuel Levinas, *Proper Names*, trans. M. B. Smith (Stanford, Calif.: Stanford University Press, 1996). The quotations from these short pieces that appear in my text are my own translations from the French texts. There is also the odd reference to Kierkegaard in other works, for example, the claim, "It is not I who resist the system, as Kierkegaard thought; it is the other," in Emmanuel Levinas, *Totality and Infinity*, 40. I have provided a fuller exposition of Levinas's comments on Kierkegaard in Dudiak, "Religion with an Impure Heart," 185–89. I will not speculate here on the degree to which Levinas may have encountered and/or been influenced by Kierkegaard outside of his explicit comments, a question that is being actively pursued by others.

14. Levinas, "Existence et éthique," 67.

15. Levinas, "A propos de 'Kierkegaard vivant,'" 77.

16. Ibid., 78.

17. Ibid.

18. Levinas is not immune to hyperbole, whether intentional or not, and his attribution of the stylistic harshness of modern thought (from Nietzsche to the neo-Hegelians to Heidegger, even National Socialism) to Kierkegaardian origin may well fall under this category. There is, moreover, a double irony here in Levinas's shock at Kierkegaard's violence, insofar as (1) Levinas appreciates Kierkegaard's refusal of the violence of totalities that is the motivation for the structures of thought in Kierkegaard in which Levinas will identify a "new violence," and (2) Levinas himself is appreciative of at least a certain kind of violence, which he terms a "good violence" (i.e., the assault of the other upon my egoism) and many a commentator has been shocked by this, Levinas's violence, in turn.

19. Levinas, "A propos de 'Kierkegaard vivant,'" 76.

20. Ibid., 89.

21. Or, better, the very constitution of the universal/communal across my answering to the other, as we shall shortly see.

22. Levinas, "A propos de 'Kierkegaard vivant,'" 90.

23. Ibid., 76.

24. Levinas, "Existence et éthique," 73.

25. One might more precisely say "the same" here rather than "the totality," but "the same" may be taken in a rough and ready way as "the totality" as it is embodied in me.

26. I must confess that trying to sort through the game of three-dimensional chess (and one in which moves are made by one player only to be taken back or taken again differently by another: four-dimensional chess?) that is the play of pseudonyms in Kierkegaard's authorship is beyond me, and I will leave that task to more accomplished readers. For my purposes, I am allowing the major themes of the major pseudonyms to pass under the name of Kierkegaard, even while I understand that by doing so I run the very real risk of playing the fool to Kierkegaard's irony. But aside from engaging in the often comical if highly sophisticated exercise of speaking of several authors in discussing the works of Kierkegaard (and I suspect that Kierkegaard might have taken some bemused pleasure in hearing that too!), I am not sure how else to proceed. I learn as I go.

27. This may correspond roughly to the Kierkegaardian distinction between Religiousness A and Religiousness B insofar as the former is something closer to a general human structure (guilt) and the latter to a specifically Christian/faith version of the same (sin).

28. Westphal, *Transcendence and Self-Transcendence*, 219–20.

29. Strange thing here, in that the Knight of Faith is excluded from all community (there is no community of Knights of Faith; each must "do" faith for himself), and yet the ethics that follows from faith is apparently "shared" by all those of faith. So Christian ethics is not faith alone but a step "beyond." And yet this "beyond" does not seem to be a "higher still," but a "consequence of."

30. Even if, as in the case of the John the apostle, it is perfected by being lived more as an indicative than as an imperative. See the translators' introduction, 15–17, and conclusion, 344–53, in Søren Kierkegaard, *Works of Love: Some Christian Reflections in the form of Discourses*, trans. H. Hong and E. Hong (New York: Harper Torchbooks, 1962).

31. Westphal quotes this too, at *Transcendence and Self-Transcendence*, 220.

32. Though also not so ironic really, since for Kierkegaard *only* the relationship with God resists mediation, not any of my other relationships.

33. I am leaving aside here as inconsequential to the present point the perhaps otherwise important distinction that Kierkegaard makes in his journals between "edifying discourses" and "reflections" in comparing the *Works of Love* to other works. Compare the translator's introduction to WOL, 11.

34. Kierkegaard devotes all of section 2, the first major section of *Works of Love* (34–98), to an exegesis and exposition of Matthew 22:39: "And a second is like it, you shall love your neighbor as yourself."

35. "Love!" is a peculiar command, because of its open-endedness and because it seems to imply an attentiveness to the specific needs of the other that most commands regarding conduct toward others, given *a priori,* lack. Although Kierkegaard does "fill it in" in some detail in *Works of Love,* I am struck by the possibility that the content of this command is no more given *in advance* of the encounter with the other than is Levinas's own "responsibility," and if so it would fail to function well as a "neutral third." Still, there are times in Kierkegaard's writings where openness to the expressed need of the other seems to be precluded by the help that one is to provide to him by, for example, "suspending him over 60,000 fathoms of water," so that he may, despite himself, be put in a position where he will turn to God.

36. In fact, the *structure* of Levinas's ethics is not dissimilar to the structure of Silentio's religion, resisting the temptation of a universal ethics in favor of an exposure

to, and responsibility for (although for Kierkegaard this latter "for" is more properly a "to"), the singular other/Other who in interrupting my security in the universal calls for a singular response—one not pre-programmed according to a pre-given standard. It is this parallel that leads Westphal to include Levinas as a leading figure, even if ultimately put aside, in his *Transcendence and Self-Transcendence*. I have also dealt with this correlation, the similarities and differences, in my "Religion with an Impure Heart," 189–94. What most distinguishes Levinas and Kierkegaard at this point is that while for Kierkegaard the singular Other who calls for an absolute response is God, turning me away at least in the interim from the human other and ethics, for Levinas the other is the human other whose call for an absolute response from me is ethics itself, even if always already the singular other is one among many and the ethical moment is converted into a concern for justice and its universality.

37. In this context Levinas is fond of Zossima's claim in *The Brothers Karamazov*: "Each of us is guilty before everyone for everything, and I more than the others," at, for example, Emmanuel Levinas, OTB, 146.

38. I lay out this argument in considerable detail throughout my book: Jeffrey Dudiak, *The Intrigue of Ethics: A Reading of the Idea of Discourse in the Thought of Emmanuel Levinas* (New York: Fordham University Press, 2001), 224–47.

39. Kierkegaard, "A propos de 'Kierkegaard vivant,'" 77.

40. From the prayer that opens the text.

41. "Middle term" is explicitly used by Kierkegaard in this context at least three times in *Works of Love*, 78, 87, 113.

42. I have not always attempted here to sort out Westphal's readings and employments of Kierkegaard from Kierkegaard himself (and given the pseudonymous authorship the very phrase "Kierkegaard himself" is problematic), partly because of the in principle barriers to/impossibility of such distinctions (the impossibility of separating an author from his/her readers, as Gadamer has convincingly taught), and partly because I am not a Kierkegaard specialist. So I concede, in advance, to those who would take me to task for "getting Kierkegaard wrong." I am interested in the broader trajectory of thinking that Kierkegaard represents, and represents over against the broad trajectory of Levinas's thought, and *that* I hope to have not entirely missed.

43. Westphal, *Transcendence and Self-Transcendence*, 179.

44. Westphal, *Transcendence and Self-Transcendence*, 201.

45. Westphal, *Transcendence and Self-Transcendence*, 179. Westphal is hardly alone in this judgment. Some of Levinas's most outstanding interpreters and advocates also read him as an atheist, Robert Gibbs among them. But Levinas's personal beliefs are, even on the judgment of his own works, not really so important here.

46. Westphal, *Transcendence and Self-Transcendence*, 200.

47. Westphal, *Transcendence and Self-Transcendence*, 202.

48. Albeit an atheism "*required* by idea of Infinity" (TI, 60).

49. Westphal rightly points out that the "intentionality" at play both in Kierkegaard and Levinas with respect to the Other/other is an inverse intentionality. "*Inverse intentionality is the key to ethical transcendence.* By contrast with the intentionality of possession, it will be one of 'dispossession'" (Westphal, 192). I am arguing that while this does characterize our relationship to God in Kierkegaard (and our relationship to the human other in Levinas), it is inadequate, along with a more conventional intentionality, to describe the God-relation in Levinas.

50. Cf. The opening section of the main body of *Totality and Infinity*, "Desire for the invisible," 33–35.

51. Cf. GWCM.

52. In reference to the witness to God in the "here I am."

53. Cf. OTB, 151: "I can indeed state the meaning borne witness to as a said. It is an extraordinary word, the only one that does not extinguish or absorb its saying, but it cannot remain a simple word. The word God is an overwhelming semantic event that subdues the subversion worked by illeity. The glory of the Infinite shuts itself up in a word and becomes a being. But it already undoes its dwelling and unsays itself without vanishing into nothingness."

54. Westphal, *Transcendence and Self-Transcendence,* 231, my emphasis.

55. Westphal, *Transcendence and Self-Transcendence,* 3.

56. Michel Henry, *I Am the Truth: Toward a Philosophy of Christianity,* trans. S. Emanuel (Stanford: Stanford University Press, 2003).

Part Three.   *Time, Alterity,*
and Eschatology

6   Hearing, Patiently:
Time and Salvation in
Kierkegaard and Levinas

David Kangas and Martin Kavka

Martin Kavka

So much for ideas.

When Aaron Simmons and David Wood first asked us to contribute individual essays to this volume, we thought that it might be more effective to write together or, more precisely, converse in public. If the editors of this volume want to establish a relationship of neighborliness between Kierkegaard and Levinas by setting up a conversation between them, what better way to accomplish this than to embark on a conversation between us? After all, we have been neighbors quite literally, with our offices twenty feet apart, and team-teaching on a regular basis. What's more, one of us publishes primarily on Kierkegaard while the other publishes primarily on Levinas.[1] But projects go awry. When we began conceptualizing this essay, I was away from Tallahassee while you were there. And once I returned, you left Tallahassee for an indefinite period of time. What could such distance philosophically produce, now that our neighborliness has become mediated by telephone calls and emails with attached files?

My instinct is to think of neighborliness as something which moves toward that which transcends; the biblical command to love the neighbor is part of a way of life that imitates or emulates divine holiness and therefore counts as historical progress, a development that leaves the "is" behind and moves toward the "ought." Nevertheless, leaving behind the "is" is dangerous, and invites all sorts of flights of fancy that would allow one the luxury of *believing* that one is being neighborly without having to cash out that belief in practice. How do I know that your absence will not lead me to turn you into someone you're not? On what grounds can I hope that this will actually be a conversation, and not simply two people talking past each other?

Email hasn't been a great boon to philosophical conversations. In this regard, I think of a 1998 email exchange between Edith Wyschogrod and John D. Caputo that they published as "Postmodernism and the Desire for God." By the end of the published transcript, Wyschogrod and Caputo have agreed that in our age of virtuality the language of religion is aptly described as an "erotics of transcendence" which is incarnated in ethical acts. However, Caputo seems in his final comments to be content to think of religion *only* in this manner. Wyschogrod both agrees and disagrees with Caputo; she affirms the ecstatic but also critiques it by invoking a Levinasian suspicion of such erotics, "this enthusiasm whose religious and secular versions have been implicated in the horrors of the twentieth century."[2] Caputo leaves Wyschogrod with the last word here. This is certainly polite of him, but the exchange comes to a crashing halt just when they could talk about how they might respond to this difference between them—a difference revolving around how the abstraction of religious desire can maintain itself and attend to the reality of genocide. The critique of metaphysics has not absolved us from the problem of metaphysics and historicity, to invoke the title of Emil Fackenheim's brilliant little essay.[3] And so their conversation—their own neighborliness—ends, just when the reader begins to wonder whether they have really heard each other at all.

At this moment, I impatiently want to break the limits of space and history in order to have a conversation with you that could be protected from such risks. This is impossible, of course, and it most likely will not surprise you to read that my reaction to this has only served to heighten my already quite significant taste for melodrama and camp. This time, I have been listening repeatedly over the last months to various recordings of Jacques Brel's "Ne me quitte pas" (so often bastardized in English as "If You Go Away"). On one hand, this *chanson* is to my mind the modern hallmark of the denial of difference and the denial of time. The relationship between the narrator and the beloved who is about to leave can only be salvaged by attending to an imperative to ignore all temporality: "Don't leave me. One must forget all that can be forgotten, all that already slips away *[Ne me quitte pas/Il faut oublier tout peut s'oublier/Qui s'enfuit déjà]*." On the other hand, it heightens the stakes of the salvation of the relationship to such an extent that the narrator's project of keeping his beloved is impossible: "Don't leave me. I will invent senseless words for you that you will understand. *[Ne me quitte pas/Je t'inventerai des mots insensés/Que tu comprendras]*." The project of sustaining the relationship seems doomed to failure, and this is why the narrator can only beg the beloved not to leave, willing the most nonsensical and ridiculous kinds of abasement in the face of this impossibility: "Let me become the shadow of your shadow, the shadow of your hand, the shadow of your dog *[Laisse-moi devenir l'ombre de ton ombre/L'ombre de ta main/L'ombre de ton chien]*."

Of course, Brel was not a phenomenologist. But insofar as the song claims that the impatient desire to forget everything (time, language) inevitably collapses into the depths of patience, into suffering the blows of history and the hope against hope for a new future (in which the beloved stays), Brel is not unlike Levinas or Kierkegaard. For all of them, salvation can only possibly occur through some kind of patient demeanor in which patience is forced upon the "subject," deferring the fulfillment that is customarily associated with salvation. The cessation of suffering and pain cannot be planned, anticipated, or calculated; articulating the state of affairs that would constitute such satisfaction only runs the risk of creating more and more *mots insensés*. On this broad point, at least, I think we can say that Levinas and Kierkegaard (and Brel) can come to hear each other's words, and be brought into conversation.

David Kangas:

To bring Kierkegaard and Levinas into conversation will bring Christianity and Judaism into conversation. And in relation to Kierkegaard and Levinas, two of the most provocative readers of the Bible in the past two centuries, this will mean to bring a Jewish reading of the Bible into conversation with a Christian one, and vice versa. In the case of Kierkegaard and Levinas, however, something decisive has happened as regards the whole question of reading the Bible: less at stake is the *content* of the Bible than the very *possibility* of the Bible as the locus of a divine word. In his essay "Revelation in the Jewish Tradition" Levinas points out that the "ontological status or régime of the revelation "primordially makes Jewish thought restless, posing a problem which must be considered before any introduction to the contents of this revelation" (BTV, 160/131).[4] Kierkegaard's short book *Philosophical Fragments* (1843) likewise constitutes a meditation on the scandal of the very idea of revealed truth vis-à-vis ontological presentation. It clarifies the revelatory event itself as to its ontological status, in particular its non-collapsibility to speculative reinscription.

The Bible becomes, as it were, an ontological category, or rather a category whereby one can think beyond the terms of ontology. Though both thinkers have absorbed Greek thought in a profound and personal way, each allows a shock to the Greek horizon, a shock provisionally associated with the Bible. How can this be specified? In any number of ways, yet I suggest that at stake is an orientation in which human existence is grasped, most basically, in terms of finding itself amid language, addressed by a word that strikes it from the outside. It is a question of a call. Commenting again on revelation in the Jewish tradition, Levinas puts the point in a way that Kierkegaard, author of *Fear and Trembling,* may well have understood: "The correct significance of the signifying of the Revelation [in Judaism] lies in its calling to the unique within me" BTV, 163/133). Attending to this call, whereby I am drawn out in my singularity, becomes a question, says Levinas, of a "hearing . . . of God's living word." A hearing of the word involves a confrontation with my singularity, the weight of my existence ineluctably bearing down. This event, the irruption of singularity, along with my response to it ("Here am I"), takes precedence over vision.

To approach the conversation between Kierkegaard and Levinas in terms of the question of revelation (i.e., the hearing of the word), then, will be inseparable from attending to a word that is heard within the two "revealed religions." Nevertheless, if it is the case, as Levinas says, that the very *possibility* of revelation is, initially at least, more significant than the *content* of revelation, then the way is open for the consideration of a hearing of the word independently from what is heard. Without having immediate recourse to the differences between the word that is heard within Christianity and the word that is heard within Judaism, one could interrogate a set of formal structures associated with hearing, for example, the way a subject's very subjectivity would involve its exposure to language, its being kerygmatically addressed by a word from beyond itself, by a command and perhaps a promise. This is a path of conversation I want to pick up. I would like to speak of a convergence between Kierkegaard and Levinas around the question of the subject addressed by a word even if, in the end, it will be essential to attend to the difference, not only between the word that is heard within Judaism and the word that is heard within Christianity, but also between the modality of response that transpires in Levinasian "ethics" and in Kierkegaardian "religion."

Within Christianity, it is undoubtedly Luther who most emphatically grasped the "hearing of the Word" *(Hören des Wortes)* in terms of its radical potential for a critique of speculative onto-theology. In his 1515 *Lectures on Romans* Luther formulates the terms of such a critique in a way that decisively shapes Kierkegaard's own critique of speculative thought:

> The apostle [Paul] philosophizes and thinks about things in a different way than the philosophers and the metaphysicians do. For the philosophers so direct their gaze at the present state of things that they speculate only about what things are and what quality they have, but the apostle calls our attention away from a consideration of the present *[Apostolos autem oculos nostros reuvocat ab intuitu rerum preferentium]* and from the essences and accidents of things and directs us to their future state.[5]

This revocation of philosophical intuition, calling thought back from the preoccupation with *what is*, with presence, and the aiming of thought at what *is not* (the future), already coincides with a hearing of the word. Whereas philosophers and metaphysicians only succeed in deriving "a happy science from a sad creation"[6] through the contemplation of what is, the proper task of thinking is to "hear creation waiting."[7] Luther, following Paul, speaks of such waiting or patience in terms of "an entirely new and marvelous theological word": the "expectation of the creation" *(expectatio creaturē)*. Luther gives great weight to the word *expectatio*, raising the Pauline term to the status of new category that systematically contests the priority placed upon presence within onto-theological thought. *Expectatio* now defines the subject in its very subjectivity—along with the whole order of "what is"—as oriented around a divine *promissio* that still "is not" or remains under withdrawal.

Luther's biblical conception of existence thus understands the subject as defined by its patience and expectancy, its waiting upon the divine promise: in short, by a redemption of what is that lies in a future that cannot be achieved through human capability. Everything is organized around *to nun kairos*, the fullness of time, in which the divine *promissio*, the object of patient expectancy —which is to say, of *faith*—is fulfilled. Nevertheless fulfillment must always be grasped within the modality of "not-yet"; only in hope, in expectancy, does it impinge upon the present. And, in his understanding of faith as hope, Luther makes a move closely relevant to what happens in Kierkegaard: he understands hope, not merely as a privation, a necessity imposed upon the subject due to the absence of the thing hoped for, but as itself already the presence of what is hoped for. Commenting on Romans 8:24 Luther says, "Thus it happens that the thing hoped for and the person hoping become one through the tenseness of the hoping . . . Thus hope changes the one who hopes into what is hoped for, but what is hoped for does not appear. Therefore hope transfers him into the unknown, the hidden . . . so that he does not even know what he hopes for, and yet he knows what he does not hope for."[8] Hope allows *non-being*—the future insofar as it does not give itself to anticipative foresight—*to be* at the heart of the "I." In this way an identity is forged, without representation or knowledge, between the one who hopes and what is hoped for. What is hoped for becomes real in the one hoping, even if it must remain *in abscondito,* claimed by an essential non-knowing. Within this understanding of existence, in which non-being is affirmed, faith does not simply oppose philosophy, but rather offers a different way of philosophizing. Luther writes, "The apostle philosophizes and thinks about things differently than the philosophers and metaphysicians do" *[Aliter Apostolus de rebus philosphatur et sapit quam philosophi et metaphysici].*[9] It is in terms of this thinking *aliter,* otherwise, that biblical "hearing" invites a more radical reflection upon existence than one preoccupied with essences and qualities: to philosophize otherwise is to begin to think temporality as real.

Kierkegaard's series of edifying discourses, collected later as *Eighteen Upbuilding Discourses* and all written between 1843 and 1844—at the very time he was writing *Either/Or, Fear and Trembling,* and others—are organized around the motifs of expectation, faith, and patience. They reproduce Luther's revocation of the philosophical gaze quite consistently. What for me will be the decisive issue in the patient thinking, or *thinking otherwise,* that happens in Kierkegaard's edifying discourses is the following: a certain understanding of fulfillment, or salvation, is overturned. All of the edifying discourses aim at "overturning of thought and speech" (*Omvæltning i Tanke og Tale;* SKS 5, 162/ EUD, 162), a destruction without which there can be no edification. Patience and expectancy cannot be thought about apart from what fulfills them. Yet the specific revocation or undoing Kierkegaard accomplishes in the edifying discourse is to make fulfillment signify, not the closure of desire, its satiation, but rather its ever-renewed opening. To need God, he will say, is not an imperfection or privation, but rather "a human being's highest perfection." Need is read *as* fulfillment, albeit a fulfillment that is not structured around completion— that is the decisive gesture of overturning at the heart of the edifying discourses. In terms of this paradoxical understanding of fulfillment, one will never be done with patient expectancy (faith). The instant of fulfillment is already there in patience itself. Hence, a *simul* between fulfillment and non-fulfillment rules over Kierkegaard's edifying discourses (a *simul* that shows precisely the impatience of all mediation).

In a discourse titled "The Expectancy of Faith" from 1843 Kierkegaard clarifies the structure of expectation. It has essentially to do with a relation to the future: "But all who are expecting do have one thing in common, that they are expecting something in the future, because expectancy and the future are inseparable ideas" (SKS 5, 27/EUD, 17). Yet the future, Kierkegaard suggests, is something that both does and does not have its origin in the projective power of self-consciousness: "The future is not; it borrows its power from [the person] himself, and when it has tricked him out of that it presents itself externally as the enemy he has to conquer" (SKS 5, 27/EUD, 18). The intentionality aimed at the future bends back upon its source, dividing it from within. Without consciousness aware of itself there could be no future; the future only *is* on condition that someone is *conscious of* it. On the other hand, the future cannot be reduced to the intentionality of self-consciousness; it withholds itself. Thus consciousness of the future becomes irreparably split and acquires an extraordinary ambiguity: the future signifies both what falls under anticipative foresight *and* what essentially withholds itself from that. Such a split appears in the "trick" that consciousness, through its awareness of temporality, becomes an enemy to itself. Kierkegaard writes, "When a person struggles with the future, he learns that however strong he is otherwise, there is one enemy that is stronger—himself; there is one enemy he cannot conquer by himself, and that is himself" (SKS 5, 27/EUD, 18). To speak of an intending of the future, in expectation for example, is to identify a modality in which consciousness becomes doubled-up upon itself: vis-à-vis the future, consciousness finds itself in a struggle with its own essential ambiguity, for the difference between the future apparent to anticipative foresight and the absolute future, which remains essentially *in abscondito*, will never be reconciled. Indeed, consciousness itself "is" that very difference, how then could it overcome it? Here the "groanings of creation" may be heard, a patience enjoined, but also the emergence of an exceptional expectation.

Kierkegaard speaks of faith as a modality of expectation. Yet with faith one often thinks of the expectation *of* something definite and representable. What then does the expectancy of faith expect? It expects "an eternity" (SKS 5, 36/EUD, 27) and in this expectation it awaits "victory" (SKS 5/EUD, 26). Nevertheless, Kierkegaard indicates that these two terms—eternity and victory—must remain open as to their meaning, for as soon as they acquire a determinant, particular meaning, the structure of expectation collapses into wish fulfillment. Thus Kierkegaard explicitly says that "the person who expects something particular or who bases his expectancy on something particular" (SKS 5, 36/EUD, 27) does *not* have faith. Faith does not refer to a particular, representable content, but rather to the future as a whole, as what remains essentially open. It is a posture toward what cannot be brought to closure, the open as such. The expectancy of faith, then, does not flee the ambiguity of existence but preserves the open character of the future. Yet in allowing the future its essential openness, a transformation becomes possible vis-à-vis the present: "But an expectancy of the future that expects victory—this has indeed conquered the future. The person of faith *(den troende)*, therefore, is finished with the future before he begins with the present" (SKS 5, 28/EUD, 19; altered). Faith is "finished with" *(færdig med)* the future not because it now knows its content, but rather because it lets it be the open that it is. Such letting-be liberates the relation to the present.

Kierkegaard's discourse "Patience in Expectancy" shows the relation to the future as one of essential patience. It meditates on the biblical figure of Anna (from Luke 2) in order to clarify the essential structure of expectation and fulfillment. Anna is "in the strictest and noblest sense: the expectant one" (SKS 5, 223/EUD, 224). On Kierkegaard's treatment Anna becomes a category of existence, for life itself is "one long night of expectancy" (SKS 5, 207/EUD, 206). She is old, childless, widowed; her life is essentially over. Of time she has nothing left to expect. Yet for precisely this reason she is the perfect figure to clarify an essential or patient expectancy. Only when there is nothing more to be expected as "the fruit of temporality" can one speak of essential expectation, which "awakens only in the person who gave up the temporal in order to gain the eternal and then found the grace so see eternity as an expectancy in time" (SKS 5, 212/EUD, 218). As long as one approaches time on the basis of the project, expectation will be a holding-in-view of some representable end. Expectation will live within the tension between "now," a moment defined by its lack, and "then," the moment of fulfillment. Yet once fulfillment arrives, expectation is essentially killed. What is at stake in Anna, however, is an expectancy that cannot be killed or even surpasses its own fulfillment—an *eternal* expectation. To "see the eternal as an expectancy in time" *(at see Evigheden som en Forventning i Tiden)*: everything depends on this *seeing as.* To expect eternity is precisely not to flee time toward some other region, dreaming of some final fulfillment; it is rather to discover a new relation to time as a whole. In the opening of new relation to time, time is fulfilled without closure.

For Anna, indeed, the object of fulfillment comes to pass on the temporal plane. She sees time fulfilled in the presentation of the child Jesus of Nazareth at the temple; her expectation is therefore not disappointed. "But," Kierkegaard asks, "in what sense was she not disappointed?" (SKS 5, 222/EUD, 223–24). The decisive question. Suppose she never saw that moment with her own eyes, what then? "Can Anna be disappointed in her expectancy; can the fulfillment come too late?" (SKS 5, 213/EUD, 215). For Kierkegaard she was not disappointed, not because she lived to see what she expected, but only insofar as she could not have been disappointed, whether the expectation was fulfilled or not fulfilled. This suggests a fulfillment that coincides with non-fulfillment: "And even if [the fulfillment] had failed to come, she still would not have been disappointed. The fulfillment came; at the same moment, just like Simeon, she desires only to wander away *(kun at vandre bort),* that is, not to remain with the fulfillment and yet in another sense to enter into the fulfillment" (SKS 5, 222/EUD, 224; altered). A strange dialectic: entering into the fulfillment means wandering away from it, letting it go. The moment of fulfillment can be appropriated only in not appropriating it. For Kierkegaard the nobility of Anna, what constitutes her prophetic status, would have to be that, in the moment time is fulfilled, she does not dedicate herself to the service of recollection *(Erindringen)*—does not orient her life around closure—but remains in the service of expectation. To remain a servant of expectation can only signify that there is fulfillment—essential fulfillment—already in the expectation itself. What Kierkegaard's dis-

course on Anna thus seeks to articulate is the destruction of the dialectical ontology that thinks fulfillment as completion or ending. Time is fulfilled, not in
the appropriation and enjoyment of its meaning but in its recommencement.
Time is fulfilled only where fulfillment is let go. It is fulfilled in patience.

Kierkegaard's discourse "To Gain One's Soul in Patience" explicitly over-
turns the dialectical (Hegelian) economy according to which the movement of
reality is thought in terms of the subject's production and realization of itself
through the moment of difference. According to such logic, the moment of beginning is of itself a poverty, an abstraction; the beginning signifies reality as
undeveloped or implicit. Hegel formulates this idea with perfect rigor in saying
that the beginning really is the beginning only at the end, namely, in terms of
what it will have brought about. Beginnings are real only as retrospectively posited.[10] A subject, then, is not real in its waiting or expectation—not real in its
desire—but only in its anticipative insight into its self-coincidence. A subject is
real in its association with closure. In "To Gain One's Soul in Patience," however, Kierkegaard reverses this: he places the moment of fulfillment, plenitude,
and self-coincidence not as the fulfilling end of the self, but at the beginning,
and then articulates a logic according to which the figure of fulfillment is undone. Kierkegaard writes, "What people aspire to—to possess the world—a
person was closest to in the first moment of life, because his soul was lost in it
and possessed the world in itself, just as the undulation of the waves possesses
in itself the restlessness of the sea" (SKS 5, 164/EUD, 164). Self-coincidence,
the subject living its own plenitude, is precisely what is to be abandoned.
The real self forgoes fulfillment—not this or that fulfillment, but fulfillment
as its fundamental project. In the strictest sense the real self accepts its own
self-dispossession. Coming to this acceptance is the work of *patience,* and in patience expectancy arises.

"To Gain One's Soul in Patience" radicalizes the notion of patience beyond its everyday sense. Generally, one is patient "in order to." The work of
patience, a deferral of gratification, is organized around some end aimed at.
When the end is achieved, patience is exchanged for enjoyment. Patience here
gains its entire sense from the moment of fulfillment defined as enjoyment or
satiation. Yet for Kierkegaard the self is an essential patience, that is, a patience
that is not "for" or "in order to." Patience is not an attribute of the subject, a
"soul strength" (virtue), but the very subjectivity of the subject. Certainly, one
"gains one's soul" in patience: but what does one gain in gaining one's soul? It
is here where Kierkegaard's discourse rigorously desubstantializes the soul. The
soul cannot be grasped in any sense as a "thing," nor for this reason is it to be
thought about in terms of a logic of entities. The law of non-contradiction, for
example, does not pertain to the soul, but only to objectivities (what Kierkegaard calls "the external"). In fact, the soul expressly "is in contradiction and is
self-contradiction" (SKS 5, 166/EUD, 166): it is, namely, "a self-contradiction
between the external and the internal, the temporal and the eternal" (SKS 5,
166/EUD, 166). Even more, the soul is *difference,* the "infinity in the life of the
world in its difference from itself" (SKS 5, 165/EUD, 165). It is all too easy to

be thrown by these formulations, which have the appearance of being dialectical or even onto-theological. Wouldn't Hegel have understood Kierkegaard here, namely, in seeing the soul as the location in which being differs from itself as the condition for its self-manifestation? But at stake here is a difference that is not taken into the service of manifestation, a difference that cannot be objectified and appropriated. The soul "is" this difference that cannot appropriate itself, an essential patience or deferral. Or again, the soul is where being no longer rejoins itself and rests in itself. Something beyond enjoyment and self-coincidence transpires.

What transpires is the "work of patience." Acquiring patience is the one and only absolute work of the self: to gain patience *is* to gain one's soul. The "work of patience" in which one gains one's soul will thus be nothing like the "labor of the negative." To gain one's soul in patience is not to produce oneself as an object in order to appropriate one's identity, for in the strictest sense nothing is gained in patience beyond patience itself. Kierkegaard comments: "'In patience.' The words do not say 'through' or 'by means of' patience, but 'in patience,' and thereby suggest that the condition stands in a special relation to the conditioned . . . In this gain, the very condition is also the object and is independent of anything external. The condition, therefore, after it has served as the gaining, remains as that which is gained" (SKS 5, 168/EUD, 167–68). *What* one gains (the conditioned) and that *whereby* one gains it (the condition) are identical. Gaining is a "redoubling repetition" (*fordoblende Gjentagelse;* SKS 5, 169/ EUD, 169). In other words, here there is a gaining in which nothing is gained. Yet one has to think about this process in which nothing is gained, not as lack or Hegel's bad infinite, but according to its essentially positive meaning as the *awakening of expectation.* In patience arises the "expectancy of an eternal salvation," something, I have suggested, which coincides with a new beginning in the present. In patience "all things are become new."

And now Levinas. In that magisterial last paragraph of Levinas' preface to *Otherwise than Being* Levinas speaks of the necessity to "*hear* a God not contaminated by being . . . a human possibility no less important and no less precarious than that of bringing Being out of the oblivion into which it is supposed to have fallen in metaphysics and in onto-theology" (OTB, x/xlviii). The revelation of the real happens through *ears;* this stands opposed to the manifestation the strikes the *eyes.* At stake here for Levinas is a possibility associated with Jewish revelation, with the word that is heard in Judaism. Levinas suggests that, within Judaism, the human being is "at the same time the person to whom the word is said, and also the one through whom there *is* Revelation" (BTV, 175/145). He continues, "Perhaps, in the light of this situation, the status accorded to subjectivity and reason should be revised" —away from the theoretical and visionary modalities that dominate "Greek" thought, up to and including Heideggerian *Dasein.* It is vis-à-vis this revision that I will want to join the conversation on Kierkegaard and Levinas.

Levinas consistently associates such hearing with the human experience of obligation. What seems decisive to me, however, is that he interprets the "you

must" of obligation as a command which "takes no account of what 'you can'"
(BTV, 176/146). In hearing he discovers an obligation that breaches human capability. This breach, which breaks the correlation between "ought" and "can"
upheld by Kant, indicates a space of essential patience in Levinas, the space
of an *unfulfillable obligation*. It is precisely here, in terms of what is unfulfillable, that one must speak of transcendence in Levinas. But the dedication to an
obligation that is unfulfillable must be thought, paradoxically—and this is a
decisive qualification—as the very fulfillment of an intrigue that transpires
between God and the human person, an intrigue that for Levinas carries the
name "ethics." Revelation transpires in or *as* the ethical, which is why "the
ethical" must be accorded priority over anything named "the religious." Nevertheless, it is not a question of a simple opposition between the ethical and the
religious, for if the religious names the modality through which the human
person bears transcendence, the ethical *is* the religious.[11] Such an ethical structure, in other words, must be grasped as prior to the distinction between the
ethical and the religious. For this reason, one should not be tempted by Levinas'
prioritization of the ethical over the religious into conflating his thought with
the Kantian program of a religion within the bounds of reason. Rather than being forged within the implication between "you must" and "you can," as in the
Kantian ethical, the Levinasian ethical opens precisely where these terms cannot coincide. Here, between ought and can, is something irreparable, something infinitely non-formal, which will bring Kantian practical reason to ruin. I
shall say in a moment that this infinitely non-formal element, preventing ought
from coinciding with can, is precisely temporality; and not only this, but that
temporality is for Levinas already itself a modality of hearing, that is, it signifies as a revelation of the Most High.

According to Kant's *Critique of Practical Reason,* what is edifying about the
human experience of obligation is that it reveals to us a capability that we could
not otherwise discover in ourselves: the capability for exercising a goodness not
oriented around the fulfillment of our affective drives—a moral, super-sensual
goodness. In striking down our self-aggrandizing drives, law sublimely reveals to us a freedom, an absolute spontaneity, that we could not otherwise see
or claim. Kant suggests that, in the consciousness of the moral law, a person
judges "that he can do something because he is conscious that he ought to do
it, and he cognizes freedom within himself—the freedom with which otherwise, without the moral law, he would have remained unacquainted."[12] In that
sense my freedom is thoroughly mediated by command. I first understand that
"I can" *because* I am addressed by the word "you must." There is revelation in
the Kantian ethical, then, insofar as obligation offers the possibility of a new
self-understanding that could not be derived from mere reflection upon *what I
am,* upon my empirically accessible capabilities. Through law, and only through
law, I grasp myself according to my absolute freedom; I learn something absolute about myself that I could not otherwise learn (my absolute spontaneity).

Yet what specifically defines this Kantian gesture and informs the whole program of a religion within the bounds of reason is the presupposition that the word that is heard in obligation emanates from the self's own interior. Revelation is the revelation of human capability. If we consider this a little more closely, we can discover the source of Kant's restriction of ethical revelation to the domain of immanence (i.e., to being a revealing of the autonomy of the will): it is the understanding of the transcendental subject as a source point for the constitution of all phenomena. At its deepest stratum, the transcendental subject posits, through its originary spontaneity, the conditions through which anything can come to presentation, or appear, at all: in the first instance, space and time. Of these two, however, it is time that must be regarded as more originary. Whereas space constitutes "the form of outer sense," time constitutes "the form of inner sense," or the "formal condition of inner intuition"[13] and "and precisely thereby also, indirectly, a condition of outer experiences."[14] In other words, time as form constitutes, in the broadest sense, the condition of any phenomenon, inner or outer.

Bypassing a host of interpretive issues, we can ask, What is the significance of Kant's thinking time as precisely *form*? The ethical in Kant is also decisively organized around the idea of form (the form of the maxims for the will). In both cases, form signifies what has its origin in the spontaneity of the subject, what the subject imposes a priori upon the givens. The formalization of time in Kant is thus linked to the move to secure both the priority of the subject to given being and the originary status of its spontaneity. As Kant says, "apart from the subject, time is nothing."[15] One can see what Kant gains here: by tracing temporalization back to the spontaneity of the subject, Kant radically secures human capability from its exposure to anything that befalls a subject "in" time, namely, against all natural drives and externalities, but also against any word that would strike it, heteronomously, from the outside. In these terms, obligation does indeed imply and reveal capability.

For his part, Levinas once remarked that "the essential theme of my research is the deformalization of the notion of time." He continued, "all human experience does in fact take on a temporal form. The transcendental philosophy descended from Kant filled that form with a sensory content coming from experience or, since Hegel, dialectically led that form toward a content. "These philosophers never required a condition in a certain conjuncture of 'matter' of events, in a meaningful content somehow prior to form, for the constitution of that very form of temporality" (EN 263/232). Thus Levinas seeks a meaningful content prior to form, prior to what the subject is capable of positing through its spontaneity—a meaningful content prior to meaning. Levinas specifies such meaning prior to meaning in a variety of ways. In *Totality and Infinity* it is the face of the Other that fulfills this role. In *Otherwise Than Being*, however, it seems rather to be temporality itself that constitutes such non-formal meaning. There Levinas articulates an understanding of temporality in which time "is not the work of a subject," something specifiable in the phenomenon of ageing. He comments (OTB, 66–67/51–52):

Temporalization as lapse, the loss of time, is neither quite an initiative of an ego, nor a movement toward some telos of action. The loss of time is not the work of a subject . . . Time passes *[se passe]*. This synthesis which occurs *patiently* . . . is age-ing. It bursts under the weight of years, and irreversibly tears itself away from the present, that is, from re-presentation. In self-consciousness there is no longer a pres-ence of self to self, but senescence. It is as senescence beyond the recuperation of memory that time—time lost without return—is a diachrony, and relates to *[con-cerne]* me.

This passage sets the terms for a critique of capability that is radical. In aging, something takes place and defines the subject that is not the work of the sub-ject. Aging is an event that transpires in a time that cannot be represented or posited, a time that has no presence. Time itself continually disjoins the sub-ject from its own present, and in such a way that "the same does not rejoin the same" (OTB, 67/52). This displacing and disjoining is its infinitely non-formal (non-positable) aspect. Real time, deformalized time, is the continual uproot-ing of the very possibility of finding my place, the impossibilization of impos-sibility, the death of absolute spontaneity. Through its temporality the subject does not stand present at its own origin; it is not originally a "for oneself," as the entire tradition of idealism would have it, but rather a "despite oneself" *(malgré soi):* "The despite oneself marks this life in its very living. Life is life despite life—in its patience and in its ageing" (OTB, 65/51).

The deformalization of time effected in the analysis of aging, then, locates the subjectivity of the subject in its patience, its absolute inability to rejoin it-self, rather than (as in Kant and every idealism) in its absolute spontaneity. If, however, owing to its temporality, a subject essentially cannot rejoin, posit, or recuperate itself, then it is exposed to something irreparable. However, "ought to" implies "can" only so long as there is nothing irreparable. The subject *ought* to be equal to itself, transparent to itself—its will ought to be universal. But what if, say, through its temporality, it finds itself ever in a position where it *no longer can?* What if, owing to the irreparability of time, whenever something is done it cannot be undone? What if the experience of obligation reveals not the will's absolute spontaneity but its having departed, beyond recall, from its own inner universality? Then the correlation between ought and can no longer holds; it is breached by the irreparability of an act. Kant, of course, struggles tremendously with this problem—a problem that threatens the very founda-tions of his ethics—in the consideration of "radical evil" and its overcoming.[16] Yet radical evil, no doubt an essentially Christian problem bound up with the divine economy of grace, is not Levinas' problem.

What I find distinctive about Levinas is to have accorded this destitution of freedom, the irreparable breach between the will and itself (and so be-tween "ought to" and "can"), an essentially positive meaning: the death of spontaneity—temporalization itself—signifies not evil and fall but the breakout from immanence, the opening to an outside. Time is itself the event of tran-scendence. In his lecture course titled "God and Onto-Theology" from 1975 to 1976, Levinas put the point concisely: "Far from signifying the corruptibility of being, time would signify the ascension toward God, *dis-inter-estedness,* the passage to being's beyond" (GDT, 232/203). This revision, thinking time as ascension, probably cannot be thought about enough. There is no question of an ecstatic thrust toward the future here, but rather of a calling back of the subject to an instant lying on the hither side of all spontaneity. This revocation of freedom underlies Levinas' effort in *Otherwise Than Being* to understand temporalization, not through intentionality and spontaneity but according to the structure of the *revelation* of the radically Other, that is, in terms of hearkening to a call from a beyond.

Hence Levinas comes to speak of temporalization (aging) in terms of an *obedience to a command:* "The temporality of time," he writes, "is an obedience" (OTB, 68/52), an "obedience prior to any voluntary decision that would have assumed it" (OTB, 69–70/54). In reference to such obedience he adds, "it is in the form of the *being* of this entity, as the diachronic temporality of ageing, that there is produced despite myself the response to a call that is *direct,* like a traumatizing blow. Such a response cannot be converted into an 'inward need' or a natural tendency. This response answers, but with no eroticism, to an absolutely heteronomous call" (OTB, 68/53). In my very ageing—in my "living corporeality," in my very skin—I already for Levinas exist within an order constituted by call, hearing, obedience, response. I exist within an ethical order characterized as "one-for-the-Other," or substitution. My ageing itself, what is most definitive of me, is *already a response to a word that has been heard*—the word of one who is absolutely Other. I exist vis-à-vis a word that does not bear a meaning appropriateable by my spontaneity, but rather calls my spontaneity into question and so provokes an infinite response.

At this point, it may be useful to raise some questions: What is it that allows Levinas to interpret temporalization according to the structure of hearing and revelation rather than in terms of the spontaneity of the subject (i.e., as an a priori *intuition*)? Is it philosophical critique alone? The critique of time as form has good phenomenological evidence, but what about the decision to interpret temporalization through the structure of command and obedience? What about the reversal of seeing time as transcendence? Is this a theological decision that expresses the historical particularities of the *content* of Jewish revelation? Is Levinas developing an understanding of existence, not simply in phenomenological evidence but as a response to the word heard within Judaism? However this is answered, we can at least say the move is a stunning one, a real coup: suddenly the entire thematic of patience—aging, lapse, loss, suffering, time, dispossession, terms which Western thought has always judged to be indicative of privative states destined to be surpassed—acquire a contrary sense. Suddenly one is able to read loss *as* the opening of meaning, the death of spontaneity as the very association with the good, and to see in patient waiting the very meaning of the human being. A voice reaches human ears in the depths of its destitution, summoning the person back from the night of senescence, making him live again—by making him responsible.

In "Revelation in the Jewish Tradition" Levinas comments on this destitution that becomes an opening in patience: "[There is] forever this bursting open of the 'less' (unable to contain the 'more' that it contains) in the form of 'the one for the other.' Here, the word 'forever' *[toujours]* signifies in its original *[natal]* sense of patience, of [patience's] diachrony and temporal transcendence. 'Forever' a coming to one's senses *[dégrisement]*, ever more profound, and in this sense, the spirituality of the spirit in obedience" (BTV, 181/150). The telos will never be reached, *not* because it keeps being deferred as a Sisyphean bad infinite but rather because completion is not essentially the modality of fulfillment. There is fulfillment in the most rigorous sense only in waiting on the end, waiting upon the Messiah. Levinas says, "The awaiting of the Messiah is the very duration of time, or waiting for God. But in that case, waiting no longer attests to the absence of a Godot who will never come, but rather to a relationship with that which cannot enter the present" (BTV 172–73/143). The advent of the Messiah, who consummates history by bringing about eschatological peace, can never arrive into any present—and thus can never become present to "objective experience"[17]—simply because his advent conditions every present, opens every present. The Messiah ends history only by renewing it, by launching it again, in each instant, from the beginning. The present itself has messianic depth.

Waiting for the Messiah, then, becomes a matter of essential patience which no longer has the structure of a temporary deferral, but rather an absolute one. Patience is the name for the human association with its own non-positable temporality. To wait for the Messiah—the true object of expectation—is not to wait *for* anything definite but rather to wait on time as such: "[essential] patience waits without waiting for; that is, it is an awaiting without anything being awaited, without the intention of waiting" (GDT, 158/139). Such waiting without waiting-for, in which patience is no longer a project, is not nevertheless not useless, but rather the condition in which time is fulfilled through the assumption of a responsibility for the Other: "Time is deferred, is transcended to the Infinite. And the waiting without something awaited (time itself) is turned into the responsibility for another" (GDT, 158/139).

MK:

With all this I want to agree. Nevertheless, must not my very assent end up negating itself? Acknowledging the strengths of these arguments about patience and deformalization involves staying in patience, and so it would go against the content of these claims to take them up in such a manner that would appropriate the relation between Kierkegaard and Levinas as one in which they coincide with each other. That would truly be a case of tarrying with the negative in the most heterophagic manner: Kierkegaard's other, Levinas—and this alterity is apparent right from Levinas' claim in "Kierkegaard: Existence and Ethics" that Kierkegaard disdains ethics (PN, 84/72ff.)—will have been converted into a Kierkegaardian. Instituting neighborliness involves the kind of bridge that you indeed have built between patience and senescence; but patience necessitates undoing any and all such claims to recognize Kierkegaard in Levinas, to see them as sharing the same soul. So, in hearing your words, I object. To narrate the concept of salvation in Kierkegaard, the gaining of one's soul, as a gaining in which nothing is gained, seems to me to be overly abstract. If the work of patience is not a project—neither in Kierkegaard nor in Levinas—how should we understand the structure of, say, *Totality and Infinity*? From its opening sentence (TI, ix/21), it seeks to defend and re-energize the modern moral project, by understanding that project in terms of an ethical subject grounded in infinity (TI, xiv/26). If the stance of this subject is aptly termed "patience"—and Levinas describes ethical acts with this word (TI, 213–17/236–40)—is it not patience-in-order-to, a patience for the sake of the fulfillment of peace and justice? At least on the surface, the claims that Levinas makes for the possibility of "messianic triumph" (TI, 261/285) can be understood in this manner. The salvation that accompanies such a triumph is concrete—outer as well as inner—and if patience makes such a triumph possible . . . well, here is a gaining in which *everything* is gained. On the other hand, it would be false to say that this is the *only* discourse of salvation or the Messiah, terms which Levinas equates in the 1947 text translated as *Existence and Existents* (EE, 156/93), in Levinas' work. Salvation can happen now, and still be to come. The Messiah can be both someone I know—you, for example—and a player to be named later. The easiest way to delineate this odd structure is to traipse through Levinas' earliest writings, which are driven by an anxiety over how, or even whether, Western humanism can free itself from the critique of it posed by Hitlerism.[18]

The brilliance of Levinas' 1934 essay "Reflections on the Philosophy of Hitlerism" lies not simply in its portrait of National Socialist ideology, but also in his argument that Hitlerism has some proper philosophical grounding to it. Too often this essay has been read as a dismissal of Hitlerism as *bad* philosophy, to be opposed to good and proper transcendental idealism.[19] But if this were to be the case, then Hitlerism would pose no threat at all; there would be no contest between it and humanism. Nevertheless, Levinas is clear in this essay that the contest runs deep, and that the future of the West hangs on strategizing how humanism can win. For Hitlerism has been determined by the philosophical history of the West, specifically by the *weakness* of transcendental idealism in its antihistoricist orientation, a weakness that becomes particularly acute when transcendental idealism is taken on its own as the only valid account of meaning. The account of the subject in liberalism and in Christianity is one of untrammeled freedom. For liberalism, humankind possesses an "absolute freedom with respect to the world and to the possibilities that solicit his action . . . Speaking absolutely, he has no history." Similarly, in Christianity, "the cross sets free, and through the Eucharist, which triumphs over time, this deliverance takes place every day" (UH, 29–30/14). Such robust accounts of freedom—again, when taken on their own—are phenomenologically false. For the flight from history is also the flight from matter and the flight from embodiment; it is always a flight done in bad conscience.

But the body is not only something eternally foreign ... The body is not only closer and more familiar to us than the rest of the world; it does not only control our psychological life, our temperament and activity. Beyond these banal observations, there is the feeling of identity. Do we not assert ourselves in the unique warmth of our bodies long before any blossoming of the Ego that would claim to be distinct from it? Do those bonds made by blood, long before the blooming of intelligence, not withstand all trials? In a dangerous sport, in a risky exercise where gesture attains an almost abstract perfection under the whisper of death, all dualism between ego and body must disappear. And in the impasse of physical pain, doesn't the sick person feel the indivisible simplicity of his being as he tosses and turns on his bed of suffering, for the sake of finding a position that will give him peace? (UH, 36–37/ 17–18)

These phenomenological claims are not ones that Levinas will later disavow. Indeed, this affirmation of the irreducibility of embodiment is echoed almost three decades later in *Totality and Infinity:* "The naked and indigent body is the very reversal, irreducible to a thought, of representation into life" (TI, 100/127). Thus, when he goes on in the Hitlerism essay to claim that the body's "adherence to the Ego is in itself valid" (UH, 37/18), one should not conclude that this is part of an improper mode of thinking, one that places too much value on immanence. Embodiment is a fact which philosophy must take into account. The problem of Hitlerism comes when it makes the fact of embodiment the *only* relevant fact for philosophy, and thus turns embodiment into an essentialist claim about human nature. It becomes a biologism that is nothing more than an acceptance of an enslavement or shackling *(enchaînement)* to our bodies, and an ethnocentrism that is nothing more than an acceptance of the chains that bind us to those who allegedly share our blood (UH, 39/19).

While Hitlerism is opposed to liberalism insofar as they have opposing hierarchies of the mind/body relation, they are mirrors of each other insofar as they are both monist ways of looking at the world. Levinas' task, then, is to develop a mode of thinking that takes account both of the embodied nature of human selfhood and of the "escape from self" that both Christianity and liberalism promise but cannot fulfill. He wants both metaphysics and historicity, yet there is nothing in Levinas' breakneck tour through the history of Western philosophy in this essay that makes such a double affirmation possible. Nowhere in this early essay does Levinas pose a philosophical answer to the problem of how to reclaim the liberal world after the turn to materialism, a turn which was justified under the weight of all existence (UH, 40/20)—by the inability to free oneself from being determined by one's body and one's history—then no individual has the strength to lessen his own burden, and no other individual has the strength that would enable her to come to his rescue. Levinas ends this essay by saying that racism "is contrary to the very humanity of humankind" (UH, 41/21), but this contest is one in which liberal and Christian humanism seem to be losing to Hitlerism because there has been no account of humanism which could out-think Hitlerism on the issue of the body, its philosophical trump card. This is the tragedy of 1930s philosophy: humanism has not yet been able to philosophically defend itself against racism's ethical offenses. From this tragedy, we need salvation.

We can find one sentence in the Hitlerism essay that delineates how Levinas wants to defend humanism (UH, 30/14): "Judaism bears the magnificent message that remorse—the painful expression of a radical impotence to repair the irreparable—announces the repentance that generates the pardon that repairs." For Levinas, Judaism supersedes both Christianity (at least when Christians are not understood as grafted into the people of Israel) and secular liberalism. Judaism's affirmation of historicity—the inability to make time go backwards so as to repair a past act—somehow generates freedom from that very historicity. Nevertheless, Levinas does not expand on how this process of generating pardon operates; neither does he expand on whether the pardoning agent is divine or human. All that the reader has from Levinas at this point is the articulation of a problem of salvation, and a possible solution that needs more data in order to be persuasive.

The essay "On Escape," published the year after the essay on Hitlerism, does not resolve the issue. Indeed, Levinas' problematization of previous claims about the possibility of transcendence becomes even knottier. Here, it is clearer than it was in the 1934 Hitlerism essay that Levinas wants to affirm the description of humanity as being "weighed down by existence" as a fact. The centrality of this weight to human existence is most obvious in Levinas' complex phenomenology of malaise. Our usual instinct is to describe malaise as a general and indefinable feeling of lack, the blankness so typical of twentysomethings. But the inability to have projects is not, in fact, what malaise actually is. For Levinas (OE, 78/58), "the fact of being ill at ease *[mal à son aise]* is essentially dynamic. It appears as a refusal to remain in place, as an effort to get out of an unbearable situation." Malaise is thus the inability to settle in any one project, something closer to what we would now describe as attention deficit disorder. In my malaise, I will engage in multiple projects for brief periods of time. For example, feeling unwell as a result of the sense that the essay I am writing is a piece of utter rot, I will try to find something to calm myself. I may read bits and pieces of a secondary source, before I become convinced that it will not help. Then I may read another, and then another, and yet another, convinced by each in turn that it is useless; no one else's intellectual labor will put me on the right track. I may then take a walk, before convincing myself that fresh air is only emptying my brain. I may then listen to a little music, before coming to the judgment that "mood music" is simply making me numb. I may pass time surfing the Internet, before concluding that information is the last thing I need. I may even attempt to glean something of importance to save my writing from its decrepit essence simply by staring into space. In all these acts, I am never being indecisive; I am always engaged in something (perhaps even multiple activities simultaneously). The problem is that no project that I undertake can deliver me from my malaise in writing. For even when I finish this sentence, or this paragraph, a future sentence or paragraph may very well make the process start all over again. It never stops. As Levinas writes,

Moreover, the satisfaction of a need does not destroy it. Not only are needs reborn, but disappointment also follows their satisfaction. We are in no way neglecting the fact that satisfaction appeases need. However, it is a matter of knowing whether this ideal of peace lies within the initial demands of need itself. We note in the phenomenon of malaise a different and perhaps superior demand: a kind of dead weight in the depths of our being, whose satisfaction does not manage to rid us of it. What gives the human condition all its importance is precisely this inadequacy of satisfaction to need. The justification of certain ascetic tendencies lies there: the mortifications of fasting are not only agreeable to God; they bring us closer to the situation that is the fundamental event of our being: the need for escape. (OE, 79/59–60)

We are needful beings. If all of our needs could be satisfied by projects, then it would not be possible for us to feel malaise. (Thus the person who is engaged in no project would not be a content person, but someone who is conscious of the impossibility of satisfying her needs, thereby confirming the insight of the phenomenology of malaise.)

The condition of the possibility of malaise is a need that can only be addressed by escape, not only from a particular situation but more fundamentally from the situatedness that is concomitant with the adherence of my body to my ego; reading "On Escape" in the context of the Hitlerism essay suggests that the dead weight is the weight of my own materiality. I cannot plan such an escape on my own. I could simply tell others that my body is irrelevant or immaterial; perhaps I could tell them that I am merely a brain in a vat. When I realize that this claim fails to persuade, I may engage in practices that attempt to deny my embodied nature. I may stop eating. I may wear extra-large cardigans, even and especially in the summer, in order to hide the contours of my body. I may drink lots of coffee to speed up thoughts in my head. I may drink lots of alcohol so that my head feels separate from the rest of me. But all of these avoidance mechanisms lead to various sensations that one might broadly describe as nausea. Not eating leads to an ever-deeper hunger. Wearing sweaters in the summer while outdoors leads to dehydration and its symptoms. Large quantities of coffee produce an upset stomach, and as for the alcohol . . . well, the end of that story is all too familiar. All of these practices designed to repress embodiment only lead to sensations which forebode the return of the repressed (quite literally, in the case of the sense of a drunk about to vomit). Attending to one's embodiment—even attending to the consequences of fleeing from one's embodiment—leads to the inability to describe oneself through any attributes of action; it is my body that weighs me down, prohibiting my most needful projects from taking flight. Only attributes of being count when projects cannot be fulfilled. As a result, to think of myself in terms of being, and nothing else, is to think of myself as fundamentally powerless (OE, 92/68): "The ground of this position [of nausea] reveals to us the presence of being in all its impotence, which constitutes this presence as such. It is the impotence of pure being in all its nakedness."

To gloss this in terms of a Levinasian critique of Heideggerean ontology would hardly be surprising. But it is still important to point out that Levinas sees the power of the affirmation of our powerlessness to escape, an affirmation that Levinas associated with paganism in his 1935 review of Lavelle's *Total Presence* (as Rolland points out in his "Annotations" to "On Escape").[20] This makes the task of philosophy all the more urgent. The task of "surpassing being" (OE, 69/71) or "getting out of being by a new path" or, in an echo of rabbinic texts that posit the starkest of antimonies between Jewish and non-Jewish cultures, overturning the "wisdom of the nations" (OE, 99/73),[21] is a task of finding a phenomenon which shows that such a surpassing is really possible. It is not a task of speculative thinking, as if the act of thinking had some kind of salvific power. Insofar as the being that thinks is always an embodied being, riveted or thrown *(rivé)* into unchosen and ungraspable structures of existence, speculative thinking can only end in failure. "Thought, by itself, [is] powerless over being," as Levinas writes in *Existence and Existents* (EE, 152, 90).

It is in this text where the tragedy of existence is explicitly linked with the concept of salvation. Getting out of being by a new path is the aim of messianic (EE, 156/93): "The true object of hope is the Messiah, or salvation." Yet at this point in the text, this is still an assertion, not an argument. How do we know that this hope is grounded in the structures of real possibility? When is this hope fulfilled? By whom? For how long? Levinas begins to answer in the sentences that follow immediately upon the invocation of the Messiah: "The caress of a consoler which softly comes in our pain . . . concerns the very instant of physical pain, which is then no longer condemned to itself, is transported 'elsewhere' by the movement of the caress, and . . . finds 'fresh air,' a dimension and a future." In other words, salvation consists in having a future time, in being able to engage in projects, in being able to do more than just be (and, unfortunately, be a body), in being able to have "another go at the adventure of existence" (TI, 258/282). And this has something to do with the caress. In *Time and the Other,* Levinas writes (TO, 82/89) that "it is not the softness *(velouté)* or warmth of the hand given in contact that the caress seeks; the seeking of the caress constitutes its essence by the fact that it does not know what it seeks." The caress is a project—it has an intentionality, that of concupiscence *(volupté)*—in which materiality is no longer impotent. The power of the concupiscent body is not that of being able to touch or grasp another's body, and thereby transcend oneself; if that were the case, then sex would only confirm the most nihilistic conclusions of a philosophy of embodiment. Rather, the power of the concupiscent body is that, in its materiality, it can attract another's caress; I can find myself caressing someone—or more broadly, taking up a stance toward someone—in which I do not know why I am doing it. Love "invades and wounds" (TO, 82/89), and yet I am conscious of myself caressing. While one could point to other modes of the affectivity of the self, it is in the analysis of the loving caress that I discover that a mode of tarrying with materiality in which I engage with a body that resembles my embodied nature, but still maintains its difference from me amidst all the sensation. *Ve-ahavta lo kamokha* "love the stranger as yourself" (Lev. 19:34); but in love I become aware that the beloved is, while like me, also a stranger. I am finally aware of something outside my body that is, even in its embodiment, something foreign to my body, something that seems to me to be foreign to all embodiment and thus to be infinite. Through this encounter with the infinite, I have finally wriggled free of the shackles of the body without leaving my body behind. I have found my way from gross materialism to a right to engage in philosophy of mind, a right to call oneself a Cartesian, a right to abstraction, and most importantly, a right to the metaphysics and reason of liberalism that Hitlerism had undone.

This argument, stretching throughout Levinas' early writings, is about history. Its aim is to show that we are not doomed to be forced to assent to the proposition that Hitlerism is the wisest of philosophies. It is to take up the identity of the modern, on the basis of the deformalization of time. This is a project. At the same time, it is a project that goes forth in awareness of its debts. So it does not have the robust flavor of that would accompany, say, a discourse of salvation in which one could figure out how to hasten the eschaton, and plan to achieve that within history. For the eschaton is already now, in the following sense: the consoler of the caresser or the person who, in his or her body, leads me to acknowledge that I do not know what I do when I caress is properly associated with the Messiah, because at this moment in the caress humanism is redeemed from fatalism. The breaking of the chains of embodiment in eros gives me confidence that my hope in the eschaton is not in vain. So while I am still a material being, unable to transcend my body in every respect, I know that such transcendence over determinism, such messianic triumph, is really possible.[22] So yes, Levinas is arguing for an account of subjectivity as oriented around the work of patience—the messiah is the one who shows me that subjectivity is open to the exterior, "incapable of closing itself off" (HAH, 122/CPP, 151)—but by means of this thinking and the possibilities that it opens up, it is ensured that Hitlerism will never have the last word. That will belong to the messiah who is to come.

This oscillation between the messiah-who-is-you-right-here and the messiah-to-come in Levinas' early writings on salvation seems, on the surface, to be quite different than the parallel God talk in Kierkegaard's *Eighteen Upbuilding Discourses*. When Kierkegaard writes at the end of "Patience in Expectancy" that "there is truly only one eternal object of wonder—that is God" (SKS 5, 224/EUD, 226), there seems to be no ambiguity here. The object of wonder is God, not the human. Anna the prophetess, in Luke 2:35–38, serves God night and day in fasting and prayer, without leaving the temple. How could this be translated into Levinas? There is no caressing in Kierkegaard's portrait of Anna; if there were, one imagines that that would be quite a violation of temple decorum, or the prohibition of mixed-gender seating, or at the very least, of Anna's solitude. While, for Kierkegaard, "every truly expectant person," that is, the one who is patient, "is in a relationship with God" (SKS 5, 220/EUD, 221), and has concern for the inner life over and above the outer life (SKS 5, 220/EUD, 222), such pietism is absent in Levinas. The instinct to read Kierkegaard as "theology" and Levinas as "ethics," and to read the two in strict opposition to each other, here becomes somewhat understandable.

But I can be a bit more patient than this, in part because it is by no means clear to me that these discourses establish a firm or simple boundary between the divine and the human. The context for the "relationship with God" passage is as follows:

> The person whose expectancy is truly expectancy is patient by virtue of it in such a way that, upon becoming aware of his impatience, he must not only judge himself but also test his expectancy to see whether this explains his impatience and to what extent it would be wrong to remain patient; if that were possible, he ought to give up the expectancy. Only the true expectancy, which requires patience, also teaches patience. But true expectancy is such that is pertains to a person essentially and does not leave it up to his own power to bring about the fulfillment. Therefore every truly expectant person is in a relationship with God. (SKS 5, 220/EUD, 221–22)

The one who expects an eternal salvation by means of human powers, projects, concepts, and measures ends up forgetting God (i.e., no longer expects God at all) because what becomes expected in this context could not possibly be qualitatively different than any temporal scene that human action could accomplish. So "God" here cannot be the content of any *ideatum*. Part of what the practice of patience involves is to let go of theological notions of God, and to do this repeatedly and constantly, in an ever more rigorous negative theology, as patience teaches itself and compounds itself. For this reason, patience, for the sake of maintaining the relationship with God, must break off that very relationship. And so Kierkegaard writes that "in patience he offers his expectancy; in patience he sacrifices it by submitting it to God" (SKS 5, 221/EUD, 222). What is left after this? Perhaps some Eckhartian God beyond God. But if the patience is complete, and if the sacrifice is total, than there can be nothing left of expectancy after the sacrifice is made; the relationship to God, or to salvation, must be kept silent, without concept.

What remains when the relationship to God is made sacred, and thereby erased, is the relationship to the community. This is the dimension of Anna's prophecy that Kierkegaard almost entirely ignores, the one in which she speaks to others (Luke 2:38): "And at that very instant she came up and began giving thanks to God, and continued to speak of Him to all those who were expecting the redemption of Jerusalem." She says nothing about the child from Nazareth. Indeed, there is nothing in Luke's narration that leads the reader to believe that Anna says any different words on this day than she has said on every other day that she has been in the temple. There is nothing extraordinary about thanking God and speaking of God in a temple. Gee, God-talk is the lingo of the place! What might be strange to moderns about Anna, though, is that her speech shifts recipients. Her thanks *to* God *(tô theô)* invisibly ends, and passes into talking *about* God *(peri autou)* with others. That group is bound together by their being the ones who expect *(prosdechomenoi)* redemption.

This last detail suggests that her patience too is for the sake of something. If Anna really amounts to nothing on account of her expectancy, then Luke 2:38 becomes a puzzling text. Why would a divinely inspired text mention this, if it is for nothing? On the other hand, one cannot say that her expectancy results in some kind of self-making. These kinds of projects Kierkegaard rightly denies: "Did she herself perhaps amount to something through her expectancy—for example, like the person who was impoverished and again became rich, the person who was toppled and then elevated again, and in a certain sense was elevated because of his expectancy?" Nonetheless, Anna does amount to something as a result of that instant when she sees Jesus of Nazareth, for in seeking to verify her patience, she speaks of God to the community. This too is to sacrifice expectancy to God. The second chapter of Luke does not end with the community drawing up a plan to develop criteria by which their fulfillment will be perfected. It ends with talking: words that caress, words that mark their own completion by being quite insignificant, no different than the God talk on any other day in the temple, as if no one special, no one more unique than anyone else, had just been presented before the Lord. Luke's narrative suggests that these words bolster the community's expectancy just the same. If her words do indeed have such an effect—and we cannot know for certain, because Luke never deigns to mention whether anyone responds to Anna's words—it is only because they sacrifice their extraordinariness. If Anna's words were truly extraordinary, truly new, then they would be cause for others' enjoyment and fulfillment; as a result, the Lukan narrative would be false when it refers to those to whom Anna speaks as *prosdechomenoi*. So if something miraculous happens in the temple on that day, it is not the vision of a child, but this: on a day when nothing different happens, and when nothing different is spoken, a community has been formed that was not there earlier, and without any natural cause that could serve as a distinguishing mark as to why the community was formed at this instant, neither earlier nor later. Something new, something undetermined by history, has occurred in history, and—given its complete ordinariness—there is no reason to think that such newness could not occur at any other later moment in history. The Messiah is thus the expectant one, who in patience can accomplish something that breaks free from the ordinary, all the while perduring within it.

Kierkegaard closes "Patience in Expectancy" with a midrash of sorts on Horace's *Nil admirari*, overturning Horace's ataraxia:

> People often lament that life is so impoverished, existence so powerless in all its magnificence, that it seeks in vain to take the soul by surprise or to captivate it in wonder, since to wonder at nothing is the highest wisdom, and to expect nothing is the highest truth. The child is astonished at insignificant things. The adult has laid aside childish things; he has seen the wondrous, but it amazes him no more . . . If, however, a person knew how to make himself truly what he truly is—nothing—knew how to set the seal of patience on what he had understood—ah, then his life, whether he is the greatest or the lowliest, would even today be a joyful surprise and be filled with blessed wonder and would be that throughout all his days, because there is truly only one eternal object of wonder—that is God—and only one possible hindrance to wonder—and that is a person when he himself wants to be something. (SKS 5, 224/ EUD, 225–26)

Anna's patience allows her to wonder at God instead of wondering at nothing, but as soon as she opens her mouth to others, she returns to wondering at nothing, now no longer understood in the sense of freedom from worry. At the end of Luke 2, the stage has been set for Anna to wonder at and to worry about those other persons who try and act as the nothing that they acknowledge themselves to be in their patient expectancy. In this manner does patience teach itself.

To read "Patience in Expectancy" in this manner threatens the tidying up that Kierkegaard does in this last paragraph, which deploys somewhat surprisingly clear dichotomies between nothing/something, child/adult, and God/human. However, such ordering, as Kierkegaard writes in "The Expectancy of an Eternal Salvation," can only be miserable (SKS 5, 261/EUD, 265). And so while a community might be formed (or re-formed) at the close of Luke 2, on Kierkegaardian grounds one must say that it can and will be unmade in the future, thrown into disorder; for otherwise expectancy would be something that could be fully known by all the members of a community and used as the basis for calculations. In this oscillation between unmaking and remaking of communal membership and boundaries there develops the freedom to try out new adventures of existence, neither assuming that the other is totally other than me (and thus beyond conversation) nor an alter ego (and thus obviating conversation). These adventures, which have a caress of words as their material, are the beginnings of neighborliness, the beginnings of new possibilities and new futures that you and I find in both Kierkegaard and Levinas.

It is also the beginning of drawing Kierkegaard and Levinas into a relationship of neighborliness with each other; but I fear it threatens to end as soon as it begins. The concreteness of Anna's speech is missing from "Patience in Expectancy," and the contributions of the other *prosdechomenoi* are missing from Luke's text. It is when Levinas supplements Kierkegaard (and Luke) that the neighborliness appears, yet that act of bringing Levinas to bear on Kierkegaard suggests that their own neighborliness is not essential, but forced. Such separation is the mark of patience, yet to remain contentedly in separation is the mark of impatience. You and I should begin again, forget all that can be forgotten, all that already slips away. *Ne me quitte pas.*

DK:

Ne me quitte pas. And yet departure is inevitable. Kierkegaard and Levinas must go their separate ways. Before the inevitable transpires, however, will you allow me a few words that perhaps risk unintelligibility? A few more words to delay the inevitable?

The thinking of Kierkegaard and Levinas, I have wanted to say, converges around patience: both consent, maturely, to the ego's radical inability to rejoin itself; both *consent to time.* Moreover, such consent, I have implied, does *not* hinge merely upon their making a good philosophical case for the unsurpassability of what Hegel called the "unhappy consciousness." A philosophical case of that sort would involve exposing the inadequacy of Hegel's account of consciousness and time as mediation—something Kierkegaard and Levinas indeed both do, at length—but these philosophical arguments will never explain the consent, the affirmation, which rings out. In both thinkers, that is, a certain surplus to philosophical evidence, a problematization of the priority ceded to evidence, finds articulation: Kierkegaard meditates on this in terms of the possibility of "faith," and Levinas in terms of "the spirituality of obedience." In both cases, so I have suggested, the surplus gets articulated in terms of a paradoxical fulfillment: patience is thought as already a modality of fulfillment, the opening to the real beyond its representation. "At the very moment where all is lost, everything is possible" (EE, 158/95): this sentence, with its striking Kierkegaardian resonance, remains valid throughout the entire Levinasian corpus.

Calling this surplus "theological" will not advance our understanding, for the precise reason that for neither thinker is it a question of arguing from "belief" in some dogmatic content. Faith in Kierkegaard is precisely not belief, no more than obedience is in Levinas. Rather, each involves a "hearing of the word," a hearing in which, one must say, *the word actually and first of all comes to be spoken.* To call faith "belief" would imply a relation to a meaningful content already available; yet faith is that wherein meaningful content first arises. Belief gets it backwards. The inclining of the human ear is the condition for the revelation of the word; the primordial act of the self is not its positing of itself, but the lending of its ear as a space of resonance. In a wonderful passage from "Revelation in the Jewish Tradition" Levinas supplies a short metaphysics of listening to the word:

> [I am suggesting] that the totality made out of the contributions *[apport]* of multiple people: the uniqueness of each act of listening carrying the secret of the text; the voice of Revelation, precisely as inflected by each person's ear, would be necessary for the All of truth. The fact that the word of the living God may be heard in a variety of ways does not mean merely that the Revelation adopts the measure of the people listening to it, but that this measure measures Revelation. (BTV, 163/133–34)

This makes hearing an act of the will through which meaningful possibilities are disclosed that are not dreamt of, neither in philosophy nor in speculative theology.

Yet what are these meaningful possibilities disclosed within hearing? If up till now I have, following Levinas' suggestion, bracketed the content of revelation in order to consider its originary possibility, these brackets must now be removed. History must be allowed back in. Immediately, the conversation between Kierkegaard and Levinas will have to be contextualized with respect to the *differend* between the Jewish reading of the Bible and the Christian one, between Jewish hearing and Christian hearing. Of course, they are not reading the same Bible. But beyond this stands the history of the Christian appropriation of the Jewish Bible according to which Judaism is said to lack, as Luther wrote, *der Sinn des Messiä,* the sense of the Messiah, the key to the intelligibility of the biblical text.[23] Jews are said to be incapable of reading their own Scriptures, consigned to the mere letter. Standing behind this appropriation is a powerful metaphysics of fulfillment as sublation: the Christian Scriptures fulfill and thereby obliterate Jewish Scriptures as Jewish. Hegel only gave decisive expression to a millennial-old logic in which expectancy is killed.

This history of reading and of hearing, with all the violence it imposes, is drawn like a shade between Kierkegaard and Levinas. A conversation between these two neighbors cannot afford to be naive about this, nor can it skirt their irreducible difference. For Levinas, the metaphysics of hearing indicated above, that revelation requires the human ear, allows one to "appreciate in its full weight the reference made by Revelation to exegesis" within Judaism, for in these terms, "the slightest question put to the schoolmaster by a novice pupil constitutes an ineluctable articulation of the Revelation which was heard at Sinai" (BTV, 164/134). In Judaism, then, it is not a question of belief, but of questioning and exegesis—specifically an exegesis accomplished in dialogue with Talmudic sources. Such listening in dialogue, implying the entire form of life of "living Judaism," constitutes the specificity of the hearing of the word in Judaism. Of this, Kierkegaard cannot speak; he must let the Other be other.[24] Couldn't one ask, though, whether or not it is possible to conceive a reading of Kierkegaard's Christianity, at least where it is organized around the paradox of a fulfillment that does not fulfill, as "grafted in" to this hearing? Doesn't the inherent pluralism Levinas identifies within revelation—so plural that every naïve question constitutes the occasion for a renewed expression of Sinai—suggest this possibility? I suppose this is what I have been asking all along.

MK:

The questioning of the rabbis that lies at their expansion of the Halakhic system after the destruction of the Jerusalem temple is guided by history, as is Levinas' questioning (which is not that of the rabbis of the Talmud), as is Kierkegaard's questioning (which is not that of, say, Justin Martyr), as is yours. If the meaningful possibilities disclosed within hearing are essentially bound up with historicism in this manner, then it can no longer be a matter of grafting Gentiles onto a reified concept of the people Israel. Neither can it be a matter of re-grafting the carnal Israel that persists in its disbelief onto Paul's spiritualized concept of Israel, now interpreted as the ones who accept Christ.[25] It is instead a grafting of conversation participants into a history in which all types of branches are broken as soon as a question is uttered, and in which therefore all grafts are temporary and ad hoc. This can perhaps open up meaningful possibilities for the participants, but the extent to which the possibilities that it opens up are recognizable as "Judaism" or "Christianity" to those who identify as Jews and Christians—the measure of the future's departure from the past, of conversation as a mode of profanation—is unpredictable.

It perhaps seems odd to write of unpredictability in a relatively streamlined essay as this; perhaps some readers will have found this essay entirely predictable. Nevertheless, upon reading and being surprised by each other's responses, we have gone back and altered our own texts, trying to hear each other better, grafting new bits of text on and cutting off other branches as the history of our conversation moved forward. Could we have reproduced the history of our conversation more accurately and still made it worthwhile for others to read? I doubt it, but I would not have wanted it anyway. This conversation is ours, bearing its own secrets that will remain hidden from others, who now have the freedom to hear, to re-inflect and re-measure the terrain of the Kierkegaard-Levinas neighborhood. Such is the adventure of hearing your words (what some might *also* call "hearing of the word") patiently, of writing and speaking to another *prosdechomenos*.

Notes

1. See David Kangas, *Kierkegaard's Instant: On Beginnings* (Bloomington: Indiana University Press, 2007); and Kangas, "Absolute Subjectivity: Kierkegaard and the Question of Onto-Theo-Egology," *Philosophy Today* 47, no. 4 (2003): 378–91; Martin Kavka, *Jewish Messianism and the History of Philosophy* (New York: Cambridge University Press, 2004); Kavka, "Is There a Warrant for Levinas's Talmudic Readings?" *Journal of Jewish Thought and Philosophy* 14, no. 1 (2006); Kavka, "Levinas Between Monotheism and Cosmotheism," *Levinas Studies* 2 (2007); and Kavka, "The Presence of God in Levinas and R. Hayyim of Volozhin," *Philosophy Today* 50, no. 1 (Spring 2006): 69–79.

2. Edith Wyschogrod and John D. Caputo, "Postmodernism and the Desire for God: An Email Exchange," in Edith Wyschogrod, *Crossover Queries: Dwelling with Negatives, Embodying Philosophy's Others* (New York: Fordham University Press, 2006), 298–315. Quoted passages from 315.

3. Emil Fackenheim, "Metaphysics and Historicity," in *The God Within: Kant, Schelling, and Historicity* (Toronto: University of Toronto Press, 1996), 122–47.

4. Throughout this chapter, parenthetical citations are first to the text in its original French or Danish, and then to the corresponding English translation. On occasion we have emended translations for clarity and precision. In addition to the titles included in the list of abbreviations at the beginning of this volume, we cite from the following texts: *Søren Kierkegaards Skrifter*, ed. Niels-Jørgen Cappelørn (Copenhagen: Bad's, 1997-), vol. 5, cited parenthetically as SKS 5 and corresponding to EUD; Emmanuel Levinas, *L'au-delà du verset* (Paris: Minuit, 1982), corresponding to BTV; Levinas, *Autrement qu'être ou au'delà de l'essence* (The Hague: Martinus Njhoff, 1974), corresponding to OTB; Levinas, *De l'évasion* (Montpellier: Fata Morgana, 1982), corresponding to OE; Levinas, *De l'existence à l'existant* (Paris: Fontaine, 1947), corresponding to EE; Levinas, *Dieu, la mort et le temps* (Paris: Grasset, 1993), corresponding to GDT; Levinas, *Entre nous* (Paris: Bernard Grasset, 1991), corresponding to EN; Levinas, *Humanisme de l'autre homme* (Montpellier: Fata Morgana, 1972), as HAH; Levinas, *Les imprévus de l'histoire* (Montpellier: Fata Morgana, 1994), corresponding to UH; Levinas, *Noms propres* (Montpellier: Fata Morgana, 1976), corresponding to PN; Levinas, *Le temps et l'autre* (Paris: PUF, 1983); Levinas, *Totalité et l'infini* (The Hague: Martinus Nijhoff, 1961), corresponding to TI.

5. *Luther's Works*, ed. Jaroslav Pelikan (St. Louis: Concordia, 1955–1986), 25, 361. Hereafter cited as LW. *Martin Luthers Werke: Kritische Gesamtausgabe* (Weimar: H. Bohlan, 1883–), 56, 370. Hereafter cited as WA.

6. LW, 362; WA, 56, 372.

7. LW, 361; WA, 56, 371.

8. LW, 12, 364; WA, 56, 374.

9. LW, 360; WA, 56, 371.

10. Hegel expresses this idea most eloquently in his preface to *The Phenomenology of Spirit:* "The True is the whole. But the whole is nothing other than the essence consummating itself through its development. Of the Absolute it must be said that it is essentially a *result,* that only in the *end* is it what it truly is." Cf. Hegel, *The Phenomenology of Spirit,* trans. A. V. Miller (Oxford: Oxford University Press, 1977), 11, para. 20.

11. A point Derrida makes in *The Gift of Death.* See *Donner la mort* (Paris: Galilée, 1999), 117; *The Gift of Death,* trans. David Wills (Chicago: University of Chicago Press, 1995), 84.

12. See *Critique of Practical Reason,* trans. Werner S. Pluhar (Indianapolis: Hackett, 2002), chap. 1, §6, 44 Ak. 30.

13. Kant, *Critique of Pure Reason,* A33.

14. Ibid., A34.

15. Ibid., A35.

16. See especially the first two parts of *Religion within the Limits of Reason Alone.*

17. In *Totality and Infinity,* Levinas points to the inadequacy of objective experience: "To be sure, the relation to infinity cannot be stated in terms of experience, for infinity overflows the thought that thinks it. Its very *infinition* is produced precisely in this overflowing . . . but if experience precisely means a relation with the absolutely other . . . the relation with infinity accomplishes experience in the fullest sense of the word *(accomplit l'expérience par excellence)*" (TI, xiii/25). Levinas speaks of such paradoxical accomplishment as eschatological or messianic.

18. In preparing the following paragraphs, I have learned much from conversations with Claire Katz about Levinas' early work, as well as Katz, " 'Before the Face of God One Must Not Go With Empty Hands': Transcendence and Levinas' Prophetic Consciousness," *Philosophy Today* 50, no. 1 (Spring 2006): 58–68.

19. See Arnold Davidson, "1933–34: Thoughts on National Socialism," *Critical Inquiry* 17, no. 1 (Autumn 1990): 35–45, esp. 43; and Samuel Moyn, *Origins of the Other: Emmanuel Levinas Between Revelation and Ethics* (Ithaca, N.Y.: Cornell University Press, 2005), 97ff. Better is the account given in Howard Caygill, *Levinas and the Political* (New York: Routledge, 2002), 32ff.

20. See also Moyn, *Origins,* 110ff.

21. The most famous example of this is, "You should not say, 'I have learned the wisdom of Israel. I shall [now] go and learn the wisdom of the nations.'" See *Sifre Deuteronomy* 34; *Sifra* 86ab. Nevertheless, also see the praise of "the wisdom of the nations" that Levinas offers in the 1982 interview "Philosophy, Justice, and Love," when describing the Israelites' desire for a king (EN, 124/106).

22. I should say something about the sentence having to do with atonement in the Hitlerism essay, since I have tended to emphasize Levinas' account of eros at the expense of his ethics. One could very well say that atonement undoes the reification of the spirit that Levinas describes as "the gravest sin" (EE, 168/101), but it seems to me that one can only defend the claim that this is what atonement means and argue against the counter-claim that atonement is a human fiction, on the basis of the phenomenology of eros. It is only because, as the phenomenology of the caress shows, I have an undetermined future, the ability to engage in projects, and the ability to always start over after moments of condemnation (when those projects fail)—a new present, showing that time does not flow from one moment into the next, but is a series of points across which the I constantly resurrects itself (EE 94)—that I have the right to talk about atonement or

Judaism as if it could accomplish anything. A theology without a doctrine of creation, without an account of the temporality in which we find ourselves (as under a natural law), is just fanciful gibberish.

23. This is from Luther's essay "Vom Schem Hamphoras," an anti-Semitic diatribe from 1543. A translation can be found in Gerhard Falk, *The Jew in Christian Theology* (Jefferson, N.C.: McFarland, 1992), 276 (German) and 223 (English).

24. A work, however, which he does not succeed in accomplishing. In spite of his critique of Hegelian sublation, it could be shown that Kierkegaard reproduces this logic in his representations of Judaism. See, for example, *Concept of Anxiety*, chap. 3.

25. The reading of Romans 11 here is heavily influenced by Daniel Boyarin, *A Radical Jew: Paul and the Politics of Identity* (Berkeley: University of California Press, 1994), 201–206.

7 Kierkegaard, Levinas, and "Absolute Alterity"

Michael Weston

For Levinas, the relation of the I to the other person (*Autrui;* henceforth the Other) is one to a transcendence, as for Kierkegaard is the relation of the I to God. But for both this transcendence is characterized by an "absolute difference" between the I and the Other or the I and God. This characterization of transcendence is determined by the *salvationist* nature of the relation. In both cases, the I cannot become truly itself through the exercise of its own capacities but requires an intervention ("trauma" in Levinas, "divine help" in Kierkegaard) from an "exteriority." This exteriority does not stand in a relative difference to the I, since that would presuppose that the I could be adequately characterized independently of it (as when one says *this* is different from *that* in these respects). Nor is the transcendent already in some sense implicit in the constitution of the I, as, for example, the soul in Plato's cave myth is already oriented toward the Good so that it can be led through its own resources to realize this and to fulfill the requirements of this relation. Rather, the identity of the I is dependent on the Other or God: it comes from a relation to the Other or God which itself proceeds from them. The texts of Levinas and Kierkegaard may, then, be seen as trying to enable a self-recognition of this inadequacy and the character of the intervention which would be required to resolve it.

Nevertheless, their texts have a very different character. Levinas compares his thought to transcendental philosophy (TI, 25): a reflection on the conditions of possibility for our experience. In this sense, his phenomenological descriptions of the life of the I must carry the conviction of self-recognition, while requiring a reference to the Absolute Other as the condition of possibility for the self-hood of the I. I shall suggest, however, that this requirement is not met, in particular, that the role of death in his phenomenological account does not necessitate a recognition of the intervention of the absolute Other but invites another possibility on Levinas's own terms. Kierkegaard's authorship is characterized by a distinction between pseudonymous works and works published under his own name. This character is determined for Kierkegaard by the nature of existential questions concerning the significance of human life and in particular by the role of what he calls "indirect communication" which precludes any demonstration or indeed phenomenological exhibition of the dependence of the I for its self-hood on God. Nevertheless, I shall argue that

Kierkegaard's account of the nature of existential questions determines a restricted range of possible responses which fails to recognize one which is, *on its own terms,* more fundamental, and which is, in fact, the possibility which Levinas's thought in spite of itself suggests.

I

Western philosophy, Levinas claims, takes place as ontology. Ontology reduces alterity to the Same: what is other to the thinker is rendered familiar and so not "other," through being encompassed by conceptual thought. Philosophy as ontology thus aims at, and presupposes the possibility of, totality, the complete mastery of alterity in a lucid comprehension of reality. As such, it is an exercise of the freedom of the thinker in relation to alterity: the thinker is free of alterity and enabled to encompass it through understanding. Philosophy, so understood, is an exercise of the autonomy of human reason. The domestication of alterity through comprehension requires the mediation of concepts which are general and neutral so that the particular in its singularity has no philosophical significance. The other becomes subject to the power of the human, possessed by an "I." Philosophy is an "egology." This characterization of philosophy is not simply a matter of concern to philosophers: this philosophy is a reflection of a civilization.[1]

Levinas asks what can put a stop to this "imperialism" and "totalitarianism" of the Same, the I, in relation to alterity and answers: the relation of the I with the other person. This relation is one with an "absolute other" which cannot be subsumed by the comprehension of the I and therefore whose otherness cannot be defined by relation to the I. The relation of the I to the other person, *Autrui* or the Other, is one in which the "relata" remain "absolute": "a relation in which the terms *absolve* themselves from the relation, remain absolute within the relation" (TI, 64). The "absolutely other" comes into a "relation without relation" (TI, 80) with the Same which remains itself "absolute." What Levinas means by this can only be approached through considering his account of what he called the "ontological adventure" (EE, 45) which, in his autobiographical "Signature" of 1963, he outlines in this way: "Enlightenment and meaning dawn only with the existents rising up and establishing themselves in (the) horrible neutrality of the *there is (il y a).* They are on the path which leads from existence to the existent and from the existent to the other, a path which delineates time itself" (DF, 295).

The *il y a* is introduced in the early *Existence and Existents* of 1947 but remains, as the above quote from "Signature" indicates, an essential notion for the development of Levinas's mature thought.[2] The *il y a* is what we become aware of when we think the complete disappearance of beings: the "Being which we become aware of when the world disappears is not a person or a thing, or the sum total of persons or things; it is the fact that one is, the fact that *there is*" (EE, 21). The end of the world is the end of illumination and what is illuminated, beings. This appears to point to the "other" of world and beings, that over against which we would be able to think their disappearance. But we see that in this "movement," the "other" of world and beings is itself brought within illumination. Levinas's friend Maurice Blanchot calls this the "other night." "Day makes the night . . . Night speaks only of day . . . Day is linked to night because it would not be day if it did not begin and come to an end."[3] But this relation to the other of illumination is illusory: "But when everything has disappeared in the night, 'everything has disappeared' appears. This is the other night."[4] When thought thinks everything has disappeared, the "everything has disappeared" appears: the repetition of the words within thought. The thought of the other of illumination, world and beings, remains a thought, and so defeats itself. We cannot escape the realm of Being: we are, Levinas says, "riveted" to existence with no way out. Our implication in the *il y a* is the impossibility of death (EE, 61) as escape from Being. In death, I return to the anonymous Being of the mere repetition of my name. The *il y a* annihilates our subjectivity (it is where the I disappears), but does not release us. We become aware of the *il y a* in moods. The thought of the impossibility of death in the annihilation of subjectivity fills us with horror, reflected in tales of the living dead, of those who cannot die. And it is manifest in the moods of fatigue, a weariness with existence which is like a "reminder of a commitment to exist, with all the seriousness and harshness of an unrevocable contract" (EE, 24), and in indolence, an "impotent and joyless aversion to the burden of existence" (EE, 29). "Being," Levinas says, "is essentially alien and strikes against us. We undergo its suffocating embrace like the night, but it does not respond to us" (EE, 23). This is the strangeness of intelligibility which aroused Plato's wonder. It is, we might say today, the givenness of language which must be taken over in order that there can be world and beings, an absence of sense which is still an absence of *sense*. I shall return to this later. Levinas's "ontological adventure" is described in terms of a liberation of the I from the *il y a*, one which is ultimately possible only through an intervention from beyond subjectivity. A sketch of this progress, the dawning of "enlightenment and meaning," is given in *Existence and Existents,* but in its developed form it constitutes the main body of *Totality and Infinity.*

The progress requires what *Existence and Existents* calls "hypostasis," the "upsurge" of an existent, the I, from the *il y a*. The I is as the "primordial work of identification" (TI, 36): its existing consists in the process of appropriation, of making what is other relative to me, mine. Its way of existing is thus possession, a result of my powers. The first form of the existing of the I, Levinas calls "enjoyment" which is a mode of appropriation in which the I is at the same time determined by what it appropriates. This is "living from": my powers (thinking, eating, drinking, walking, and so forth) are exercised for themselves but that exercise depends on the alterity which their exercise humanizes, comprehends. The "things" my powers in their exercise encompass, the food, drink, the lane walked, appear within a context Levinas calls the "elements," earth, sea, light, city, for example (TI, 131). This is the non-possessable background in which alterity may be comprehended as "things." The "elements" in this way form the first level of the appropriation of anonymous Being out of which the "things" from which the I lives may appear, and as such they stand in a funda-mental relation with the *il y a*. "The element extends into the *there is*" (TI, 142). The elements appear in the process of individuation of the I, but do so out of what essentially resists humanizing, "an ever-new depth of absence, an exis-tence without existent, the impersonal par excellence," the *il y a*. This other of the elements is the "very strangeness of the earth" (TI, 142).

This otherness of the elements, the strangeness of the earth, precipitates a further development in the process of individuation which is the I, since it in-troduces into the initial enjoyment of the exercise of my powers in the con-text of the elements, *insecurity* and so a sense of the future. The resistance of the *il y a* which underlies the appropriation of the I, the rendering of alterity into the Same, manifests itself in the disruption of the possession which is en-joyment. Insecurity must now be mastered through labor and so possession re-established, the rendering of the other into the Same as the mode of exist-ing of the I. Labor requires representations of some kind, articulation of the na-ture of the insecurity and proposed ways of dealing with it, and representations are held in common: they make a claim not only for me but for others. The pos-sibility of mastery of alterity through labor requires self-consciousness (the I who represents) and a relation to human others, those one cannot possess but who are possessors themselves. Labor creates a human world in which we dwell with others, a site of familiarity and predictability. The human other of dwell-ing Levinas refers to as "feminine," a human other whose "presence is discreetly an absence" (TI, 155). In the formation of a familiar world in which language is exercised in an unreflective way and the "things" of "living from" become per-manent substances, "furnishings" of the human world, the human other is pres-ent in a relation of familiarity. She addresses me in terms of community in the formation of a common home.

The realm of the familiar human world, dwelling as domestication of al-terity, is invaded by an alterity which cannot be domesticated: death. Death cannot be possessed: it is not an event in life, but its invasion by the *il y a* re-turning it to the realm of anonymous Being. Death makes a mockery of the "alienable subjectivity of need and will, which claims to be already and hence-forth in possession of itself" (TI, 245). Death disrupts the capacity of the I as the process of individuation to exercise itself: it reveals the limit of the freedom of the I to appropriate alterity and since it cannot be mastered, it throws in question the meaning which the process of appropriation gives to the existence of the I. "Mortality renders senseless any concern that the ego would have for its existence and its destiny" (OTB, 128–29). Rather, in order that the I as the freedom of the process of appropriation can now find meaning, it must be re-lated to what can give meaning to that freedom. What can do this must be something beyond the I. This Levinas claims is the human other as absolutely other, *Autrui*. The Other is not the human other of community, my other alter egos, but the Other who requires the I to live for the Other: the relation of the I to the absolute Other is one of absolute obligation. I am responsible for and to the Other in the sense of being required to respond, to justify myself and my world. The absolute Other puts me and the familiar world in question. In this way, the world becomes a theme in which the permanent "furnishings" of the familiar world, of dwelling, become freed of possession so I can "see things in themselves" (TI, 171). The absolutely Other, addressing me from a height as a summons to justification and so responsiveness, makes possible the realm of "truth," founding the "universality of reason" (TI, 201), the formation of representations which claim universal justification. In order for the absolutely Other to summon the I to give the possessed world, the Other must lack all characteristics save the height, the transcendence of the human world, from which the summons to respond comes. The Other is therefore "destitute," "naked," and its address is the "appealing to me with its destitution and nudity" thus "arousing my goodness" (TI, 200). Ethical obligations in the usual sense and the realm of "objective truth" are thus made possible by the relation of the I to the absolute Other in its transcendence. In putting my world in question so as to render it subject to universal justification, the Other looks at me with the eyes of humanity: the third party who is another other is present in the face of the Other (TI, 208). And because of this, I am an other for others, and so there is justification for concern for myself, but only because my existence has been given meaning by the Other. The transcendence that questions and judges the I and its world, that makes the Other the absolute Other, is called by Levinas "illeity" or "God": in the other's face "is the manifestation of the height in which God is revealed" (TI, 79). In relation to God or illeity "I am brought to my final reality," to serve the Other (TI, 178–79).

What, then, is meant by speaking of an "absolutely Other" which comes into a "relation without relation" with the I which is the "Same" absolutely? The I is the "Same" absolutely because its existing is as the process of appropriation, of rendering what is other into the comprehended. But this process founders on death, the eruption of an alterity which cannot be domesticated by the I. The existence of the I, its possessing of its world, can only be given sense by something beyond it which could grant significance, an Other which cannot be possessed and which is the manifestation of authority for the I as a whole. But this cannot occur through the I establishing a relation with the Other, which would be an exercise of the powers of the I which would bring the Other into its world. Rather, the "relation" erupts upon the I, breaking in upon the complacency of the dwelling of the I in the familiar world, bringing to it a source of meaning which defeats the absurdity which death threatens. The Other is absolutely Other in being that source which the I as the process of appropriation cannot provide for itself. The relation which is "without relation" is the breaking in of that source into the apparently self contained life of the existing subject.

This, then, in brief is the trajectory of Levinas's thought. From the *il y a*, impersonal, undifferentiated Being, arises the I living from the elemental in enjoyment. The implication of the elemental in the *il y a* reveals itself in what enjoyment cannot encompass, the absence of sense which leads to insecurity. This is mastered in the appropriation of labor in forming a common human world which is familiar and predictable. But alterity again disturbs the identifying process of the I in the form of death which cannot be domesticated. The absurdity with which death threatens the significance of life to the I is overcome through the "relation without relation" to the absolute Other which gives meaning to death in summoning the I to give itself and its world to the Other, to live for the Other. The Other can do this because its summons proceeds from a position of transcendence to the I and its world: this transcendence, this authority, is illeity or "God." The *il y a* is finally overcome and the I achieves its final reality in being for the Other, and so judged by God.

Levinas asks what can put a stop to the "imperialism" and "totalitarianism" of the I in its rendering of alterity as the Same, which is manifest in existing as dwelling and its reflection in the philosophy of the West. What disrupts this imperialism is death which cannot be mastered, and which therefore threatens the existing of the I with senselessness. The plausibility, therefore, of Levinas's account depends on accepting the unavoidability of the move to transcendence to counter the threat of death to life's meaningfulness. But is this unavoidable, is it, on Levinas's own terms, phenomenologically persuasive? Do Levinas's own analyses perhaps point in a different possible direction?

There are texts which at least seem to raise this possibility. One lies in his remark that God as "other with an alterity prior to the alterity of the other *(autrui)*" is "transcendent to the point of absence, to the point of a possible confusion with the stirring of the *il y a*" (CPP, 165–66). Another is the strange introduction in *Time and the Other* of the notion of absolute alterity through a discussion of death. The "approach of death indicates that we are in relation with something that is absolutely other, something bearing alterity not as a provisional determination we can assimilate through enjoyment, but as something whose very existence is made of alterity" (TO, 74). As translator Richard A. Cohen notes, the terms Levinas uses here and in the subsequent paragraph in the description of death "conjure up the encounter with the alterity of the other person" (TO, 75 n.). It is as if the phenomenological description of our relation with the Other (*Autrui*) risks sliding into one of our relation with the *il y a*.

In "Philosophy and the Idea of Infinity" Levinas characterizes my relation to the Other in three respects which counters the imperialism of the Same: (a) I encounter a resistance which is not one of power (but one which Levinas claims is ethical); (b) I have a relation to what I can absolutely not possess; and (c) which therefore shows our freedom is not only arbitrary but unjust (CPP, 53). But these respects could equally be accorded to my relation to the *il y a*. (a) In relation to the realm of the dissolution of the I, we are powerless, but not rendered such by a power. The *il y a* is no being which exercises power. (b) We cannot possess or in any way encompass the *il y a*, (c) and so our relation to it shows that the totalizing ambitions of the freedom of the I are unjustified. Furthermore, the phenomenological descriptions of the approach of the Other to the I which are a central concern of *Otherwise than Being* often seem indistinguishable from those which would apply to our relation to the *il y a*. It is a trauma (OTB, 12), creating a restlessness of the Same disturbed by the other

(OTB, 25). The approach de-poses or desituates the subject, stripping one of every quality, tearing up oneself in the core of one's unity (OTB, 49). "The *despite oneself* marks this life in its very living" (OTB, 51). Passivity characterizes the relation with the Other, it is a relation with what cannot appear (OTB, 100). And when we are told that "there is a non-coinciding of the ego with itself, restlessness, insomnia . . . pain which confounds the ego or in vertigo draws it like an abyss, and prevents it from assuming the other that wounds it . . . when it posits itself in itself and for itself . . . an overflowing of meaning by nonsense" (OTB, 64) this sounds only too appropriate for our relation with the *il y a*. When Levinas continues that then "sense bypasses nonsense-that sense which is the-same-for-the-other," I wonder why we should accept that this is phenomenologically justified as a reference to the Other *(Autrui)* and not to a coming into explicit relation with the *il y a*, a possibility I will consider shortly.

Or consider the issue of the temporality of the address of the Other. Time arises in dwelling in a familiar world through the emergence of the mastery of labor in relation to the insecurity of enjoyment of the elements. This temporality is that of purpose and the enjoyment of the elements, the projection of ends into a future horizon of illumination, out of a past horizon within which insecurity has manifested itself, revealing a present within which beings can be "mastered," revealed as permanent beings. It is the temporality of the realm of illumination of the familiar world, of the time "in which beings and entities show themselves in experience" (OTB, 31), of what Levinas calls "clock time." It is this temporality which is disrupted by the trauma of the proximity of the Other. Since this puts in question the I and its familiar world, the address of the Other "occurs" in a time other than the time of the world of illumination. "The proximity does not enter into the common time of clocks. . . . it is a disturbance" (OTB, 89). This is what Levinas calls "diachrony" (OTB, 31). The familiar world and its time are put in question by a summons which cannot be understood in terms of the present or a past present. The address has always already "occurred" in a "past more ancient than any present, a past which was never present" (OTB, 25). As a disturbance the I finds itself already always responsible for the Other, summoned to respond out of a time noncommensurable with the time of the world of illumination. The I is subjected to the order from the Other before hearing it (OTB, 150).

But again, couldn't this temporality equally be accorded to the disturbance of the familiar world by the *il y a*? The horizons of the familiar world stand in an essential relation to the *il y a*: the "element I inhabit is at the frontier of a night" and this "nocturnal dimension of the future" is the *il y a* (TI, 142). The relation to the *il y a* is outside the temporality of experience within which beings can manifest themselves. The *il y a* "is" in "a past more ancient than any present" too, and its disruption puts in question the familiar world from out of that past, and does so without the possibility of mastery, of illumination: it is the "ever-new depth of absence" (TI, 142). The disruption of the *il y a* seems phenomenologically indistinguishable from the proximity of the Other.

The point here is that it is the relation to the *il y a* which shows the impossibility of the "imperialism" of the Same, of totality, or the mastery of reality in a total comprehension. The *il y a* is "beyond thought" but in the sense of the impossibility of finality within human forms of thought which have contact with "reality." We might say: meaning is always generated in relation to resistance, to a fundamental concealment or mystery, which can provoke new thinking. This is what makes forms of thought and life which contain a conception of the real *binding* in a way the normativity of the rules of a game are not. We can change such rules in terms of human desires and purposes, but the normativity of language games which contain a conception of the real is independent of desire and purpose. If we can account for the authority of such forms of thought in this way, then there is no need to refer them to a transcendent authority. Levinas seems to feel that without such a reference to a position transcendent to the historicality of human life, the life and thought of dwelling would lack the authority for us which would allow us to talk of contact with the real. He thinks, therefore, that we must divest the contents of such life and thought from "possession" (from being merely human) in order to see them "as they are" in terms of the relation to the transcendent Other. But this is to fail to recognize that the relation to alterity which is essential to the production of meaning on Levinas's own account may be sufficient to account for the authority required to show a connection with the way things "are." The unreflective language of "dwelling" contains within itself what can provoke reflection since its forms of thought have been formed in an essential relation to alterity. As containing what prevents finality, they embody already what puts them in question.

There are a variety of models for this within modern European thought. Heidegger's understanding of the "truth of Being" as the unconcealment/concealment structure of the illumination ("world") within which beings can presence, and so of the essential otherness of the real in respect of any particular dispensation within which beings can appear, is central here. It is precisely this otherness, this mystery, which is the source of authority of the historically given ways within which beings can manifest themselves. As Heidegger remarks in the "Letter on Humanism," "Only so far as man, eksisting into the truth of Being, belongs to Being can there come from Being itself the assignment of those directions that must become law and rule for man."[5] It may be thought however, as with Blanchot and Derrida, that this reference to Being sounds too much like a reference to a ground beyond concrete forms of thought, while what is needed is to emphasize that the resistance to totality lies *within* thought itself. I mentioned above the connection between Levinas's *il y a* and Blanchot's "other night." The other night is what resists finality in thought; it is the incessant murmur which "speaks" in language when it says nothing which is the possibility of meaning otherwise which inhabits any sense that we make out of language. Blanchot too calls this "anonymous, impersonal being, the Non-true, the Nonreal yet always there."[6] Derrida's *tout autre*, the "absolute other," may also be cited here. We formulate determinate meanings only through a relation to what destabilizes, undermines the finality of any meaning, and so in a relation to a future. But this is not a future present, which is the realm of the possible, that which may be present in the future, but to the "absolute future," that which makes all future presents possible but which can never be present. It cannot be conceived: it is impossible. It is known only through its effects, the destabilizing of meaning, the impossibility of any final meaning. Other "others" are that relation to which gives the effect of meaning to anything present, whereas the absolute other is what makes possible this differential play. It functions only as opening up the present to the unconceived and is, therefore, inconceivable, beyond conceptuality. Derrida speaks of this as one way of saving the name of God, but it is not transcendent in the Levinasian sense, not a position from which history may be held to account. Rather, it is "within" historical forms of language as the necessary possibility of meaning otherwise. It functions as, we might say, the essential relation to the *il y a* of such forms.

This is not the place to discuss the merits of these and other similar developments. What I have wanted to suggest here is rather that the resources of Levinas's own position may be used to obviate the need he clearly feels for the move to transcendence. Ostensibly, the invasion of the *il y a* into subjectivity through death threatens the life of dwelling and the I's existence with meaninglessness. That life and existence can now only be given meaning by a relation to what is beyond them, the absolute Other, which puts them in question and summons them to live for the Other. However, there seems no reason why the relation to death may not rather prompt a reflection on the necessary presence of the *il y a* in the formation of meaning and a conscious relating to that presence. The *il y a* would then appear as the resistance which provokes meaning and which prevents finality within language itself. It would then be precisely this resistance which gives authority to our forms of thinking, making them "binding" on us, while at the same time putting these forms of thought in question from within. It may be further suggested that such an "immanent alterity" may then be appealed to in order to justify a significance which human beings and the world have over and beyond our conceptions of them, and so serve to provide a basis for human ethics and a renewed notion of the sacred which can support an environmental concern which does not depend on human purposes (something to which Levinas's thought seems alien). Levinas's phenomenological analyses cannot motivate the move to transcendence, to the absolute Other, and can, in fact, be used to suggest the recognition of the "absolute other" within the language of dwelling itself.

II

Kierkegaard would not have been surprised by the failure to provide a phenomenological exhibition of human life which requires for its description the relation to God. It is a form of philosophical demonstration which is inappropriate in respect of the individual's relation to ethical and religious concerns. The individual has a relation to her own life which she cannot have to any other: ethics and religion constitute forms of that relation. They are responses to the question of the meaningfulness of the individual's life, a question which can only be raised in the first person. They are not, therefore, subject to a demonstration which is the result of disinterested enquiry which claims an impersonal validity. Christianity is an "existential communication": it is not an objective claim but an answer to this question. Climacus says, "Christianity, therefore, protests against all objectivity: it wants the subject to be infinitely concerned about himself. What it asks about is the subjectivity; the truth of Christianity, if it is at all, is only in this; objectively it is not at all. And even if it is only in one single subject, it is only in him" (CUP, 130).

An existential communication is one in relation to subjective truth—that notion of truth which relates to subjectivity, the relation of the I to their own life. In respect of this kind of truth certain kinds of communication are appropriate which are not those concerned with objective truth. These forms of communication characterize Kierkegaard's authorship. On the one hand are the upbuilding discourses: "An upbuilding discourse about love presupposes that men know essentially what love is and seeks to win them to it, to move them" (JP, entry 641). It addresses fellow devotees, encouraging, strengthening and clarifying their commitment to, in this case, Christian life. On the other hand, we find what Kierkegaard calls "reflective" discourses, which include the pseudonymous authorship. This kind of discourse, in the case of Christendom, is required because Kierkegaard suspects that those who claim to lead the Christian life do not do so because they do not understand the nature of that life. Reflections are directed toward getting the recipients to attain a self-knowledge, that they are living in illusion. In Christendom, where Christianity has been proclaimed for centuries, "one does not reflect oneself into Christianity; but one reflects oneself out of something else."[7]

The character of the illusion is that Christianity is not understood as subjective truth, as a response to the personal issue of the meaning of life, an issue which is always in the first person, but in an objective or quasi-objective way. There is an intellectual and a non-intellectual form to this. The latter is thinking that being a Christian is simply a matter of doing what others do in a Christian society like that of Denmark. The intellectual form is to think that the issue of the meaning of life is the subject of disinterested, scholarly inquiry whether philosophical or historical. Both of these are ways of evading the responsibility of the "I" for the meaning of her own life: that responsibility is off loaded onto tradition or onto the nature of reality. In this way, the illusion of the modern age is to have "abolished the 'I', the personal 'I'" through making "everything objective" (JP, entry 656). Kierkegaard's indirect communications are directed toward intervening in this illusion, in recalling readers to themselves, to the responsibility they have for their own lives, to regaining what he calls a "primitive impression" of existence. The age has forgotten "what it means to be a human being" (JP, entry 649.3): each one of us is an "I," each one for themselves. Each of us has a relation to our own lives which we cannot have to any other.

The removal of such illusion leaves the individual alone, to make what she will of her life. The formula for such communication is "to stand alone by another's help" (JP, entry 650.15). The communicator "stands behind the other man, helping him negatively"[8] so the "entire work is repulsion" (JP, entry 6574). The ethical and the ethico-religious "can only be communicated by an I to an I" (JP, entry 656). In indirect communication, there is no doctrine, and the communicator does not try to persuade the other. The communicator disappears, for the recipient must remove her own illusion to be able to be left to herself. "To stop a man on the street and to stand still in order to speak with him is not as difficult as having to say something to a passerby in passing, without standing still oneself or delaying the other, without wanting to induce him to go the same way, but just urging him to go his own way—and such is the relation between an existing person and an existing person when the communication pertains to the truth as existence-inwardness" (CUP, 277). But what, then, are the possibilities of making sense of one's own life when one has a "primitive impression" of existence?

In *Either/Or* Judge William identifies an existence relationship as a life view, "a conception of the meaning of life and of its purpose" (E/O II, 179) and claims that one must either live an aesthetic or an ethical conception of this significance.[9] Such a view is supplemented rather than negated by a religious conception which appears as an accentuation and concentration on the relation to the infinite or eternal which is already involved, as the Judge repeatedly asserts, in the ethical. One can only come to the religious through the ethical, and the ethical maintains its claim, although relativized now by the primacy of the claim of the infinite itself.

The aesthetic Kierkegaard refers to in the *Journals* as the "secular" view (JP, entry 492) and is characteristic of paganism (CUP, 387). It locates the significance of life in finitude, that is, in the achievement and maintenance of conditions within time. It is quite compatible with, indeed requires, valuing some of these conditions unconditionally, that is, with love.[10] It is compatible too with a universal, in the sense of human, interpretation (as opposed to its individual or group form), and with the development of a morality in which one recognizes one's duties to others in terms of the unconditional valuing of certain earthly conditions.[11] What differentiates the aesthetic view from the ethical for Kierkegaard lies in its finding the value of life as lying in some temporal conditions (human happiness, say, or the excelling characteristic of Greek aristocratic ethics).

The ethical requires the rejection of this valuing of finitude; it requires seeing the vanity of all things (E/O II, 212). In turning away from the temporal to the eternal or infinite, one turns toward what is universal in the sense of being able to encompass any human condition whatever, as opposed to the "relativism," resting on differences between persons, of the aesthetic (JP, entry 492). It is, therefore, a religious orientation (Kierkegaard is thinking primarily of the ethics which those calling themselves Christians should recognize), but one which is lived actively in the world by living human relationships and activities in a relation to the eternal so that what occurs cannot affect the value of the individual's life. One transforms one's temporal attachments into eternal and so unconditional *commitments* so that how things go cannot abnegate them. The religious cast of the ethical is marked by the fact that Kierkegaard says that it must keep open "the place for the extraordinary" who live their lives in terms of sacrifice (JP, entry 4469). Ethical individuals must recognize the primacy of the eternal, God, and so the God relationship in their lives, and therefore the primacy of the specifically religious vocation which is not universal (in the sense of being religiously required by all) but particular, in being a matter of vocation. However, the ethical individual, engaged in transforming her attachments into eternal commitments remains therefore attached to the worldly. In this way, the temporal maintains a hold on the value the individual finds in her life, although, insofar as she is true to the ethical, this will be subordinated to the demands of the eternal.

The religious summons is to turn inward in "dying to the world," actively severing one's attachment to the world so that suffering in terms of human attachment to the temporal is replaced by the suffering involved in voluntarily giving up one's earthly attachments. Kierkegaard characterizes it as "martyrdom" (JP, entry 2643), witnessing to the direct relation to the eternal through this asceticism. He says it is solely concerned with the individual's own salvation (JP, entry 2053). This constitutes the position of Religiousness A in *Concluding Unscientific Postscript*. As active asceticism, it is something we can take on in terms of our own powers, but we cannot of those powers transform ourselves into beings who solely and perfectly will the infinite (our will would become God's will). It is here that the Christian belief in the atonement and salvation enter. To have faith is to believe that one's failure to will what is God's will is forgiven and that one is promised the eternal happiness which would unite one's will with God's. Religiousness B in *Concluding Unscientific Postscript,* and the Knight of Faith in *Fear and Trembling,* present this possibility, which, if it occurs, does so by grace alone. We cannot of ourselves achieve atonement or the hope of eternal happiness. Christ is the pattern of the human whose will is solely God's will so that all human sufferings (poverty, wretchedness, sickness, loss of status, and so forth) are reckoned as nothing (JP, entry 483). This is the good news and why this doctrine is the offense for those who live in terms of human values. Even if one suffers the greatest misfortune humanly considered, this is still conceived as a good (JP, entry 957) so that one gives thanks always.

This religious context is articulated by Kierkegaard in terms of "absolute difference" and the "paradox." A paradox is not nonsense, but rather something which cannot be demonstrated to thought and which is offensive to the realm within which things can be demonstrated. The paradoxes of the religious concern belief in God as the Absolute and faith in Christ. The first paradox is to know the "absolute difference" between God and the human (JP, entry 3081): that the measure for human life lies outside it, the manifestation of which requires an intervention into human aesthetic life. The second paradox is that God in this sense is identical with an individual man, Christ. The absolute paradox is that we are to become like Christ, which is only possible through the Atonement and the promise of an eternal happiness. These paradoxes cannot be demonstrated or exhibited, and if they are believed this itself is a matter of grace and not the result of the exercise of human capacities.

What, then, are the possibilities for the selfhood of the I in terms of these life views? The self has a history, and its nature is given by the sort of continuity involved in the story it can tell about itself. The aesthetic self has her history of strivings for finite goods, her successes and failures due to contingencies. The ethical individual has her internal history of strivings to choose herself in relation to the eternal. The religious individual has her history of dying to the world and the activity of grace in her life. Kierkegaard is a Christian writer addressing an audience which takes itself to be Christian. He therefore recognizes that true (Christian) selfhood is attained only in a relation to an eternal happiness and what that then requires, and expects other Christians to do so too. But, as Christianity is an existential communication, this at the same time requires Kierkegaard to recognize that this cannot be regarded as a demonstrable truth. Ethico-religious and even more so Christian life require recognition of the activity of the Infinite/God: whether one sees the primacy of the eternal and gives oneself to it, or whether one believes in the "eternal in time," are acts of "grace." But the aesthetic individual will regard these as illusions: she doesn't believe in grace or the activity of the eternal. The most Kierkegaard's interventions can hope for, on his own understanding, is to return the individual to a "primitive impression" of existence and so create an opening within which "grace" can operate. Kierkegaard may be regarded as a thinker of *faith*, of what that concept really requires us to accept.

But there remains a question: Why do the existential possibilities take just these forms? The answer seems to be that Kierkegaard takes it for granted that the notion of a self can only be formed in terms of some fixed telos. Such a goal is provided by an ideal toward which development or from which degeneration is measured: for the Christian, the person of Christ, for the ethical individual, the responsible citizen, for the Greek pagan perhaps Pericles or some other hero or heroine. The division would then be between an eternal standard which one can neither recognize nor achieve of oneself (Christianity), an eternally validated standard which the (Christian) ethical individual recognizes as an intervention of grace but which she can strive toward, and a temporal standard given in time and to be achieved in time. Kierkegaard makes clear this assumption in his criticism of Schlegel in *The Concept of Irony* for not possessing such a goal. Unlike the Christian, the ethical individual or the aesthetic Greek, he says, Schlegel does not have an absolute objective. Only if the individual has such a conception can she become for herself *(für sich)* what she is in herself *(an sich)*. The Schlegelian ironist has no fixed point at which his life is aimed since for him all roles are simply material for play (CI, 282).

I have argued elsewhere[12] that this misrepresents Schlegel and fails to recognize the radicality of his position. I read Schlegel as proposing a new model of the self and one which connects up with the developments I referred to above in connection with Blanchot and Derrida. What is essential to such a model is that it does not have a coherence given by a relation to a telos given by aesthetic nature or the eternal, but rather through a relation to the source of change, of the new, to what cannot be grasped, over which there can be no mastery, since it is the source of the concepts which are the instruments of understanding and control. One relates to it only in the attempt to think or live differently, to remain open to the advent of the new. Such a life can indeed have a continuity and a history, but not that toward a given ideal, but something more like we find in the development of a tradition of art, where the continuity is seen retrospectively rather than prospectively. It would have a new sense of self, having the continuity not of fate (the aesthetic self) nor will (the ethical self) nor grace (the religious self), but perhaps of living history which unfolds in an attempt to keep the future open.

We can argue that Kierkegaard himself ought to recognize such a possibility. I have a relation to my own life which I cannot have to any other: this necessitates that I take over my existence for myself. This is the "primitive impression" of existence through which I am summoned to responsibility for my own life. But this means that this breaking open of responsibility reveals the *horizons* of temporality for my life: the future is open and the past not fixed but a source of possibility. Kierkegaard objects to the quasi-objective understanding of existence which seeks to evade responsibility through seeing the past as fixed and the future as already conceptually determined. Yet he then proposes the only subjective responses to subjectivity to lie in the projection of fixed ideals, thus once again enclosing the future in conceptual determination and the past in determinate judgment. This fails to recognize the more fundamental alternative: relating to the temporality of subjectivity itself. (No doubt this is what Heidegger had in mind when he claimed that Kierkegaard's analyses remained at the *existentiell* level and did not attain the *existential*.)[13] This is a relation through which the conceptually new may manifest itself: it is a relation which recognizes the historicality of human life and that historicality involves the emergence of new forms of thought and life as *binding* on us. What is it which makes this possible? It is the opacity of language in terms of which we have our lives and the world and which renders them resistant to a final reading. This is perhaps, as Blanchot maintains, revealed in literature, where life and the world are manifest in their ambiguous linguistic form. It is the givenness of language which is Levinas's *il y a*. The temporality of the *il y a*, as we have seen, is that of a past beyond a past present, and a future beyond any future present, a givenness beyond presentation, which if thought results in paradoxes. It makes itself felt, rather, in the summons to responsiveness to what is given us in language. We always have to take over the past so that the future and past always exceed what can be made present. This responsiveness perhaps requires now above all a recovery of a sense of the opacity of existence, its mystery, and through this perhaps a sense of the sacredness of the earth as what we are dependent on but which is in no way dependent on a human vocation for an eternal happiness or a relation to a transcendent Other. And, of course, it is only because the texts of

Kierkegaard and Levinas are implicated in the *il y a* that they remain to be interpreted.

III

We may then contrast two senses which might be given to the notion of absolute difference, one we may term "deconstructionist" and the other "salvationist." The former recognizes what we could call the radical contingency of meaning. The production of meaning depends on a relation to what at the same time makes meaning in the sense of unity impossible, a relation to what prevents finality. The later Heidegger's notion of the granting of historical worlds which means that Being is always excessive to any particular historical horizon provokes the thought of Blanchot and Derrida toward recognizing a difference within meaning. Meaning depends on difference, on context, but there is nothing which can bring the play of difference to an end, there is no final context. But then the identity of the differends is itself fissured: in order to be the meanings they are, they must contain, if you like, the possibility to mean differently. This "other in the same" is what disrupts the unity of meaning while making possible new meaning. If "relative difference" presupposes the identity of the relata whose qualities may then differ, then this sense of "absolute difference" is of a difference within the relata which, while making possible the appearance of identity, prevents it in the sense of a determinate unity. The *il y a* in Levinas has this character.

That the absolute difference in Levinas allows the I to overcome the *il y a* suggests that we might characterize the salvationist notion as nullifying the role of radical contingency in relation to meaning. The I as the process of identification, unable to master alterity and so attain unity, is granted an overall sense by the absolute Other in being summoned to give itself. Alterity is overcome not by mastery but by sacrifice. Similarly, in Kierkegaard the absolute difference of God is what enables the self to attain the unity of a relation to an eternal happiness beyond the power which contingency has to disrupt both the pagan attainment of *eudaimonia* and the ethical task of commitment to the eternal over against one's attachment to the temporal. If relative difference presupposes the identity of the relata whose qualities may then differ, then here absolute difference is what grants identity to the self over and beyond its own capacities.

Perhaps philosophically we cannot go beyond sketching these differences. If there is faith, or, I would also say, the approach of the Other in Levinas's sense, then this is by grace alone: that is, Wittgenstein would say, a "grammatical remark." But whether there is grace, or if it is not rather an illusion, that is not something to be determined philosophically.

Notes

1. "Philosophy and the Idea of Infinity," in CPP, 50.
2. See, for example, TI, 142, 160; OTB, 164.

3. M. Blanchot, *The Space of Literature,* trans. A Smock (London, 1982), 167.

4. Ibid.,164.

5. M. Heidegger, *Basic Writings,* ed. D. Krell (London, 1978), 239.

6. Blanchot, *The Space of Literature,* 31.

7. S. Kierkegaard, *The Point of View for My Work as an Author,* trans. W. Lowrie (London, 1962), 144.

8. Kierkegaard, *Point of View,* 43.

9. "Aesthetic" in Kierkegaard can either refer to an existence lacking a "primitive impression" of existence and which is living, therefore, in illusion, or a concrete "life view," characteristic, for example, of paganism.

10. See, for example, JP, entries 1955, 2417, and 1823.

11. See, for example, JP, entries 1509 and 2420.

12. M. Weston, "Kierkegaard and the Origins of the Post-Modern 'Self,'" *European Journal of Philosophy* 10, no. 3 (2002): 398–412.

13. M. Heidegger, *Being and Time,* trans. J. Macquarrie and E. Robinson (Oxford, 1967), 494.

8 What Kierkegaardian Faith Adds to Alterity Ethics: How Levinas and Derrida Miss the Eschatological Dimension

John J. Davenport

Introduction: Three Higher-Ethics Approaches to *Fear and Trembling*

In recent decades, a number of scholars have argued that a close relationship exists between the alterity ethics of Emmanuel Levinas and Jacques Derrida on the one hand, and Kierkegaard's agapic ethics and portrayal of faith as a subjective process of individualization on the other. While I agree with M. Jamie Ferreira, Merold Westphal, John Caputo, and others that there are fruitful connections to be developed between Levinas's version of agapic duty and Kierkegaard's neighbor love ethic, I will argue (1) that Derrida's version of infinite responsibility offers little for the Kierkegaardian project of developing a sound agapic ethic and (2) that the distinguishing element of Kierkegaardian faith is eschatological hope, the significance of which is appreciated neither in Levinas's critique nor in Derrida's defense of *Fear and Trembling*. This argument is part of a larger critique of what I call "higher-ethics" interpretations of the "teleological suspension of the ethical" discussed by Kierkegaard's pseudonym Johannes de Silentio in the first Problema of *Fear and Trembling* (FT, 56).

In general, higher-ethics readings hold that when Silentio says Abraham's faith goes beyond the ethical, he means that Abraham obeys a higher duty, calling, or type of obligation that is contrasted with Hegelian social morality or (more broadly) with moral laws or universal precepts derived from any rational ground of understanding (Aristotelian, Kantian, utilitarian, moral sense, etc.). Thus the movement from Kierkegaard's ethical stage to the religious life-view consists primarily in a transition from ethics as the herd or the philosopher understands it to a singularizing ethical attitude that transcends all common moral codes sanctioned by tradition, government, culture, or even natural reason in general.[1] In particular, most higher-ethics readings of *Fear and Trembling* hold that the telos toward which ordinary moral laws are suspended is the duty to obey a revealed commandment to love others for their own sake, that is, an agapic ideal.

In a recent essay, I distinguish three main genuses of this approach.[2] The *strong divine command* interpretation (SDC) holds that Abraham's faith consists in absolute obedience to God's commands, which are arbitrary in the sense that they are not themselves governed by any independent standard. This view identifies Kierkegaardian faith—at least in *Fear and Trembling*—with the strongest form of theological voluntarism according to which all genuine moral obligation derives from general or singular divine imperatives, the right-making authority of which does not depend on them being constrained by any prior motives or principles: since God's authority rests purely on His power (or ownership of all He creates), He could command *any* X and thereby make X a duty for us. The passage that best supports this reading is: "He knew . . . that no sacrifice is too severe when God demands it—and he drew the knife" (FT, 22). Even though the singular imperative to Abraham seems to contradict all known duties, Abraham has a higher duty to obey it, no matter what. Patrick Gardiner suggests this reading, for example, when he says that for Kierkegaard, someone might be given an "'exceptional' mission, to be fulfilled at *whatever* the cost."[3]

By contrast, agapic command ethics (ACE) readings say that in Kierkegaardian faith, our highest duties—if not all moral obligations—derive from the commands of a *loving* God.[4] While this view is more plausibly attributed to Kierkegaard, especially in his late signed writings such as *Works of Love*, it does not so obviously apply to Abraham in *Fear and Trembling*: while sacrificing Isaac can easily be seen as obedience to an arbitrary singular divine command, how can it be seen as obedience to the commands of a God whose authority lies in His being Love? Perhaps God has a right to demand back any gift that He gave us if it is misused, or if its receiver loves it too possessively; or perhaps God has a secret good purpose that Abraham does not know; but Silentio does not consider any such explanations in *Fear and Trembling*.

Thus plausible ACE readings must hold both that the ethical which is suspended in faith is only Hegelian *Sittlichkeit* or Kantian *Moralität* rather than the agapic command ethics of Kierkegaard's religious works, and that belief in the love commandments would make it virtually impossible for us to be justified in believing that God issued a command to kill an innocent person.[5] If this is right, then the Abraham example in *Fear and Trembling* turns out to be of limited value for understanding religious faith: it only gives us the schematic outline of faith as loyalty to a God whose loving will is a higher standard than *Sittlichkeit*, without reflecting much of its higher ethical *content*. Its main point, as C. Stephen Evans puts it, is to defend "the transcendence of the divine."[6] Similarly, Westphal suggests that "the teleological suspension of the ethical is thus the movement of faith that recognizes the will of God and not the laws and customs of my people as the highest norm for my existence."[7] Gardiner agrees: "The absolute sovereignty of the ethical" in the social or immanent sense is "transcended by a perspective" in which the individual may be "subject to the demands of a unique calling."[8] But on ACE readings, such a calling could not result from a singular command to despise others, fail to love them, or harm them just for the sake of harm.

As my description is intended to emphasize, the distinction between SDC and ACE views depends on the concept of agapic love having some content that is understandable by us, however imperfectly, prior to accepting the authority of God's will as the highest (or even sole) source of moral normativity. ACE collapses into SDC if "loving my neighbor" is simply defined as obeying *any* decree taken as divine will, whatever its content. There is now a lively debate about whether this is what *Works of Love* teaches. Against Evans, Westphal agrees with Jack Mulder[9] that for Kierkegaard, love of God and love of human neighbors can never conflict just because what counts as loving anyone is determined by God's will (rather than the reverse): "This means that for the knight of faith who is commanded by God to sacrifice his son, that sacrifice becomes the right way to love the son."[10] Presumably this means that an act whose final end is *simply and only* obedience to such a command could count as loving.[11] But if the content of agapic love is this fungible, then God's nature as Love could not ground His authority in the way Evans envisions: His commands would bind solely because of His absolute power and they would count as loving only by definitional tautology.

The third main genus of the higher-ethics approach I call aretaic love ethics (ALE); it rejects universal rules and regards only singular responses to unique situations as authentically loving. This third approach itself comes in several varieties, some of which are inspired primarily by neo-Aristotelian critiques of Kantian and utilitarian efforts to unify moral norms in a single ultimate principle, or to ground morality in rational autonomy or natural sympathy. Among these, the most subtle and insightful is Edward Mooney's carefully developed aretaic conception of ethical responsiveness as including awareness of dilemmas, sensitivity to the uniqueness of individuals, and wholistic evaluation of concrete circumstances.[12] Mooney emphasizes that Silentio assumes "an objectivity of moral value. He never doubts that fathers should love their sons or that Abraham should love his God."[13] But a conventionalist or rationalist ethics "eliminates anything like separate, individual persons, each of priceless worth" and is not flexible enough to account for the virtues of integrity and freedom in developing one's own unique identity. Thus

> Faith is "higher" than social, civic, or rational morality. But not because it provides grounds for overriding ethics . . . Faith is "higher" because for someone having weathered its ordeals, it can be felt, retrospectively, to have transformed and completed a moral outlook all-too-familiar yet finally provisional. Faith enscribes space for a new ethics.[14]

In Mooney's view, then, it is only at the level of religious faith that the full value of individual persons as unique objects of essentially particularistic care is recognized; we become individuals in an absolute relation to the God who transforms lower ethics in this personalistic way, giving us back what was valuable in "the universal" by a divine response tailored to our unique identity. This is similar in important respects to Evans's idea that "the selves we must become" are unique both in the sense that our universally human duties apply differentially to our particular situation and in the additional sense that "there are genuinely individual tasks as well."[15] This accurately reflects Kierkegaard's idea that each person has a distinct and divinely ordained calling.[16]

In this chapter, however, I will focus on the alterity ethics species of ALE, by which I mean readings that see Kierkegaard's conception of faith as anticipating the Levinasian idea that moral obligation arises from a fundamental relation or experience of another person (or the plurality of persons) as absolutely unique in value and/or status, beyond knowledge or constitution by the transcendental ego. Like Kantian accounts of moral necessity, alterity ethics emphasizes that the basic obligation to respond to others is *involuntary* in an important sense: it is binding without contract or optional undertaking on our part. Like Kant, Levinas requires a motive that is pure of self-interest, since it is not even formally aimed at one's own self-realization or *eudaimonia*. Kant and Levinas also agree that the moral *faktum* that obligates us, to which this pure motive responds, is prior to all theoretical knowledge and inseparable from the standpoint of responsible agency. This makes the revelation of duty in the face of the other somewhat like a revealed command beyond natural knowledge, despite Levinas's insistence that it is distinct from all "revealed opinions of positive religions" (TI, 23). Unlike Kant (and neo-Kantians such as Korsgaard and Habermas), alterity ethicists (alteritists?)[17] do not allow this originary responsibility to be explained as an implicit commitment of free rational agency, or to be captured in any articulable norm applying symmetrically to myself and the other. Drawing on ideas that trace primarily to Martin Buber and Franz Rosenzweig, alteritists hold that since what commands us to responsibility is the radical otherness of the person as unique neighbor, justice or goodness in its originary sense cannot be reduced to a principle or set of principles, but instead transcends any lawlike system of norms.[18] The duty of absolute generosity or self-donation subtends anything like a list of basic human rights.

Alterity ethics therefore tends to be *antitheoretical*, resisting any rational explanation of the origin of obligation in the requirements of shared *eudaimonia* or the inviolable value that autonomous agency must see in itself. Rather, the difference between persons from which responsibility arises subverts the adequacy of any universal moral laws: for the most basic moral motive made possible by our openness to (or constitution by) alterity is an *absolutely singular* response to the neighbor that transcends linguistic fixity. It is enacted in *how* we speak and respond (the "saying"), not in *what* we say or the determinate content of our acts (the "said"). Rules, rights, and laws may retain an important place in our practices, but since they can only govern the content of actions rather than the adverbial *how*, they are consigned to a derivative and always incomplete level of ethical understanding. They are mere *dianoia* next to the transcendent ethical *noesis* of alterity.

There are many interesting questions about the potential of such an alterity account as an explanation of the agapic ideal.[19] While there are other versions of agapic ethics, alterity versions tend to suggest the challenging possibility that an existential virtue ethics focusing on agape as its *pros hen* may really be a fourth basic position in normative ethics, irreducible to utilitarianism, *eudaimonist* virtue ethics, or even deontological theories of obligation and the good life. This distinct position is hardly without content; in particular, it holds that the moral status of persons is based on what I call their *unappropriability:* the metaphysical difference between myself and another person lies not in contingent physical or psychological variances, but in an absolute independence from my will and thought that makes it impossible for me to *possess* him. I can never acquire a right to own another because I cannot create alterity; and even if I have another person in my power, my control can never be absolute. This is an important and novel way of reinterpreting Kant's central idea that persons deserve respect because of their freedom and capacity for moral motivation. The agapic approach deepens the idea of individual uniqueness and expands the kinds of moral motivation possible in response to this uniqueness beyond the conception of duties in classical deontology. Yet the antitheoretical bias of alterity ethics, combined with the tendency among Christian philosophers to see agapic duty as strictly limited to theological contexts (assuming that its obligatory status depends solely on revealed divine command), have conspired to keep the full potential of an agapic virtue ethics from being recognized and developed as a fourth basic type of moral theory.

Notably, Aquinas and Kierkegaard agree that to understand and respond well to agapic obligations requires faith, making agapic virtues part of a "second ethics" that lies beyond any natural law accessible to human reason and natural sentiments. This is why it has proven so tempting simply to *identify* Kierkegaardian faith with this second ethics: faith then consists precisely in loving obedience to God and loving service to human neighbors.[20] Yet this thesis, which is shared by all the higher-ethics readings of the pseudonymous works, is wrong: it misses the *eschatological* core of "faith" or religiousness in Kierkegaard's sense. In what follows, I will argue that this error explains how alterity accounts of *Fear and Trembling* became possible.

The Eschatological Element in Existential Faith Versus Levinasian Alterity Ethics

The Absolute as Source of Eschatological Possibilities

Here is a brief summary of the eschatological reading of *Fear and Trembling* to which I've alluded:[21] the telos toward which Abraham suspends his ethical duties to Isaac is the absurd possibility of Isaac's survival *despite* God's requirement that he be sacrificed. The scenario involves all the following elements:

1. *An ethical ideal* E that is *not* rejected or transcended as a moral imperative: the agent must continue to recognize and to will this ideal. (In Abraham's case, he must love Isaac with his whole soul.)
2. *An obstacle* O to the ethical ideal: the human agent is prevented from achieving his or her moral ideal by some misfortune, problem, or set of circumstances that make it practically impossible for the agent to secure it by his or her own powers. (In Abraham's case, the obstacle itself is religious: it is God's mysterious and terrible command to give Isaac back to Him, as it were.)
3. *Infinite resignation* (∞R): having concentrated his or her entire identity in commitment to E, the agent accepts that E is humanly unattainable because of O: E is accessible to his or her agency only as an ideal in atemporal eternity.[22] Thus the agent either stops actively pursuing E by his or her own endeavors, or pursues it out of pure principle without any hope of thereby realizing E. (Abraham is resigned in this sense; he accepts that he cannot save Isaac if God demands him.)
4. An *eschatological promise* (from God or His prophets) that E will be actualized by divine power within the created order of existence—either *within time*, or in *the hereafter* as a new temporal series (rather than as a Platonic *aeternitas*). (In Abraham's case, God has promised him that Isaac will become the father of a holy nation to bring the Word to all peoples.)
5. *The absurd:* the content of the eschatological promise, which is only eschatologically possible given O (and thus appears unintelligible outside of faith). (For Abraham, the absurd is Isaac surviving by God's power to fulfill his promised role, *despite* being sacrificed.)
6. *Faith,* in what we may call the "existential" sense, is defined in terms of elements 1–5 above: the agent infinitely resigns E, yet trusting entirely in the eschatological promise, stakes her/his identity on the belief that E will actualized by God. ("Even in the moment when the knife gleamed," Abraham believed that he would get Isaac back "by virtue of the absurd" [FT, 36]).

Existential faith is thus a type of eschatological hope. Eschatology in its most general sense refers to the final realization of the Good by divine power in this temporal order or its successor.[23]

A command to transgress familiar ethical norms is *not* essential to existential faith on this analysis: usually the obstacle to E is *not* a divine command to violate E, but something more familiar, like sin, finitude, or mortality, for example. Nor does Abraham really violate the universal moral requirement (already known at his time) that the father shall love the son: for, given his existential faith, he does not believe that he *is* murdering Isaac—permanently ending his life. The ethical is suspended toward the telos of eternal salvation (FT, 54) or the eschatological Good in just the sense that for Abraham, the moral law can be *fulfilled*—not rejected or abrogated—only with the aid of grace: his striving to uphold ethical ideals depends for its ultimate significance or meaningfulness on revealed eschatological possibilities. Thus in faith, we relate to the universal moral law *through* our personal trust in the covenantal God, the Person who promises eschatological resolutions not deducible from natural theology (FT, 70).

The basic idea developed in this eschatological interpretation of Silentio's Akedah is not new: it is found in Alastair Hannay's commentary[24] and plays a larger or smaller role in a number of ACE readings. Edward Mooney especially emphasizes Abraham's belief "that the very God who requires Isaac will also provide for his safe return." Thus "Kierkegaardian faith is not blind obedience."[25] Similarly, Evans points out that Abraham's faith is not demonstrated by his willingness to sacrifice Isaac, but rather by "Abraham's ability to receive Isaac back again with joy"[26] because he never lost trust that God would return Isaac (FT, 20–22). "He believes that even though God has asked him to sacrifice Isaac, somehow Isaac will not be sacrificed, or that if he is sacrificed, God will raise Isaac from the dead" (FT, 36).[27] Westphal concurs: both the knights of resignation and faith are willing to give up what is most precious. "The difference is that the latter, in the person of Abraham, hopes, by virtue of the absurd, to get Isaac back in this life."[28] Similarly, Gardiner says that Abraham "was prepared to resist the dictates of ordinary morality" and "he further believed—against every rational expectation—that he would in some fashion 'receive back' the son he had been commanded to sacrifice."[29]

But none of these interpretations adequately *connect* this trust in a miraculous fulfillment of ethical duty on the strength of God's initial promise with the higher agapic ethical ideal. If an ethical standpoint that respects individual uniqueness above universal law is what's central to Kierkegaardian religiousness, why not develop this idea without the "baggage" from revealed religion? This is the logic behind the alterity approach to *Fear and Trembling,* in a nutshell. For example, Mooney speaks of a "God so placed as to return Isaac or to provide a ground of value or to underwrite individuality."[30] But are these the same or inseparably connected aspects of the divine? Do we need the first disjunct, if the goal is to find a basis for the incomparable preciousness of each person *qua* individual? Levinas seems to do without Kierkegaard's hope for salvation, yet still to find himself "vulnerable both to the intrinsic value of persons . . . and to an ultimate source of their value."[31] Thus if the point of Silentio's Problema II is simply that "God transcends the social order" and so "an absolute duty to God would . . . relativize one's ordinary ethical duties,"[32] then why not replace God with my neighbor or the Levinasian other? This is exactly what Derrida does in his argument that God is "to be found everywhere there is something of the wholly other," namely, everywhere a human person exists: "What can be said about Abraham's relation to God can be said about my relation without relation to *every other (one),*" since the relation is "secret" and singularizing in both cases.[33]

Thus it may seem that the agapic ideal can be reframed for a time in which the idea of God or the authority of divine commands has become virtually unthinkable for many people. If the main goal is to identify a transcendent standpoint from which "radical challenge to existing values" is kept an open possibility,[34] then Levinasian transcendence seems to do the job as well as Kierkegaard's God, but in a way that is open to more people, many of whom have sincere reasons for atheism or agnosticism (such as the problem of evil, naturalistic explanations of religion, and other atheological arguments). A bit less radically, if the point of faith is "a clear sense of the difference between God and my culture,"[35] so that (among other things) I can recognize the infinite ethical tasks of confronting poverty and suffering rather than resting satisfied with "the American way of life,"[36] then do I really need the incarnate Christ or "absolute paradox" for this? Since imitating Christ is only one way to understand this transcendent ideal, can't we have what is vital in Westphal's Religiousness C without the distinctive element in Religiousness B (the absolute paradox), or more broadly without miracles of the kind to which Abraham trusted his whole self?

In short, if the ACE readings of *Fear and Trembling* were right, then Derrida would have a strong point. Or, equivalently, Levinas's attempt to show the validity of agapic obligations without reference to biblical commands or to the authority of any historical religion is a serious challenge not only to Kierkegaard's own explanation of agapic duty, but to the indispensability of God for religiousness or faith as interpreted in any ACE account. This point is independent of acknowledged problems in Levinas's own critique of Kierkegaard; in fact, it is only *strengthened* by the response that Kierkegaard's agapic ethics is similar to Levinas's in several respects—except that Kierkegaard's also requires us to believe that God is not dead! Within the ACE project, Levinas and Derrida seem to have Ockham's razor on their side. This is a good reason to consider carefully if there is anything in Kierkegaardian faith that ACE readings leave out.

Answering Levinas's Critique of Fear and Trembling

Since Levinas's critique is addressed by other chapters in this volume, I will assume that readers are familiar with it and comment only on how it sets the stage for the chief error in later alterity readings of *Fear and Trembling*. Notably, Levinas himself does not read Kierkegaardian faith as anticipating alterity ethics; instead, he *rightly* focuses on the soteriological content of "religiousness" in *Fear and Trembling* and the Climacus works. He criticizes Kierkegaard's emphasis on the possibility of salvation as simply a more refined form of egoistic "thirst" or erosiac desire for self-completion.[37] In Levinas's view, despite Kierkegaard's defense of a subjectivity prior to totality, or individuality against "impersonal *logos*," he has not made a deep break from Hegel's "egocentric" conception of the subject.[38]

I will contest this objection later. Yet in my view, the fundamental problem with Levinas's critique lies not in raising this worry about religious egoism but rather in failing to see the answer already present in *Fear and Trembling*. Though Levinas recognizes that Kierkegaardian faith is primarily about salvation rather than ethical obligation (of any kind), he entirely misses the point that in *Fear and Trembling,* the soteriological element is *Isaac's* being spared or passed over. He overlooks Silentio's evident emphasis on Abraham's absurd-by-rational-standards belief that obeying God's mysterious command will *not* result in murdering Isaac (i.e., causing his permanent death)—that the command is really a perilous test of faith in God's original promise to Abraham rather than a betrayal of that promise.

This oversight is clearest when Levinas suggests that Kierkegaard did not identify the best interpretation of the Akedah: "The high point of the whole drama could be the moment when Abraham lent an ear to the voice calling him back to the ethical order."[39] He fails to see that Kierkegaard agrees! In Silentio's version of the Akedah, this moment not only is the high point but is even expected as such: Abraham trusts absolutely in a prior divine promise which implies that *the ethical order will be restored*—whether by his being called back from the sacrifice, or in some other unpredictable and marvelous way. In Levinas's version, the point is that Abraham lends an ear to the command to stop the sacrifice when the surprise comes; in Kierkegaard's version, Abraham trusts from the outset that such a surprise will come. Faith does not consist in Abraham's being violently forced by the command "to abandon the ethical stage (or rather, what it took to be the ethical stage) in order to embark on the religious stage, the domain of belief."[40] The point of Silentio's story is not to laud sheer obedience to the command to sacrifice—which in my analysis would mean taking *the obstacle* as the ultimate authority or final word (which is despair). Rather, existential faith consists in trust that all obstacles to the complete realization of the ethical will be overcome "in the end," as God has promised, even though this outcome infinitely transcends the finite powers of our agency, strivings, and predictions. This is certainly not an assurance one can get from the alterity of human others; it requires eschatological divinity.[41]

The right understanding of the soteriological element in Silentio's narrative also lays to rest Levinas's worry about religious egoism. In *Fear and Trembling,* Abraham's existential faith concerns Isaac's life, Isaac's survival; his own good is affected only because he is *already selflessly devoted* to Isaac. Thus the content of his eschatological hope is what we may call an "agent-transcending" good.[42] The eschatological good to come is, in itself, the miraculous realization of an agapic ideal in time. Abraham's devotion to this ideal and his trust in its fulfillment are both independent of any erosiac attraction to his own beatitude: Isaac's reprieve gives Abraham infinite joy only because of his prior devotion to Isaac, which is pure to the point of infinite resignation. To see this, imagine that instead of telling Abraham to stop and sacrifice the ram instead, the angel called out, "Abraham, now release Isaac and plunge the knife into your own breast, and Isaac will be saved." This would have been just as good as the ram to Silentio's Abraham; he would have died knowing that God's promise had come true: his belief was simply that Isaac would be saved, though he knew not how.

Thus eschatological hope and the ethical willing/caring it presupposes are arguably like what Levinas (rather misleadingly) calls "metaphysical desire," namely, a motive state not driven by lack or need in the motivated subjected but rather generated by the agent looking beyond her own good.[43] While ethical willing is generated by the agent projecting ends not needed for his completion, that to which the agent is committed in faith is not a goal of intentional action at all (since he knows that he cannot bring it about by his efforts), but rather a state that confers ultimate meaning on moral motives that are purely willed for the sake of their rightness. As Silentio says, the knight of infinite resignation values his ethical ideal apart from any result in finite temporal world: he knows that in loving others, one should remain "sufficient unto oneself" (FT, 44) or free of need in Levinas's sense. In short, eschatological hope that our moral efforts are not ultimately fruitless or without eternal significance supports the purity of agapic love as its consolation. Hope for such consolation or final meaning does not make our love egoistic.[44]

Mooney is thus correct both that "mere obedience cannot distinguish faith" and that faith as Kierkegaard understands it might even be compatible with "Abraham *refusing* God's command."[45] But this is not because Abraham's situation is a moral dilemma with conflicting duties in which universal norms cannot guide us. It may be true that no sincere agapic ethics can provide an algorithmic procedure to decide what is best in Abraham's situation. Yet the perilous divine command functions as an *obstacle* to his prophesied future—as if a dangerous power in a fairy tale had acquired a terrible right to his life in bargain.[46] Given this, Abraham might reject the command, knowing that this move is just as powerless to save Isaac as obeying the command would be: either way, Isaac's fate is in God's hands. However, as Mooney sees, obeying is more clearly free of possessive attachment and recognizes that Isaac was an unmerited gift.

Contrast with Westphal's Response

It is helpful to contrast this reply to Levinas with the response given by Merold Westphal in this volume, which I take to represent the ACE view. Westphal argues that Levinas (1) does not distinguish the different senses of the ethical in Kierkegaard, and so misses the religious agapic ethics that is not teleologically suspended in faith; (2) that, while misconceived love of God can crowd out love of neighbor, Christian hope for heaven properly understood cannot be egoistic; and (3) that demanding that God's word meet pre-established ethical criteria sounds a lot like Kant's and Lessing's universal rational religion, which is open to the charge of onto-theological violence against the divine.[47] Do these replies adequately answer Levinas's concern that by suspending the ethical as *Sittlichkeit* in a relationship with God rather than in the alterity of the human other, Kierkegaard is justifying possible historical faith in immoral commands?[48]

I agree that Levinas seems to be unfamiliar with the religious ethics of *Works of Love*, which is similar in some respects to his own agapic ethics. But as I suggested, Levinasians should respond that the love-commands only make the alleged problem with *Fear and Trembling* more difficult. For Levinas holds that if our responsibility to love our neighbor has any deontic force *at all*, it must at the very least prohibit ever intentionally taking innocent life (TI, 194, 198): in fact, the command not to murder is almost *equivalent* to the Face whose vulnerability calls us to care for this other person in his uniqueness (TI, 199).[49] But Isaac lying on Mount Moriah is even more vulnerable and innocent than Abel was before Cain (the example Levinas frequently cites). So any command to murder Isaac arguably conflicts not only with ancient Hebrew *Sittlichkeit*, but also with core of Kierkegaard's agapic ethics.[50] As we have seen, the eschatological reading is able to answer Levinas quite directly on this point, while the ACE approach is not.

Nor can we can save Kierkegaard from the charge of religious egoism by interpreting the desire for salvation in an afterlife as a desire "to make permanent and perfect the welcoming of the Other, both divine and human."[51] Described this way, faith becomes a desire for righteousness that Levinas would argue should be treated as a moral ideal resting on the phenomenology of otherness rather than any historical revelation. But this ideal is incomplete: while the eschatological goods in which Christianity, prophetic Judaism, and Islam have faith surely include this perfecting of our love, they must also include the *realization* of goods we legitimately willed (however imperfectly) for others and ourselves—and thus some final meaning to all good human efforts and striving. In other words, the perfection of the promised hereafter in which I trust must be *more* than the purification of my will: it must include the fulfillment of a pure heart's wish to see the kingdom of heaven realized for all who can participate in it. To give one concrete and poignant example, if my will was perfected and united with God, but Anne Frank was still dead and her father's soul still in despair, I do not think I could be in heaven. But this kind of restoration or renewal goes beyond our ethical intentions and works, even in their highest agapic form: it requires the cosmogonic power that created the world to recreate it anew, with every distortion straightened, every evil answered, every good effort or striving given final positive significance, and more beyond all imagination.[52] The absolute reconciliation of enemies that Westphal cites from Kierkegaard's discourse on eternal salvation (EUD, 265)[53] is another good example: As much as I might long for such a reconciliation and work for some part of it with my whole mind and body, honesty requires infinite resignation to my inability to bring it about, since it requires free choices on the part of others who I cannot control.

This is the infinite comfort provided by the expectancy of salvation: the belief that striving for ethical ideals need not all be *for naught* in the final scheme of things. The boundless joy of this eschatological state is beyond description, but it not egoistic; for this joy is a by-product of willing the good of others *for its own sake* and seeing them flourish infinitely, beyond all finite earthly hopes, in the end. This answers Levinas's worry without reducing eschatological happiness to the self-respect or dignity that a person of goodwill can find purely in the rightness of her own ends, which is possible even without any hope of achieving her righteous goals.[54] The eschatological fulfillment of all ethical hopes is much more than an infinitely good conscience.

Derrida: Faith as Dilemmic Obligation Without Eschatological Hope

Derrida on Abraham's Silence

I explained above why Derrida's approach to *Fear and Trembling* makes some sense as a response to familiar SDC and ACE readings. However, Derrida's account in *The Gift of Death* not only follows Levinas's basic error and eliminates the distinctive element in Kierkegaardian faith, but also makes nonsense of the agapic ethical ideal that is supposed to replace the duty to God in this particular alterity interpretation (though not in all ALE readings). This is ironic for several reasons, including that Derrida accuses several other twentieth-century authors of offering us "a nondogmatic doublet of dogma" in place of the *mysterium* of revealed religion,[55] when this *mysterium* actually centers in the eschatological.

Derrida starts off well, associating religious fear and trembling with being seen in secret by the hidden, silent, God who judges.[56] He then emphasizes the Knight of Faith's silence, by which he "transgresses the ethical order" or "betrays ethics."[57] Silentio's Abraham is silent not to save Isaac, Derrida writes, but rather because speaking would imply that the duty involved is one for which he can answer in public, not one that singles him out. This is bizarre for two reasons. First, the idea that "no one can perform in my place"[58] the duty assigned uniquely to me hardly seems to require secrecy; in fact, people say things like this all time, and are often understood: this task is given to me; no one can perform it but me, and so on. For example, Frodo says such things several times in Tolkien's *Lord of the Rings,* and Sam understands him, though not completely until he too has borne the Ring.

Second, in Problema III, Silentio's statements concerning why Abraham cannot explain himself have little to do with the idea that authentic responsibility is an aporia of unique, singular, nonsubstitutable demands in contrast to "the generality of ethics" (as understood by lower minds—lawyers, philosophers, the rabble);[59] it is rather because Abraham's trust that he will get Isaac back cannot be rationally comprehended. Silentio is very clear that he is talking about "speech" *as rational explanation:* "If I cannot make myself understood when I speak, then I am not speaking" in the relevant sense (FT, 113). Abraham can certainly *say* that "he is going to sacrifice [Isaac] because it is only an ordeal" (FT, 113).[60] Yet "only an ordeal" *means* that Isaac will still live despite being sacrificed: "But it will not happen, or if it does, the Lord will give me a new Isaac, by virtue of the absurd" (FT, 115). By all "human reckoning" (FT, 115), this makes no sense; it sounds utterly crazy.[61] We can view this as an aporia of human reason or "human language" (FT, 114), but it is not the aporia of higher-ethical election that Derrida has in mind.

Kierkegaard's God, then, is "jealous" of other *false gods*, but not of the ethical ideal He promises to *fulfill*. The religious life view contains the ethical ideal within it; its content *mentions* the actualization of the ethical ideal, and thus is defined in relation to it. The ethical *per se* is not "renounced."[62] This religious life view only denies the *existential sufficiency* or stability of a life devoted to the good but forlorn of all eschatological hope. The idea of a religiousness beyond, or without, or "against" ethics[63] is thus in total contradiction to Kierkegaard's account of cumulative existential "stages." Such a description instead suggests a Nietzschean religiousness, if that is conceivable. It does not help to respond that "Kierkegaard still follows the Kantian tradition of a pure ethics or practical reason that is exceeded by absolute duty as it extends into the realm of sacrifice,"[64] as if the ethics that is superseded is only deontological obligation. For, like some other higher ethics interpretations, this one creates a total *opposition* between (a) the level of ordinary responsibilities that it substitutes for "the ethical" and (b) the higher level that it substitutes for "the religious" stages in the pseudonymous works,[65] although Kierkegaard clearly regards the relation between (a) and (b) as more like nested concentric circles. Moreover, since the higher calling of "respect for absolute singularity" still amounts to another *ethical* standpoint, this reading also makes it impossible to distinguish clearly "between the ethical and the religious."[66] This is not a correction to Kierkegaard but a result of misreading his Akedah as primarily a *metaphor* for "the paradox constituting the concept of duty and absolute responsibility."[67]

Of course, Derrida could not adopt the eschatological reading of *Fear and Trembling* proposed above because he thinks that even *hope* for a response from the other, or for success in one's self-sacrificing efforts, implies egoistic interest in a "return," or what he calls "economy." Only the gift that forgets itself in the giving, and even forgets the very idea that the receiver might respond with gratitude or some other kind of reciprocation, is truly generous rather than "economic." If we start with this contentious premise—more extreme than anything in Kierkegaard's *Works of Love*—then eschatological trust as I've defined would have to be selfish.

Derrida is certainly correct that in *Fear and Trembling*, Abraham's obedience is not an investment or clever wager to maneuver Isaac's reprieve: "Abraham is in a position of nonexchange with God" and expects no "reward" from him.[68] But that is because he does not conceive obedience to the perilous command as *the condition* for God's reversing the order or giving Isaac back; so he conceives the fateful decision to sacrifice Isaac neither as causing nor as earning Isaac's emancipation.[69] Hence Derrida badly errs, on Kierkegaard's view, in describing God's "decision" to "give back the beloved son" as a *result* of Abraham's obedience, let alone a result of Abraham giving to God "a gift outside any economy, the gift of death."[70] For one certainly cannot give (let alone give disinterestedly) what one does not *own*, and Derrida sees as clearly as Mooney that Abraham is renouncing any claims to possess Isaac in Silentio's narrative. Hence Abraham's obedience to the command is not intended as a gift to God:[71] Abraham hopes to receive Isaac back *in spite of* his sacrifice, not *because* of it (as if he could earn Isaac's return).

By contrast, Derrida thinks that in Silentio's story, Abraham's sacrificing Isaac is a gift to God, made because God demands this gift; the gift is pure because Abraham does not even hope for Isaac's return, yet he gets Isaac back as a result of the purity of his gift to God:[72]

> ... having renounced winning, expecting neither response nor recompense, expecting nothing that can be *given back* to him, nothing that will *come back* to him ... he sees that God gives back to him, in the instant of absolute renunciation, the very thing that he had already, in the same instant, decided to sacrifice. It is given back to him *because* he renounced calculation.[73]

Here we see the central error in Derrida's analysis: he reduces Abraham's faith to infinite resignation without eschatological hope. This is why he has to conclude erroneously that Silentio or Kierkegaard sees Isaac's return as caused by the purity of Abraham's gift. Certainly Abraham does not "expect" Isaac back in the sense of any rational calculation about how it might happen, or how he (with or without help from others) might bring it about. But he certainly does expect Isaac to live by virtue of the absurd, because he trusts in God's original promise. This promise becomes eschatological in significance when its fulfillment is apparently blocked by a horrifying obstacle, namely, a command that almost seems to come from a different God. In this case, the inexorability of the obstacle involves God's power and absolute ownership rights, but this only clarifies that accepting the obstacle in resignation does not amount to giving a gift.

In short, Abraham "expects" Isaac back in a sense of "expectancy" that is not investment or manipulation. Thus we can modify Derrida's formula that "God asks that one give without knowing, without calculating, reckoning, *or hoping,* for one must give without counting, and that is what takes it outside of sense."[74] On the contrary, while the absurdity of Isaac's return despite being sacrificed cannot rationally be counted on or strategically engineered, Abraham can still hope for it, and even *trust* in it, without becoming "economic." This holds just as much for hope to see "the kingdom of heaven," or trust in the eschatological promises made by Christ.[75]

Agapic Duty as Pure Dilemma

Suppose, however, we want to know if agapic ethics is possible without eschatological faith. Perhaps, but if so, agapic duty still cannot be plausibly be conceived as Derrida interprets it. While there is much to recommend his discussion of the biblical neighbor love commands and the secrecy of an invisible God,[76] in trying to make agapic duty paradoxical, unsayable, and contrary to the universal to match Silentio's description of "faith" (as he understands it),

Derrida distorts the requirements of neighbor love to make them impossible even *in principle* to fulfill. Let me distinguish four aspects of this complex distortion.

(1) If we define this absolute duty as totally incomprehensible or as beyond any explanation, as "a gift or sacrifice that functions beyond both debt and duty,"[77] it follows that *too many things* can count as a "gift," that agapic love is an infinitely plastic—or empty—concept. I might absentmindedly toss a cigarette out of my car window and thus perform an act of pristine generosity to a bum on the sidewalk. I might doodle on a piece of paper with no thought of any appreciation by others and thus donate a pure gift to the next person who finds the paper on my bus seat. An act of random harm to someone not done for any pleasure or as a means to any other good, which we usually call cruelty for its own sake, is also not inscribed in any economy of exchange (that is precisely what's perverse about it). When malice transcends vengeance based on a (corrupted) sense of justice, it too would stand beyond all universal law as a pure gift—indeed perhaps as the gift of death to the other.[78] For the ideal of agapic love to give any real guidance in practical deliberation, it presupposes at least some background conception of harms and goods, both in human welfare and other types of intrinsic value and disvalue in the world (such as beauty in nature or the diversity of species). These have the characteristic of being evaluative universals, although they may always be manifested in unique concrete gestalts.[79] Without such background concepts, we cannot even meaningfully say that agapic love generally intends to *help* rather than to *harm* people or the world. If agapic love simply requires "the betrayal of everything that manifests itself within the order of the universal generality" then (even ignoring Derrida's usual failure to grasp the distinction between the *universal* and the *general*),[80] we can achieve agapic generosity just by thumbing our nose at conventions or even by being "demonic" in Kierkegaard's sense. For example, the Grinch in Dr. Seuss's classic tale[81] transcends the *Sittlichkeit* of Whoville, and Dostoevsky's underground man transgresses Kantian universals in a most avant-garde fashion; both are also responding, in their way, to the alterity of the Other.[82]

(2) Derrida makes agapic duty into a *simple contradiction* rather than a paradox in Kierkegaard's quite different sense of that polyvalent term. In his view, the higher-ethical demand of alterity deconstructs the mundane ethics of everyday life and of "moralizing moralists" (the kind Nietzsche despised) because it denies the very possibility of "good conscience."[83] The sacrifice of Isaac in *Fear and Trembling* "illustrates" or stands for the point that, in my singular response to a specific other person (or God?) to whom I owe an absolute duty, I *must always* sacrifice others, betraying my equal responsibility to third parties:

> I cannot respond to the call, the obligation, or even the love of another without sacrificing the other other, the other others. . . . As a result, the concepts of responsibility, of decision, or of duty, are condemned *a priori* to paradox, scandal, and aporia. . . . As soon as I enter into a relation with the other, with the gaze, with the look, request,

love, command, or call of the other, I know that I can only respond by sacrificing ethics, that is, by sacrificing whatever obliges me to respond, in the same instant, to all the others.[84]

Here at least we have a clear thesis: beneath all the rhetoric, Derrida's whole analysis depends on this one claim. Such a claim, given its extraordinary nature, requires a frank response. Note that "ethics" in the last sentence of this passage refers not to lower Kantian or Hegelian ethics, but rather to agapic obligation itself—here read as requiring us to be everywhere on Earth at once, responding in heartfelt proximity to every person, or entering a singularizing I-Thou encounter with everyone, one by one or (even better) simultaneously.[85] This duty to become God (for that is what it implies) is certainly "absurd," but not at all in Kierkegaard's sense. Agapic duty on this alterity interpretation is immediately "paradoxical" in the cheapest sense imaginable, namely, what it demands of us is not only physically and psychologically impossible under our laws of nature, but probably also impossible for any nondivine being in any universe with natural laws and a form of life *anything* like ours. Yet we would see no profound "paradox" in telling insects to write poetry, or telling a single individual to feed all the starving with one loaf.

Derrida's conception thus introduces the thesis, novel to moral theory, that we are always in a moral dilemma, whatever we do, at all times, with respect to everyone. Other philosophers have thought it difficult to establish that moral dilemmas can *sometimes* occur a person's life without tracing to previous acts of wrongdoing by that person.[86] But Derrida leaps over such old-fashioned debates in metaethics, and goes much further; with a few words, he poetically transforms *every* decision into an underivative moral dilemma of the strongest kind: "By preferring my work, simply by giving it my time and attention," I may be fulfilling one duty but "I am sacrificing and betraying at every moment all my other obligations: my obligations to the other others whom I don't know, to billions of my fellows . . . who are dying of starvation or sickness."[87] Since I could always help someone by doing something other than what I'm doing now—even by sending a dollar to some random person on a far continent rather than writing this sentence, for example—I'm always doing something wrong. Never mind that human beings are so constituted that we need to have meaningful endeavors and relationships other than merely providing for people's basic needs;[88] I am personally responsible to ensure that no one is suffering anywhere from deprivation of any kind, but especially (it seems) basic material deprivation.

It has been considered a very powerful objection against act-utilitarian moral theories that they demand too much, or cannot leave room for loyalty to one's own family, social roles, and identity-defining commitments. But that widely recognized problem would appear vanishingly small in comparison to the conceptual problems created by Derrida's theory. Even if I religiously followed what sometimes seems to be Peter Singer's prescription and turned myself into a mere utility maximizing machine, reducing my consumption to the lowest possible amount consistent with maintaining the most lucrative career available to me while avoiding total psychological breakdown so that I can contribute as much as possible to poverty relief, I would have barely scratched the surface of what Derrida thinks the alterity of my neighbors demands of me. And to think I felt good just for coaching little league this spring!

What is most *comical* about these statements is that Derrida simply assumes that this is the right understanding of agapic duty, thus begging the question against all saner interpretations of the neighbor love commands, and against (as far as I know) all moral theory in world history before him. Not everyone agrees with the Kantian principle that ought entails can, but no one else has ever asserted that ought, properly understood, always implies *can't*!

What is *arrogant* in Derrida's stance is that he puts himself, with perhaps a few others sufficiently gifted with deconstructive insight to see the aporetic nature of our agapic duties, in the position of Abraham as a kind of martyr to the ethical, tortured by his own defiant claim that he is in the same position as Abraham. Contrast the humility of Silentio, who would never dream of comparing himself to Abraham. It is arrogant to romanticize this kind of fetishism for aporia as a higher, more authentic life view that distinguishes one from ordinary moral thinkers.

What is *frightening* about Derrida's ethic is that it is a recipe for despair. It means that because of the existence of others, I'm never entitled to anything—a quiet moment by the fire, a bit of fun playing a game with my children, the pleasure of a chocolate chip cookie—for every instant of time or bit of material could instead have been devoted to alleviating the poverty of someone somewhere. But since I'm *equally and infinitely* in the wrong whatever I do, I may as well eat, drink, and be merry and forget about it (or worse)—for it is all the same, as regards my moral worth, whether I live the life of Donald Trump or Mother Theresa (all "moral ledgers" having been rendered passé by the infinite demands of all others upon us).[89]

Of course, we are all familiar with the common experience of being pulled in different and contingently conflicting directions by what Ross sanely called prima facie moral claims,[90] and this holds for agapic ethics just as much as for Ross's intuitionist theory of the right. There is nothing ethically profound, let alone religious, in this. But by a simple non sequitur, Derrida turns this prosaic truth of our existence into an absolute dilemma and associates it with transcendence by rhetoric like "responding to the call of each other as absolutely other" and so on.

Many intelligent philosophers have been misled by such rhetoric into thinking that there must be some great insight here. Caputo, for example, says that Derrida is more authentically ethical than all the "moralizing and self-approving critics of Derrida, who are given to praying in public."[91] Yes, Derrida is much more profound; he ventures "beyond duty," beyond all public ethical ideals into the singularizing paralysis of totalized moral dilemma; he accepts the martyrdom of impossible ethical demands, which sanctimonious analytic philosophers won't admit. He is daring; who else could have gone beyond even Levinas, who still saw the origin of responsibility in the singular face as compatible with universal duties.[92] One should recall here the assistant professors mocked by Kierkegaard for thinking themselves profound because they had gone "beyond faith." Derrida's rhetoric is pure idolatry of aporia, worship of contradiction, sanctification of dilemma—an aestheticization of movement beyond ethics.

It would significantly mitigate these problems if we thought that institutional relationships mediated by the "force of law" can count as primary ways of fulfilling our agapic obligations to distant strangers and future generations, and that the main requirement for such institutional relationships is that they be just in some non-maximizing sense definable by various universal norms. But Derrida simply assumes that global markets are unjust without giving any diagnosis of the specific injustices. If anyone is "allowed to die" anywhere without our personal and direct intervention as private citizens who transcend global politics, then we are murderers in his reckoning.[93] Thus we are all murderers, like Abraham. Yet this highly offensive claim is not followed by any explanation of what institutional arrangement would suffice for us to avoid ending up on a moral par with Manson (there can be none, since we are *necessarily* murderers). Derrida condemns civilized societies for "the monotonous complacency of their discourses on morality, politics, and the law, and the exercises of rights (whether public, private, national, or international)" because they allow third world debt and poverty.[94] But does he tell us how global markets should be structured and limited by law so as to be just? Of course not; to enter into such details would be to descend from his heights into the casuistry of general/universal normative discourses, the paltry calculations of common mores, or the pale abstractions of ethical theory.

Likewise, the current global political order is criticized as if there were clear moral criteria for critiquing it when there can be none in Derrida's totality of moral dilemmas. Derrida rightly condemns the fact that millions are left to die or suffer from systematic injustice at the hands of tyrants, or abused by those who fight wars to stop tyrants—though again, he outrageously puts these opponents on a moral par.[95] But does he call for a new federation of the world's democracies to create a global order in which the atrocities of Iraq, Sudan, Rwanda, Bosnia, Kosovo, Congo, East Timor, Zimbabwe, and so on, are not possible, and each nation (even France) does its fair share to stop tyranny and terrorism? Of course not. Derrida is not Habermas; he proposes no institutional solution. Yet his defenders often call Habermas arrogant.[96] In reply, it might fairly be asked how their deconstruction of ethical theory has helped created a more just global order.

(3) All this said, however, I think Derrida's ethic is *nominally* close to the truth, or at least to Kierkegaard's view that ethical responsibility is "infinite." That it so badly misconstrues this central idea in perfectionist accounts is part of its tragedy. In the *Postscript*, Climacus explains the perfectionist ethical demand in the section on the totality of guilt.[97] We are "essentially guilty" because

we are subject to perfectionist moral judgments: being morally responsible makes it possible to be guilty or not guilty in particular cases.[98] The obligations that make us responsible are ultimately owed to God, who is infinite and thus incommensurable with even the slightest fault on our part.[99] But it is crucial that contingent guilt (as opposed to the essential condition of being morally responsible before God) is not inevitable *in principle* on Climacus's account: it is metaphysically and psychologically possible for us to fulfill our perfect duties.[100] Our responsibility is *qualitatively* infinite, since it is governed by a perfectionist ideal:[101] it always extends beyond what we have actually done, but not beyond what we could in principle have done. Thus it does not violate one relevant version of the ought-implies-can principle.[102] By contrast, Derrida interprets the totality of guilt as an actual failure to live up to our duty that *necessarily* results from our finitude.[103]

In Kierkegaard's view, our agapic duties do not aim to *maximize* any numerical quantity (CUP, 536): they require that perfectly earnest love be operative toward everyone, leaving room for universal norms (involving comparative judgments and finite criteria) to fill out *how* this motive is best expressed in different spheres of life. What matters qualitatively is "constancy in the relation" or ongoing commitment of the will to the perfect good and thus to the recollection of guilt, since we always *in fact* fall short of that to which we are committed (CUP, 535). Derrida externalizes this perfectionist conception of duty, making it into the task of attending personally to each one of roughly 6 billion unique individuals. This confusion has been aptly diagnosed by Knud Løgstrup, who argues that we need to distinguish the radical character of a demand for selfless motives from a quantitatively unlimited "responsibility for everything under the sun," and from a maximizing concern for "what best serves the welfare of everyone."[104]

Climacus's qualitative conception of infinite duty also explains why resignation to our inability to fulfill our duties on our own, which stands at the outer limit of the ethical, is called "infinite" resignation: it is the same as the totality of guilt before a perfectionist ideal. The totality of guilt transcends anything found in the "comparative, conventional, external, bourgeois conception of the ethical" with its discrete list of dos and don'ts (CUP, 546).[105] But note that this category is *before* faith as its necessary precondition in both Climacus's and Silentio's writings: infinite responsibility to each person according to the love commands is not faith itself. Thus it is also prior to recognizing sin as contingent rebellion against divine authority in each person's life.

(4) Finally, despite his emphasis on the singular, Derrida cannot avoid a type of *universality* in the duty to love all neighbors, given his claim that we are responsible "at every moment for every man and every woman"[106] as unique individuals rather than simply as numbers in some calculus. Rightly understood, this means that our agapic duties are universal *in scope*, reaching to all persons and requiring us to show agapic regard to them all as precious, free, creative, beings capable of autonomy but needing relation, whose status as per-

sons gives them inviolable basic dignity. This type of universal scope is quite compatible with my duties to particular others being historically unique or unrepeatable because of their singular place in the web of human life stories, which makes my role in these contexts "irreplaceable": no one else could take my place, because to be in this place is part of what it is to be *me*. Thus Derrida is wrong to think that singularization of duties to specific individuals in this time/place contradicts the universal scope of agapic obligations: turning toward a single individual in love does not require putting their interests or demands *above* those of all other unique individuals (including even oneself).[107] Derrida simply mistakes this universality in *scope* for a duty that is identical in *material content* to each other at the same time, and so is impossible to fulfill.

In sum, agapic love for others is not "exclusive" in the same sense as existential faith. It is a universal duty to all persons, which means that what is owed to every individual is formally identical; but this does not entail the same material relationship of direct caring interaction with each. The faith-relation is exclusive because only one being can make eschatological goods possible; so that being is different from all other persons. God's Alterity is not the otherness of persons in general, the alterity that grounds agapic obligation to them: it *exceeds* this interhuman alterity, just as one order of infinity exceeds another.

Conclusion

We have seen that trying to assimilate the singularity of faith to agapic duty leads Derrida to misconstrue not only what Kierkegaard means by religious faith, but also the content of agapic duty itself. Kierkegaard's portrayal of eschatological trust in the story of the Akedah is turned, by rhetorical art, into a quick excuse for rejecting all ethical theory, a fast way of rejecting universal ethical norms. God is replaced with the human other, and the absolute relation of trust in the eschatological promise is replaced with absolute moral dilemma. Poor Kierkegaard, to have a disciple like that.

Thus more is at stake in the right understanding of *Fear and Trembling* than simply the question of how best to read a single famous text by an old Danish author. For higher-ethics interpretations that fail to distinguish faith from individual vocations or singular moral callings not only miss the eschatological center of Kierkegaard's conception of God, but also threaten to give us versions of agapic duty that overstress exclusive care relationships that are possible only with a few others in this life. When universalized, such agapic duty becomes sheer impossibility, rather than infinite resignation looking toward eschatological hope. The singularity of the absolute relation is indeed crucial to faith, but this absolute relation is something added to ethical obligation and our volitional response to such obligation, rather than a replacement for them. Only the eschatological reading preserves the right relation between universal agapic duties to all human persons and the higher duty to have faith in God's promise that the ultimate aims of agapic love will be realized, here or hereafter.

Notes

1. Note that it is not only the materialist philosopher who is transcended here, nor only the herd who deny any non-physical reality: all rationalist ethics is overcome. My description intentionally highlights the danger of elitism or even gnosticism that is built into the higher-ethics approach. We "faithful" have a sacred calling that is higher than these petty bourgeois with their legalistic rights, these casuists with their traditional moral precepts, these eudaimonists with their virtues, or these Kantian calculators with their hidebound categorical imperatives. However, defenders of this approach to Kierkegaardian faith usually hold that the higher-ethical attitude or insight is available in principle to all. But claims that true faith requires a teleological suspension of concern for human welfare in mystical detachment, or a suspension of all rules of just war for the sake of forcing revealed truth on all nations, or a suspension of all scientific knowledge in order to adhere to the creed of some illuminati, would all count as other species of the higher-ethics family. This is uncomfortable company to keep.

2. Davenport, "Faith as Eschatological Trust in *Fear and Trembling*," forthcoming in *Ethics, Love, and Faith in Kierkegaard: Philosophical Engagements,* ed. Edward F. Mooney (Bloomington: Indiana University Press, 2008), chap. 15.

3. Patrick Gardiner, *Kierkegaard: A Very Short Introduction* (1988; Oxford University Press, 2002), 67 (my italics). Gardiner is sensitive to Silentio's point that the ethical is *not* rejected or "dispensed with" in being made relative to the absolute or denied "ultimate or supreme" status (66). However, the SDC reading cannot make sense of this point, which is only explained on the eschatological reading.

4. C. Stephen Evans, *Kierkegaard's Ethic of Love* (New York: Oxford University Press, 2004). Evans follows Robert Adams in connecting divine commands to "God's broader teleological vision of the good" (9). God's commands are not arbitrary, since they are "successfully directed toward human flourishing" (300). Thus if God did issue a command to murder an innocent child, it would have to serve some purpose independently recognizable as good, such as teaching that human sacrifice is forbidden (306–307). God cannot command anything that is evil, and this is not a tautology in Evans's view (315). Our duty to obey God depends on our knowledge of "God himself as a good and loving person," which in turn depends on some prior (even if imperfect) understanding of "what is good and loving" (316). On this view, the authority of divine commands clearly rests on the idea that God embodies perfect love.

5. Ibid., 62–84, 305–10. It is hard, however, to square this with Evans's idea that one goal of *Fear and Trembling* is to show, in a fictionalized Abraham, "what true religious faith would be like in a person who is perfectly ethical" (82). For by Evans's own analysis, in the counterfactual case that such a human person existed, she or he would know and follow the love commands, and could not then believe that God commands her or him to sacrifice an innocent child.

6. Ibid., 76.

7. Merold Westphal, "Kierkegaard's Religiousness C: A Defense," *International Philosophical Quarterly* 44, no. 4 (December 2004): 535–48, 538.

8. Gardiner, *Kierkegaard,* 67.

9. Jack Mulder, "Re-Radicalizing Kierkegaard: An Alternative to Religiousness C in Light of an Investigation into the Teleological Suspension of the Ethical," *Continental Philosophy Review* 35, no. 3 (2002): 303–24.

10. Westphal, "Kierkegaard's Religiousness C," 539.

11. As we will see, the eschatological interpretation has a quite different explanation of how Abraham's act can be loving, which depends on his having a purpose *other* than mere obedience to God as creator or infinite power. The dispute is not over the thesis that, rightly understood, loving God and loving the neighbor cannot conflict; it is over the reason *why* they cannot conflict in the second ethics, and whether this reason is implied in *Fear and Trembling*.

12. See Edward Mooney, *Knights of Faith and Resignation,* chaps. 4–8; Mooney, *Selves in Discord and Resolve* (Routledge, 1996), chaps. 4–6. Another version of ALE is found in Jerome Gellman's reading of the teleological suspension as defending a kind of proto-Sartrean individualistic ethic: Gellman, "Kierkegaard's *Fear and Trembling,*" *Man and World* 23, no. 3 (1990): 295–304. I briefly mention these approaches along with John Caputo's version of ALE in "Faith as Eschatological Trust in *Fear and Trembling,*" but my focus there is on SDC and ACE readings.

13. Mooney, *Knights of Faith and Resignation,* 92.

14. Ibid., 94.

15. Evans, *Kierkegaard's Ethic of Love,* 25.

16. Ibid., 26–27. Evans emphasizes that for Kierkegaard, human agents must exercise "creative freedom" in discovering this divine vocation and fashioning an authentic practical identity on its basis. But I suggest that the radical uniqueness of individuals required for Kierkegaard's agapic ethics involves something more than this, namely that the identity I'm "called" to develop is *intrinsically* ambiguous in certain key respects— like a quantum state in superposition—waiting for my freedom to interact with it. If that is right, then persons cannot be individualized by "individual essences" that pick them out metaphysically prior to their existing and choosing (ibid., 15 n. 15). This does not mean the "call" must be as abstract as in Heidegger's account; it only means that neither Molinist haecceities nor singular divine commands can fully define the agent's cares and the unique way that she pursues her devotions.

17. We cannot call them "alterity *theorists*" because, although they *are* defending a moral theory that includes specific metaethical propositions (so my summary claims), they often want to believe that their theory is only a praxis without any pure theoretical elements, or that it is only an engagement with others to improve the world rather than an address to philosophers looking for any rational explanation of morality or way to understand ethics. In this regard, however, Derrida seems to be more honest than most; he knows he is providing a kind of moral theory.

18. On this idea, see in particular Derrida's famous essay, "Force of Law: The Mystical Foundation of Authority," in *Deconstruction and the Possibility of Justice,* ed. Drucilla Cornell, Michael Rosenfeld, and David Carlson (New York: Routledge, 1992).

19. I have raised some questions about Levinas's version of agape in "Levinas's Agapeistic Metaphysics of Morals: Absolute Passivity and the Other as Eschatological Hierophany," *Journal of Religious Ethics,* Fall 1998, 331–66. The irony is that rather than divinizing each other, as Derrida would have it, Levinas unwittingly collapses the uniqueness of individuals into a single transcendent divinity: "plurality" can only be stipulated because the theory lacks an adequate metaphysical conception of personal individuality (admittedly this is a hard problem for any agapic metaphysics of morals to solve).

20. That said, I do not concede that Kierkegaard's *Works of Love* presents a strong divine command ethics or defends the ontological thesis that divine command is what makes a norm obligatory for us. See Zachary Manis's careful critique of this position in

chapter 3 of "Virtues, Divine Commands, and the Debt of Creation: Towards a Kierke-gaardian Christian Ethic" (Ph.D. diss., Baylor University, 2006).

21. For the full story, see John Davenport, "Faith as Eschatological Trust in Kierke-gaard's *Fear and Trembling.*" A summary that focuses more on the two main conditions of existential faith is given in "Kierkegaard's *Postscript* in Light of *Fear and Trembling: Eschatological Faith,*" forthcoming in *Revista Portuguesa de Filosofia* (2008).

22. Note that this is distinct from the non-corporeal afterlife anticipated in various forms of Religiousness A, such as Socrates' faith; it is a pure ethical ideal accessible only in contemplation, expecting no hereafter.

23. See John Davenport, "The Essence of Eschatology: A Modal Interpretation," *Ultimate Reality and Meaning,* September 1996, 206–39.

24. Hannay, *Kierkegaard* (London: Routledge & Kegan Paul, 1982), 80–81.

25. Mooney, *Knights of Faith and Resignation,* 4.

26. Evans, *Kierkegaard's Ethic of Love,* 71; he follows Mooney's essay, "Getting Isaac Back: Ordeals and Reconciliations in *Fear and Trembling,*" in *Foundations of Kierke-gaard's Vision of Community,* ed. George Connell and C. Stephen Evans (Atlantic High-lands, N.J.: Humanities, 1992), 71–95. Also see Kierkegaard's remark that "Abraham was great not because he sacrificed Isaac, but because he had faith, because he was cheerful and willing" (JP, IV B 73 n.d., FT Suppl. 249).

27. Ibid., 73. The parallel between Isaac's return and Christ's return helps clarify the sense in which Isaac's liberation is an eschatological good or miraculous restoration of the right ethical relationship.

28. Westphal, "Kierkegaard's Religiousness C," 540. However, he immediately adds that "nothing in this account concerns the question of Abraham's duty" nor the idea that God is "the highest authority," which is "doubtless why Silentio calls this discussion 'pre-liminary'" (Ibid.). This remark *assumes* both that Abraham's "duty" is something other than to trust in God's original promise, and that the teleological suspension concerns this other duty to God *rather* than the absurd hope to get Isaac back (which is reduced to a merely "preliminary" matter). I would draw the opposite conclusion and infer that, since the task of the "Preliminary Expectoration" section is to set out the essential struc-ture of "faith" that is only elaborated in all the subsequent Problemata, the teleological suspension and absolute duty to God are *aspects* of "faith" and so must also be explained by the way that trust in the eschatological outcome transcends the ethical principles re-spected in infinite resignation: the duty to God is precisely to make the second move-ment that takes the agent beyond infinite resignation and into second immediacy (as de-scribed in the "preliminary" section).

29. Gardiner, *Kierkegaard,* 68. Unlike Hannay, Gardiner does not explain any integral connection between this absurd belief and Abraham's willingness to obey God.

30. Mooney, *Knights of Faith and Resignation,* 96.

31. Ibid., 100. Note that Levinas still seems to recognize a divine trace ("illeity") be-hind the human Face in his philosophical works, and a transcendent God as revealed in scripture in his religious commentaries, though in neither case does God function ex-actly as a "ground" of responsibility.

32. Evans, *Kierkegaard's Ethic of Love,* 77.

33. Jacques Derrida, *The Gift of Death,* trans. David Wills (Chicago: University of Chicago Press, 1995), 78.

34. Evans, *Kierkegaard's Ethic of Love,* 79.

35. Westphal, "Kierkegaard's Religiousness C," 541.

36. Ibid., 545.

37. Levinas, "Existence and Ethics," reprinted in *Kierkegaard: A Critical Reader,* ed. Jonathan Reé and Jane Chamberlain (Oxford: Blackwell, 1998), 26–38, 27. My citations are all to this later reprint version, in which the essay is translated by Reé.

38. Ibid., 28. It is not entirely clear that Levinas is right about Hegel; nor do I agree with Levinas's insistence that Heidegger's description of *Dasein* as existing "in such a way that its existence is always an issue for it" makes *Dasein* essentially egoistic (30).

39. Ibid., 33. Levinas repeats this point in more detail in the first of "Two Comments on Kierkegaard" immediately following "Existence and Ethics" in *Kierkegaard: A Critical Reader,* 34.

40. Ibid., 31.

41. This is why Derrida completely ignores the prior divine promise to Abraham (which was so absurd to Sarah) when he is describing Abraham's free decision to obey the command to sacrifice. Derrida recognizes that Abraham does not *know* what is going to happen, but he simply stops with this negative aspect, which he compares to "heading off towards the absolute request of the other, beyond knowledge" in Levinas's sense (*Gift of Death,* 77). By contrast, the *positive* element of trust in a good to come (beyond all prediction or manipulation) cannot be so easily conflated with anything coming from the human other on Levinas's account, so Derrida conveniently leaves it out. Turning his own rhetoric on him, we might even say that this is the lacuna on which his entire text depends: *the suppression of the eschatological* turns out to be the "truth" of deconstruction. While eschatological hope is explicitly rejected as spite in Nietzsche's *Zarathustra,* its rejection is concealed in Derrida.

42. See the discussion in *Will as Commitment and Resolve* (New York: Fordham University Press, 2007), chap. 5. It is also a good that is non-targetable in the sense explained in chapter 5 §2.4.

43. See the discussion of Levinas in *Will as Commitment and Resolve,* chapter 9 §4.

44. I use Hans Küng's theology to defend this point in response to Levinas in "Eschatological Ultimacy and the Best Possible Hereafter," *Ultimate Reality and Meaning* 25 (2002): 36–67, 39–42.

45. Mooney, *Knights of Faith and Resignation,* 85.

46. For example, compare Isaac's situation to Gawain's in *Sir Gawain and the Green Knight.* Gawain, of course, is a knight of resignation rather than faith, since he does not hope by virtue of the absurd to live when he comes to the Green Knight's chapel. We might also compare Isaac's situation to Edmunds's in C. S. Lewis's *The Lion, the Witch, and the Wardrobe,* in which the evil witch queen Jadis acquires a claim on Edmund's life through his own sins. His return through Aslan's sacrifice is an example of what Tolkien calls a "eucatastrophe" (a theme discussed in my essay, "Faith as Eschatological Trust in *Fear and Trembling*"). While the Green Knight is associated with the sacred, and the witch with the profane (like the Snow Queen in Andersen's famous story, on which Lewis's witch is based), God in the Akedah shows *both* sacred and profane sides, as do divine figures throughout world mythology.

47. Westphal, "The Many Faces of Kierkegaard as a Reader of Levinas," in this volume. My remarks here are drawn from my response to an early version of this chapter presented to the Kierkegaard Society session at the Eastern Division meeting of the APA (December 2002).

48. This is also pretty much how John Llewelyn summarizes Levinas's critique of Kierkegaard in his book, *Emmanuel Levinas* (Routledge, 1995), 3.

49. In this respect, Levinas follows not only Kant—whose absolute moral *faktum* of

the free rational agent as an end-in-himself, the secularized *imago dei*, surely underlies much of what Levinas says about the call of the Other—but a long line of rabbinic and Christian theologians.

50. Indeed, Timothy Jackson defends this thesis at length in his essay, "Is Isaac Kierkegaard's Neighbor?" *Annual of the Society of Christian Ethics* 17 (1997): 97–119.

51. Westphal, "The Many Faces of Kierkegaard as a Reader of Levinas," p. 9.

52. Thus the Apostle Paul's faith does not consist primarily in his ethical obedience to God's call to ministry, but rather in his trust that somehow, beyond anything he can achieve by his own power, the churches that God has founded through him will succeed and have a place in the glory of the final kingdom to come. Without this hope, his faith would be pure obedience without any consolation—something closer to the Levinasian ethical ideal.

53. Westphal, "The Many Faces of Levinas as a Reader of Kierkegaard," p. 12.

54. I agree with Westphal's point that on his ACE reading, "Abraham does not appear as an egoism tensed on itself, but as a deeply decentered self" (Ibid., p. 14). Our disagreement concerns the direction of the decentering. If it is toward God as arbitrary omnipotent commander, of what value is it? If it is toward God as Love, how is that compatible with the command to kill an innocent child? If it is toward God as the source of eschatological possibility, then it makes sense and we agree.

55. Derrida, *Gift of Death*, 49.

56. Ibid., 56–57.

57. Ibid., 59.

58. Ibid., 60.

59. Ibid., 61. Again, my rhetoric is intentionally polemical here, but this is necessary in response to John Caputo's polemics, such as his insistence that obligation has to be incomprehensible to the agent to be authentic obligation: see *Against Ethics* (Bloomington: Indiana University Press, 1993), 8–10. It is unclear why he thinks this, because the *involuntariness* of obligation hardly entails its unintelligibility to reason or its heterogeneity to language.

60. Derrida quotes this passage because it ends with the ethical as a "temptation." But Silentio does not mean that the ethical makes us "irresponsible" (Ibid.); rather, the temptation refers to stopping with infinite resignation inside the ethical, rather than *adding* to infinite resignation the second movement of faith in the "absurd."

61. For further evidence in favor of this reading of Problema III, see my essay, "Kierkegaard's *Postscript* in Light of *Fear and Trembling*" §II.

62. Derrida, *Gift of Death*, 62.

63. See Caputo, *Against Ethics*, 18: "In short, Johannes de Silentio writes a eulogy to obligation without ethics" (in the sense of ethical theory or normative principles).

64. Derrida, *Gift of Death*, 92–93.

65. Ibid., 63: "The absolute duty that binds me to God himself, in faith, must function beyond and against any duty I have" in the ordinary sense of "duty" as respect for the moral law.

66. Ibid., 84. Derrida adds here that Levinas's ethics is also already "religious" because it cannot distinguish between "the infinite alterity of God and that of every human." This seems to be incorrect, because Levinas does distinguish between ipseity and alterity. But even if it were correct, that would not make Levinas's ethics "religious" in the eschatological sense—the sense that actually distinguishes religious categories from all natural knowledge and naturally accessible categories, including the phenomenology of the Face.

67. Ibid., 66.

68. Ibid., 96. Indeed, nothing given *because* demanded could ever count as a gift in Derrida's sense of gratuitous or pure generosity; demands for gifts are violent and even self-defeating, since they prevent free giving by ordering it.

69. Derrida is correct that Abraham does make this decision and it is only within this "instant" between decision and completed action that God stays his hand. He is also correct that "it is as if he [God] did not know what Abraham was going to do, decide, or decide to do" (Ibid., 95). This is one of many points in the pseudonymous works that suggest what would now be called an "open" conception of God that preserves human leeway–libertarian freedom (though in signed religious works Kierkegaard does affirm complete divine foreknowledge).

70. Ibid., 96.

71. Derrida implies more than once that God demands that we give him gifts, as if God *needed* us to set aside our debts and duties to other human beings to turn to Him (Ibid., 72). By contrast, the eschatological interpretation says that the love God demands consists primarily in following His moral laws in interacting with human persons and the world, and *having faith* in His promise that the ideal behind these laws will be fulfilled within time or at its end.

72. Caputo emphasizes these points in "Instants, Secrets, and Singularities," 219: "Abraham is willing to make a gift of the life of Isaac." Kierkegaard would regard this as pure nonsense, not paradoxical sublimity: for my sacrifice of X to count as a gift of X, I must think that I am the rightful owner of X. Though parents may at one time have seen their children as property, Silentio certainly does not describe Abraham this way.

73. Derrida, *Gift of Death*, 96–97 (last set of italics mine). Note that if this were right, then a clever calculator could anticipate it and have himself hypnotized or trained not to barter with God but rather to give freely, in order to get the reward. This would be a theological version of Derek Parfit's self-effacing egoistic strategy in *Reasons and Persons*. Thus Caputo is right that on Derrida's reading, God turns Abraham's act "into an economy of sacrifice" in which the agent gets a return ("Instants, Secrets, and Singularities," 229). But Caputo does not see how dramatically this counts against Derrida's interpretation!

74. Ibid., 97 (my italics).

75. To which Derrida refers on 99.

76. Ibid., 100–10, but I am focusing on the negative in this chapter. In doing so, I fear I will offend many persons of goodwill whom I do not wish to offend, perhaps even some friends. But someone had to say it: in the analysis of Kierkegaard, Emperor Derrida has no ethical clothes, despite the fine terms in which these clothes are often praised.

77. Ibid., 63.

78. For a discussion of non-erosiac forms of evil motivation, see Davenport, *Will as Commitment and Resolve*, chap. 10.

79. See G. E. Moore, *Principia Ethica* (New York: Prometheus, 1988), §59, p. 99.

80. Compare Caputo, "Instants, Secrets, and Singularities," 223.

81. Dr. Seuss, *How the Grinch Stole Christmas* (New York: Random House, 1957). This applies even more clearly to the expanded storyline in the new movie adaptation, *The Grinch*, directed by Ron Howard, with Jim Carey as the Grinch (Universal Studios, 2000). The Grinch steals the gifts and thus unwittingly gives a greater gift. His return of the Christmas gifts in this story is another eucatastrophe, in which it turns out that Christmas means "a little bit more" than economy.

82. If the underground man example seems odd, consider that Derrida seems to cele-

brate Bartleby's refusal to speak as a "sacrificial passion" (75), rather than recognizing it as aesthetic spiritlessness.

83. Derrida, *Gift of Death*, 67.

84. Ibid., 68 (my italics).

85. Actually, I don't think this goes far enough. On the banal logic behind this interpretation of agapic obligation, we might as well extend it to require that I be present for each other at every point in history as well, and indeed on every other planet in the universe on which personal beings exist, and call the physical impossibility of doing so part of the "paradox" and angst of the higher-ethical attitude that makes it so fraught with torment. On the other hand, when everyone can become a knight of faith simply by accepting the ubiquity of moral dilemma in every circumstances, hasn't the price of faith come down a bit? Why feel so lonely and singularized by the impossible call?

86. See, for example, Christopher Gowans, *Moral Dilemmas* (New York: Oxford University Press, 2001).

87. Derrida, *Gift of Death*, 69.

88. Several conceptions of agapic love leave too little place for forms of love or devotion that are "partial" or particularistic; arguably, Kierkegaard himself fails to recognize that parental, filial, and romantic love can sometimes be appropriate expressions of agapic regard or ways of fulfilling agapic duties. But the problem with Derrida's account should be distinguished from this well-known problem of reconciling agape with other forms of love: for on Derrida's account, it is not possible to show agapic regard to a single other person without failing in one's agapic duty to all the rest; acts of parental devotion, *philia*, or *eros* are betrayals in the same sense, not in a distinct sense.

89. Perhaps I just don't understand Derrida. For after forty years, I have got no further than the ethical, while Derrida has passed right beyond the everyday ethical concerns that worry me into a higher kind of religiousness above my meager powers of comprehension.

90. W. D. Ross, *The Right and the Good* (Indianapolis: Hackett, 1988), 20.

91. Caputo, "Instants, Secrets, and Singularities," 217.

92. Ibid., 225.

93. Derrida, *Gift of Death*, 86.

94. Ibid., 86. I fear that we are meant to infer that no market system whatsover, however limited, could ever be just to individuals qua individuals. For this issue, we'd have to look at *Specters of Marx*.

95. Ibid., 86–87.

96. Caputo, *Against Ethics*, 37. I'm happy to be corrected, but I do not recall Derrida calling for ground troops from France to stop the slaughter in Rwanda, Bosnia, or Kosovo; but then why would he, if standing idly by and allowing ethnic cleansing and genocide is no better than using force to try to stop it, because either way we are sacrificing all the other absolute others, and so on?

97. See Kierkegaard, *Concluding Unscientific Postscript*, trans. Howard Hong and Edna Hong (Princeton, N.J.: Princeton University Press, 1992), "The Decisive Expression of the Existential Pathos," 525–55.

98. Ibid., 528–29.

99. Ibid., 530.

100. Ibid., 532; this is one of the differences between "guilt" and "sin," which is also not determined but in fact always already present in each of us. Thus strictly speaking, we should say "possible in the *initial* development of our agency." On this theme, see Kierkegaard's *Concept of Anxiety*.

101. Ibid., 548. The "silent relation to the ideal" in inwardness that blames only itself rather than others for its faults concerns the purity of our motives and the strength of our will, rather than (only) our outward acts.

102. On this point, see John J. Davenport, "My *Schindler's List:* A Personal Kierke-gaardian Reflection," *Religious Humanism* 34, no. 2–3 (Summer-Fall 2001): 13–23. In the terms of this chapter, Derrida's idea of infinity in duty seems to be a quantitative infinity or aggregation of tasks summing to infinity. However, specifying the right version of the ought-implies-can principle remains a tricky business because of the complexity of the relevant sense of "can."

103. Derrida, *Gift of Death,* 51. Note that this implication seems to be a de dicto *metaphysical* necessity.

104. Knud Løgstrup, *The Ethical Demand,* intro. Hans Fink and Alasdair MacIntyre (Notre Dame, Ind.: University of Notre Dame Press, 1997), 46–47. I do not comment here on Løgstrup's own critique of Kierkegaard's conception of agapic duties in his "polemical epilogue," since that deserves detailed treatment. However, Løgstrup's own version seems to require intermediate principles (or secondary precepts, as Mill would have called them) to guide judgment concerning what love for the other whose life or well-being rests in our hands requires for us in different types of circumstance. I think this is the right way to go: otherwise an agapic version of moral perfectionism turns into an empty situation-ethics that can provide little practical guidance.

105. Though Climacus does not discuss the love commands explicitly in the way that *Works of Love* does, it is still clear that he thinks the totality of guilt does not occur in *Sittlichkeit,* since legal or conventional systems are restricted to particular lists of acts to be done or avoided and lack any qualitatively infinite background demand on our motives (e.g., 537). This aligns the totality of guilt with the second ethics of the religious stage, and indeed Climacus characterizes it as part of Religiousness A: it requires absolute divine authority (544).

106. Derrida, *Gift of Death,* 78. He stresses that God is just a name for the fact that "every other (one) is every (bit) other" (77).

107. Here is the origin of Caputo's error in replacing Levinas's "excess" of the other with "infinite partiality" to a single other person (*Against Ethics,* 19).

Part Four.

Ethico-Political Possibilities

9 The Challenge of Justice: The Ethics of "Upbuilding"

Edith Wyschogrod

Can it not be argued that Emmanuel Levinas's assertion that ethics is grounded in the primacy of the other person's claim upon the self in effect sanitizes the moral life by unrealistically detaching it from social actuality? Does he not also contend that an ethics of otherness at its deepest level depends upon the impact created by the presence of another, that an ethics of for-the-other lies beyond predication, beyond the possibility of utterance? In response, it can be said that when duality is ruptured by the advent of another other, the entry of a third party, one who is neither the self nor the first other, the need for justice is born and that justice necessitates juridical regulations. Social existence that is termed "just" is contingent upon the enactment of laws that govern the relations of multiple others to one another. How, it must then be asked, are these juridical sanctions to be grounded? Is one's relation to the other that is grounded neither in rational rules nor in the calculation of the consequences of actions based upon empirical observation not imbricated by default, as it were, in yet another relation, a relation to a transcendent Other? If so, the connection to transcendence must affect the ways in which one acts towards others in actual existence. Is there then not the necessity for a formative discourse, a mode of "upbuilding," a term favored by Kierkegaard, that would take account of the social responsibilities incurred when multiple others are involved? What is more, does not the single individual whom Kierkegaard addresses not become everyone? (EUD, 505 n. 6) Although Levinas does not refer to upbuilding, some of the multiple meanings attributed to the term by Kierkegaard resonate throughout his work.

Upbuilding: The One or the Many?

The Danish word *opbyggelig*, the adjective in the title of Kierkegaard's numerous *Upbuilding Discourses*, is generally rendered as upbuilding rather than as edifying, a term that in current usage rarely brings to mind the constructing of an edifice but may instead imply reproachful correction. By contrast, upbuilding, as Kierkegaard maintains in *Works of Love*, suggests height but also, inversely, depth since building high requires a foundation. "If one wished to erect a tower that reached the sky . . . if it lacked a foundation it would not actually be built up" (EUD, 504). Upbuilding also should not be confused with the German *Bildung* with its resonances of education, refinement, and cultivation. In the works authored pseudonymously, Kierkegaard upbuilds through duplicity, through the donning and doffing of numerous personas. Determining the perspectives of one who speaks pseudonymously in a Kierkegaardian opus has, it goes without saying, resulted in countless interpretations to which his own ironic response, that he is both secretary and "the author of the author or authors" of those writings, can be given. In contrast to the pseudonymous writings, in the works labeled *Upbuilding Discourses*, Kierkegaard maintains that he is literally the author of their every word.[1] The discourses, he stresses, are not sermons. Nor are they the works of a teacher in which the author designates himself an authority and the reader a learner. In prefaces to these numerous discourses, the addressee is the reader as "the single individual . . . by whom [his book] wishes to be received as if it had arisen in his own heart" (UDVS, 5). Upbuilding does not mean increasing one's abstract knowledge but rather being driven between alternatives and learning to exist with passion. It is all too easy for the single individual to avoid the realization that, tossed between "eternity [as] a winged horse infinitely fast, and time [as] a worn out jade, the existing individual, is the driver" (CUP Swenson/Lowrie, 276).

To be the single individual, Kierkegaard maintains, means having the responsibility to will one thing in truth and intending that this one thing be the good. One must avoid at all costs "double-mindedness that wills the good with a kind of sincerity, but only to a certain degree" in that willing the good admits of no gradations (UDVS, 78). The adumbration of this doubleness can be framed in terms of the subvention of skepticism understood as "the cutting short" and "disarming" of doubt, not through knowledge that sets doubt at rest but through accepting God as the good and as the condition for the overcoming of doubt. "The good is from God. If it were bestowed upon the single individual by the person himself or some other person then it would not be the good . . . God is the only one who gives in such a way that he gives the condition along with the gift" (EUD, 134). Yet Kierkegaard insists upon a precondition of this condition, a sine qua non for overcoming doubt, namely, the individual's renunciation of the desire to be something. Only when the individual who struggles for an explanation for the conditions of existence fails to discover it and experiences himself as reduced to nothing can God imprint himself in him. The problem is not one that is amenable to cognitive resolution. Far from receiving an explanation as he desires, by rendering himself nugatory, the one who struggles is transfigured. I hope to show that, similarly for Levinas, the relation of the good to transcendence is not one of cognition but of self-abnegation, a relation that is inextricably bound up with humility. But crucial for Levinas is the claim that this self-abnegation is constitutive of the ethical relation.

Still, Kierkegaard concedes, in everyday existence there are complex situations in which deliberation is required. One can sink into double-mindedness should one persist in remaining mired in deliberation so that one fails to act. When required to do so by the good, one must act and bear the responsibility for acting. Kierkegaard admits that in the world of time unlike that of eternity "we are cross-questioned about one thing and another" so that it would be illusory to imagine that we could escape "the compounded complexity of interaction" (UDVS, 131). Is the single individual then not inevitably hurled into a world of others? Does Kierkegaard not envision himself as called upon in Levinasian terms to act as teacher or, using Kierkegaard's preferred term, as author, one who solicits passion and who tries to prevent his addressee from escaping into general truths arrived at through rational inquiry. "Generality is not for upbuilding *(opbygges)* because one is never built up in general. Only when the right words are said by the right person in the right situation in the right way," Kierkegaard declares, "only then has the saying done everything it can to guide the single individual to do honestly what one is otherwise quick to do—to refer everything to oneself" (EUD, 276).[2] It would seem that upbuilding allows for, indeed mandates, a place for another, the author and the single individual whom he calls to order.

In addition to the soliciting voice of the author, are there not also the multitudes who live alongside the single individual, those whom Levinas would see as "the neighbor?" Kierkegaard does not fail to notice that in inhabiting a heavily populated world of others, one can lose oneself in the crowd, in what Heidegger came to identify as the perspective of *Das Man*. Kierkegaard maintains that individuals have become abstractions, entities that replicate one another's behavior and, fueled by the popular press, merge into a faceless whole he calls the public (UDVS, 130–31).[3] Fastening upon the deliberate and libelous falsehoods disseminated by the journalists of his day with whom he was famously embroiled, Kierkegaard contends that "almost everyone can have a superficial opinion about everything," the result being that no one assumes responsibility for anything. Yet, he argues, in response to the widespread abnegation of responsibility is one not, by relating to an outside world in effect relating to oneself as a single individual who retains "eternal responsibility"? From the perspective of eternity one is not asked whether he shares the opinion of the crowd nor whether he will give up his usual occupations, but rather whether his convictions are his as those of a single individual (UDVS, 134–35).

Is there then, after all is said and done, a road, a way to be pursued, a path that is upbuilding, that one must find and follow? One ought not, Kierkegaard avers, to ask *where* it is but rather *how* it is trodden. "In hardships" is his answer. What is crucial in his reply is the claim, "It is not the road that is hard but hardship that is the road." The road becomes no easier as one traverses it, but there is also a joy in the knowledge that this is the road: *"This is the joy: That it is not a quality of the road that it is hard but it is a quality of hardship that it is the road"* (UDVS, 300, italics in original). Are we then to assume that the adamantine way, the road is itself the goal or, on the contrary, that hardship is, in fact, a subsidiary good that leads to something beyond that is other than itself? Is hardship then not a sine qua non for the formation of the single individual and, as such, a prime modality of upbuilding? And does Levinas's depiction of persecuted truth not present an apposite conception of the Kierkegaardian subject and the vicissitudes of upbuilding?

Questioning the Self, the Self in Question: Kierkegaard and Levinas

Contesting Hegelian idealism's identification of the subject with thought and its object and the view of philosophy as proclaiming the oneness of thought and being is, Levinas holds, indebted to Kierkegaard for "maintaining human subjectivity . . . as absolute, separated, standing on the hither side of objective being." Inaccessible to cognitive apprehension, subjectivity is a "tensing on oneself [tension sur soi] an undergoing experienced as "a thorn in the side" or more specifically as the Christian sense of sin (PN, 66–67). What is significant in Kierkegaard's critique of antecedent views of knowledge is, for present purposes, his contesting of what Levinas calls "truth triumphant," the assumption that truth is understood in terms of the rational apprehension of existence. The alternative for Kierkegaard, belief, is not conceived as an inferior mode of rational knowledge whose insufficiencies require correction, but rather as a relation to that which "no outside could contain." Crucial for Levinas in this context is Kierkegaard's bringing to the fore the nature of subjectivity as needy and indigent (PN, 69). Thus, Levinas notes, Kierkegaard links belief to a truth that suffers and is persecuted and by way of which the divine manifests itself. It is not the opposition between faith and knowledge that is new in Kierkegaard but rather his insistence on the difference between truth triumphant and truth persecuted. Far from refusing to grant meaning to truth, for Kierkegaard persecution and humility are themselves seen as modes of truth.

Nonetheless, Levinas faults Kierkegaard for what he perceives as a subvention or downgrading of the ethical in that Kierkegaard identifies ethics with the universal so that when subjectivity is lived as ethical existence the singularity of the I is lost (PN, 76).[4] But for Levinas it is not the I of Kierkegaard's singular individual that can undo generality but rather the impact of the Other who resists cognitive grasp and who puts the I into question. It could be argued that Kierkegaard's view of singularity more closely resembles Levinas's conception of the passive subject (a notion to which I shall turn) than Levinas acknowledges here. In any event, to convert the Other into an object of thought is to obliterate the Other's alterity by reducing otherness to a content of one's own consciousness so that otherness becomes what Levinas calls "the Same." When the "egoism" and "imperialism" of the I are put into question by the Other, the I changes from being for itself to being for the Other, is singularized as one who is responsible for the Other. In sum, "Subjectivity is responsibility and only irreducible subjectivity can assume a responsibility. That is what constitutes the ethical" (PN, 73). The singular individual is not a monadic I but an I fractured by the incursion of another.

Still, must there not be an individual anterior to the intrusion of alterity, an existent who is simply a living being, one whose needs must be satisfied and who also seeks the gratification of desires? Must the one who is in quest of satisfying basic needs not attempt to transform the environing world through varied physical, affective and cognitive activities and, as such, master it? Levinas's account of the formation of the ethical subject, of *its* singularity or ipseity, must be distinguished from that of the one who undertakes these mundane activities, the individual existent who has emerged from what he calls the *il y a*, there is, sheer presence that is simply there in the absence of things, a kind of pleroma without aperture.[5] Heidegger's depiction of the condition of human existence as thrownness, being cast into the world, is supplanted by Levinas's account of the emergence of an existent as an event that occurs within the anonymity of being, an event of the mastery of being. Such an existent is a vital self, the self as life, one who fulfills its bodily needs.

For Levinas the manifestation of mastery that is of paramount importance is the upsurge of consciousness in that it is as consciousness that the experience of an individual "something" is born. Being now not only inheres in a "something" that is the object of consciousness but is also experienced by the subject as a property attributable to himself. Consciousness cannot coincide with itself in that "what makes consciousness what it is, is that there can be departure from and a return to self, a process of identification that enables the existent to renew his existence as solitude."[6] It is worth noting that for Levinas solitude is not the consequence of removing others as a negative reaction to social existence, but in his early works, solitude appears (counter-intuitively, as it were) before there are others. Consciousness comes into being having itself as a starting point and discovers in its very individuality a refuge from being. At the outset consciousness is an event, that of emerging from being, but it is subsequently hypostatized into a substantive. It is as solitary existents that we bestow significations upon the world.[7]

The Tutelage of the Other: "I Fear for You"

We have seen that, especially in Levinas's earlier works, the subject is not only the subject as consciousness but is also an independent existent who is in the world as a body, a vital self whose needs must be satisfied. The stance of the existent toward undifferentiated being, the *il y a*, is one of horror in that the *il y a* can only be envisaged by one already in a world as the destruction of all that is. Maurice Blanchot refers to the horror of a subject's detachment from any fixed anchorage as a "disaster" in an etymological sense as detachment from a star. However, the independent self of everyday existence is a self of mastery that attempts to erect a bastion against the anonymity of the all-engulfing *il y a*. Even the transformative character of the new technologies, Levinas warns, does not eradicate the threatening formlessness of the *il y a*. Far from precluding a return to the world of self and ontology, the *il y a* lies beyond them.

The subject who attempts to control the world is also an affective being, a subject of feeling who inhabits an environment that Levinas designates the elemental, a backdrop without differentiable form—earth, sky, sea, light—that, in contrast to the *il y a,* can support life lived as visceral enjoyment. When immersed in the elemental, a non-possessable environment exterior to it, the independent existent can experience a joy that is irreducible to thought and is lived as affective intentionality. Although the elemental itself cannot be owned, it is the sine qua non for possession. "Every relation or possession is situated within the non-possessable which envelops or contains without being able to be contained or enveloped."[8] Amenable to neither cognition nor use, it can be dominated but still remains what it was before, the backdrop for instinctive biological needs and drives now lived as joy. In *Totality and Infinity,* the *il y a* is that into which the elemental is extended so that the possibility for the withdrawal of enjoyment can be envisaged as a swallowing up of the elemental itself. Because existence in the elemental is that of natural man it is, as such, innocent, devoid of the taint of original sin. As existence that has not yet been penetrated by the Other as other, it is also atheistic.[9] Thus understood, human existence is not a fall, a decline from a better state, but rather a condition for the emergence of consciousness whose upsurge is for Levinas necessary. In sum, life in the elemental appears to be a prerequisite for the upbuilding of an ethics into which the Other enters. On this account, could it not then be argued that the prelapsarian innocence of enjoyment is itself a necessary part of the process of upbuilding? Still, satiety and pleasure do not exhaust affectivity in that ethics itself requires still another mode of affectivity, a primordial non-intentional passivity that awaits the advent of the Other and to which I shall return in detail.[10]

Before grappling with the tensions inherent within this passivity, it may be helpful to explore the diremptions in the Levinasian conception of the active ego and its overcoming as an inversion of the dialectical relation of mastery and bondage depicted in Hegel's *Phenomenology.* Hegel's reading of the relation of two consciousnesses neither of which is yet aware of itself as self-consciousness has, needless to say, made its influence felt in numerous trenchant recent interpretations from Adorno to Sartre and Derrida to name a few. For Hegel, when "life" is the natural setting of consciousness and death its natural negation, two living beings may engage in a struggle in which each perishes. If both die, no conscious entity remains from which self-consciousness could emerge.[11] But when one of the contenders wishes to persist as an independent being, he realizes that life is essential to him and fearing for his life, he surrenders to the other. However in so doing, he exists in bondage to the other who managed to conquer fear and is now *eo ipso* master.

Levinas's claim that, with the advent of the Other, the self fears not for its own life but for the life of the Other can be read as a double inversion of the preceding segment of Hegel's narrative. A self, willing to go proxy for the Other, to substitute itself for the Other when the Other is endangered, lives in fear *for* not *of* the Other. In fearing for the life of another, the self is in bondage to the Other for whom he fears. At the same time in fearing for the Other it is also he, the one who is in bondage to the Other, who *confers* mastery upon the Other and is, as such, master. In contrast to Hegel's bondsman, the Levinasian self as a living self is willing to risk his life in the interest of that Other but thereby remains subservient to the Other but paradoxically, in conferring mastery, expresses the self-mastery of not fearing for himself. Can fear for the Other experienced from each of these perspectives not be viewed as modes of affective upbuilding? Is the Other in each case not higher than the self and, as such, is s/he not in effect my teacher?

Justice: The Challenge of *le Tiers*

For Levinas, Hegel's bequest to philosophy is the view that "the labour of thought wins out over the otherness of things and men,"[12] a legacy that continues in the primacy attributed to thought in Husserl's depiction of consciousness as intentional. Consciousness aims at apprehending its objects thereby making them its own. What Husserl calls the transcendental reduction "suspends all independence of the world other than that of consciousness itself." The I is master both of its own nature and of the world.[13] To be sure, Levinas in conformity with the later Husserl, Merleau-Ponty and others also speaks of the I that constitutes the world as a bodily I, an I that is corporeally imbricated in the world that consciousness is said to constitute. However, in addition, there is alongside of consciousness' grasp of its world and of itself, a non-intentional consciousness that accompanies intentional acts. "Indirect, implicit, aimless without any initiative that may refer back to an ego, [it is] passive like time passing and aging me without my intervening."[14] Its temporality is that of pure duration as duration, as a lapse in time and whose role is the effacing of presence. Unlike the Hegelian subject, this self refuses to return to itself and recoils before self-identification. This self, Levinas claims, is not guilty but accused, "responsible for its very presence." Does upbuilding in this context not occur as a challenge to the self's justification of itself and as an affirmation of its primordial passivity? The non-intentional is passivity in and through which "the very justice of my position within being, my right to be, is placed in question."[15] Is the pre-originary self insofar as it is one whose passivity is a reproach to egoity and subject to an unincorporable Other not, in this call to humility, called as the single individual who is in effect Kierkegaard's addressee?

Is the one who is altogether other not one who is higher than the self? But the Other is also one who is nigh, who in her/his proximity to me is another who is my neighbor. "The other as other, as neighbor, is in his presence never equal to his proximity. . . . Between the one I am and the other, for whom I am responsible, there gapes open a difference, without a basis in community." Proximity as difference is indescribable. But my responsibility is non-indifference to the Other, itself a primordial mode of signification, a reason prior to thematization "a pre-original reason that does not proceed from any initiative of the subject, an anarchic reason" (OTB, 166). Yet far from sinking into a mode of irrationalism, Levinas develops a critical distinction, the difference between the Saying, language that signifies otherwise than propositionally, and the said, the language of being. A doubleness or what Levinas calls the amphibology of being is manifested in the said both as the designation of identities and as the verb in predicative propositions in which substance dissolves into modes of being and temporalization (OTB, 40). However "from the amphibology of being and entities in the said we must go back to the Saying which signifies prior to essence, prior to identification on the hither side of this amphibology. Saying states and thematizes the said by signifying it to the other, the neighbor" with a meaning that is different from what is actually stated in the said (OTB, 46).

How can the Saying that signifies otherwise than propositionally convey its meaning in the said? "Saying taken strictly is a 'signifyingness dealt the other,' prior to all objectification" and signifies as proximity (OTB, 47). As such, "proximity can remain the signification of the very knowing in which it shows itself" (OTB, 157). As a relation between two individuals, proximity fits the Levinasian paradigm of self and Other but becomes a problem with the entry of the third who is also other and therefore an equal source of responsibility, one whom I must not harm. As such, the third, *le tiers,* gives rise to the need for justice, for thought and philosophy. "Justice is necessary, that is thematization . . . intentionality and the intellect, the intelligibility of a system." In turn this need for intelligibility and thence in what is crucial for my present purposes is a prerequisite for the ultimate desideratum: "An equal footing before a court of justice" (OTB, 157).[16] To be sure, philosophy allows for the intrusion of the Saying into the said. What is crucial, however, in the context of upbuilding is that philosophy is essentially required by the juridical, by what is called to thought by justice. The third does not provide an entering wedge for an ethics of calculation but rather is experienced as obsession. In the Other all the others obsess me, an obsession that cries out for justice. What is significant is that the law is "in the midst of proximity." Justice is not primordially understood as a subsuming of cases under a rule but rather as presupposing proximity (OTB, 159–60). Nonetheless, the path from the immediacy of primordial responsibility to justice in its worldly manifestations requires rational control, the search for a principle. It is in this context that philosophy can bring into discursive clarity the difference between the one and the other while remaining subservient to the Saying.

The Claims of Law

The assertion that if there is to be justice there must be law derives for Levinas from his study of rabbinic literature, of Halakhah, the legal literature of the Bible and the Talmud. It is particularly the literature of the Talmud upon which Levinas focuses and that functions for him as a paradigmatic mode of upbuilding. Insofar as rabbinic discussion is not confined to case law but is aimed at uncovering multiple meanings implicit in a juridical text that help to determine the legal principle from which a concrete decision should be drawn, the rabbis themselves uncover rational meanings in biblical passages. Thus, Levinas holds, a philosophical approach to their significations is justified.[17] He refers to his own philosophical task as one of translation, a rendering of Hebrew into Greek. In addition to the casuistry of the Halakhah, Levinas often resorts to Aggaddic or homiletical texts in that they graphically reflect philosophical concepts. Thus he writes, "in fact it is a *Halakhah*, a lesson that teaches conduct to be maintained, that states a law. But the *Halakhah* in the text itself, and *without provocation by an interpreter,* transforms itself into *Aggadah,* a homiletic text" a mode transposable into philosophical expression but which then itself morphs into Halakhah.[18]

Levinas attributes this view to his Talmud teacher in Paris, a certain mysterious Shushani, rather than to his early education in the subject in a Lithuanian yeshiva. The influence of the latter is not to be underestimated as may be inferred from Levinas's essay devoted to the influential nineteenth century Lithuanian rabbi, Chaim of Volozhin, whose life and work are for him exemplary.[19] Legal scholar Chaim Saiman in an article unrelated to Levinas depicts this approach and draws out its implications. Unknown to American or German schools of legal science, Saiman writes, "in the small Lithuanian town of Volozhin, a group of legal scholars were creating their own fusion of law theology and science. . . . [a] method known as the Brisker *derekh* or simply Brisk . . . a conceptual and 'scientific' vision of *halakhah.* Brisk revolutionized the study of Jewish law by recasting the multitude of [its] detailed rules into a system of legal concepts."[20] Although they were relatively insulated from developments in European legal thought, those who labored there could not avoid being affected by widespread general secularization. A key feature of the Yeshiva, the house of study founded by Reb Hayyim Volozhin was Torah *lishma,* Torah studied for its own sake, a standpoint that prioritized the study of Talmud over other expressions of religious life. For Volozhin, to know God is to be familiar with God's law.[21] Levinas has on occasion radicalized this precept in the admonition to love the Torah more than God, an admonition that can be interpreted as love for the text as that which in the order of human existence goes proxy for a transcendence that is beyond access. Although the practical case related outcomes of study were not ignored, "the curriculum was weighted against decision rendering," focusing instead on argumentation.[22] In conformity with this style, positions in a dispute were matched with one of two *hakira* [two sides of a legal dispute]. The Halakhic interpreter showed how "perhaps equal from the standpoint of both reason and tradition, each position is acceptable," a principle to which Levinas adverts when he writes, "the recorders of the Talmud text recorded the opinion that was rejected. . . . It is still written down" (BTV, 114). In effect, legal details are used in the interest of eliciting core concepts.[23]

The attention paid to legal detail can be interpreted as attesting the primacy of the particular but, paradoxically, the particular as such can play an important role in Talmudic casuistry. Halakhic discourse does not undermine the particular but rather deploys it to prevent what might otherwise occur as the overturning of a general principle by converting it into its opposite. The vantage point of the particular when brought to bear upon a general principle can foil what Levinas refers to as a principle's "Stalinization," the ideological inversion of the rule's ethical intent.[24] It is significant that the appeal to a particular decree does not halt the dialectical process that determined it but opens further discussion. Rather, controversy reflecting multiple rabbinic perspectives is itself an expression of the flourishing of Halakhic discourse (LR, 200).

Entweder Oder: Staging the Third

The juridical and philosophical contexts in which justice as a relation to another other, a third, is seen does not exhaust the meaning of the third. In order to expand upon yet another sense in which the third must be understood, it is necessary to return once again to the *il y a* in order to distinguish it from another mode of exclusion from being and non-being, a beyond that Levinas designates *illeity.* The third person pronoun, *il,* is converted to a noun that refers to a third as another that is other than the Other and, as such, can have reference to God. Outside ontological discourse and united by their ineffability, the *il y a* and *illeity* constitute a new polarity, a dyad of ineffables. The *il y a* is encountered in a movement of descent into that which is infra-cognitive, a pre-originary state prior to emergence of a self whereas *illeity* is encountered as a movement of ascent towards the good. Levinas is compelled to speculate whether "if [god] is transcendent, to the point of absence [there could be] a possible confusion with a stirring of *there is,*" terms that, as Hent de Vries notes, Levinas means to be functionally distinct while the question of their interactive alternation remains.[25] In sum, in the absence of predicable characteristics, the notions of physical or conceptual space are inapplicable to both. And, if there can be no distance between the *il y a* and *illeity* such a whole could be construed as sheer absence, as nothing, so that nihilism would be the outcome and upbuilding rendered moot. To be sure their difference remains beyond cognitive grasp but, I would maintain, the ineffability through which they have become indistinguishable does not undo a difference in placement, a hierarchical staging of the there is and transcendence.

For Kierkegaard, stages of existence are depicted as markers of identity, determinants of like and unlike. Even if, in the manner of the aesthetic and the religious, they may resemble one another with respect to their affective intensities, a radically disjunctive logic is strengthened by the claim that one cannot avoid choosing. "I shout it to you, Either/Or, *aut, aut,* for the introduction of a single *aut* does not clarify the matter," Kierkegaard proclaims (E/O II, 38). Even in what is often regarded as the *locus classicus* of the tension between stages, the teleological suspension of the ethical as played out in *Fear and Trembling* most frequently glossed as faith triumphing over the ethical, can it not be said be said that Abraham holds both moments in their disjunctiveness, each a reproach as it were to its alternative.

In his account of the either/or, the aut/aut, Kierkegaard looks at choice not as a situation of reasoned deliberation about specifiable alternatives but rather as an existential involvement in the options at hand. "That which is chosen has the deepest relation to the one who is choosing" (E/O II, 63). Thus the ethical as a quintessential moment of choice is embedded in an existential context. If choice is indissolubly bound up with the ethical, can the ethical ever be transcended? In what can be construed as a Levinasian gesture, a concession to the other, Kierkegaard reflects upon a paradox within the ethical itself, upon what it means to be in the wrong. If I think I have done right by the other but discover that I am being ignored by the other who goes his own way or does otherwise then I have done wrong by the other. But doing wrong is edifying, a lesson in upbuilding. To be sure, it is painful to be in the wrong but, Kierkegaard asserts, upbuilding calls me to attention so that the more often I am in the wrong, the more upbuilding.

What is more, upbuilding opens the way to understanding the relation between the finite and the infinite. "Wishing to be in the wrong is an infinite expression of a finite relationship" (E/O II, 348). Since the infinite builds one up, is it not paradoxically upbuilding to be in the wrong? Yet Kierkegaard asserts "in your relationship with God, you would be freed from the contradiction." To be sure, one wants God to be in the right, but in so doing, one would have lost the upbuilding. He concludes powerfully that our upbuilding is always being in the wrong relation to God. Just as one is forced by love to want to be in the wrong in relation to the beloved because one loves that person, the love of God places one as always in the wrong in relation to God. In wanting to be in the wrong vis-à-vis God, one concedes that God is always in the right but the thought that God is in the right cannot then be Upbuilding. And if one is always in the wrong in relation to God, will being in the wrong not paralyze the will, become anesthetizing however upbuilding? On the contrary. By destroying doubt, this thought "inspires to action" (E/O II, 53).[26] "What I really lack is to be clear in my mind *what I am to do* . . . The thing is to understand myself, to see what God really wishes *me* to do; the thing is to find a truth which is true for me, to find the idea for which I can live or die"[27] For Levinas, what I am commanded to do, that for which I can live or die and what God wants of me, is to respond to the cry of the Other.

Notes

1. See Kierkegaard, "First and Last Declaration," in *Concluding Unscientific Postscript*, trans. David F. Swenson and Walter Lowrie (Princeton, N.J.: Princeton University Press, 1941), appendix. Hereafter cited parenthetically as (CUP Swenson/Lowrie) followed by a page number.

2. See also EUD, 475.

3. See also "The Present Age" in TA.

4. For a critical examination of Levinas's critique of Kierkegaard as identifying the ethical with the universal, see Hent de Vries, "Adieu, à dieu, a-Dieu," in *Ethics as First Philosophy: The Significance of Emmanuel Levinas for Philosophy, Literature, and Religion,* ed. Adriaan Peperzak (London: Routledge, 1995), 210–22.

5. See Levinas, "There Is: Existence without Existents," in LR, 29–36. See also TO, 46–49.

6. See Edith Wyschogrod, *Emmanuel Levinas: The Problem of Ethical Metaphysics,* 2nd ed. (New York: Fordham University Press, 2000), 17.

7. Ibid., 18. For a concise account of Levinas's relation to Husserl and Heidegger, see Adriaan Peperzak, *Beyond: The Philosophy of Emmanuel Levinas* (Evanston, Ill.: Northwestern University Press, 1997), 38–52). See also Michael Purcell, *Levinas and Theology* (Cambridge: Cambridge University Press, 2006), 7–22.

8. Wyschogrod, *Problem of Ethical Metaphysics,* 67–68.

9. Ibid., 187. See also Purcell, *Levinas and Theology,* 60–63.

10. For an account of two modes of affectivity, see Andrew Tallon, "Non-intentional Affectivity: Affective Intentionality and the Ethical in Levinas's Philosophy," in Peperzak, *Ethics as First Philosophy,* 107–22.

11. G. W. F. Hegel, *Phenomenology of Spirit,* trans. A. V. Miller (Oxford: Oxford University Press, 1977), 111–18.

12. Levinas, "Ethics as First Philosophy," in LR, 78.

13. Ibid., 79.

14. Ibid.

15. Ibid., 81–82.

16. For an analysis of the third in its relation to the political, see Bettina Bergo, *For the Beauty That Adorns the Earth: Levinas Between Ethics and Politics* (Dordrecht: Kluwer Academic, 1999), 177–85.

17. Robert Gibbs, *Correlations in Rosenzweig and Levinas* (Princeton, N.J.: Princeton University Press, 1992), 170–71.

18. Ibid., 170. The text cited by Gibbs, p. 171, is a translation from Levinas, *Du Sacre au Saint* #16 (Paris: Les Editions de Minuit, 1977), 155.

19. See Levinas, "'In the Image of God' according to Rabbi Hayyim Volozhiner," in BTV, 151–67.

20. Chaim Saiman, "Legal Theology: The Turn to Conceptualism in Nineteenth Century Jewish Law," *Journal of Law and Religion* 21, no. 1 (2005–2006): 39–100, 40. This article was first brought to my attention by Menachem Butler, a student at Yeshiva University, New York, in connection with the thought of Talmud scholar Joseph B. Soleveitchik.

21. Ibid., 43.

22. Ibid., 44.

23. Oona Eisenstadt maintains that the appeal to a particular that calls a law into question in a juridical ruling is situated not between ethics and politics but on the level of the political. "Levinas in the Key of the Political," in *Difficult Justice: Commentaries on Levinas and Politics,* ed. Asher Horowitz and Gad Horowitz (Toronto: University of Toronto Press, 2005), 74.

24. Levinas, "The Pact," in LR, 220.

25. Levinas, "God and Philosophy," in LR, 177.

26. In her explication of transitions in Kierkegaard, Jaime Ferreira speaks of a leap *to* faith and not a leap *of* faith—a leap spurred by passion, not volition. "Faith and the Kierkegaardian Leap," in *The Cambridge Companion to Kierkegaard,* ed. Alasdair Hannay and Gordon D. Marino (Cambridge: Cambridge University Press, 1998), 226.

27. Kierkegaard, *The Journals of Søren Kierkegaard,* ed. and trans. Alexander Dru (London: Oxford University Press, 1938), 15. Journal entry dated August 1, 1835.

10 Levinas and Kierkegaard: Ethics and Politics

Zeynep Direk

I

Although Kierkegaard and Levinas are both religious philosophers, there are reasons to suspect that Levinas is disturbed by Kierkegaard's philosophy more than any other philosophy he engages. The symptoms of this can be encountered in Levinas' texts even though explicit references to Kierkegaard are often absent. Although communication with Kierkegaard is incessant, the final judgment seems to be crude and harsh, if not violent. In this chapter I shall explore the possibility that both Kierkegaard and Levinas can be read as thinkers of the political beyond their concern with the "ethicity of ethics" and the "religiosity of religion." However, before taking up the question of ethics and politics, I would like to point out that Levinas has a more complicated response to Kierkegaard's thought, beyond what seems to be a rapid dismissal.

Levinas' allusions to Kierkegaard in *Totality and Infinity* and other works and his brief evaluation of Kierkegaard's position in *Proper Names* show that in Levinas' reading, Kierkegaard's critique of ontology in the name of subjectivity remains within the egoism of the I and the care for the self. This final judgment that Levinas has passed on Kierkegaard's philosophy cannot surely foreclose the possibility that Kierkegaard's writings remained a source of inspiration for Levinas.[1] Derrida, the first major commentator on Levinas' work, was also the first philosopher to comment on Levinas' reception of Kierkegaard's thought.[2] In "Violence and Metaphysics" Derrida cites Levinas' phrase "the egoistic cry of a subjectivity still concerned with Kierkegaard's own happiness or salvation"[3] in order to establish that for Levinas Kierkegaard's anti-Hegelian existentialism remains a "violent and pre-metaphysical egoism."[4] Levinas confirms and elaborates this reading in his brief commentary entitled "Kierkegaard: Existence and Ethics."[5] Derrida's inquiry into Levinas' interpretation of Kierkegaard belongs to his thematizing of Levinas' break with phenomenology and ontology, and especially Levinas' objection to Husserl's strategy in the fifth of *Cartesian Meditations*[6] in which the other's alterity appears first as a question of the other's egoity. Derrida insists against Levinas that the alterity of the other human being remains a question of subjective existence, and therefore implies that Kierkegaard in his defense of subjectivity cared not only for himself but also for the others: "The philosopher Kierkegaard does not *only* plead for Søren Kierkegaard . . . but for subjective existence in general (a noncontradictory expression); this is why his discourse is philosophical, and not in the realm of empirical egoism."[7] Indeed Levinas admits in the final analysis that to conceive alterity in the form of egoity or subjective existence would be to reduce it to totality or anonymous universality. However, this is not the accusation that Levinas makes to Kierkegaard, for in his view Kierkegaard appeals to pre-philosophical experience and provides a non-philosophy in his defense of subjectivity against idealism. Derrida, on the other hand, makes the point that to deny this universal form of egoity and the truth or essence of subjectivity to the Other would not only be to renounce philosophical discourse, but also to exercise the worst violence on the Other. Hence he suggests that Levinas' empirical altruism risks even more violence than the Kierkegaardian philosophy of subjectivity.

Derrida represents Levinas as saying, "Søren Kierkegaard pleads *only* for Kierkegaard." Although this is a fair reformulation of Levinas' final judgment on Kierkegaard's existentialism, its grounds are not clear at all unless we go back to Levinas' critique of idealism. "Kierkegaard: Existence and Ethics" begins by indicating that Kierkegaard's strong notion of existence derives from his critique of idealism. First, it is in that very critique that Kierkegaard opens the dimension of interiority for human subjectivity in European thought. Even though Kierkegaard continues to rethink subjectivity in terms of "self-knowledge," he accounts for it in non-epistemological terms by concentrating on the stages of the subject's self-constitution in the world through "a sacrificial dialectic."[8] This sacrificial dialectic of inwardness is not detached from the subject's situation in the world, its pre-philosophical experiences of its own worldly situations. I think that Levinas' enterprise to rethink the genesis of subjectivity in non-epistemological terms such as hypostasis, enjoyment, economy, dwelling, encounter with the other, and so on, is essentially Kierkegaardian.[9] His Kierkegaardianism shows itself especially when he proceeds to account for the separation of the I in terms of interiority and refers to absolute separation as a relation with the *incognito* of exteriority which interrupts totalization. Second, in Levinas' account Kierkegaard is the first philosopher who has sensed that idealism's totalization implies "the impossibility of discourse, the shadow of evening in the midday sun" (PN, 68). Idealism ends in political totalitarianism "in which human beings are no longer the source of their language, but reflections of the impersonal logos, or roles played by figures" (PN, 68). *Totality and Infinity*'s critique of idealism may shed some light on this. In this work Levinas argues that idealism's strategy of reducing objectivity to the universality of thought renounces the singularity of reason. In idealism, the autonomy and the sovereignty of the person are accomplished in the universal. Personal and particular acts of thinking of separate thinkers count as rational only insofar as they figure as the moments of "unique and universal discourse" (TI, 72). Thus the thinker is comprehended in what he thinks, the speaker is assimilated in his language understood as a system of signs. Kierkegaard has challenged idealism in the name of the inassimilable truth of subjective existence, while for Levinas, in contrast, the problem of idealism is its incapacity to allow for the possibility of the revelation of the Other as another reason in language.

In order to reflect further on how Kierkegaard stands in Levinas' critique of idealism, I shall take into account a few remarks that Franz Rosenzweig makes on the significance of Kierkegaard's philosophy.[10] In the beginning of *The Star of Redemption*[11] Rosenzweig explains that philosophy's original question concerned the knowledge of the All. According to him Hegel represents the coming-to-an-end, the fulfillment of this philosophical task of the knowledge of the All in which the debate between knowledge and faith is also included. In Hegel's philosophy "this knowledge no longer includes merely its object, the All, but also includes itself with no remainder, with no remainder at least according to its own claims and its own particular modalities."[12] He thus not only reconciles the dichotomy of being and thinking but also the problem of knowledge and faith. The truth of Revelation is philosophically confirmed by showing the innermost connection of knowledge and faith. Kierkegaard challenged both the solution brought to the question of faith and the claim of the self-completion of knowledge as nothing but "appearance." Rosenzweig writes, "A highly apparent appearance at any rate, for if the presupposition that was mentioned first is valid, and if all knowledge concerns the All, if it is enclosed in it while being all powerful in it, then that appearance was certainly more than appearance, then it was the truth."[13] Therefore, "whoever still wanted to raise an objection had to feel under his feet an Archimedean point outside of that knowable All."[14] Kierkegaard puts into question the fundamental philosophical presupposition that the All is knowable, by making the point that individual consciousness is irreducible to the All, precisely because it is the Archimedean point where totalization can be opened to question. The subjectivity of the subject must be thought anew by refusing to reduce it to a knower of the All. Not only is pluralism impossible if the subject is dissolved in the All, in the universal, but Kierkegaard also knows that God exceeds the universal, the All; the subject's relation to God is irreducible to the philosophical tradition of knowing the All, taking care of all beings. However, the Archimedean point from which Kierkegaard contests the Hegelian integration of Revelation into the All must be tested by the translatability of the individual consciousness to the universal, which is of course the fundamental presupposition of the Hegelian enterprise. In Rosenzweig's view, Kierkegaard can hold his position against Hegel even if the possibility of translation is real: even if everything in it (the individual consciousness) could be translated into the universal—there remained the fact of having a first and last name, the most personal thing in the strictest and narrowest sense of the word, and everything depended precisely on that personal reality, as the bearer of these experiences asserted."[15] The name is the untranslatable bearer of the experiences that may well be ultimately reintegrated into the All by way of translation. Thus the untranslatability of the proper name is the very opening of the pluralism, the beyond of philosophy in the classical sense.

Rosenzweig had called the philosophical concern "the knowledge of All," the equivalent of this in Heideggerian language would be "taking into consideration beings as a whole." In its attempt to take into consideration the totality of beings, philosophy's task is to meditate the question of the Being of beings. If we turn to Levinas' early critique of idealism, as it is manifest for example in *On Escape*, idealism appears to be a more advanced philosophical position than realist materialism, because it raises the question of the Being of beings without reducing the question of transcendence.[16] Nevertheless, because that question could not exceed the framework in which it appears in terms of knowing the Being of beings, idealism does not give any "exit from Being." Although I cannot pursue here the development of the question of transcendence in Levinas from the 1930s to the 1960s, I can point out that in *Totality and Infinity* Levinas takes the face-to-face relation with the Other as the concretization of a structure of transcendence which he explains with reference to Descartes's idea of infinity. The face-to-face is for Levinas the primordial event of signification. The face as the origin of the sign function cannot be reduced to a differential relation between the signs it emits, but signifies itself by itself, *kath'auto*. Its signification cannot be adequately grasped by my *Sinngebung*, but overflows it. In this way Levinas rethinks the irreducibility of the exteriority of the Other to a system of signs, the revelation of the Other as another Reason who teaches me by putting my rationality into question. Here we can read Levinas as responding to Rosenzweig's interpretation of Kierkegaard, in which the proper name gives itself as the Archimedean point from which totality can be put into question, the irreducible place of a religious experience with God who exceeds the universal, by making the claim that the religious experience in the Kierkegaardian sense, namely, as knowing one's self in the inward relation to the Absolute remains an "ethical egoism." Given this mediated background, the formulation "Søren Kierkegaard *only* pleads for Kierkegaard" is fair because the irreducibility of the proper name, whatever that name may be, whether it be Søren Kierkegaard, a pseudonym, or Emmanuel Levinas' own proper name, cannot be the basis of pluralism or of opening to the beyond of totality. Without the irreducibility of the signification of the Other, the Other as signifier signifying itself to a system of signs in terms of which the Same identifies itself, totality remains intact. This is perhaps why Levinas writes, "The same is essentially identification within the diverse, or history, or system. It is not I who resist the system, as Kierkegaard thought; it is the other" (TI, 40). Without doubt, the accusation of ethical egoism brought to Kierkegaard's philosophy presupposes a specific conception of the identification of the Same in terms of care for the self or as *conatus essendi*, but it is also based on a fundamental philosophical disagreement on the possibility of a break of totality.

Levinas argues that Kierkegaard's concern with subjectivity as such would still be an egoistic cry if it misses the ethicity of ethics, namely, ethics as the relation to the Other beyond an anonymous and totalizing universalism. Arguably, Levinas and Kierkegaard do not agree on what the term "ethics" signifies.[17] Judge William says in *Either/Or* that "the task of the ethical individual is to transform himself into the universal individual" (E/O II, 261). And yet this universality does not permit the subject's relation with the beyond. Levinas is critical of ethics as a system of prescriptions or rules of action for everyone and agrees with Kierkegaard that this universalism does not permit a relation with the absolute alterity beyond an anonymous universalism. However for Levinas this relation with absolute alterity is what constitutes "the ethicity of ethics," and not religious experience understood as the solitary inward relation of the person with God who is a transcendent Being. Clearly, there are important differences between Kierkegaard's and Levinas' understandings of the beyond. For Levinas the responsible subject cannot relate to God except through the face of the Other and God can be said to be present at the Other's face, only as a trace of its retreat. In concluding this section on Levinas' reception of Kierkegaard's philosophy, I would like to point out that Derrida's remarks on this reception miss the complexity of the level at which Levinas has been engaging with Kierkegaard's thought. Even though Kierkegaard appears very rarely in *Totality and Infinity,* he is surely present as an interlocutor at every crucial step that Levinas takes in this work. For Levinas, Kierkegaard was already putting the totality in question, yet he could not really open up the pluralism he sought for since he lost sight of ethics as a religious experience.

II

It is possible to be misled by Levinas' critique of politics as a power game, totalization, war by other means, pursuit of one's own interests at the expense of the others, and so on, and by Kierkegaard's efforts to distance himself from politics as a question of identity, collectivity, and common praxis, devotion to one's own worldly interest or to the others in the world. Levinas opposes politics to ethics, and Kierkegaard to religious experience. On the other hand, as I shall show, it is unfair to read either philosopher as an apolitical thinker.

It may appear at first sight that an orientation by the question of politics will not take us very far to the heights or depths of Kierkegaard's philosophy. At its best, political life belongs to the category of the ethical life which aims to equalize the interior and the exterior and thus means a turn away from the secret of subjectivity. The ethico-political stage of life has to be overcome in pure faith. The soul becomes spirit by the turn to inwardness in which the self is known through a relation with the Absolute. One cannot know one's self by taking seriously one's worldly facticity and the historical forces that pervade it. To interpret the self as the product of such forces would be to deny the possibility of its freedom and the ideal of a true self beyond the meaningless contingency of existence. Kierkegaard also denies that the self is created by its own actions, that is, through what it brings into the historical world by its ethical, political, and artistic deeds. In contrast to what the pagans would think, immortality or eternity is not achieved by great human deeds. Devotion to the universal, ethical, or political way of life does indeed deserve respect in comparison with the aesthetic way of life, but it is nonetheless a way of fleeing at the face of one's self. To struggle to achieve a better and more just or more equal life for everyone living in the world can be a way of busying one's self with the world. This representation of Kierkegaard's thought is not incorrect, though it hides a lot from our view and does not explain why Kierkegaard is so concerned with the question of history in *The Concept of Anxiety*. Kierkegaard pretends to set a person's inner history in opposition to an external history which includes the realm of the political. His discourse appears to rest on the presupposition that the inner history of the soul's becoming spirit does not depend on the external history. But on the other hand, Kierkegaard attempts to think the possibility of the historicity essential to Christianity, and which lies at its doctrine of hereditary sin. If the question of historicity displaces and hides the political in Kierkegaard's philosophy, his account of the hereditary sin in *The Concept of Anxiety* cannot amount to an apolitical psychology or anthropology. Kierkegaard has preferred to reflect on individual human existence instead of concerning himself in an abstract way with the metaphysical, ethical, and political questions of philosophy. However, such questions cannot be properly dealt with by ignoring that not only the subject's own existence but all incarnated existence calls for thinking in anxiety. The feeling of anxiety is a mark of inwardness which Vigilius Haufniensis calls "an understanding, but in concreto" (CA, 142).

In interpreting his claim that a life devoted to political or ethical affairs, a life invested in the care for the others may serve as an alibi for not caring sufficiently for the self, it is useful to refer Kierkegaard to the Socratic tradition, in *Alcibiades,* that sets the care for the self as the condition for the knowledge of the self.[18] "Care for thyself" means turn to your soul, take an interest in it before engaging yourself with the world of public affairs in order to care for the well-being of others. Nevertheless, in this tradition caring for the soul really means turning toward the rational part of the soul through which all that is real and intelligible is known. Knowing one's self means knowing all that is knowable. Without that kind of knowledge one would remain ignorant and harm not only oneself but also the others in trying to care for them. This gesture is a way of delaying politics to make it depend on inner knowing. In Kierkegaard's critique of the Platonic theory of recollection which provides to the Socratic pair care for the self and the knowledge of the self their proper epistemological ground, we are face-to-face with a Christian transformation of the whole setup for the care for the soul and the meaning of the knowledge of the self. Now what is at issue is the knowledge of the soul in relation to the Absolute, the absolute difference of the transcendent God that cannot be treated as an object of knowledge. It would be a mistake to think of Kierkegaard as a philosopher who is not concerned with action at all, because what he really needs is to achieve clarity in the face of the question, What should I do? rather than the question, What can I know? Self-understanding is important precisely because it is necessary for me to see what God wants me to do, to find an idea for the sake of which I could live and die. Not only the search for objective, systematic, theoretical knowledge, but also a political theory of government, the construction of an ideal political order has no worth in comparison to the knowledge of the meaning and purpose of life. This is another way of saying that all theoretical knowledge must be concretized in my own life. Kierkegaard does not condemn reflection on political questions as worthless or secondary; he only demands that knowing bears an inward relation to the knower's living the essential knowledge. This is not the classical unity of words and deeds, not a way of equalizing the interior and the exterior. All knowledge that does not relate itself inwardly to existence is not essential knowledge. And the historical existence gets its ultimate meaning in the momentary unity of the finite and the infinite which transcends bare existence.

How would one be justified in engaging one's self in politics if one does not know the Good and has not concretized it in one's own life? For Kierkegaard the Good is to be found nowhere in the empirical world and the world of history,[19] but reveals itself only in this existential relation with the Absolute—God. In *Fear and Trembling* the question of obedience to God's command takes precedence over the question of the knowledge of the Good. In other words, the subject cannot know the Good outside of its relation with the Absolute. Abraham has faith and hope: he has faith in God and hopes that Isaac will live, and for Johannes de Silentio this Knight of Faith Is beyond hesitation over the nature of the Good; the Good is not an object of knowledge but what God requires us to do. But if the relation between me and the Absolute cannot be totalized, that is, universalized, Kierkegaard cannot give himself the possibility of any politics in the higher sense, no matter how much his philosophy invites us to the self knowledge in relation with the Absolute. I shall try to argue that Kierkegaard's strategy is to overcome abstract universality of ethics and politics in order to open the way for taking up the ethico-political issues from within the subject's singular relation with the Absolute.

What is the sense and necessity of offering a psychology as a supplement to dogmatics if Kierkegaard is not seeking for the possibility of a religious ethics and politics? *The Concept of Anxiety* is the work in which Kierkegaard takes up Christian dogmatics and thereby engages himself with the question of historicity. The question of historicity is tied to the problem of inwardness (self knowing as transcendence) by means of a psychology. In this context he defines ethics as a philosophical discipline of an ideal science that imposes itself on human reality without taking into account that the essential limit of human existence is sin. This first ethics that ignores sin altogether rests on metaphysics, which asks the question of being as being without excluding a theological reflection from it. What Kierkegaard calls *secunda philosophia* in contrast to Aristotle's *prote philosophia* deals with the actual manifestations of sin, judges and accuses it where ever it appears, though not with its origin. *Secunda philosophia*, which Kierkegaard also names "second ethics," needs to be supplemented with a psychology in the new sense. This new psychology is not concerned with the study of what the soul produces from within itself or what it has already repressed, but focuses on the abiding restless predisposition from which the possibility of the sin becomes real or actual (CA, 21). Whereas the second ethics is concerned with the actuality of sin, psychology addresses only the possibility of the sin (CA, 23). Kierkegaard claims that psychology completes dogmatics, the discipline that thematizes hereditary sin or explains sin as an ideal possibility. Hence the question of the relation of psychology to dogmatics depends on the relation between the real possibility of sin to the ideal possibility of sin. Kierkegaard construes this connection as the passing over of the doctrine of the "subjective spirit" to the doctrine of the "absolute spirit." He contrasts the first ethics and the second ethics and attempts to ground the latter not in pagan metaphysics, but in psychology and history. History comes into the picture not as a sequence of events in time, but as the religious history of the human psyche, through Christian dogmatics. Kierkegaard says that the real possibility of sin takes its historical sense from the ideal possibility of sin, the origin of which is paradoxical. The origin of history is paradoxical, for Adam's sin lies outside of history as its origin, even though as a member of the race Adam has to be conceived as in history (CA, 28). The origin of history as the transition from an a-historical to a historical state is construed as a "qualitative leap" of the individual, without which neither can the race have a history nor can the individual be both himself and the race at the same time. In this leap not only lies the ground of ethics, but also the possibility of politics. Dogmatics serves to connect the inner history of the person to the external history through the unity of the "race." The historicity of inwardness—the soul as already marked by the hereditary sin in its relation to the Absolute—is the ground of Kierkegaard's universal anthropology for which the individual can at the same time be the whole human race. He writes:

> At every moment, the individual is both himself and the race. This is the individual's perfection viewed as a state. It is also a contradiction. A contradiction, however, is always the expression of a task; a task, however, is a movement; but a movement that as a task is the same as that to which the task is directed is an historical movement. Hence the individual has a history. But if the individual has a history, then the race also has a history. (CA, 28)

When he interprets Kierkegaard's discourse on sin, Adorno says that hereditary sin "as an anthropological and equally as a historical constant is supposed to illuminate the essence of historicity itself."[20] Adorno argues that the recommencement of Adam's sin in every sin may be taken to solve the paradox of history, but it "negates any authentic history as the constitutive transformation of the individual," leaves the unique out of history, erases the singularity of the historical fact.[21] Kierkegaard tries to save the singularity of each first sin by appealing to the leap as the "secret of the first." This secret concerns the singularity of the individual's belonging to the human race. However, I believe what is at stake in this discussion is also a rethinking of universality beyond the Kantian categorical imperative, beyond autonomy because the individual is identified with the whole race as having in some sense already transgressed the law of the Absolute, therefore as sinful, as always already heteronomous. It is possible to say that Kierkegaard's conception of subjectivity is at the final account political, for it is determined in terms of historicity. Even though it is marked by the uncritical duality of the body and the soul, it is concerned with the possibility of the absolute spirit. Even if it rests on the dichotomy of the inside and the outside, it is in search of the possibility of a connection with the whole human race from within an internal relation. And we should not forget that requiring one to know that which is inside before that which is outside is to ask for a clarification of the internal sense of the outside and to incarnate that sense in one's own existence.

Anxiety for incarnated existence is the state of mind in which a concrete understanding becomes present to the consciousness without which freedom would close itself off against unfreedom. Thus Kierkegaard never considers ethical and political issues by presupposing the autonomy of the human will or reason, for unfreedom is not simply the risk of being enslaved by the others and their authority, or by one's passions but more fundamentally enclosure within one's self, namely, lack of communication. The essence of communication is not immanence; its truth does not rest on the recollection of the essential truths that the soul brings with itself. Communication is transcendence and repetition.

Without doubt Kierkegaard lends himself to a reading as a thinker who distances himself from politics understood as a worldly power game or pursuit of one's own interests. Whether it is corrupted or not, a life of struggle for power would be a betrayal of inwardness and the closing off of unfreedom against freedom. Politics as collectivity, common praxis, identification with the others on the basis of common opinions or existential interests may also bring about the loss of the self and the reduction of its inwardness in the average way of being in the world. However, insofar as sin plays the role of unifying the history of the human race and the identification of the individual with the whole race, it necessarily opens the question of universality pertaining to ethics as well as to politics. Politics as occupation with the real so as to open it to its other possibilities, to the possibility of its being otherwise, involves the dimension of the religious if the human spirit is understood on the basis of sin and as having always already lost its innocence, hence as guilty. Hereditary sin implies a conception of humanity as guilty prior to having committed a crime and thus is a manner of taking responsibility more seriously and more historically than in a politics of innocence.

We can question Kierkegaard at this point. Even if we grant to him the premise that the knowledge of the self can only be reached in my relation with the Absolute, his claim that the identification of the individual with the whole race is only possible through the hereditary sin is problematic because it cannot give us the possibility of a politics in a universal scale. It seems to me that only Christians can identify themselves with other Christians through this specific mark (hereditary sin) in relation to the Absolute. Kierkegaard forgets that the world is inhabited by other types of relations to the Absolute, in which the self does not interpret its sameness with the human race by way of hereditary sin. Kierkegaard does not seem to be willing to take into consideration other religious experiences in which the humanity of the human shines forth. He proposes a certain interpretation of the humanity of the human in Christian terms, by completely ignoring that not all humanity is Christian. Insofar as he does not ask the question of other traditions, historicities, ways of relating to the Absolute he cannot open the possibility of the communication between the different ways of inhabiting the world, knowing the Self and incarnating that knowledge in existence as a condition for comporting ourselves politically in order to care for all incarnated existence. In spite of Kierkegaard's resistance to totalization, which assimilates the subject in an anonymous universalism, his own new universalism through self-knowledge in relation to the Absolute amounts to a very problematic universalism, which is, in my view, totalizing.[22]

Levinas has not been attentive to the political aspect of Kierkegaard's interpretation of historicity. He reads sinfulness as an essential trait of religious subjectivity. In "Kierkegaard: Existence and Ethics" he argues that Kierkegaard brings into our view a subjectivity that suffers, a "persecuted truth," which is Christian. However, Levinas seems to lose sight of the way hereditary sin seems to have marked all inter-human relations by making possible the identification of the individual with the whole race. On the other hand, from a Levinasian perspective this account of historicity is another political form of the totalization of the relation with the alterity of the other human being. Sinfulness would then be the condition of the experience of the encounter with the Other or what the Other and me have in common. In contrast to Adorno's critique, we could say from this point of view that Kierkegaard erases the unique and the singular as it interrupts history (including history understood in terms of hereditary sin). Kierkegaard's politics as care for the others does not only presuppose self knowledge in relation to God but also the recognition of one's self as a member of the human race, of the universal in history, and so on, in that very relation. It is therefore impossible to accuse Kierkegaard of ethical egoism, unless ethical egoism includes the reduction of the singularity of the Other to "the dialectic of the Absolute."[23] To sum up, first, Levinas can be represented as being critical of Kierkegaard for following up the ancient tradition of the care for the soul, for which, from the outset Levinas substitutes the problem of excendence, because he believes that the inward turn is after all a way of mediating the relation with alterity. Second, we can go further than Levinas and argue that on his conception of historicity Kierkegaard reduces the relation with the Other to a relation with the whole human race, to the relation with the third. The latter problem would have disappeared if Kierkegaard's relation with the Absolute were a relation with the Other in Levinas' sense. The essential disagreement between Kierkegaard and Levinas lies in the fact that Kierkegaard allows for a relation with the transcendent God beyond the ethical relation, whereas for Levinas this relation is bound to remain demonic insofar as it is not an openness to the other human being.

Both Levinas and Kierkegaard would agree that the politics of identity is totalization. Insofar as politics of identity rests on my identification with a certain culture, nation, religion, race or sex, what we have in Levinas' terms is the identification of the diverse, the Same. Transcendence is only possible if such an identification is interrupted and called into question by the Other. For Kierkegaard such an identification would give rise to the problem of the reduction of subjectivity. And this is why a Kierkegaardian type of critique can always be seen as an inexhaustible source of resistance against totalization by way of identification. But, in spite of his critique of orthodox official Christianity for reducing the transcendence of the subject, in spite of the fact that the religious experience he describes in *Fear and Trembling* disturbs religious identification, Kierkegaard's notion of historicity constitutes a ground for religious identification.

III

Even though Levinas is not a thinker of the political for most of his readers, I shall argue that his conception of ethics and his critique of ontology are profoundly political. Let us begin with his critique of ontology. As it is well-known *Totality and Infinity* confers the honored status of "first philosophy" not on ontology, whose task is to understand and dominate beings, but on ethics. Understanding is to reduce the Other to the same, by way of intentional *Sinngebung*. This reduction to the Same rests on the spontaneity and freedom of the understanding (TI, 43). This curious statement seems to imply that the categorical intuition that must be in play in our act of giving sense to the manifold in *noema* and its evidence rests on the spontaneity and freedom of *noetic* acts. To claim that this freedom is arbitrary before it is put in critique by the Other, amounts to saying that the eidetic essences that made our experience of beings possible are constructed and somehow arbitrary. Levinas translates the question of freedom into the identification of the same; its becoming what it is through the recognition of itself in the other; its return home from its journey to elsewhere. Even our eidetics is a kind of politics of universal domination and a way of establishing the primacy of the free subject as it is given in European philosophy, including Husserl's phenomenology. However, Levinas does not thereby block the possibility of another way of theorizing. What he calls "first philosophy" is not the ontology whose ultimate question is freedom, but metaphysics in the sense of "theory as respect for exteriority" (TI, 43). Ethics is a theoretical effort to respect alterity before all classical efforts to issue universal rules for action.

In *Totality and Infinity* Levinas argues that not only political totalitarianisms that require homogeneity for political unity by denying the equality of the heterogeneous, but also liberal politics that aims at the equality of all on the grounds of the freedom of the I rest on the "ontology of power."[24] He thus puts into question both the alternatives of totalitarianism and liberalism[25] by claiming that justice as the relation with the Other interrupts the ontology of power. Hence it is possible to say that Levinas' revolutionary conception of the ethicity of ethics as the relation with the Other makes him a thinker of the political, but he will thereby also be accused of assimilating politics to ethics. Reflections on the essence of the political can always represent Levinas as a thinker who belongs to the era of the recession of political, in which politics disappear by being assimilated to the domains of economy, law, or ethics (morality). Derrida's later work can be used to argue against such an interpretation. According to him, Levinas is not an apolitical thinker for he re-opens the question of politics by the presence of the third who makes the demand for justice as equality on the asymmetrical ethical relation with the Other. Indeed, Derrida has significantly contributed to the explication of the aporia in which ethics and politics question one another: Even though the third party can never represent or totalize the relation with the Other, it is constantly there to question my infinite responsibility for the Other. Levinas did not only point out that the relation with singularity is open to be questioned from the point of the view of the universal, but also that the universal has to be tested from the point of view of the singular. According to Levinas all political institutions presuppose the face-to-face encounter, the primitive society of the I and the Other, and therefore are open to an interrogation in terms of it. For Derrida in the *The Force of Law* the performative event which institutes a State or its legal system is a violence that is neither legal nor illegal at the moment of its institution.[26] And it is always possible to think of it not only as violence exercised on the previous legal order, but also on the Other. Thus no political order can be pluralistic in the radical sense insofar as it closes itself against being haunted by the singularity of the face. It is possible to go further and argue that in *Totality and Infinity* Levinas goes beyond the demand for the test of the universal by the relation with singularity when he attempts to rethink the relation with the Other as language, conversation. It seems to me that to conceive the relation with the Other as the relation with another reason and to take that as the condition of the constitution of a new universality paves the way for politics in the pluralistic sense, beyond an anonymous universalism.

Robert Bernasconi's recent work has fundamentally contributed to the reading of Levinas' political philosophy.[27] On this reading, Levinas appears to be a political thinker, starting from his "Reflections on the Philosophy of Hitlerism"[28] until his second major work *Otherwise Than Being*, beyond the contrast he makes between ethics and politics. The critique of freedom offered in "Reflections on the Philosophy of Hitlerism" applies also to Kierkegaard's Christianity. Levinas notes that European culture conceives man's destiny in terms of the spirit of freedom, and in European philosophy man is fated to be free. He defines the spirit of freedom as "a feeling that man is absolutely free in his relations with the world and the possibilities that solicit action from him."[29] This feeling is in its essence "Christian" for it declares that man can eternally renew himself despite the resistance of history—his fundamental limitation. By annulling the past that cannot be recuperated, Christianity's forgiveness opens a genuine realm of freedom in which a person can repeat actions or processes differently and can make up for past failures. Thus in Christianity man is no longer impotent in the face of the irreversibility of the past as he was in Greek tragedy. There can be no engagement which ultimately determines freedom, if one is free to choose and can give up what one had freely chosen before. A person chooses himself over and over again—freedom is always something to be conquered anew. This critique of the spirit of freedom in European philosophy for not taking facticity seriously can be read as Levinas' earliest critique of Kierkegaard's philosophy. Indeed, it seems to be directed to Kierkegaard's notion of "repetition forward." As "Kierkegaard: Existence and Ethics" notes, repetition forward is still identification. In this kind of repetition the soul becomes pure spirit, and yet one forgets the rivetedness of the I to its body. I am seen as a Jew in 1935 or a Muslim in today's Europe or America. Even though none of these identifications are part of my essence, no consciousness I take of my situation can get me out of my rivetedness to myself when I am seen as a particular embodiment of them. This situation is not an external addition to me like the color of the dress I wear; rather, it constitutes the foundation of my being. I cannot escape from the body that I experience under the gaze of the other. Racism rests on a truth ignored by both Christianity and the European notions of philosophical and political freedom: my body participates in myself, inseparable from who I am. As Bernasconi argues, the consciousness of the impossibility of escaping from one's own body, of being riveted to one's own being, is the site from which Levinas undertakes to think the possibility of transcendence. We can add that Levinas' discourse challenges Kierkegaard's account of human being in terms of the duality of body and soul and of the possibility of their unification in terms of the soul's becoming free spirit. Levinas is perhaps pointing out that this is not quite possible for everyone, if we take the question of one's facticity in the radical sense, a facticity that takes into account our materialization under the gaze of the others.

Levinas downplays the importance of Kierkegaard's politics of resistance to the extent that it is still grounded on freedom as repetition forward. For him, totality breaks only by the Other's questioning of my arbitrary freedom. The Kierkegaardian notion of subjectivity is indeed based on the freedom of the I, but it is also fundamentally an openness to the outside. It is difficult to see how this freedom, which is ultimately the freedom to know one's self and the experience of the ambiguity of the instant where eternity touches time, may lend itself to a reading in terms of egotism and power. Levinas' argument for this is through Spinoza and Heidegger: "Egotism is not an ugly vice of the subject's, but its ontology, as we find in the sixth proposition of part 3 of Spinoza's *Ethics:* "Every being makes every effort insofar as it is in it to persevere in its being"; and in Heidegger's expression about existence existing in such a way that its Being has this very being as an issue (PN, 71). Both Kierkegaard and Levinas are critical of the autonomy of freedom and rethink freedom as heteronomy. However, Levinas argues that freedom as it reveals itself in the religious stage of life as Kierkegaard conceives it, is still a concern with one's own being. In *Totality and Infinity* the arbitrariness of the freedom of the I is put into critique and opened to heteronomy with the reception of the command of the Other. This heteronomy interrupts ontology and the politics based on it and renders the subject capable of going beyond the care for its own being, in being responsible for the needs of the Others. Compared to this kind of heteronomous ethics, heteronomy of the religious stage in which Kierkegaard conceives a subjectivity beyond ethics is, in Levinas' view, still demonic.

In *Otherwise Than Being* Levinas continues to oppose himself to Kierkegaard when he points out that the "secret of the self" will be lost if we look for it in a subjectivity that begins in person and in the person who begins in freedom. Kierkegaard had argued that the secret of the self is to be found not in relation to a past that we need to recollect but in the repetition forward of the religious state. Levinas, in re-situating this secret back into our relation to the past, takes it out of the domain of reminiscence by characterizing it as irrecuperable. In contrast to Kierkegaard's religious subjectivity who freely commits himself to the Absolute, Levinas fashions the subject of infinite responsibility as responsible beyond what he freely committed himself, as in charge of a world that is not issued out of his own free will, as being incessantly subjected to everything in absolute passivity. In having the Other under one's skin, the self is absolved of itself, it thus "liberates itself from its enchainment to itself" (OTB, 124). Levinas insists that the Self does not choose the Good, it is chosen by it in the first place, and this is perhaps the irrecuperable origin that accounts for the infinitely responsible subject. Levinas continues to communicate with and respond to Kierkegaard's reading of Abraham when he construes the genesis of the structure of the responsible subject in terms of "being disturbed by the Other" and therefore as "exposure prior to commitment" and when he defines this exposure as more ancient than the freedom of the ego. More explicitly, the notion of persecution which is fundamental in Levinas' reading of Kierkegaard's notion of sin as it pertains to religious subjectivity in history, marks also the structure of the responsible subjectivity in *Otherwise Than Being*. Levinas thinks of the ethical subject as persecuted: "The self, the persecuted one is accused beyond his fault before freedom" and "cannot defend himself by language" (OTB, 121). Nevertheless, he at the same time takes the precaution to protect his own appeal to persecutedness against a possible Kierkegaardian interpretation: "One must not conceive it to be the state of original sin, it is, on the contrary, the original goodness of creation" (OTB, 121). My view is that Levinas takes persecution out of its Christian context: for Kierkegaard the individual comes into being as a sinner and this is the consequence of a Deity's presence in time (an historical fact); in sin consciousness the individual becomes conscious of his difference from the human in general and at the same time becomes conscious of the sin of the whole race.[30] On the other hand, persecution in Levinas is not a historical fact, and it does not imply that humanity is sinful.[31] Moreover, "the consciousness of difference from the human in general" is reconstrued as "election," namely, as being more responsible than everyone else. There is a sense in which Levinas' responsible subject is still religious subjectivity. But in this religion the elements of the care for the soul and the knowledge of the self in relation to the Absolute have disappeared and replaced by the infinite responsibility for the Other.

In both Kierkegaard and Levinas the question of religion is profoundly political. First of all, one must account for religion in the sensible realm and the question of transcendence is understood as the attestation to the infinite within the finite. In *The Concept of Anxiety* the task is to reveal how the religious expresses itself in the sensible world. Although Levinas argues that the infinition of the face of the Other overflows its sensible form, he will not allow for a personal relation with God beyond the relation with the face of the other human being. The fundamental disagreement between Kierkegaard and Levinas is that for the former a personal relation with God can only be truly experienced in the ambiguity of the instant in which the religious subject is even ready to transcend the respect for the human face, whereas for Levinas this surrendering to one's own destiny in the movement of transcendence is a return of paganism within religion. Indeed against the sacrificial figure of Abraham in *Fear and Trembling*, Levinas opposes the figure of Abraham who attempted to save the innocent men of Sodom from God's destructive rage.[32] This negative reception of Kierkegaard by Levinas should not, of course, hide their affinity—their taste for paradox, their phenomenology of interruption, their critique of universalism, their call for a rethinking of subjectivity, and the fact that guilt plays a central role in their accounts of subjectivity. However, Levinas claims that Kierkegaard has not attained to a profound conception of responsibility, and has misconceived the paradoxes of ethical subjectivity and the ways in which ethical subject is both religious and political.

Notes

I thank the Research Fund of Galatasaray University, Istanbul, Turkey, for supporting this project.

1. For example, Merold Westphal in his essay "The Transparent Shadow: Kierkegaard and Levinas in Dialogue" has persuasively argued that "Phenomenon and Enigma" (in CPP) is the most Kierkegaardian of Levinas' essays: "The Kierkegaardian overtones are more overt when Levinas speaks of this move "beyond reason" as a kind of madness or folly" (61–62). See "The Transparent Shadow: Kierkegaard and Levinas in Dialogue," in *Kierkegaard in Post/Modernity*, ed. Martin J. Matuštík and Merold Westphal (Bloomington: Indiana University Press, 1995), 266.

2. Jacques Derrida, *Writing and Difference*, trans. Alan Baas (London: Routledge & Kegan Paul, 1985), 79–153.

3. Ibid., 110.

4. Ibid.

5. We do not know if Derrida had access to "Kierkegaard: Existence and Ethics" in 1964, for it was originally published in German in *Schweizer Monatshefte* 43 (1963).

6. Edmund Husserl, *Cartesian Meditations*, trans. Dorion Cairns (The Hague: Martinus Nijhoff, 1960).

7. Derrida, *Writing and Difference*, 110.

8. The renunciation of the self-dispersion by the choice of choosing between either good or evil in the ethical stage *(Either /Or)* and then the transition to the religious stage by the sacrifice or suspension of the ethical *(Fear and Trembling)* makes possible a reading of Kierkegaard's dialectical account of the self as a sacrificial dialectic.

9. But here we need some reservations: First, interiority in Levinas is foreign to in-

wardness in the sense of Kierkegaard, for it is constituted through intentional relations with different forms of alterity. Levinas is more Hegelian than Kierkegaard wants to be. Just like Levinas, Hegel does not make a real distinction between inside and the outside and lets the actuality of the subjectivity rest on the identity of the inside and the outside. Levinas' account of interiority differs from Hegel's insofar as Levinas describes enjoyment already as separation. In contrast, Kierkegaard in his attempt to rethink the actuality of subjectivity begins by presupposing the duality of the inside and the outside. Second, Levinas' dialectical account of the constitution of the self in its interiority is not sacrificial. The element of self-sacrifice is only to be found in Levinas' representations of ethical subjectivity in terms of substitution and persecution.

10. Levinas writes in the preface of *Totality and Infinity*, "we were impressed by the opposition to the idea of totality in Franz Rosenzweig's *Stern der Erlösung*, a work too often present in this book to be cited" (TI, 28). If Rosenzweig's influence cannot just be isolated by way of citation to this or that constitutive idea of Levinas' thought, the way Rosenzweig reads Kierkegaard as a critique of idealism may also be worth taking into account. This is not to presuppose that Levinas agrees with Rosenzweig at all points, but just to ask if Rosenzweig may not have been an important point of reference when Levinas attempts to situate Kierkegaard's philosophy with respect to totality.

11. Franz Rosenzweig, *The Star of Redemption*, trans. Barbara E. Galli (Madison: University of Wisconsin Press, 2005).

12. Ibid., 12.

13. Ibid., 13.

14. Ibid.

15. Ibid.

16. Levinas argues that idealism seeks to surpass being *(l'être)* in its aspiration, but because of the attachment of thinking to being, it fails to do so; it only modifies the structure of the existant and attributes existence to the realm of the ideal, of consciousness, and so on, without saying anything about existence. "Those intellectual relations into which idealism dissolved the universe are no less its existences—neither inert nor opaque to be sure—and they do not escape the laws of being *(l'être)*." Cf. OE, 71–73.

17. The Kierkegaardian conception of ethics is usually characterized with reference to texts such as *Either/Or* and *Fear and Trembling* in which pseudonyms such as Judge William and Johannes de Silentio describe the ethical subjectivity in terms of a transformation of the individual into a universal individual. But if Kierkegaard's critique of Hegel is taken seriously, then it may seem problematic to attribute a Hegelian or sometimes Kantian conception of ethics straightforwardly to Kierkegaard. Thus there is a legitimate tendency to distance Kierkegaardian ethics from the ethical sphere described by particular pseudonyms. Indeed there may be some ambiguity involved in Kierkegaard's use of the term "ethics." In contrast to ethics in the Kantian sense, Kierkegaard may be envisaging the possibility of a religious ethics. A similar ambiguity can be found in Levinas' use of the term "ethics." Although he is employing the term in the sense of justice in *Totality and Infinity,* he also says elsewhere that his main concern is not ethics as a system of universal rules of action, but the experience of saintliness or holiness.

18. See Michel Foucault, *L'herméneutique du sujet,* Cours au Collège de France, 1981–1982 (Paris: Gallimard Seuil, 2001), especially Cours du 6 Janvier et 13 Janvier 1982.

19. Here I thank J. Aaron Simmons for pointing out to me that Kierkegaard, in *Works of Love*, mentions various sorts of actions, relations, and attitudes that signify as good in

the world of history. However, these are the works of love and not the love or the good itself.

20. Theodor W. Adorno, *Kierkegaard: Construction of the Aesthetic,* trans. and ed. Robert Hullot-Kentor, Theory and History of Literature 61 (Minneapolis: University of Minnesota Press, 1999), 33.

21. Ibid., 34.

22. One may object, "what if Kierkegaard is right about the truth of Christianity and as such other traditions, historicities, ways of relating to the Absolute are false? If so, the hereditary sin would be something that holds for everyone and it is merely that Christians have been able to recognize this reality in their own lives." The problem in this objection lies in its use of truth and falsity claims. Different traditions may believe that their own way of relating to the Absolute is the right one, but as human beings we can never assume a divine point of view to judge such claims to truth. Johannes Climacus in *The Concluding Unscientific Postcript* says that there is more truth in worshiping a false God with passion than in worshiping the true God without passion. This statement—beyond being a praise of passionate worshiping—pretends to distinguish between a true God and a false God and qualifies its own religious experience as universally valid, at the expense of the other experiences of worshiping. My point is that the theological self-assertion over against the other historicities of religious experience jeopardizes the possibility of a truly universal ethics and politics, which takes its inspiration from various religions and religious experiences.

23. The expression comes from Adorno (*Kierkegaard: Construction of the Aesthetic,* 34).

24. The term "ontology of power" is often read as alluding to Spinoza's *conatus essendi.* However, Heidegger's reading of metaphysics as culminating in the technological epoch in the will to power may also be constituting the background of Levinas' use of the term. Heidegger uses this Nietzschean term to point out a way of maintaining one's self in the midst of the real in order to dominate beings and their reduction to resources which stand in reserve. Heidegger takes up the question of freedom in turning towards to what the common sense considers as that which can be futile to dwell on, namely, meditation on the sense of Being. Within this strategy Heidegger offers a severe critique of politics and its category of action. Freedom understood as letting beings be is the essence of truth. Man does not possess freedom but is possessed by it. For Levinas such a notion of freedom remains anonymous and moreover arbitrary insofar as it is not put into question by the other.

25. Levinas understands liberal democracy ultimately as *conatus essendi*—the pursuit of one's own interests at the expense of a just distribution of wealth by means of which we could respond to the needs of the others in the world. This critique of liberal democracy highly contrasts with the critique of it in Carl Schmitt's sense, for example. According to Levinas, the origin of the political unity of the state and of sociality in general is not antagonism or the political association of friends and the exclusion of the enemies, but the ethical relation with the Other, which is the putting of my freedom into question. No doubt, Levinas prefers liberal democracy to totalitarianisms such as fascism and Stalinism, even though for him liberal democracy is still totalitarian insofar as it fails to understand responsibility as transcendence.

26. Jacques Derrida, "The Force of Law: The 'Mystical Foundation of Authority,'" trans. Mary Quaintance, in *Deconstruction and the Possibility of Justice,* ed. D. Cornell, M. Rosenfeld, and D. G. Carlson (London: Routledge, 1992).

27. See Robert Bernasconi, "The Third Party," *Journal of the British Society for Phe-*

nomenology 30, no 1 (January 1999): 76–87; and "Strangers and Slaves in the Land of Egypt: Levinas and the Politics of Otherness," in *Difficult Justice*, ed. Asher and Gad Horowitz (Toronto: University of Toronto Press, 2006), 246–61.

28. Emmanuel Levinas, "Reflections on the Philosophy of Hitlerism," trans. Sean Hand, *Critical Inquiry* 17, no. 1 (Autumn 1990): 63–71. In "Reflections on the Philosophy of Hitlerism" Levinas had to account for how this Hitlerist culture relates to European culture and how the European philosophy of freedom could give rise to the philosophy of Hitlerism in order to explain the sense of his own lived experience of racism.

29. Ibid., 64.

30. Søren Kierkegaard, *Concluding Unscientific Postscript*, trans. David F. Swenson and Walter Lowrie (Princeton, N.J.: Princeton University Press, 1974), 517–18.

31. Persecution in Levinas is not a commitment "in the form of original sin" (OTB, 113) but "the infinite passion of a responsibility, in its return upon itself goes further than identity." If this is right, persecution in the form of hereditary in the Kierkegaardian sense remains within the limits of the return to one's own identity.

32. In *Fear and Trembling* Johannes de Silentio mentions that Abraham pleads with God to stop destroying Sodom, in order to save the just men who live in the city. Perhaps Levinas wants to point out that this text does not sufficiently concentrate on this apparition of Abraham in the Bible and fails to play it against the Abraham who is willing to sacrifice his innocent son in a test of his fidelity to God.

11 Works of Justice, Works of Love: Kierkegaard, Levinas, and an Ethics Beyond Difference

Stephen Minister

Do Kierkegaard and Levinas have any insights for us into practical ethical action? Even if they do, can their insights be brought together in anything but a polemic manner given Kierkegaard's reputation as the defender of radically anti-social individuality and Levinas's reputation as the advocate of the other who completely overwhelms the I? This chapter will attempt to answer both of these questions in the affirmative by offering readings of Kierkegaard and Levinas that take us beyond their exaggerated reputations. Despite differences of both the merely apparent and real varieties, Kierkegaard and Levinas find common ground in arguing that some sense of ethico-religious subjectivity is the central task and ultimate concern in human life. One of the key developments in recent scholarship on Kierkegaard's notion of ethico-religious subjectivity is the increasing recognition of the essential sociality of this subjectivity. There is also within the community of Levinas scholars a growing appreciation of the significance of the political as the context in which all interactions with others take place and in which the I has the requisite capacities for deliberative action. Fortunately much work has already been done to lay the foundations for this project so that this essay will be at once synthesizing the insights of other commentators while also building upon them in an attempt to reach new heights.

Though it is anachronistic to say so, Kierkegaard and Levinas can both be considered postmodern thinkers because of the manner in which they reject the epistemological aspirations of the Western philosophical tradition. Since Plato, the dominant movements in this tradition have conceived of the goal of thinking as the attempt to ascend the divided line, to pull ourselves up from appearance-based beliefs to knowledge of reality. Kierkegaard and Levinas both raise serious questions about the legitimacy of this mythical journey. They both embrace a hermeneutics of finitude, acknowledging the essentially perspectival nature of thinking, which does not merely limit our capacity for reaching objective truth but undermines traditional conceptions of objectivity altogether.[1] They also supplement this critique with a devastating hermeneutics of suspicion, according to which motives other than the pursuit of truth infect our allegedly theoretical endeavors. This possibility, in tandem with the opacity of oneself to oneself, irreparably undermines any claim to disinterested knowledge.[2]

Kierkegaard and Levinas are postmodern ethicists insofar as they both reject any necessary or universal ethical principles not only because all alleged ethical principles would be inadequate to encompass our responsibility, but also and more importantly because any alleged ethical principle would undermine the radically singular character of our ethico-religious subjectivity and the radical alterity of other subjects. And yet. And yet Kierkegaard and Levinas set themselves apart from many other postmodern ethicists by their willingness to endorse a positive vision of the good capable of inspiring deep commitment and positive action and of making life meaningful, or as Kierkegaard puts it, "the idea for which I am willing to live and die" (JP, 5:5100). Their positivity is rooted in the realization that our inability to ascend the divided line induces skepticism, cynicism, or resignation only if we retain the epistemological aspirations of the tradition. In contrast to this traditional goal, the main thrust of both thinkers' work is to articulate the primacy of a different, non-epistemological task, the task of ethico-religious subjectivity. Once this more primary task is freed from the straitjacket of the demand for objective, disinterested truth, we find ourselves not condemned to a non-cognitivist ethics, but liberated to articulate possibilities for meaningful action and commitment. I contend that Kierkegaard and Levinas go beyond, by going through, difference and singularity to unashamedly articulate such possibilities. I will therefore devote the bulk of this chapter to drawing out these possibilities before concluding with some brief reflections on them.

Levinas and the Work of Justice

I would like to start this investigation into the positive, practical endorsements of a Levinasian ethics with an example of ethical goodness that Levinas gives. Though commentators sometimes explain Levinas's philosophy by pointing to the courageous persons who willingly hid Jews in their homes and communities during World War II,[3] Levinas himself seems to have more enthusiasm for a fictional episode from Vassily Grossman's novel *Life and Fate*. This episode takes place toward the end of World War II in the recently liberated Stalingrad and, as Levinas tells it, consists simply of a Russia woman "in a mob unleashed against a conquered German soldier, the most detested in a group of prisoners, [who] gives him her last piece of bread" (RTB, 81).[4] While this episode, like the stories of sheltering Jews, depicts a person who willingly acts against social pressures and her own self-interest in response to the vulnerability of another, two important differences between this episode and the stories of sheltering Jews come to the fore. First, whereas those who welcomed Jews into their homes were helping the innocent, giving them assistance they deserved, the German soldier, who was the most detested because he had been the harshest and most unjust prison guard, was not innocent and did not deserve assistance. Thus this story powerfully illustrates the value of mercy for practical ethical response. Goodness shows concern not only for the victims, but also the victimizers. Second, whereas the welcome of a persecuted person into one's home is a private act, the success of which depends on it remaining private, the Russian woman gives her bread to the German soldier in "the full light of the public order," as Levinas would say. She does not wait for the cover of darkness to reach out to the other, but instead lends him aid in front of an angry mob in the full light of day. Though for Levinas goodness always happens in interpersonal interactions, it need not for that reason be private or hidden.

Levinas develops this latter point in connection with his notion of the third party. Far from ethical goodness occurring in "a private relation and a clandestinity," which Levinas regards as "forgetful of the universe," Levinas claims that any response to another "differs from the 'reaction' that the given gives rise to in that it cannot remain 'between us,' as is the case with the steps I take with regard to a thing. Everything that take place here 'between us' concerns everyone, the face that looks at it places itself in the full light of the public order" (TI, 212–13). Levinas's notion of the third party refers to this fact that all human interactions are public, even when just between two persons. This explains the ubiquity of the third, which Levinas consistently claims is always already present in every encounter of another (TI, 213; OTB, 158). It also carries with it the implication that though the significance of the other transcends any thematization, any response to another is subject to public investigation, thematization, scrutiny, explanation, and justification. One can always be asked to give reasons for the action one undertakes.

Because of this, the encounter of the face, as Levinas repeatedly states, calls us to reason, that is, to reflective, honest, reason giving. Thus he calls the face "the starting point of philosophy"; claims that his project is not the "denunciation of intellectualism but to its very strict development"; issues the exhortation that "one must not sleep, one must philosophize"; and sees philosophy's potential to be "the wisdom of love at the service of love" (CPP, 59; TI, 109; GWCM, 15; OTB, 162 et al., respectively). According to Levinas, our responsibility for others should inspire not an emotionalism or "disdainful spiritualism," what Kierkegaard might call an "abstract sentimentality," but critical reflection, interpersonal reason giving, and action (TI, 69; SUD, 31, respectively). All of these are aspects of the work of justice.

"Justice is necessary, that is, comparison, coexistence, contemporaneousness, assembling, order, thematization, the visibility of faces, and thus intentionality and the intellect, and in intentionality and the intellect, the intelligibility of a system" (OTB, 157). Even though his endorsement of systematic thought is qualified by the ethical task of ongoing critique, Levinas, unlike some of his neighbors in the field of postmodern ethics, does not advocate the abandonment of systematic thought in favor of, for example, a fragmentary "poetics of obligation."[5] Instead, the comparing of incomparables begins by regarding the other not qua face as unique and incomprehensible, but qua individual as a member of a genus, as a human being among human beings. "For beings are not compared as faces, but already as citizens, as individuals, as a multiplicity in a genus and not as 'uniquenesses'" (EN, 205). Levinas goes so far as to say, "We must . . . *de-face* humans, sternly reducing each one's uniqueness to his individuality in the unity of the genus, and let universality rule" (RTB, 246, cf. 116). Comparison is only possible for items sharing some common ground. It is as human beings, as participants in a common nature, that we are able to compare other persons. In order for this comparison to be helpful in discerning to whom we should respond, we must also have some ideas about what it means to be human and which features of humanity are relevant to ethics. Thus in one place Levinas equates "comparing what is incomparable" with "knowing men" (RTB, 115). Ethical action requires getting beyond difference to a theory of human nature.

Levinas's turn to reason in order to scrutinize our responsibilities to others should remind us not of Kant's *Groundwork* but of Plato's *Republic*. Levinas does not think that reason can deliver a priori a necessary and universal supreme moral principle. Instead, like Plato, Levinas thinks the answer to the question of justice will require something more than pure reflection on the nature of willing. It will require an interpersonal dialogue regarding philosophical anthropology, ontology, and epistemology. I would like to suggest that Levinas's writings offer us his contribution to this dialogue and so present us with various aspects of his philosophical anthropology, ontology, and epistemology as well as his reasons for them.[6] It is from these reasoned positions that we can draw positive, practical ethical guidance. Given the focus of this chapter, I will only develop the way in which Levinas's philosophical anthropology recommends certain concrete ideals for ethical response to others.

The attempt to articulate a practical ethics based on Levinas's work has an obvious starting point. Levinas repeatedly claims that the face of the other announces a specific command: Thou shall not kill. "The first word of the face is the 'Thou shalt not kill.' It is an order. There is a commandment in the appearance of the face" (EI, 89; cf. TI, 199, et al.).[7] At times Levinas even seems to suggest that this commandment comprises the content of the face. "What is there in the Face? . . . the 'Thou Shalt not Kill'" (EN, 104). But this raises a problem. Does not Levinas insist that the face is not a phenomenon and that it is prior to any culturally embedded meanings? Yet what is a content or a proclamation if not a phenomenon? What is the commandment "Thou shall not kill" if not culturally embedded? How can these claims be reconciled or, more broadly, how should the "thou shall not kill" of the face be understood?

While Levinas consistently argues that the face is prior to and a condition for all language and constituted meaning, I think the "Thou shall not kill" is best understood as Levinas's attempt, even though one he recognizes is necessarily inadequate, to make present in language the ethical significance of the face. To articulate this point in terms of Levinas's important distinction between meaning and sense, we could say the "thou shall not kill" presents a meaning that attempts to express the primordial sense encountered in the face of the other.[8]

Though this sense is not experienced phenomenally and cannot be thematized, the responsibility it produces can, and for the sake of responsibility must, be thematized and said, that is, presented as a meaning. Locating the commands of the face on the level of meaning rather than on the level of sense has a couple of important implications for our understanding of these commands.

First, this command does not, like the face, resist thematization, but rather is a thematization, indeed an interpretation, of our responsibility for others based on a conception of what it means to be human. The face as a sense that orients human subjectivity does not itself immediately reveal practical commands, though it makes them both possible and necessary.[9] Instead, practical commands are derived from an interpretation of the possibilities for destitution within human existence. Hence mortality as a fundamental and permanent vulnerability of the human condition serves as the content for the first command. Levinas thinks Heidegger was right to identify death as a fundamental ontological reality of human existence, but wrong to think that one's primary orientation is toward one's own death.[10] It is rather the mortality of the other that should concern me before my own as a site of the concretization of my responsibility for the other.

Though the mortality of the other provides content for the ethical command not to kill, it is clear that by itself it remains impracticably vague and thus in need of further interpretation to apply it to concrete situations. Perhaps no ethical principle has needed more interpretation, both historically and presently, than the imperative "Thou shall not kill." The deceptive clarity of this imperative conceals the difficulty of discerning its applicability during wartime, in cases of self-defense, and to issues such as capital punishment and euthanasia. Though Levinas does not offer any calculus or practical syllogism for discerning the morally best action in specific situations, he does offer further interpretation of the "thou shall not kill" that serves as a further fleshing out of our responsibilities to others.

"There are a variety of ways to kill. It isn't always just a matter of killing, say, with a knife. The everyday killing with a good conscience, the killing in all innocence—there is such a thing as well" (RTB, 132, cf. 53). According to Levinas, responsibility for the mortality of the other extends beyond an injunction against directly taking another's life to any indirect contribution to the death of the other. Since Levinas includes neglect as a form of indirect killing, he denies any ethically meaningful distinction between killing and letting die and thereby interprets "thou shall not kill" as a call not to non-interference but to active attention to and involvement in the lives of others. Hence Levinas finds "thou shall not kill" to be equivalent to all of the following commands: "thou shalt not leave me alone in my dying"; "you shall defend the life of the other"; "you are responsible for the life of this absolutely other other"; "thou shalt cause thy neighbor to live"; and "love thy neighbor" (RTB, 145, 192; EN 168; AT, 127; RTB, 132, respectively). The final two articulations of one's responsibilities to others clearly indicate that justice demands not only the non-violation of others, but also provision for others of the means of life, such as food, shelter, and medical care. "To hear 'You shall not kill' is to hear 'Social justice'" (DF, 8–9).[11]

However, one might wonder, by developing a Levinasian practical ethics out of the "thou shall not kill," even with its expanded scope, does not such an ethics interpret the human only in terms of its capacity for victimization? If so, then does not this ethics fall prey to the objection that, though it may provide for the easing and elongating of life, it fails to make life positively meaningful and, given the inexorability of death, is ultimately futile?[12] While the majority of Levinas's treatment of practical imperatives is focused on preserving the biological life of others, Levinas does at times indicate that responsibility is not limited to this concern. Indeed, the command to "love thy neighbor" seems to exceed concern merely for others' material subsistence, though it does not indicate in what way. Such an indication can be found, I believe, in Levinas's insistence that one is responsible not only for another's life, but also for her faults and responsibility.[13] Though this claim may seem rather puzzling at first blush, in the context prepared by the preceding interpretation, Levinas's meaning can be made clear. Developing an interpretation of our responsibilities to others requires a conception of what others qua human beings are like. Levinas's conceives of humanity not only as a *conatus essendi,* but more fundamentally as constituted by a responsibility for others. Hence responsibility for others must be interpreted not only, or even primarily, as responsibility for their biological preservation, but also, more significantly, as responsibility for their responsibility, that is, for their existence as a responsible subject. One has a responsibility not only *that* another lives, but more importantly *how* the other lives. This subordination of the preservation of another's life to responsibility for her also prevents the fetishization of biological life so that, for example, we can responsibly allow others to put their lives at risk for the sake of a worthy cause.[14]

Though Levinas points us in this direction, he himself does not explore it in depth, perhaps because it seems fraught with the possibility for paternalistic violence. For Levinas, the fallibility of one's own conception of how to live in addition to our capacity to use or manipulate others, even unintentionally, renders loving another, including concern for how she lives her life, a risky endeavor. We could recall here the story Levinas recounts of the mother of the Russian czar who tells a dying soldier that he must be proud to die for his country.[15] The concern for others as ethical subjects requires that we respect their freedom since freedom, though not the source of responsibility for Levinas, is required for ethical action. Nonetheless, responsibility toward others is incompatible with allowing others to live in certain ways. The risky nature of ethical action for others underscores the point that, for Levinas, ethical responsibility is never simply a matter of rule following or personal virtue, but requires ongoing attention to the good for another as it emerges in particular contexts, including how that other expresses her own sense of her good.[16] However, since the other may ask to be treated in ways that diminish her possibilities for ethical action, it might not always be responsible to do whatever she asks and so judgment is always ethically necessary. Though the risk of paternalism is inescapable, since such judgments are never completely free of interpretation, it is a risk that must be run for the sake of the other.

The other's status as an ethical subject also opens up the possibility for reciprocity. Though for Levinas responsibility is asymmetrical—responsibility for others is in no way contingent upon others having a reciprocal responsibility—the recognition of others as ethical subjects allows for the possibility of reciprocity. While treating another in a certain way in order to elicit a self-serving response is in no way ethical, Levinas explicitly argues that the ethical subjectivity of others implies equality and reciprocity.[17]

Reading Levinas's ethical commands as attempts to articulate the sense of responsibility on the level of meaning also implies that they are necessarily socially and historically conditioned. Whereas Levinas argues that the fundamental orienting sense is not so conditioned, meaning for Levinas can only open up from a socially and historically conditioned perspective. Consequently, the ethical commands Levinas ascribes to the face must be regarded as Levinas's own conditioned interpretations of responsibility. Indeed, he makes no effort to try to hide this, as the commands not to kill and to love thy neighbor are clearly drawn from the Hebrew Bible, while the injunction not to usurp another's place in the sun comes from Pascal's *Pensées*. The fact that these commands are derived from a particular tradition does not undermine their ethical import, nor give us reason to dismiss them or regard them as arbitrary. It does, however, mean that these articulations of responsibility are not absolute, but can be criticized and revised. Of course, the point that all meaning is socially and historically conditioned does not commit Levinas to an ethical relativism, since he maintains that the encounter with the face is universal. This understanding of the relation between the source of normativity and ethical commands allows Levinas the flexibility to acknowledge the possibility for a variety of ethical commands among varied cultural and historical settings, while also maintaining a universal standard for ethical responsibility.

The ability to criticize and revise our articulations of responsibility makes possible, Levinas thinks, the creative improvement of existing social norms and political structures. "The feeling that there is still violence evokes a search for a better justice. A progressivism of justice belongs to this, as does the possibility of creating out of my singularity something for the other. The relation of the one to the other does not vanish in justice, but rather the I always hears the call to create something" (RTB, 134). The call to critique issuing from the other is not only, or even primarily, a negative call to deconstruction of existing institutions, but a positive call to deconstruction of existing institutions for the sake of the creation of better institutions. Openness to the questioning of others allows us to break out of our lived habits, our economic structuring of the world, in order to see creative possibilities we had not previously considered but which might be better than the existing norms and structures.

Levinas's advocacy of the ongoing task of creatively rethinking social and political structures parallels Derrida's claim in "Force of Law" that law, because it is always constructed, can be continually deconstructed.[18] For Derrida the term "justice" plays the role that "the ethical" plays for Levinas, so that deconstruction of the law is both a practical possibility and an ethical necessity because of the undeconstructibility of justice. Derrida explains that the deconstructibility of law on account of justice should not be received as bad news, since such deconstruction in fact makes possible progress. Derrida goes so far as to suggest that "deconstruction is justice."[19] While Derrida acknowledges that "incalculable justice commands calculation" and so "should not serve as an alibi for staying out of juridico-political battles," and though he even gives a ringing endorsement of the "classical emancipatory ideal," he nonetheless confesses the following in a later work: "That is sometimes what I am charged with: saying nothing, not offering any content or any full proposition. I have never 'proposed' anything, and that is perhaps the essential poverty of my work."[20] Despite the apparent recognition that justice demands both construction and deconstruction, Derrida remains reluctant to engage in the former. By contrast, though Levinas acknowledges the ethical necessity of something like deconstruction, he is also willing to engage in the ethically necessary task of positive systematic philosophy to articulate ethical norms and values.

Kierkegaard and the Works of Love

This willingness to articulate ethical norms and values is also found in Kierkegaard despite the teleological suspension of the ethical and the endorsement of radical individuality. One of the persistent objections to Kierkegaard's philosophy is that his advocacy of a radical individualism renders the Kierkegaardian subject antisocial and apolitical. If this accusation was correct, then the project of eliciting practical ethical guidance for our interactions with others from Kierkegaard's work would be doomed at the outset. However, as has been repeatedly and decisively demonstrated in Kierkegaard scholarship of the past thirty years, this accusation is false.[21] Since this has been adequately shown elsewhere, I will assume that Kierkegaard's individual does not have the essentially antisocial character some critics claim it does, but instead is always already a social being. I will, however, draw from this scholarship to briefly rehearse a few major points about the social nature of Kierkegaard's individual that are relevant for this essay.

As Merold Westphal points out, Kierkegaard freely adopts Hegel's rejection of compositional individualism, instead insisting that there are no I's "that do not already essentially say We," that is, exist in a socio-historical and linguistic context formed by others.[22] Why then does Kierkegaard so strongly emphasize the need for the individual to distinguish herself from and in some sense transcend the "We"? In short, the answer is that Kierkegaard thinks that Hegel's philosophy, in its tendency to deify the "We," downplays the significance of the "I" aspect of the dialectical understanding of the individual. Kierkegaard might not have felt compelled to defend this individualism so ardently had he thought that it was simply a philosophical position held by Hegel and other academic philosophers. Instead, his passion comes from his belief that in his "present age" people live like Hegelians, tending toward the self-deification of their own "We" at the expense of the dialectical individualism that keeps open the possibility of a passionate, ethico-religious commitment that requires an "I." As Westphal puts it, "Kierkegaard seeks to unsocialize the individual in order to un-deify society."[23] This unsocialization does not entail the complete disengagement from nor abandonment of society, but instead recognizes that it is not the "absolute foundation and end" of the individual.[24] This enables the individual to relate absolutely to the absolute (God), while relating relatively—*but still genuinely relating*—to that which is relative (*Sittlichkeit*).

So what practical ethical guidance does Kierkegaard have for us then? The first point to be noted is that whatever practical ethical guidance Kierkegaard has for us does not strictly speaking follow from his account of the individual. Though this account forms the context in which we strive to live out our responsibility to others, in itself it does not tell us what we ought to do. While the individual must find the idea for which she is willing to live and die, Kierkegaard does not tell us once and for all what this idea and its practical implications are. Fortunately for the project of this chapter, Kierkegaard's writings are not confined to distinguishing the individual from the wrongly deified society, but also include an attempt to clarify the demands and practice of neighbor-love. This attempt is found, of course, in *Works of Love*.

One of the key points to understanding love that Kierkegaard makes is that genuine love always involves not only two persons, but also God. "Christianity teaches that love is a relationship between: a person—God—a person, that is, that God is the middle term" (WOL, 107). This need not imply, as some critics have argued, that the particularity of the other is lost in being just another window on the divine. Kierkegaard's point is not that the God relationship overwhelms or short-circuits the love relationship, but that that the God relationship makes possible the genuine love relationship between two particular human beings. Without the resources of the God-relation, Kierkegaard does not think one can love a particular other as that particular other ought to be loved. The fact that the love relationship originates in God has a very significant implication for Kierkegaard: "It is God who has placed love in the human being, and it is God who in every case will determine what is love" (WOL, 126). As the originary source of all genuine love, God is the final authority on what it is that constitutes love. As Jamie Ferreira puts it, "This means that God's view of what is 'good' is the standard for what we should do for the other or want the other to do for us."[25]

Kierkegaard contrasts the recognition of God as the middle term and final authority in the love relationship with the world's opinion on love. According to worldly wisdom, love is a relation between two persons without a middle term. Since there is no middle term to serve as the standard for love, Kierkegaard thinks that worldly wisdom must rely on the beloved as the sole standard. It is the beloved who "is to determine whether devotion and sacrifice have been shown, and whether the devotion and sacrifice shown are love" (WOL, 107). Kierkegaard here anticipates Nel Noddings's account of caring in which she argues that an action is caring only if the one cared for regards it as such.[26] While Kierkegaard shares Noddings's concern that acting on the basis of self-assured principles can lead to a dangerous inattentiveness to others, he would regard Noddings's suggestion as simply replacing one fallible human being (the lover) as the standard of love with another fallible human being (the beloved) as the standard of love. Rather than resolving the fundamental problem, this simply repeats it. Thus when the beloved has wrong ideas about what constitutes love, he "will regard a false kind of devotion and sacrifice as true love and will regard true love as lovelessness" (WOL, 107). For Kierkegaard, the resolution to this problem comes through the recognition of God as an essential part of and source of the standard for the love relationship.

This has an important implication that parallels one of Levinas's points made above. As Ferreira puts it, "If we recognize that we are under God's judgment of what love is and that we both 'belong' to God, there will be times when we simply cannot give what the other asks."[27] Ferreira continues on to add that it "is in this context that Kierkegaard's provocative discussion of 'hate' must be understood."[28] It is in connection with the command to love one's enemy that Kierkegaard explains the notion of hating one's beloved.[29] In the same way that the former defies the other's expectation (of animosity) by responding with concern, so the latter defies the other's expectation (of compliance) by responding with concern. While the enemy might consider such a response suspicious, the beloved, absent the recognition of God's standard for love, might consider such a response unloving, that is, hateful.[30] This need not, and indeed should not, make us insensitive or inattentive to the particular needs of others. Such inattentiveness would be justified only if one knew with certainty what the other needed at each given moment. But since the individual cannot know this about herself, how could she possibly know it about another? The fact that the beloved is not the final authority on what action toward her is loving in no way implies that her perspective on her situation can be disregarded. It simply points out that her perspective is not the whole story. If the standard for love is not simply determined by what the beloved desires, but is instead rooted in God, then what can we know of it? As it turns out, for Kierkegaard, quite a lot.

Rather than issuing a broad call to protect differences, Kierkegaard emphasizes, at least at times, that becoming oneself, and so by extension others becoming themselves, is not primarily a matter of attaching to one's differences, but embracing what is true of all persons. Thus Kierkegaard writes:

> To will to be an individual human being (which one unquestionably is) with the help of and by virtue of one's difference is flabbiness; but to will to be an individual existing human being (which one unquestionably is) in the same sense as everyone else is capable of being—that is the ethical victory over life and every mirage, the victory that is perhaps most difficult of all. (CUP, 356)

As Kierkegaard argues elsewhere, this commonality is not found only in the God-relation, the primary context for becoming a self, but even in the neighbor relation, which is after all an extension of the God-relation. Consider this:

> Yet if someone is truly to love his neighbor, it must be kept in mind at all times that his dissimilarity is a disguise . . . Christianity has not wanted to storm forth to abolish dissimilarity . . . but it wants the dissimilarity to hang loosely on the individual . . . When the dissimilarity hangs loosely in this way then in each individual there continually glimmers that essential other, which is common to all, the eternal resemblance, the likeness. (WOL, 89)

While love for the other ought to allow her to become who she is, who she is is not, Kierkegaard thinks, mired in absolute difference, but is something to which we can in some way relate. It is because we can relate, because we have something in common, that we can help and encourage her to become who she is. But how do we do this?

As a Lutheran, Kierkegaard believed that we ought to strive to be like the historical Christ. As Kierkegaard describes him, "It certainly must never be forgotten that Christ helped also in temporal and earthly needs . . . [He] healed the sick, the lepers, the deranged; he fed people, changed water into wine, calmed the sea, etc." (JP, 1:347). As this passage clearly illustrates, love as Christ exemplified it is not simply a matter of "spiritual" giving but includes a concern with the material situation of particular others. In fact, as Ferreira notes, our capacity for "spiritual" giving has some distinct limitations. "Since we cannot be called to do what Christ did in the sense of imitating his soteriological achievement (we cannot redeem humanity), what we are called on to do is to follow the example he set in his human nature. Kierkegaard sees Christ as the prototype in meeting earthly needs."[31] The recognition of the importance for genuine love of addressing lived, material needs should not come as a surprise since Kierkegaard elsewhere criticizes as infinitude's despair the "abstract sentimentality" that feigns concern for others but is not expressed in any outward, concrete action. For love to be genuine, it must be sensitive to the finite, material situation of the other, even though the other's self cannot be reduced to its finite, material situation. Because, as Kierkegaard's description of Christ's attention to earthly needs makes clear, other persons are in a variety of finite, material situations (sick, diseased, mentally ill, hungry, humiliated, endangered, etc.), loving response to another must be attentive and responsive to the other's particular situation and her particular needs within it. Such responsiveness to the particular needs of another is perfectly exemplified by the story of the merciful Samaritan, which Kierkegaard references on a number of occasions in *Works of Love.*[32]

Another significant aspect of the imitation of Christ is the concern shown for those who are marginalized, disadvantaged, or suffering. Kierkegaard's embrace of this concern[33] leads Mark Dooley to claim that the ethical significance of Kierkegaard's work is best expressed through Derrida's notion of a deconstructive justice that seeks to loosen up constructed laws and norms for the sake of excluded others. Referring to Kierkegaard's position, Dooley suggests that "to be born to the world anew through the saving power of God in servant form is to liberate oneself from the despair of the age . . . by affirming what is anathema and alien to the established order."[34] Later Dooley writes, "To practice Christianity, however, requires that one affirm what is out of power, what the law looks at with suspicion, and what offends and repulses our most sacred beliefs and mores."[35] While Dooley recognizes that the Kierkegaardian individual is not antisocial or apolitical, but instead must engage the present age, he overlooks the fact that Kierkegaard's primary goal concerning *Sittlichkeit* is not to abolish it, but relativize it, not to show that it is absolutely wrong, but simply that it is not the absolute. Dooley's focus on *what* the established order represents rather than *how* it represents it gives rise to the claim that we should embrace *what* the established order marginalizes rather than *who* the established order marginalizes. Neighbor love for *who* the established order marginalizes does not imply an affirmation of *what* the established order marginalizes. In certain cases there may be reason to affirm what the established order marginalizes, but that the established order marginalizes it is not in itself sufficient reason.

Just as the self is not only its finite material situation, but is a synthesis of the finite and the infinite, the temporal and the eternal, so too the other is not only its finite material situation. Consequently, love of the other requires attention to not only the other's temporal needs, but also her eternal needs. Thus Kierkegaard writes, "to love God is to love oneself truly; to help another person to love God is to love another person" (WOL, 107). An essential aspect of the work of love is to encourage the other person in her God-relation, only through which can she come to properly love herself. This proper love of self embraces one's dialectical individuality so that one recognizes that as a member of a particular, non-absolute socio-historical community one is fallible but that one can nonetheless relate absolutely to the absolute. To help another to embrace this individuality is "to help him to stand by himself, to become himself, to become his own master . . . to become free, independent, oneself" (WOL, 277–78). It would of course be a contradiction in principle to attempt to help another become free and independent through means of coercion or in such a way that the other becomes indebted to or dependent upon the helper. Indeed, as Kierkegaard puts it, with regard to the other's relation with God, the lover plays merely a "background" role, as is perhaps fitting for one who remains, even in genuine loving, fallible.

Lest we think that in helping others to become the free, independent individuals they are, we are encouraging them to become antisocial, isolated beings, we must remember that an important aspect of being oneself truly and loving God truly is striving to love one's neighbors truly. Hence, insofar as love of another helps that other to become herself, it also helps her to love other persons. That is to say, to love another person is to help her to be responsive to the material, spiritual, and ethical needs of others. One of the perhaps unexpected implications of this is that it makes possible a legitimate notion of reciprocation. While Kierkegaard rejects *ad nauseam* any attempt to induce reciprocation as unloving, the possibility that the lover's love for the beloved will lead to a situation in which the beloved loves the lover as well need not be rejected. The problem with inducing reciprocation for Kierkegaard is not that is it wrong to be loved—indeed, Kierkegaard explicitly acknowledges the value of being loved and helped by others[36]—but rather that it keeps another trapped in the economy of the same. Hence, in the same way that Levinas comes to embrace the possibility of reciprocity through the recognition of the other as an ethical subject like me, so too Kierkegaard embraces the possibility of reciprocity through the recognition of the other as a subjectively existing individual like me.

Despite the criticisms that Kierkegaard fails to give any concrete or actionable content to our ethical responsibilities to others, we have seen that Kierkegaard's work recommends three key aspects of love for others that are rooted in his understanding of what it means to be human; that we are a synthesis of the finite and the infinite, able to relate relatively to the relative and absolutely to the absolute, and on account of the latter called to neighbor-love. Consequently, to love another person is to be responsive to her particular material needs, to encourage a proper self-love through love of God, and to support her efforts to love her neighbors.

Conclusion

In at least one work on Levinas's thought, the author has cleverly chosen to end his piece with a section entitled "In-conclusion."[37] While still affirming the fallible, revisable nature of Kierkegaard's and Levinas's work and my own thinking, I will resist this pun as, in part, an artifact of the reading of Kierkegaard and Levinas that fails to subordinate their points about epistemic limitation to their insistence on the urgency of the ethical task of subjectivity. Ethical urgency does not allow indefinite inconclusiveness. We must concede the point that no book will ever arrest the need to question, criticize, and write anew, while nonetheless being willing to articulate norms, values, and ideals worthy of guiding practical action. Kierkegaard and Levinas can serve as our inspiration in this endeavor since their commitments to fallibilism allow them to articulate and commit themselves to particular norms, values, and ideals rather than keeping them from doing so. As this paper has demonstrated these norms, values, and ideals are themselves rooted in Kierkegaard's and Levinas's thinking about human nature beyond difference. While they certainly do not give us the last word, as they are eager to concede, they give us words worthy of discussion, though as they are eager to exhort, the fact that discussion is always ongoing should not paralyze us in our attempts to love our neighbors in the fullness of their humanity.

Notes

1. At least for us humans in Kierkegaard's case.

2. I will not defend the claim that Kierkegaard and Levinas both practice the hermeneutics of finitude and suspicion, as this claim has been adequately defended elsewhere. See, for example, Merold Westphal, *Becoming a Self* (West Lafayette, Ind.: Purdue Uni-

versity Press, 1996); Robert Bernasconi, "The Ethics of Suspicion," *Research in Phenomenology* (1990); and Stephen Minister, "Is There a Teleological Suspension of the Philosophical? Kierkegaard, Levinas, and the End of Philosophy," *Philosophy Today* 47, no. 2 (Summer 2003).

3. See, for example, James Mensch, *Ethics and Selfhood: Alterity and the Phenomenology of Obligation* (Albany: State University of New York Press, 2003), chap. 4.

4. Levinas also recounts this story at RTB, 89.

5. John Caputo, *Against Ethics* (Bloomington: Indiana University Press, 1993), 21.

6. For Levinas's acknowledgment that such thinking is necessary and that this is what he is doing, see OTB, 155–63.

7. Levinas uses "thou shall not kill" (*Tu ne tueras point;* e.g., EI, 89) and "thou shall not commit murder" (*Tu ne commettras pas de meurtre;* e.g., TI, 199) synonymously as commands from the face.

8. For this distinction see "Meaning and Sense" in CPP.

9. For a contrary interpretation, see Mensch, *Ethics and Selfhood,* chap. 4. It is not clear to me, as Mensch suggests, that when confronted with a vulnerable other we experience the absolute value of life.

10. See CPP, 92; GDT, pt. 1.

11. Levinas recognizes that concern for the lives of others requires concern for a host of material conditions. Thus he argues that social justice requires that people have the opportunity for "education and participation in political power . . . work, rest, a place to live, freedom of movement . . . social advancement" (OS, 120; cf. AT, 146).

12. See Alain Badiou, *Ethics: An Essay on the Understanding of Evil,* trans. Peter Hallward (London: Verso, 2001), chaps. 1–3.

13. See OTB, 117; CPP, 123; EI, 99.

14. We could also potentially allow for death in certain circumstances, such as some cases of euthanasia or in a just war, though Levinas explicitly opposes capital punishment as a flight from responsibility for the condemned (RTB, 51, 55).

15. " Dialogue with Emmanuel Levinas," in *Face to Face with Levinas,* ed. Richard A. Cohen (Albany: State University of New York Press, 1986), 31.

16. On this point, a Levinasian practical ethics finds itself in proximity to some feminist thinkers' development of an ethics of care. See, for example, Gilligan, *In a Different Voice: Psychological Theory and Women's Development* (Cambridge: Harvard University Press, 1982); and Noddings, *Caring: A Feminine Approach to Ethics and Moral Education* (Berkeley: University of California Press, 1984). For treatment of the relation between Levinas's project and an ethics of care, see Katz, *Levinas, Judaism, and the Feminine: The Silent Footsteps of Rebecca* (Bloomington: Indiana University Press, 2003), especially 106–107; and Bookman and Aboulafia, "Ethics of Care Revisited: Gilligan and Levinas," *Philosophy Today* 44, Supplement (2000).

17. See OTB, 158; RTB, 214; EN, 107, 229.

18. Derrida, "Force of Law," trans. Mary Quaintance, in *Acts of Religion,* ed. Gil Anidjar (New York: Routledge, 2002), 242–43.

19. Ibid., 243.

20. Ibid., 257, 258; Derrida, "Hospitality, Justice, and Responsibility: A Dialogue with Jacques Derrida," in *Questioning Ethics: Contemporary Debates in Philosophy,* ed. R. Kearney and M. Dooley (New York: Routledge, 1999), 74.

21. For these arguments, see Merold Westphal, *Kierkegaard's Critique of Reason and Society* (University Park: Pennsylvania State University Press, 1991), Bruce Kirmmse, *Kierkegaard in Golden Age Denmark* (Bloomington: Indiana University Press, 1990);

Bruce Kirmmse, "Call Me Ishmael—Call Everybody Ishmael: Kierkegaard on the Coming-of-Age Crisis of Modern Times," *Foundations of Kierkegaard's Vision of Community: Religion, Ethics, and Politics in Kierkegaard,* ed. George B. Connell and C. Stephen Evans (Atlantic Highlands, N.J.: Humanities, 1992); and Mark Dooley, *The Politics of Exodus: Søren Kierkegaard's Ethics of Responsibility* (New York: Fordham University Press, 2001).

22. Westphal, *Kierkegaard's Critique of Reason and Society,* 32.

23. Ibid., 34.

24. Hegel, *Philosophy of Right,* trans. T. M. Knox (Oxford: Oxford University Press, 1952), ¶142.

25. Ferreira, *Love's Grateful Striving: A Commentary on Kierkegaard's Works of Love* (Oxford: Oxford University Press, 2001), 71. This is a lucid and insightful commentary and the interpretation of love I develop is indebted to it.

26. Noddings, *Caring,* 68–69.

27. Ferreira, *Love's Grateful Striving,* 74.

28. Ibid., 74.

29. See WOL, 108.

30. Hence, *pace* Elsebet Jegstrup's argument in "A Questioning of Justice: Kierkegaard, the Postmodern Critique and Political Theory," *Political Theory* 23, no. 3 (August 1995), there may be times when love demands that we not just let the other do "whatever she wants" (442).

31. Ferreira, *Love's Grateful Striving,* 82.

32. WOL, 22, 317, 323. Both Jegstrup and Mark Dooley argue that Kierkegaard would endorse an ethics of *Gelassenheit.* See Dooley, *Politics of Exodus,* 229–46; and Jegstrup, "A Questioning of Justice," 434–42. While Kierkegaard emphasizes the importance of neighbor love not placing demands on others that are merely artifacts of one's own thought or desires, the proactive involvement of the Samaritan, involvement that might even be characterized as paternalistic since there is no record of the victim requesting the treatment the Samaritan provides, renders the notion of "letting be" at the least highly misleading and at the worst just plain wrong as a description of Kierkegaard's notion of love.

33. See, for example, PC, 12–15.

34. Dooley, *Politics of Exodus,* 137.

35. Ibid., 142; my emphasis.

36. See WOL, 107.

37. Richard A. Cohen, *Ethics, Exegesis, and Philosophy: Interpretations After Levinas* (Cambridge: Cambridge University Press, 2001), 326.

12 "More Than All the Others": Meditation on Responsibility

Martin Beck Matuštík

Each of us is guilty before the other for everything, and I more than any.

—Fyodor Dostoyevsky, *The Brothers Karamazov* (374, 386)

We are all responsible for everyone else—but I am more responsible than all the others.

—Emmanuel Levinas, *Otherwise Than Being* (146)

Biographical Preface

This chapter examines one aspect of the wide-ranging philosophical background of the intellectual and dissident movement for human rights in onetime Communist Czechoslovakia. On January 1, 1977, Charta 77—a manifesto for human rights in Czechoslovakia—was issued by three spokespersons, Václav Havel, Jan Patočka, and Jiří Hájek and initially signed by 242 signatories. Professor Patočka studied philosophy in Freiburg with Edmund Husserl as well as Martin Heidegger, and he became Husserl's close friend. That friendship emerged within the philosophical genealogy of modern Central Europeans from Tomáš Garrigue Masaryk, the first Czechoslovak president (1918–1935) and philosophy Ph.D., who encouraged his Moravian compatriot, Husserl, to study philosophy in Vienna, to the playwright Havel who learned philosophy in the underground Prague seminars from Patočka.

When Nazis took power in Germany and Husserl was forced to leave Freiburg University, Patočka, on behalf of the Prague Linguistic Circle, invited him to lecture in Prague. In 1935 Husserl delivered at Charles University one of his Crisis lectures (also given that year in May in Vienna), which constituted the core of his late work, *Crisis of European Sciences and Transcendental Phenomenology*. Husserl died in 1938, and Patočka endeavored to save his archive in Prague. When Hitler occupied Czechoslovakia in March 1939, the Husserl archives were smuggled by Herman van Breda across Europe to Louvain. Although Prague, unlike Louvain or Freiburg, never had long enough periods of postwar freedom to become again the world center of phenomenology, Patočka imparted his philosophical originality in thinking that learned from both his teachers, Husserl and Heidegger, and yet inflected both with an ethical heart later found chiefly in postmodern turns of phenomenology in Levinas and Derrida.

I was eleven in 1968 when the Soviet tanks invaded Prague, twelve a year later when Jan Palach, a nineteen-year-old philosophy student, immolated himself in protest of the Soviet invasion, and nineteen when Charta 77 was issued. Patočka died on March 13, 1977, after suffering a brain hemorrhage under police interrogation. I was the first student of psychology at Charles University. I attended one of Patočka's last home seminars devoted to the question of death. I was detained by the state police at one of the home gatherings and again at Patočka's funeral. After my arrests, the secret service both invited me to work as their agent at the university and threatened me if I refused. Later as a condition for remaining at the university I was ordered by Dean Ráb and the Communists to publicly denounce Patočka and Charta 77 at the September assembly of all university students and faculty. Given the stark choices before me—collaborate and feel spineless, have my life destroyed at twenty as an unknown protesting youth, or flee—I had to make a quick yet life-impacting decision. Under cover of secrecy and with considerable help from a female admirer at the university Communist youth organization, I obtained an invitation to a summer camp in India, and with that I secured a state permit to leave for the West. I departed in August of that year officially traveling to India but journeying via Austria, where I spent eight months in a refugee camp, only to land in the Americas in early 1978. Instead of denouncing the dissident movement as demanded of me by the authorities, I signed Charta 77 and left my homeland, never to return. I have always wondered if the branch that issued my permit communicated with those who interrogated me. I know that many people were in trouble because of my "disappearance."

I was not allowed into Czechoslovakia even as U.S. citizen until 1988, toward the end of the Gorbachev years. In the fall of 1989, I commenced my Ph.D. research as a Fulbright student of Jürgen Habermas in Frankfurt. The Berlin Wall came down and the Velvet Revolution took place in November. At thirty-two, I witnessed Havel's ascent to the Prague Castle as the first post-Communist president returned, and later I delivered a series of lectures at Charles University. My dissertation was published as a book, *Postnational Identity,* and it reflects on those historical and intellectual currents so well embodied by the figures that impacted my life—Havel and Habermas—on the two sides of the old cold war divide.

On April 22–28, 2007, I was invited to present this essay at the centennial celebration of Patočka's birth and the thirty-year commemoration of his death at a conference jointly organized in Prague by Ivan Havel's Center for Theoretical Study and the Husserl Circle. This event marked also thirty years since the birth of Charta 77 and thirty years since I had to leave Prague. This remarkable event marked in many ways the end of an era—a caesura in which students of Patočka or those, who like me discovered his thought in their youth precociously but who were impacted by his Socratic death, came of age either as thinkers or public figures. The conference thus wore the Janus-like intellectual and public faces of scholarly panels, public events with nightly receptions hosted by one of the sponsors, Charles University, the Czech Academy of Sciences, the Czech senate, French embassy, the Polish Institute in Prague, Austrian Cultural Forum, and the Goethe Institute in Prague.

Dr. Ivan Chvatík, the person who conceived and organized this event, was among those chiefly responsible for saving Patočka's archives from the Communist secret service. During the dark years he began to organize the unpublished writings into what today are several volumes of published works. Patočka archives are housed at the Center for Theoretical Study of the Philosophical Institute of the Academy of Science of the Czech Republic. Erika Abrams received an honorary doctorate from Charles University for her lifetime work as translator of Patočka's works, and three distinguished scholars, Ivan Dubský and Jiří Polívka from Prague, and Klaus Nellen from the Austrian Institute for the Sciences of Men, were awarded Patočka's Medals of the Academy of Science of the Czech Republic for their significant contributions to Patočka scholarship.

Among the public figures, Martin Palouš, former Czech ambassador in Washington and now the Czech ambassador to the United Nations, presented a paper on Patočka's Socratic message for the twenty-first century, while Petr Pitthart, the first vice president of the Czech senate, spoke about questioning as a prerequisite for a meaningful protest and then hosted a reception in the beautiful rooms of the Wallenstein Palace that houses the senate.

The conference opened with a prelude, "Music As Philosophy," Patočka's beloved composer Beethoven's 1st and 4th Symphonies, and it concluded with the original version of Beethoven's 9th Symphony for Cello Solo at the Gothic House at the Stone Bell. Václav Havel opened the conference sessions with three vignettes. He described how at fifteen, he discovered Patočka's first book in the library, but it was hidden "on the index" among the *libri prohibiti,* and so he had to convince a friendly librarian to let him read it on the sly. In the 1960s, when Havel was employed as a stage hand in *Divadlo na zábradlí,* Patočka used to come after hours to lecture late into the night on philosophical topics to actors and writers. In 1976, Havel was among those who persuaded Patočka to become the spokesperson for Charta 77. Havel recalled that Patočka deliberated for some time whether or not to emerge from his philosophical vocation into a decisive public role, but once he did cross that Rubicon, he embraced it with all he was—unto death.

Introduction

Václav Havel echoed both Dostoyevsky and Levinas when he wrote at the end of entry 122 of his *Letters to Olga* that "responsibility founds an asymmetrical ethical situation," namely, the "thought that 'someone must begin.'" This at once Kierkegaardian and Levinasian transcription of responsibility found in Dostoyevsky cannot be "preached, but only borne," writes Havel. It would be strange both for Kierkegaard's or Dostoyevsky's existential recovery of Christianity and Levinas's ethically anchored Judaism to specialize in discoursing on responsibility but not to become responsible. Havel recalls this lived sense of responsibility in his dramas when he places the most impressive ethical discourses into the dialogues pronounced, absurdly so, by cowards and opportunists. By taking recourse to Dostoyevsky, Derrida, and Patočka as a bridge between Kierkegaard's second, religious ethics and Levinas's meontological ethics, I want to show how Kierkegaard and Levinas come to support the Havelian view that responsibility begins with an ethical response of one's own. Yet is there not something uncanny, if not Atlas-like and Pelagian, in the infinitizing (whether Jewish or Christian) demand that increases one's responsibility in an infinite measure by claiming that "I am responsible for the state of the world"?

I will meditate on Jan Patočka's finite responsibility, Derrida's Kierkegaardian, albeit aporetically inflected emphasis on the infinite dimension of responsibility, and Levinasian-Dostoyevskian-cum-Kierkegaardian ethico-existential variations on in/finite responsibility. Havel alludes to hyperbolic (second in Kierkegaard, first in Levinas) ethics in a parenthetical remark on the birth of the manifesto for human rights in Czechoslovakia, Charta 77. With this three-pronged examination, the question before us is this: Which dimension of responsibility appears at this ethico-political birth, or to put it otherwise, what sort of responsibility is born in care for the soul and polis?

Patočka's Finite Responsibility

In the fifth heretical essay, Patočka inquires into the sources of decadence of technical civilization.[1] The core issue turns on the question of the peculiar quality of our being in the world, responsibility, which bespeaks human interest not only in the truth of but also ethical response to existing. Humans are furthermore distinguished by seeking the sacred festival dimension that would transform our everyday toil and suffering. Festival lifts the weight of finite life by inserting it in larger meanings and forces. From time immemorial festival was the dimension of the orgiastic passion—from the erotic to the sacred to the demonic self-forgetfulness.[2] The question of civilization and its discontents, to echo Freud's last work, is how the yearning for orgiastic ecstasy, the sacred, becomes related to responsibility otherwise than by a flight from it or its overcoming. The demonic must become transformed within a new relation with responsibility, and this very movement from the orgiastic to responsible existence—in what is a very Kierkegaardian translation of the religious as a task of becoming self and discovering oneself as spirit—gives birth, says Patočka, to the religious. The religious is instituted in the existential overcoming of the sacred as demonic; by contrast, the resurgence of the orgiastic demonic, whether in religion or politics, destroys the religious in its Kierkegaardian sense of responsible existence.[3]

What is responsibility but birth of the religious itself? What is religiousness so understood but birth of the responsible self freed from anonymous everydayness and the anonymous orgiastic demonic? Patočka offers us the most succinct and moving understanding of the self when he describes the I arising from responsible and sober questioning of everydayness as well as from active courage to face the dizziness of possibility. These are the core themes found before Martin Heidegger in Kierkegaard's reflections on anxiety and despair. Patočka's ethico-religious reception of them even while commenting on Heidegger is without doubt inspired by the stress on singular responsibility found in Kierkegaard as much as Husserl. The ordinary can be overcome without the forgetful flight from self into the orgiastic demonic.[4] Human history is punctuated by the struggle to give birth to care for the soul and polis.[5] The Platonic cave dramatizes an allegory of blind and so dark faith of impersonal cults and mysteries yielding to care for the soul. What is the notion of immortality but the holding site of responsibility for oneself before the other, and ultimately for one's death?[6] The Platonic philosopher transforms everydayness by a festival of soul's assent to the good. Everyday time and the time of the festival differ in kind, yet the philosopher in the Platonic sense partakes of the latter to transform the former. This is what Plato means by the ascent of the soul to the good. Unlike the disintegrating dispersion into the orgiastic sacred, philosophy is born of soul- and polis-making. The philosopher who thus overcomes the orgiastic demonic is a magician more akin to Prospero's than to Faust's care for the soul and death. Prospero and Faust are both magicians, and yet the philosopher of the Platonic type is unlike modern Faust, and in that both care differently for soul and death.[7] Philosophical conversion to the good and true and beautiful provides an incomplete resistance to the demonic, and for Patočka it is only with the Judeo-Christian revelation of the good as agape that we reach the deeper root and greater intensity of responsibility. What the discovery of the responsible self means becomes truly revealed only in the personal or, to borrow from Jean-Luc Marion, iconic relation of the soul with the wholly Other who sees one without being seen.[8] The question of living in truth is no longer reducible to the truth of insights or idols but rather becomes the iconic truth of one's existential responsibility to one's destiny. To vanquish the anonymity of everydayness and the orgiastic demonic takes on a recognizably *religious* inflection of redemptive care for the soul. Patočka affirms the key Kierkegaardian insight that one is a finitely responsible individual in relation to the infinite love.[9]

The discontents of modern technological civilization arise from the incompleteness and gaps of the Platonic as well as Judeo-Christian attempts at overcoming of everydayness and orgiasm.[10] When Faust wins over Prospero, when boredom wells up in new intensities of the demonic, then the eschatology of everyday non-personality carries the day. What is so imprecisely called today *the return of the religious* is often a surge of the orgiastic demonic both in secular forms within the established democracies and in a garden variety of religious fundamentalism in all great Abrahamic religions of the Book—the Bible.[11] In this critique of the contemporary return of the fake religious, or resurgence of religious aestheticism and despair of the infidel-faithful, we find a Kierkegaard-inspired unmasking of fundamentalism. Patočka writes about the twentieth century as an era of war and new orgiasm.[12] The most pernicious form of orgiasm is the need to demonize the enemy in order to underwrite one's moral superiority. The resurgence of the use of capital punishment is the extreme case of the religious morality underwritten by the orgiastic. The technological power of modern civilization becomes a demonic light that can create as much as destroy.[13] With global technology, communication, and markets, the old civilizational discontents have assumed planetary proportions.[14] Patočka views human history as nothing else but the trembling of any given, thus finite certainty of meaning. It is, indeed, the Abrahamic fear and trembling out of which are born both our crises that draw us into the demonic and our calls to responsible solidarity. All civilizations live or die with human courage to face the crossroads of fear and trembling. This is the claim which Kierkegaard recorded in *Practice in Christianity* (PC, 88) as a complement and corrective to *Fear and Trembling*, explaining by the latter that we are in the process of becoming from which no power that be, and no established order can be exempt. All civilizations live or die with taking responsibility for their history.

Derrida's Aporetic Responsibility

Is Derrida justified in reading Patočka as replicating an existential, flat-footed Christian notion of responsibility?[15] It hinges on what is meant by "Christian," and it will be a reading of Kierkegaard that will split the difference between what Patočka meant by it and what Derrida says that Patočka meant. A certain reading of Kierkegaard (and of Christianity) will open a possibility for carrying a fruitful dialogue with Levinas (and Judaism).

Evink clarifies the nuance between "a non-Christian thinking through of the Christian tradition,"[16] which he discerns in Patočka's non-dogmatic religiosity and Derrida's aporetic reading of Patočka. Derrida reads Patočka's "logic at bottom" against Patočka, whom he views as having failed to think the logic of the gift non-dogmatically as "the possibility of religion without religion."[17] Derrida deploys certain Judaic messianicity against what he perceives to be Patočka's Christian messianism, namely, the latter's notion that "Christianity represents to this day the most powerful means—never yet superseded but not yet thought right through either—by which humans are able to struggle against their own decline." How does then Patočka's Christianity underwrites the rebirth of the responsible self as well as of an authentic care for the polis or *Europe*?[18]

There lies an aporia at the core of every movement of responsibility that intends infinite goodness but can never meet up to it in an intuition of its finite irreplaceable singularity. The infinite exceeds in intuition what I can grasp in my finite conceptuality. Derrida distills this aporia out of a certain reading of Christian responsibility. Infinitizing responsibility of finite creatures who are to bear the whole world on their shoulders is always already implicated in one's ethical guilt. "I am guilty inasmuch as I am responsible,"[19] and my guilt arises from this infinitizing horizon of goodness before which singular "responsibility is always unequal to itself." Responsibility clearly turns aporetic in Derrida's infinitizing movement of human singularity, and so does therefore his reading of Kierkegaard whose pseudonymous midrash on Abraham's sacrifice of Isaac will be the chief exemplar for this aporia. Yet Patočka's third movement of human existence signals a finite breakthrough to truth and freedom within the life world to which the Knight of Faith or perhaps a dissident returns,[20] that is within the established regimes of the ethical-universal that are challenged by those who dissent. Responsibility cannot lie in an aporetic flight of the Knight of Resignation, which would seem to be more akin to Derrida's reading of Kierkegaard. Patočka's two turns from the orgiastic demonic—by way of Platonic *anabasis* to the good and in Christian self-relation to the agapic love—bears a finite, and so never a Pelagian or Atlas-like, responsibility. Something else than what is manifestly attributed by Derrida to Patočka as flat-footed Christian apologetics is gained by Derrida's corrective reading. In fact Derrida's corrective is already adumbrated by Patočka's sober responsibility.

I arrive at the scene of the infinite call to responsibility not only late, thus ontologically guilty (and this is Climacus's discovery in the autodidactic school of existential pathos) but also existentially inadequate to its lived requirement to care for every other. I am found not only guilty with regard to time and finite existence but also ethico-religiously sinful in terms of the requirement. This aporetic situation of originarily guilty and ethically compromised, thus sinful, responsibility, in Derrida's judgment, threatens us anew with the return of the orgiastic demonic even under the disguise of the ethico-religious. Derridean (unlike Kierkegaardian) faith never resolves in act the aporia of infinite responsibility. It is always already compromised, perhaps overburdened like Dostoyevsky's underground man, by too much undecideable reflection. The orgiastic offers a sense of false innocence, and now it is lost over and over by the hyperconsciousness of responsibility. The fundamentalist resurgences of the religious: what are they but so many postmodern reassertions of the orgiastic? Like the autoimmune response that attacks its own body, Derrida insists, the orgiastic religious tears apart all sense of responsibility from within. Reacting to the orgiastic religious from without, fundamentalist political wars on the orgiastic lose the ethico-political sense of care for the soul and polis. What ensues from this suicidal loop is the new decline of technological civilization.

Offering a fresh midrash on Kierkegaard's own midrash of Abraham's sacrifice of Isaac, Derrida counsels us to recover from this experience of the impossible yet a more finite sense of responsibility. This is his Kierkegaardian corrective to the purported flat-footed Christianity of Patočka. The aporia of love's or faith's gift would no longer be lived in responsibility to infinite sacrificial love that one can never live up to (this marks Derrida's parting with the exclusive sacrificial cult of Christianity), but rather in discovering that Abrahamic sacrifice of Isaac (the gift of life and death) occurs in the ordinary and everyday (the Abrahamic as well as the Christ event marks every face-to-face encounter). Every other is wholly, irreplaceably other.[21] This offers us at once a Christian and Judaic reading of ethico-religious responsibility. Derrida deploys a uniquely Kierkegaardian-Levinasian reading of fear and trembling that heightens responsibility of the singular individual to every other who is wholly other. In Derrida's view this is the only way to safeguard Patočka's existential demand that we work against returns of orgiastic religiosity whether within the state, the economy or the church.

Levinasian-Dostoyevskian Ethico-Existential Responsibility

In *Letter to Olga* 122, Havel writes on March 4, 1982, that the thought of asymmetrical responsibility, namely, that I am responsible more than all the others, stood at the birth of Charta 77. That I am responsible for the state of the world, he writes, "this is how we thought about it five years ago." The manifesto of Charta 77 evokes the "feeling of solidary responsibility and faith in the meaning of civic engagement," while Patočka's January 3 addendum clarifies that Charta 77 is an outgrowth of a conviction that one has an obligation to resist injustice.[22] In Patočka's text from March 8, Charta 77 is represented as a radical citizen education for liberation and responsibility. "Every person must learn for himself . . . Education means coming to understand that there is more to life than fear and gain. . . . It is the hope of Charta 77 that our citizens may learn to act as free persons, self-motivated and responsible."[23]

What is the meaning of this ideal and yet concrete responsibility? As a human being, how could I be guilty toward the infinite love or be required to give as God gives and loves with divine infinite embrace?[24] But I am guilty and responsible "more than all the others" because of the injunction of shared solidarity with and "insatiable compassion" for the human race. This is my lived injunction, not a structural aporia. Derrida's responsibility is conceptually aporetic or undecideably reflective and hyperconscious; Kierkegaardian-Levinasian-Dostoyevskian responsibility, shared by Havel and Patočka in co-founding Charta 77, is actively ethico-existential in performance. Derrida's infinite responsibility marks an aporetic condition of im/possibility of ethical relation.[25] Ethico-existential responsibility exceeds the ordinary morality and justice by a higher obligation to act first, yet this injunction is lived in finite concretion. Derrida tries to implicate Patočka in a guilt-ridden Christianity (as if reading certain Kierkegaardian-Levinasian against Patočka) that aims to tame the orgiastic with what for humans is an *impossible* feat of infinite love and divine sacrifice. Yet Kierkegaardian-Levinasian responsibility is human and so finite even as it reveals the trace of the infinite Other in every human encounter. We find the Kierkegaardian faith marking our finitude inscribed into Patočka's third movement of existence and set within a contextual horizon with no ultimate foundations or justice.[26] For Derrida, the finitude of responsibility that intends the infinite suffers an aporetic deficit because in taking up my singular responsibility to one human person, I sacrifice my responsibility to another. I can do nothing other than always already care for the other (every human other) ir/responsibly. I suffer the hyperconsciousness of my split or aporetic duties to be responsible.

In Derrida's Judeo-Christian heresy (his midrash on Patočka's heresy), Mt. Moriah or Kierkegaard's *Fear and Trembling* occur in every ethical relation where I, like Abraham, am willing to sacrifice Isaac.[27] And this Derridean, at once Judeo-Christian midrash marks the end of all theodicy—God spares Isaac and also reveals in Jesus Christ the end of all blood sacrifice and so the birth of responsible love. Yet unlike Derrida, Patočka's responsibility, even the Levinasian-Dostoyevskian thought that I am more guilty and responsible than all the others, does not sacrifice the other for the sake of attending to the one. Existentially lived responsibility is never an abstract conceptual aporia; rather, I am called to a finite act, whereby I am bound by my historical and singular situation. Kierkegaard's existential concretion and Levinas's substitution complement and so correct Derrida's hyperflective and intertextual, hence ir/responsible undecideability.

In order to transform the aporetic impasse into a lived injunction, we must recover the finite ethico-existential motive of hyperbolic responsibility behind Charta 77 and in Patočka's Socratic death in the hands of the secret service. We find the same sentiment in Havel's claim made in his first New Year's speech as president and then in another form again in Oslo, Salzburg, and Jerusalem, namely, that we are all responsible for the totalitarian past of which we are all but recently released prisoners. The key to finding the hidden motive behind the notion of "more than all the others" lies in Levinas's figure of substitution (OTB, chap. 4). "More than all the others" does not mean actually having done *X* more than others or having to carry the entire world on my shoulders or safeguard its redemption with my works alone.[28] That lifting of the world by my own efforts would be hyper-Protestantism or simply a Pelagian heresy. For Levinas the "more" means that I find Thou when I seek myself. His I-Thou tilts into an un-Buberian asymmetry of my stance before the other that saturates *my* ethical responsibility with a "surplus" (OTB, 100) of neighborly, caring, divine anarchy. My ethical responsibility, Levinas says, is "justified by no prior commitment" or ontology. In acting with hyperbolic responsibility, meontologically, I am a refugee exiled in oneself (OTB, 102ff.).[29]

After Auschwitz, Jewish thinkers such as Levinas, Hans Jonas, Etty Hillesum, or Elie Wiesel answer the problem of human evil by admitting the figure of a suffering, weak, affected, becoming God. The Christian weak God meets the post-Holocaust suffering God.[30] As if reinscribing the terrain of low Christology, in which the God of Abraham, Isaac, and Jacob is revealed in Jesus' "useless" and thereby redemptive suffering, this is where Dostoyevsky's (and in that also Kierkegaard's) existential Christianity impacts Levinas's post-Holocaust Judaism, and so both impact Patočka's heretical responsibility. I believe this nuance offers a corrective to Derrida's a/theistic messianicity without messianism, which he deploys in his aporetic reading of Patočka's existential religiosity without the orgiastic-religious. With low Christology there is always already a certain messianicity without messianism (and this is one possible bridge for a dialogue with Renewal Judaism) because it is a religion of responsibility without theodicy and so without the orgiastic-demonic return of the religious. The Messiah will come, says Franz Kafka, when we no longer need him or her. What is to come once faith resolves despair and justice is love's true revolution? Kierkegaard defines the God event very simply as *that there is possibility*. This is likewise the Judaic messianic expectation that destroys hopelessness as the essence of all idolatry. The exilic ethics affirms quintessentially a Judaic, Job-like response to human suffering, which in Levinas (US) is deemed *useless* because never justified. Only in the ethical call does the useless suffering of another become "the just suffering in me for the unjustifiable suffering of the Other," and this *redemptive* sense of the substitution "opens upon the suffering the ethical perspective of the inter-human" (US, 159). In Dostoyevsky only this ethical responsiveness (or religion in the sense of hearing the call and responding to the other) names the redemptive dimension suffering. In Levinas as much as in Kierkegaard the Judaic and the Christian meet in the hyperbolic figure of substitution that integrates the double commandment (proclaimed in Torah and affirmed by Jesus of Nazareth as the core of faith) to love God with all one's heart and the neighbor as oneself. In existential finitude I can only love God non-reciprocally, yet this loving does not dictate an impasse of conceptual aporias. The thoroughly self-interested love, the clause of the "as oneself," transforms into interested responsibility for the other greater than that of all the others. The commandment to love my neighbor inverts my self-interested loving—just as does my prayer for forgiveness in the Lord's Prayer that pivots on the "*as*" in "as we have also forgiven our debtors"[31]—into a hyperbolic care for the other.[32]

Religiously, one is bereft of any recourse to theodicy: suffering is useless and even obscene when sought or explained *that* way, orgiastically, demonically, or in a perverse masochistic substitution against which Derrida obliquely warns (see his "Hostipitality") the Christian as much as Jewish fans of Levinas. Even the *Dialogues of the Carmelites* reveal as much about the pure unsolicited martyrdom of the nuns in the French Revolution. Suffering becomes redemptive in the ethical responsibility of the present individuals and generations whose response has been awaited in the messianic expectations by the victims of history.[33] The thought of shared Adamic guilt (we share it as a human race; hence, this is a substitution in bad) and the hyperbolic Judeo-Christian ethics of responsibility (we can assume it; hence, this offers paths to our substitution in good) is redemptive. For example, new generations share the original guilt (though not personal responsibility) of genocide inflicted on the native peoples of the Americas and yet the future generations can redeem this inherited liability (though not personal guilt) for the past by their present acts of responsibility.

No innocent suffering can be justified. In Levinas's Judaic midrash on the commandment to love God and the neighbor there is a double substitution—the love of God is fulfilled in one's love of the neighbor—and there is a substitution of oneself who responds to the other. This is why a redemptive response to useless suffering is always already ethico-religious. Just as the Christian God is revealed in low Christology in a suffering God of the divine substitution, so also the Jewish God is encountered only indirectly in the love of one's neighbor. This is one and the same God; God is One.

Mitya Karamazov, without having killed his father, accepts his Siberian sentence on behalf of others, be it the Grand Inquisitor's nihilism or Ivan's despair. The ideality of Charta 77 and the reality of Patočka's death were both assumed without reciprocity or future guarantees. Perhaps a fitting complement to Patočka's existential idea of dissidents who act to overcome the orgiastic and the totalitarian extremes of human sociality in a solidarity of the shaken would be the Judeo-Christian solidarity of substitution in which everyone is becoming more oneself in becoming more ethico-existentially responsible than all the others. In contrast to Derrida's aporetic reading of Kierkegaard's and Patočka's Christianity, post-Holocaust thought accepts that redemptive suffering marks all acts of responsible solidarity. One must remain without recourse to human reciprocity or divine theodicy. After Auschwitz, Dostoyevsky's silent Jesus standing before the Grand Inquisitor becomes a modern Job-Levinas who, like Kierkegaard, answers the surplus of innocent suffering, existential guilt, and despair in the world with non-reciprocal and risky freedom to be responsible. Low Christology mirrors the Judaic law of anti-idolatry, in that solidarity can break their bread and bless their cup of wine. This mutual rediscovery of the two biblical religions in their ethical solidarity with dissidents and victims of history alike is perhaps their shared *heresy* yet to be loved by both.[34] I am responsible "for the freedom of the others" (OTB, 109), "for the responsibility of the other" (OTB, 117, cf. 43), for which I too have to answer without the guarantees of reciprocity and theodicy (OTB, 84). Indeed, with Alyosha Karamazov and Father Zossima, Kierkegaard and Levinas, Patočka and Charta 77, I must act first because I am more responsible than all the others (cf. LR, 1, 182).

Notes

This chapter first appeared (in a slightly different form) in *Critical Horizons: A Journal of Philosophy and Social Theory* 8, no. 1 (August 2007): 47–60. It is reprinted here by permission.

1. Jan Patočka, *Kacířské eseje o filosofii dějin* (Praha: Academia, 1990), 105–26.
2. Ibid., 108.
3. Ibid., 110.
4. Ibid., 111.
5. Ibid., 112.
6. Ibid., 113.
7. Ibid., 114.
8. Ibid., 115.
9. Ibid., 116.
10. Ibid., 118.

11. Cf. Jacques Derrida, "Faith and Knowledge: The Two Sources of 'Religion' at the Limits of Reason Alone," in *Acts of Religion*, ed. Gil Anidjar (New York: Routledge, 2002), 42–101; 58, 64f.

12. Cf. Patočka, 120f., and the sixth heretical essay.

13. Ibid., 123f.

14. Ibid., 125.

15. Jacques Derrida, *The Gift of Death*, trans. David Wills (Chicago: University of Chicago Press, 1995), chaps. 1–2.

16. Ed Evink, "Patočka and Derrida on Responsibility," *Analecta Husserliana* 89 (2006): 307–21, 311.

17. Derrida, *Gift of Death*, 49.

18. Patočka, 116f., quoted in Derrida, *Gift of Death*, 50; translation edited.

19. Derrida, *Gift of Death*, 51.

20. Patočka, 48–52.

21. Derrida, *Gift of Death*, 53–115.

22. Patočka in *Jan Patočka: Philosophy and Selected Writings*, ed. Erazim Kohák (Chicago: University of Chicago Press, 1989), 340–43. Hereafter cited as Kohák.

23. Ibid., 346.

24. Cf. Evink, 313f.

25. Ibid., 318f.

26. Ibid.

27. Derrida, *Gift of Death*, 68, 78–81, 82–86.

28. Derrida implies that there is a danger lurking behind the self-sacrificial impulse of substitution, namely, a desire to redeem if not to convert the other with one's own martyrdom. Gift of self for another has to be free even from this proselytizing desire for the good of the other. In what sense can "useless suffering" ever become redemptive? This is a key question for the Jewish-Christian dialogue about responsibility or substitution in the post-Holocaust, non-orgiastic, and non-triumphalist sense of the ethico-religious. See Derrida's discussion of the pitfalls and scruples of Louis Massignon and of the Badaliya prayer communities of Christians living among the Muslims. Derrida, "Hostipitality," in *Acts of Religion*, ed. Gil Anidjar (New York: Routledge, 2002), 365–80. This intervention suggests an indirect critique of Levinas's Judaic substitution when used in a self-flagellating manner, and I am not saying whether or not this has been Massignon's case. It is reminiscent of Derrida's critique of Patočka's purportedly triumphalist Christian responsibility discussed above. Such charges were leveled, in a secular veneer, against the purported Czech dissident elitism of the solidarity of the shaken that arose out of Charta 77 and ushered into the Velvet Revolution of 1989. In this chapter I seek a way to respond to all three charges against substitution, redemptive suffering, and dissident solidarity by underscoring the Judaic law of anti-idolatry, the low Christology, and an existential sense of shared finite responsibility of those who care for the soul and polis.

29. If, as Edelglass shows, there is an intrinsic connection between *The Brothers Karamazov* and Levinas's figure of substitution, then the very figure reinscribes and transforms the territory shared by Judaism and Christianity. "Asymmetry and Normativity: Levinas Reading Dostoyevsky on Desire, Responsibility, and Suffering," *Analecta Husserliana* 85 (2005): 709–26, 717. See note 28 above on Derrida's suspicion of certain self-inflicted Christian martyrdom in Massignon and note 34 on the post-Holocaust possibilities of a Judeo-Christian dialogue.

30. Compare Caputo with Jonas and Hillesum; John D. Caputo, *The Weakness of*

God: A Theology of the Event (Bloomington: Indiana University Press, 2006); Hans Jonas, *Mortality and Morality: A Search for the Good After Auschwitz,* ed. Lawrence Vogel (Evanston, Ill.: Northwestern University Press); Etty Hillesum, *An Interrupted Life: The Diaries of Etty Hillesum* (New York: Pantheon, 1984).

31. Cf. Derrida's emphasis in "Hostipitality," 397.

32. Murav shows that Dostoyevsky, Derrida, and Levinas share the view that "religion has to do with answerability or responsibility to the other." Harriet Murav, "From Skandalon to Scandal: Ivan's Rebellion Reconsidered," *Slavic Studies* 63, no. 4 (2004): 756–70, 759. Thus the heart of Ivan Karamazov's rebellion has to do with the im/possibility of responding to the other's suffering. But "hell" is hardly a conceptual aporia. It is clear that for Dostoyevsky and Levinas, this annihilating suffering is an existential issue that goes to the heart of nihilism. No wonder that Dostoyevsky defines hell, unlike Sartre, as "the suffering of no longer being able to love." *The Brothers Karamazov,* trans. David McDuff (London: Penguin, 2003), 417. Dostoyevsky's answer to nihilism of this living hell is precisely substitution or redemptive suffering.

33. Walter Benjamin, *Illuminations: Essays and Reflections,* ed. and intro. Hannah Arendt, trans. Harry Zohn (New York: Shocken, 1968), 254.

34. The Judaic law of anti-idolatry and the low Christology share minimally the following three heresies regarding useless and redemptive suffering. These heresies could be added to underwrite Patočka's heretical thinking about the birth of responsible self and care for the polis out of the overcoming of the orgiastic religiosity:

1. The God of Abraham, Isaac, and Jacob is revealed in the face-to-face relations of responsible ethics, and Jesus is a perfect prototype of the double commandment to love God with all one's heart and the neighbor as oneself.
2. The God revealed in the life, death, and prayers of Jesus is the same God revealed to Abraham, Isaac, and Jacob.
3. The weak God of post-Holocaust ethics of responsibility who empties God's Godhood of all omnipotence (*tzimtzum,* self-contraction of God of the Lurianic Kabbalah) and relies on humans to help God complete creation is revealed in the *kenotic* God of low Christology.

Contributors

JOHN J. DAVENPORT is associate professor of philosophy and associate director of environmental studies at Fordham University. He has published widely on topics in free will and responsibility, existentialism, virtue ethics, self hood and motivation, theories of justice, and philosophy of religion. With Anthony Rudd, he edited *Kierkegaard After MacIntyre*, and most recently has published *Will as Commitment and Resolve*. Currently Davenport is working on essays dealing with Kierkegaard's *Fear and Trembling* and *Concluding Unscientific Postscript*, global government, and the democratic limits to religion in the public sphere.

ZEYNEP DIREK is associate professor of philosophy at Galatasaray University, Istanbul, Turkey. She is editor of *Sonsuza Tanıklık: Emmanuel Levinas'tan Seçme Yazılar* (Attesting to the Infinite: Selections from Levinas) and author of *Başkalık Deneyimi: Kıta Avrupası Felsefesi Üzerine Denemeler* (The Experience of Alterity: Essays on Continental Philosophy). She has also authored essays on Levinas and Bataille in English.

JEFFREY DUDIAK is associate professor of philosophy at the King's University College in Edmonton, Canada. A Quaker philosopher grounded in the Continental tradition, he is working and writing in the areas of philosophy of religion and ethics. His principal publication to date is *The Intrigue of Ethics: A Study of the Idea of Discourse in the Thought of Emmanuel Levinas.*

M. JAMIE FERREIRA is Carolyn M. Barbour Professor of Religious Studies at the University of Virginia. Her numerous publications include *Love's Grateful Striving: A Commentary on Kierkegaard's "Works of Love"; Transforming Vision: Imagination and Will in Kierkegaardian Faith; Scepticism and Reasonable Doubt; The British Naturalist Tradition in Wilkins, Hume, Reid, and Newman;* and *Doubt and Religious Commitment: The Role of the Will in Newman's Thought.*

DAVID KANGAS is adjunct associate professor of philosophy and religion at the Graduate Theological Union and lecturer in the department of philosophy at the University of California–Berkeley. He is author of *Kierkegaard's Instant: On Beginnings* (Bloomington: Indiana University Press, 2007) as well as numerous articles on Kierkegaard and German idealism. He serves on the editorial board and as translator for the forthcoming critical edition of Søren Kierkegaard's *Journals and Notebooks.*

MARTIN KAVKA is associate professor of religion at Florida State University. He is the author of *Jewish Messianism and the History of Philosophy* (New York:

Cambridge University Press, 2004) as well as of several articles on Jewish philosophy and theology. He is completing a manuscript on the relationship between covenant theology and the public sphere in modern Jewish thought.

JOHN LLEWELYN has been reader in philosophy at the University of Edinburgh, visiting professor at the University of Memphis, and Arthur J. Schmitt Distinguished Visiting Professor of Philosophy at Loyola University of Chicago. Among his publications are *Beyond Metaphysics? Derrida on the Threshold of Sense; The Middle Voice of Ecological Conscience; Emmanuel Levinas: The Genealogy of Ethics; The HypoCritical Imagination; Appositions: Of Jacques Derrida and Emmanuel Levinas; Seeing Through God: A Geophenomenology;* and *Margins of Religion: Between Kierkegaard and Derrida.*

MARTIN BECK MATUŠTÍK is professor of philosophy at Purdue University, where he has been teaching since 1991. Matuštík is author of six single-author books, two edited collections, and a co-editor with Patricia Huntington of New Critical Theory, a series at Rowman & Littlefield. Among his books are *Radical Evil and the Scarcity of Hope: Postsecular Meditations; Postnational Identity: Critical Theory and Existential Philosophy in Habermas, Kierkegaard, and Havel; Specters of Liberation: Great Refusals in the New World Order; Jürgen Habermas: A Philosophical-Political Profile;* and editor with Merold Westphal of *Kierkegaard in Post/Modernity.*

STEPHEN MINISTER is assistant professor of philosophy at Augustana College in Sioux Falls, South Dakota. He has published articles in *Journal of the British Society of Phenomenology, Heythrop Journal, Philosophy Today, Symposium,* and *Philosophy in the Contemporary World.* Recent essays include "Forging Identities and Respecting Otherness: Levinas, Badiou, and the Ethics of Commitment" and "From Perpetual Peace to the Face of the Other: A Levinasian Reframing of Human Rights."

J. AARON SIMMONS is visiting assistant professor of philosophy at Hendrix College. In addition to editing the present volume with David Wood, Simmons has also published on topics in philosophy of religion, phenomenology, and political philosophy in *Journal of Religious Ethics, Philosophy Today, Symposium, Philosophy in the Contemporary World,* and *Journal for Cultural and Religious Theory.* Among his essays are "Is Continental Philosophy Just Catholicism for Atheists: On the Political Relevance of *Kenosis*" and "What About Isaac? Re-Reading *Fear and Trembling* and Re-Thinking Kierkegaardian Ethics."

MICHAEL WESTON is senior lecturer in philosophy at the University of Essex, U.K. He is author of *Kierkegaard and Modern Continental Philosophy* and *Philosophy, Literature and the Human Good,* and of papers on the philosophy of religion and the philosophy of literature.

MEROLD WESTPHAL is Distinguished Professor of Philosophy at Fordham University in New York City. In addition to two books on Hegel and two on Kierkegaard, he is author of *God, Guilt, and Death: An Existential Phenomenology of Religion; Suspicion and Faith: The Religious Uses of Modern Atheism; Overcoming Onto-Theology; Transcendence and Self-Transcendence: An Essay on God and the Soul;* and *Levinas and Kierkegaard in Dialogue.*

DAVID WOOD is Centennial Professor of Philosophy at Vanderbilt University, where he teaches Continental philosophy and environmental thought. In addition to editing the present volume with J. Aaron Simmons, Wood is author of *Time After Time; The Step Back: Ethics and Politics After Deconstruction;* and *Thinking After Heidegger.*

EDITH WYSCHOGROD is J. Newton Rayzor Professor of Philosophy and Religious Thought Emerita at Rice University. Her works include *Crossover Queries: Dwelling with Negatives; Embodying Philosophy's Others; An Ethics of Remembering: History, Heterology, and the Nameless Others; Saints and Postmodernism: Revisioning Moral Philosophy; Spirit in Ashes: Hegel, Heidegger, and Man-Made Mass Death;* and *Emmanuel Levinas: The Problem of Ethical Metaphysics.*

Index

ject), 25, 112, 139, 165; and Socrates, 30. *See also* God; Judaism; religion(s)

cogito, 31; Cartesian, 29

command(s) (commandment), 59, 233, 235; God's (divine), 12, 23, 26, 33–34, 45, 70, 106–107, 170–71, 173–75, 178, 209; "strong divine command," 170, 190n20; Ten Commandments, the, 23, 89; first commandment, the, 23, 31; second commandment, the, 23, 31–32; "thou shalt not kill," 13, 34, 93, 179, 232–34; to kill, 51, 170 (*see also* Abraham). *See also* law(s), the; response; *and under* God; love

community, 55, 57, 145–47

conscience, 77–78; bad conscience, 139; good conscience, 59, 180, 183, 233

consciousness, 72, 202–204, 213, 223; and intentionality, 205. *See also* Husserl, Edmund; *and under* self, the; sin

conversation, 10, 126–28, 147, 149, 222; between Levinas and Kierkegaard, 125, 127, 148–49

cultural imperialism, 36

Czechoslovakia, 14, 244–45. *See also* "Charta 77"; Havel, Václav

de Vries, Hent, 53, 208

death, 25–26, 38n20, 73, 80, 85–86, 153, 155, 161, 233–34, 248; (im)mortality, 174, 248; as undomesticated alterity, 156–58 (*see also* alterity). *See also under* Derrida, Jacques; God; life

decision (deciding), (choosing), (deliberation), 14, 72, 184, 194n69, 200–201, 222–23; choice, 208–209; "ir/responsible undecidability," 15, 252. *See also* freedom; will

deconstruction (deconstructionist), 5, 167, 185–86, 192n41, 235; of the law, 235–36. *See also* Derrida, Jacques; philosophy

demonic, the, 13, 183, 220, 224

Derrida, Jacques, 4, 37n8, 44, 79–80, 160–61, 166–67, 169, 175–76, 180–88, 190n17, 192n41, 211–12, 215, 222, 235–36, 247, 249–54; "deconstruction is justice," 236, 239; and economy, 181, 183; "Force of Law," 235; *The Gift of Death*, 180; *tout autre*, 160; "Violence and Metaphysics," 211. *See also* deconstruction; gift; hospitality

Descartes, René, 76. *See also under* cogito

despair, 185, 248

destitution, 137, 157, 233. *See also under* face, the

determinism, 144. *See also* freedom

diachrony (diachronic), 136–37, 159

"diacony," 51

difference(s) (dissimilarity), 13, 117n1, 126, 132–33, 167, 205; absolute, 9, 153, 164, 167, 216, 239; and commonality/likeness, 238–39; relative, 153, 167. *See also* same, the

discourse, impossibility of, 24, 212. *See also* language; philosophy

Dooley, Mark, 239–40

Dostoyevsky, Fyodor, 14–15, 42, 104, 246, 253

doubleness (double-mindedness), 200, 206

doubt, 21, 30, 36n1, 37n1, 41, 103, 200, 209. *See also* knowledge; *and under* God

dwell (dwelling), 157–61, 212

ec-static(ness), 69, 73

egoism (egoistic), (egocentric), (egotism), 6, 7, 21, 25–26, 29–30, 32, 41, 45–47, 59, 69, 103, 113, 118n18, 176–79, 181, 194n73, 202, 211–12, 214, 220, 223. *See also under* philosophy; self, the

elements (elemental), 155–56, 159, 203–204

embodiment, 53, 139–40, 142–44, 223. *See also* body

enjoyment, 155–59, 204, 212

environment, the, 31, 161

equality, 75, 83, 91–92, 235

eschatology (eschatological), (eschaton, the), 12, 138, 144, 151n17, 174; divinity, 177; faith, 182; fulfillment, 180; good, 179, 188, 191n27; happiness, 179; hope, 169, 174, 177–78, 181–82, 188; and mystery, 180; promise(s), 174, 182, 188; trust, 181, 188, 191n28. *See also* Messiah; salvation

eternal, the (eternity), 26–28, 73–74, 77–78, 84, 97n33, 130–31, 163–65, 167, 174, 200, 215; and happiness, 25–31, 37n12, 79, 164, 167; life, 27–29, 38n20; responsibility, 201; and truth (*see under* truth). *See also* temporality

ethic(s) (ethical, the), (ethico-), (ethically), (ethicality), 1, 4, 21–22, 25, 35–36, 49–50, 64n41, 69, 71, 74, 76, 109, 181, 202, 209, 214, 218, 221, 231, 236; action, 234 (*see also* action); act-utilitarian, 184; asymmetry (dissymmetry), 90–92, 95, 222, 235, 246, 251–52; beyond/surpass/overcome, 7–8, 13, 43, 48–51, 53, 57–58, 104–106, 169, 180, 220 (*see also* priority); deontological(ly) (deontology), 27–28, 173, 181 (*see also* Kant, Immanuel); Derridean, 12, 185–86 (*see also* Derrida, Jacques); ethicity of, 211, 214–15, 221; ethico-existential, 14, 251–52; ethicopolitical, 2–3, 8, 215, 217, 247, 250; ethico-

47–50, 54, 56, 105, 127–28, 219–20; communication, (in)direct, 2, 153, 162–63; impersonal logos, 24, 103, 212; origin/source
of, 6, 212, 214; social embeddedness of, 2, 5,
222; speak in tongues, 49–50, 63n38; speech
(*logos*), (ability to speak), (speaking), 43–45,
80, 149, 180, 208; word(s), 127–28, 146–48
law(s), the, 10, 12, 21–22, 31, 33–34, 50, 110,
160, 172, 186, 199, 206–207; and Jesus, 23,
26, 31. *See also* command(s); responsibility;
and under deconstruction; God; moral
Lessing, G. E., 2, 35, 178
Levinas, Emmanuel: being for-the-Other, 12,
85; biography, 3–4, 51–52; "diacony," 22,
38n20, 51; *il y a*, 11, 154–56, 158–61, 166–67,
203–204, 208; illeity, 77, 80, 121n53, 157–59,
191n31, 208; and Judaism (Jewish), 1, 4, 71,
78, 92–93, 207, 247 (*see also* Judaism); lapse,
3, 135, 205; "me," 8, 72–73, 112 (*see also* I,
the); saying/said, 172, 205–206; Third, the
(*le Tiers*), 34, 205–206, 208, 220, 222; third
party, 13, 72, 157, 183, 199, 222, 231. *See also*
under conversation; ethic(s); neighbors
Lewis, C. S., 25–26
life: care for others, 12, 216, 220; and death,
204; and history/historicality, 166; "living
from," 155–56; significance/meaning, 153,
158, 162–63, 217, 230, 234. *See also under*
eternal, the
love, 7–9, 12, 27–28, 36, 70, 72, 237–41; and
command, 1, 5, 8–9, 39n32, 70, 83–86, 93–
94, 119n35, 170, 178, 182–83, 185, 187; *eros*,
144, 195n88; genuine, 239–40; and God,
10, 26, 29, 31, 57, 70, 72–73, 83, 99–100,
106–107, 116, 171, 178, 209, 240, 241, 253;
and the neighbor, 8–10, 14–15, 22–23,
26–29, 36, 38n20, 57, 70, 73, 82–85, 88–90,
93, 99–100, 106–107, 125, 171, 173, 178–79,
233–34, 237, 239–41, 253; *philia*, 195n88;
preferential, 70, 83, 86, 97n33; for strangers,
28, 143; unconditionality of, 27, 83, 87, 93.
See also under agape; God; politics; responsibility; self, the
Luther, Martin (Lutheran), 7, 27, 46, 88–89,
92, 128, 148. *See also under* Kierkegaard,
Søren

malaise, 141–42
marriage (married), 1, 64n40
materialism, 140, 144, 214
meaning, 14, 167, 232–33, 235; as conditioned,
235; destabilizing of, 160–61; finite certainty of, 14, 249; formation/production

of, 160–61, 167; source/possibility of, 157,
160. *See also* language; sense
Messiah (messianic), 138–39, 143–44, 146, 148,
151n17, 249, 252–53; triumph of, 73, 139,
144. *See also* eschatology; salvation
metaphysics, 5, 34, 74, 126, 140, 177, 217, 221;
as ontotheologically constituted, 34–35
(*see also* Heidegger, Martin). *See also* philosophy
Mooney, Edward, 171, 175, 178, 181
moral (morally), (morality), 34–35, 156, 163,
173, 185; dilemma, 184–86, 188; *faktum*,
172, 192n49; law, 11, 134, 169, 172, 174–
75, 193n65, 194n71 (*see also* law(s), the);
and modernity, 139; motive, 172–73, 178,
196n101; and rational autonomy, 171 (*see*
also reason); theory, 173, 190n17. *See also*
ethic(s); *and under* faith; responsibility
Moriah, 71, 104, 108, 179. *See also* Abraham;
Isaac

need(s), 129, 141–42, 203–204, 239–40
neighbors (neighborliness), 9, 22–24, 28, 30–31,
59, 70, 72–73, 82–86, 125–26, 138, 147, 201,
205; between Kierkegaard and Levinas, 5,
6, 10, 125, 147, 149; conception of, 70, 83,
97n25; equality and kinship, 9, 83; infinity
of, 46, 63n30; love (*see under* love); neediness
of, 9, 86. *See also* other, the; responsibility;
and under God
Nietzsche, Friedrich, 22, 29, 32–33, 50, 78
nihilism, 208, 256n32
Noddings, Nel, 14, 237–38
noesis (*noema*), (*noetic*), 172, 221. *See also*
Husserl, Edmund

obedience, 137–38, 148, 175, 181; and faith,
178; to God's (command), 28–29, 33,
170–71, 173, 177, 217
offense, 30, 36n1, 37n1. *See also* doubt
ontology (ontological), 34–36, 39n41, 43, 108,
127, 154, 221; critique/contestation of, 1, 2,
221; Heideggerian, 142; "ontological adventure," 154–55; of power, 221; reality, 233; relational conception of, 5. *See also* being(s);
philosophy
ontotheological (theo-ontology), 34, 94, 101–
102, 128, 133. *See also* ontology; theology
orgiastic demonic, 247–48, 250, 253
other, the (Other, the), (other being, the),
(other person, the), (Otherness), 6–9, 22,
24, 26, 31, 46, 52–53, 57, 69–71, 153, 204,
240; absolute Other/Alterity, 11, 153–54,

156–58, 161, 215; and absorption, 55; demand of, 34, 185; face of, 6, 34, 53, 85, 90, 105, 135, 157, 172, 215, 225, 232 (*see also* face, the); as God or as human, 74–76, 105, 108, 111, 120n36 (*see also* priority); infinite debt to, 5, 84; my other, 79–80; as negative of the same, 69; non-human other, 39n41, 80; openness to, 13, 109, 112, 172, 220, 235; relation(ship) with/to, 56–57, 73, 76, 154, 158–59, 183, 199, 220, 222, 235; sacrifice of, 183–84, 195n96, 251; summons/ call of, 157–58, 185; "the first you," 73, 83. *See also under* alterity; fear; God; Levinas, Emmanuel; life; priority; response; revelation; singularity

parallelism (parallel), 10, 101, 109
Parmenides, 3, 44
passion, 54, 201, 210n26, 219, 227n22, 228n31, 247
passivity, 112, 159, 204, 224; passive subject, 202, 205
patient(ly) (patience), 10, 126, 128–39, 144–47; and gaining, 138–39; patience-in-order-to/ for the sake of, 139, 145
Patočka, Jan, 14–15, 244–52, 256n34
Paul, Saint, 28, 72, 128–29
persecution (persecuted), 224, 226n9, 230. *See also under* God; self, the; truth
Peter, Saint, 28
phenomenology (phenomenological), 11, 43, 52, 76, 245
philosophy (philosophical), (philosophize), 2–7, 11, 21, 24, 43–44, 52, 75, 104, 108, 118n11, 128–29, 140, 142, 154, 158, 202, 211, 213, 229, 248; as "egology," 154; epistemology (epistemological), 5, 229–30; existentialism, 54, 211–12; forms of thought, 160–61, 166; goal of, 13, 229; history of, 21, 139, 140; and justice, 206; logocentric (logocentrism), 44, 47; pedagogical responsibility of, 2; and religion (*see under* religion[s]); systematic, 29, 42, 236; thinking otherwise than, 129; transcendental, 135, 153; and truth, 43. *See also under* ethic(s)
Plato, 77, 153, 174, 232, 248
pluralism (pluralistic), 213–15, 222
politics (political), 4, 7, 13–14, 22, 25–26, 36, 75, 210n23, 215–19, 222, 224, 227n25; care for the polis, 247–50, 255n28, 256n34; consequences/results of, 14, 58; critiques of, 36, 215, 227n24; of identity, 13, 220; of justice, 36; liberalism, 139–41, 221; of love, 36;

thinkers, 12, 211, 221; totalitarianism, 24, 32, 212, 221. *See also under* ethic(s)
possession, 155–57, 160, 204
postmodern (postmodernity), 1, 4, 229–30
power, 5, 47, 155, 157–58, 223. *See also under* ontology; struggle; technology; will
priority, 4; of ethics, 34, 111; of God (*see under* God); to the indicative, 114; order of, 8, 73; of the other, 1, 7–9, 90–91, 100; relational, 47; reversal of, 6, 24, 46, 113; of the subject, 135
proper name, the, 213–14
prophecy (prophetic), 63n38, 131. *See also* language
Prospero, 248
Pseudo-Dionysus, 102
psychology, 217–18

questioning (question), 149, 246, 248
quietism (quietistic), 2, 12, 59; Panglossian resignation, 58. *See also* action; fear

race, 218–20; racism, 140, 223, 228n28
reality (real, the), 154, 157, 160, 162
reason (rationality), 22, 25, 35, 76, 104, 214, 231–32; autonomy of, 154, 219; singularity of, 212; universality of, 157. *See also under* moral
reciprocity (reciprocation), 95, 181, 235, 240–41, 254
reconciliation, 28, 179
relation(al) (relationality), 23, 46, 60, 69, 74, 86; absolute, 48, 188; to the Absolute, 219–20; interhuman, 74, 220; "relation without relation," 74, 154, 157–58
religion(s) (religious), (religiousness), 6, 24, 32, 58–60, 71, 74–75, 79, 112, 126, 224, 227n22, 247, 249; "absolute relation to the Absolute," 4, 13, 49, 104, 237, 240–41; agnosticism, 176; asceticism, 164; atheism (atheist), (atheistic), (a/theism), 10, 24, 34, 37n8, 102, 111, 113, 176, 204; exclusivity, 4; historical, 35, 176; martyrdom, 164; paganism, 79, 142, 163, 225; pluralism, 4; redemption, 128, 145; relationship with philosophy, 1–2; the return of the religious, 248; and soteriology, 176–77; stage, 22, 29, 32, 48, 169, 223–24; subjectivity (*see under* subject); theodicy, 15, 252–54; and violence, 35, 105, 108. *See also under* ethic(s); Kierkegaard, Søren; transcendence
renunciation, 29, 200; absolute, 182; of self, 29–30; of self-sufficiency, 30

response (respond), (responsiveness), (responsivity), 85, 137, 156–57, 166; ethical, 14, 171, 232, 247, 253 (*see also* ethic[s]); to others, 14, 69, 87, 94, 105, 172, 184, 231, 253 (*see also* alterity; other, the); particularity of/singular, 83, 171–72, 183. *See also* responsibility

(ir)responsibility (duty), (obligation), 3, 5, 9, 14–15, 21–22, 24–26, 28, 31, 36, 53, 58, 72, 85–87, 91, 105, 109, 116, 133–34, 138, 166, 172, 183, 187, 193n59, 201, 205, 219, 230–35, 246–51; absolute (inescapable), (unconditional), 22, 25–28, 37n8, 48, 50, 72, 84, 105, 109, 156, 175, 181, 183; and abstraction, 14, 53; aporetic, 249–51; ethical/moral, 13–14, 115, 157, 170, 172, 177, 188, 234, 241, 252–53; existentially lived, 15, 252; finite (infinite), (infinity), (unlimited), 3, 14, 38n20, 51, 61n2, 84, 91, 94–95, 100, 169, 186–87, 222, 224, 247, 249–51, 255n28; and love, 9, 86–87 (*see also* love); origin of, 172, 186; sober, 14, 250; uniquely assigned duty (irreplaceability), 180, 188; and universality, 172, 187–88. *See also* moral; *and under* Christianity; decision; eternal, the; existence; history; philosophy; self, the; subject

revelation, 10, 29, 35–36, 127, 133–37, 148–49, 172, 213, 248; human conditions for, 148–49; of the Other, 213–14

Robbins, Jill, 52–53, 61n2

Rosenzweig, Franz, 13, 15n2, 42, 70, 90, 172, 213–14; *Star of Redemption*, 42, 213

sacrifice, 194n73, 212. *See also under* other, the; self, the

salvation (salvationist), 11, 25–30, 49, 58–59, 66n82, 73, 94, 103, 126, 138–41, 143–45, 153, 164, 167, 174, 176–77, 179. *See also* eschatology; eternal, the; God; Messiah

same, the, 202, 214, 220; "imperialism"/ "totalitarianism" of, 154, 158, 160, 202. *See also* difference(s); *and under* alterity

Sartre, Jean-Paul, 54

Schlegel, Friedrich, 165

secrecy (secret), 44, 48, 54, 75, 148, 175, 180, 218, 224. *See also* language; *and under* subject

self, the (selfhood), 7, 9, 11–12, 15, 24–26, 30, 53, 55–56, 58, 72, 94, 133, 140, 153, 166, 202–205, 208, 215, 224, 240, 248; abnegation of, 200; aesthetic, 22, 165–66; affectivity of, 143, 203; "become oneself," 238–40; care of/ for, 211, 214, 216, 223; concern about, 54–55, 60, 162; consciousness (conscious), 130, 136, 156, 204; decentered (decentering), 29, 99,

102, 106, 112–13; dispossession of, 12, 142; egoity, 205, 211–12 (*see also* I, the); esteem, 9, 92; and God, 76, 112; and justification, 205; and knowledge, 13, 162, 212, 216, 219, 220, 224; love, 9, 14, 26–29, 70, 73, 88–94, 102, 240–41; as "persecuted hostage," 86, 90, 112, 224; relation to oneself, 57, 59; renunciation of (*see under* renunciation); responsible self, 27, 31, 248–49, 256n34; sacrifice, 9, 86, 164, 167, 181, 226n9; self-coincidence, 132–33; self-deification, 237; and society/ history, 56, 165; and *telos*, 165–66; transformation, 10, 101, 114. *See also* other, the; subject; *and under* alterity; Christianity; fear; renunciation; transcendence

senescence, 136–38

sense, 155, 157–59. *See also* meaning

Sheil, Patrick, 5

Shushani, Monsieur, 207

sin (sinfulness), 25, 30, 45, 57, 59–60, 89, 103, 106, 119n27, 174, 195n100, 202, 204, 217–20, 224; actuality/possibility of, 217–18; concept/definition of, 7, 46, 84; confession of, 3, 27; consciousness of, 8, 53, 58–60, 224; forgiveness of, 27, 37n13 (*see also* forgiveness); hereditary, 13, 216–20; real/ideal possibility of, 218. *See also* Adam; atonement

Singer, Peter, 184

singularity (singular), (single), (solitary), 4, 7, 13, 23, 127, 154, 181, 184, 248; elimination of, 42, 50 (*see also* totality); imperative/ command, 170–71, 190n16; of individual, 2, 4, 54; of the I, 2, 202 (*see also* I, the); of the other, 2, 10, 79, 237 (*see also* alterity; other, the); relationship with God, 3, 59–60; subjectivity (subject), 8, 43, 103 (*see also* subject); and universality (universal), 13, 49, 222. *See also under* faith; individual, the; reason; response

skepticism, 200, 230

society (societal), (social), (sociality), 58, 237; civilized (civilization), 154, 186, 247, 249; unsocialization, 237

Socrates, 4, 43

Sodom and Gomorrah, 51, 225. *See also* Abraham

solitude, 54–55, 57, 59, 203

soul, the, 132–33, 138, 153, 217, 223; care for, 220, 224, 247–50, 255n28; and the good, 248; and spirit, 215–16, 223

Soviet Union, 31

Spinoza, Benedict, 25, 45, 102, 223; *conatus essendi*, 25–26, 29, 31, 45, 214, 227n24, 234

Stalinization, 208

state, the, 21, 222. *See also* politics

struggle, 46, 55, 200, 204; of existence, 60; for identity, 4; for power, 219

subject (subjectivity), 1, 4–5, 8, 21–25, 32, 51, 61, 64n41, 69, 126, 128, 132, 135, 139, 144, 161, 162, 203, 224; annihilation of, 155; authentic, 14; ethico-religious (sociality of), 13, 229–30, 237; existential, 57; genesis of, 212; and inexpressible secret, 45, 103 (*see also* secrecy); as needy and indigent, 202; religious, 48, 50, 57, 220, 224–25; and responsibility, 202, 224, 234; self-absorbed, 43; separated, 103, 111, 202; singular (*see under* singularity); subjectivity of, 38n20, 127–28, 132, 136, 213; temporality of, 166, 205; tensing on oneself/itself, 7, 25, 29–30, 45, 50, 55, 59, 103, 202 (*see also* Kierkegaard, Søren); transcendental, 135. *See also* other, the; self, the; *and under* Christianity; ethic(s), existence; "immodesty"; Kierkegaard, Søren; passivity; priority; truth

substitution, 137, 226n9, 252–54. *See also* Levinas, Emmanuel

suffering, 28, 30, 79, 86, 126, 140, 164; redemptive, 253–54, 255n28; useless, 15, 252–54

surprise/wonder, 146, 149. *See also under* God

systematicity (system): critique of/resistance to/opposition to, 2, 7, 22, 24–25, 54, 69, 103, 214; intelligibility of, 206, 231; thought, 231. *See also* totality; *and under* Hegel, G. W. F.; philosophy

task(s), 9, 84, 87

Taylor, Mark, 42, 52–53

technology (technologies), 1, 203, 227n24; and civilization, 247–50; and power, 249

temporality (temporal, the), (temporalization), 3, 11, 27–28, 126, 129, 131, 134–37, 159, 163–64, 166–67, 206. *See also* eternal, the; time

Tertullian, 1

testimony, 14

theism, 113–15. *See also* God

theology (theo-logy), 2, 24, 34, 45, 113, 115

time, 10, 72–74, 126, 131–32, 135–36, 147, 151n22, 163, 200; "absolute future," 77, 161; ageing, 135–37; beginning, 132; "clock time," 159; duration, 205; finitude, 163, 174, 187; forever, 137–38; future (futurity), 3, 28–29, 77, 128–31, 143, 156, 161; "not-yet," 128; present, the (presence), 43–47, 128, 130, 133, 138. *See also* eschatology; *and under* world, the

totality (totalizing), (totalization), (totali-

tarian), 2, 4, 7, 9, 32, 42, 44–45, 47, 49–50, 54, 56, 75, 79, 104–105, 118n9, 154, 160, 212–15, 220–21, 223. *See also* Hegel, G. W. F.; systematicity; *and under* being(s); guilt; politics

transcendence (transcendent), 8, 32, 35, 47, 52–53, 60, 74, 101, 103, 110, 134, 153, 157–58, 214, 219–20, 223, 225; cosmological, 10, 101–102, 113–15; epistemological, 10, 101–102, 114–15; "erotics of transcendence," 125–26; infinite, 71; religious-ethical, 10, 101–102, 114–15; self-transcendence, 101–102, 111–12, 114; "transascendance," 52, 53; "transdescendance," 52, 53; of the word, 75–76. *See also under* God

trauma, 32, 35, 153, 158–59

truth (true, the), 1–3, 5, 7, 21, 29–30, 36, 44–45, 47, 54, 73, 148, 151n10, 157, 201–202, 227n24; demonstrable, 165; eternal, 21; and falsity, 227n22; and humility/invitation, 3, 202; and knowledge, 47, 103; new modality/view of, 43–48, 103; objective, 157, 162, 229–30; as persecuted, 3, 7, 46–48, 63n32, 103, 115, 202, 220 (*see also* persecution); subjective, 162; as triumphant, 3, 7, 24, 44–47, 63n32, 103, 202; (un)certainty of, 3, 5, 47, 55 (*see also* foundationalism). *See also under* God; Kierkegaard, Søren; philosophy

understanding (comprehension), 154, 160, 166, 221

universality (universal), (universalism), 21, 29, 49, 105, 212, 215, 218–20, 232; ethics, 104, 106, 109–10, 219, 230; logic, 49; norms, 187–88. *See also under* God; reason; responsibility; singularity

upbuilding (*opbyggelig*), (edifying), 12, 199–209; and ethics, 204; and hardship, 12, 27, 201; interpretation of, 12, 199; path/road to, 201; vs. *Bildung*, 200. *See also* Kierkegaard, Søren

victim(s) (victimizers), (victimization), 231, 234

violence (violent), 6–7, 32–36, 39nn40,41, 43, 47, 50–51, 57, 59, 100, 104–105, 107, 113, 148, 194n68, 211–12, 222, 235; good violence, 113, 118n18; new violence, 118n18; paternalistic, 234; verbal, 32

Wahl, Jean, 7, 8, 43, 51–57

waiting, 10, 128, 132, 138

war(s), 22; holy, 34, 36. *See also* violence

Westphal, Merold, 5, 9–10, 14, 41, 43, 46, 50–51, 58, 101, 111, 120n36, 170–71, 175–76, 178, 236; *Transcendence and Self-transcendence,* 101, 111, 120n36

Wiesel, Elie, 3

will (willing), 25, 28, 135–36, 148, 164, 173, 179, 187, 209, 232; ethical, 177–78; and freedom, 72, 219, 224; God's, 33, 164, 170–71; to power, 29, 31, 227n24; willing the good, 200

Wittgenstein, Ludwig, 5, 167

world, the, 79, 101, 160; end of, 154; enjoyment of, 72; familiar, 156–57, 159; of history, 217; of lived existence, 13; of time, 201

writing, 2, 32; rhetoric, 32–33

Wyschogrod, Edith, 125–26